SAN FAIRY ANN?

MOTORCYCLES AND BRITISH VICTORY 1914-1918

MICHAEL CARRAGHER

FIRESTEP
Press

FireStep Press
An imprint of FireStep Publishing

Gemini House
136-140 Old Shoreham Road
Brighton
BN3 7BD

www.firesteppublishing.com

First published in Great Britain by
FireStep Publishing, 2013

© 2013, Michael Carragher

ISBN 978-1-908487-38-4

Cover design by Ryan Gearing

Typeset by Graham Hales

Printed and bound in Great Britain

SAN FAIRY ANN?

Table of Contents

Acknowledgements

THIS BOOK GREW out of my course in First World War Studies at the University of Birmingham, a wonderful experience that I can recommend heartily. Sincere thanks go to my instructors, Drs John Bourne, Rob Thompson, Gary Sheffield, Peter Simkins and the late Bob Bushaway. Thanks also go to all my colleagues, from whose presentations I learned a great deal.

My esteemed friend David Minton offered encouragement and practical assistance, factual information and advice, from the very start; Annice Collett of the Vintage Motorcycle Club could not have been more helpful; Richard Rosenthal, Steve Wilson, Nick and Martin Shelley, Chris Roberts, John Quirke, Peter Smith and Bert Thurling all helped, as did Dr Terence Zuber and Eorna Walton. Thanks also go to Barbara Levy and the Estate of George Sassoon for kind permission to quote Siegfried Sassoon's "Does It Matter?"

The illustrations that are reproduced are individually acknowledged where possible. Every effort has been made to locate ownership of all rights, and if I have inadvertently breached any I will be glad to make that right.

Closer to home, I owe my abiding interest in history to my old schoolmaster, Charlie Curtis, whose Irish Nationalism inculcated passion, and to my grandfather, Mickl Murphy, who had known some of the horrors of the Irish Revolutionary years and seen through the high rhetoric. Thus I came to confront the complexities of the past, and the notion that it's as simplistic as any mythology or ideology would define it, while sustaining the passion for it.

Mickl, born shortly after the Franco-Prussian War, had lived through many of the events I was studying at school and he was able to make them seem ... well, alive; just beyond the horizon of my birth; things I'd barely missed, and whose effects were all around me. It's thanks to Pop that long before I heard of William Faulkner I knew that "The past is never dead, it's not even past", no sort of "diminishing road but, instead, a huge meadow which no winter ever quite touches", for those who have lived through it—and, vicariously, those who will listen and learn. Though far removed nationally, culturally and socially from the like of Captain Watson and Lieutenant West, Pop shared many of the values of the men of 1914, in particular a well-honed sense of duty and a "greedless and fearless straightness". *Ní fhaicamuid a leitheid arís.*

7

A portrait of Pop's brother-in-law, Hugh Coburn, looked down from the wall over my childhood. Uncle Hughie had emigrated to New Jersey but returned to Europe in 1918 in a doughboy's uniform. On 14 October, during fierce fighting in the Meuse-Argonne Offensive, he went to the assistance of Dinny Murphy, who was not just a brother-in-arms but a childhood friend and neighbour from back home in Ireland. He was killed by shellfire. His looming presence, and my grandmother's occasional tears, made me aware from an early age not just of the tragedy that was and remains the Great War, but of the sacrifice that so many, of so many nationalities, made.

By no means least: without the unstinting support and encouragement of my partner, Consuelo, and our sons, Oisín and Ronán, this book could never have been written. *Míle buíochas.*

To the memory of Don R, 1914-1918.

And to that of PFC Hugh Coburn, AEF, who
laid down his life for his friend on
14 October 1918.

Glór na Trumpaí go Ghlosaidh Siad.

If one considers how small an amount of success is due to one's individual self, and thro' what weak instruments God manifests his greatness, it is a simple matter to be modest.

—Field Marshall Sir Douglas Haig.

Of all the crimes the worst
Is to steal the glory
From the great and brave,
Even more accursed
Than to rob the grave.

—Robert Frost.

Clear the road! I am a-coming through!

—"Cannonball" Baker, pioneer motorcyclist.

Foreword

THE WORLDWIDE SUCCESS of the recent stage and film adaptations of Michael Morpurgo's*War Horse* (1982) has brought renewed interest in the role of the horse in the First World War. The war was undoubtedly horse-drawn. There were 25,000 horses in the British Army in August 1914; by August 1918 there were 828,360. 226,204 horses died from various causes in the British Army in France and England during the war. Maintaining horse numbers in the face of these casualties and the increasing demands for horse transport became a major enterprise: 417,685 horses (and 209,618 mules) were landed in the United Kingdom, principally from Canada and the United States. The war could not have been conducted without this enormous amount of animal power.

Although the First World War did not bring to an end the military importance of horses, which remained a major factor on many fronts in the Second World War, the replacement of animal by mechanical power became apparent. The British Expeditionary Force (BEF) went to France in August 1914 with 334 lorries, 133 cars, 166 motor cycles and 63 aircraft; by November 1918 it had 31,770 lorries, 3,532 ambulances, 7,694 cars, 14,464 motor cycles and 1,782 aircraft.

The role of the horse in war was essentially four-fold: to deliver 'shock' on the battlefield; to reconnoitre the enemy; to pull supplies and guns; and to facilitate communications. Mechanical means began their displacement of the horse from these activities almost from the start of the war. Aircraft played a vital part in reconnoitring German movements during the battles of 1914 and later became central to the development of effective artillery fire. From September 1916 the nascent tank offered a new, if unreliable, means of producing battle 'shock'. And the increasingly sophisticated logistics network became more and more reliant on motor transport.

Nowhere were these changes more instantly apparent, however, than in the realm of communications. Even before the BEF deployed, the War Office was urgently trying to recruit motor-cycle despatch riders, principally for the Intelligence Corps. One of these daring young men was Roger West, a Cambridge engineering graduate, who spoke French and German, and was a keen motor cyclist. West rode over a thousand miles trying to volunteer before he was given a commission 'for six months or the duration of the war'. By 12 August, a week after British mobilization began, West and his army-issue motor bike were on the quay at Southampton ready to go to war.

West and his machine were a portent. In Michael Carragher, a writer with a fluent pen, the know-how of a mechanic and the soul of a poet, motor cycles and their riders have at last found a historian worthy to tell their story.

Dr J.M. Bourne
Director Emeritus
Centre for First World War Studies
The University of Birmingham

Introduction

Who'll Ride With Me!

Who'll ride with me when the wind beats high,
Thrashing the clouds as it flicks them by?

Who'll ride with me when two must go,
Lest Death is waiting out there in the snow?

Who'll ride with me though it's ten to one
We'll both be scuppered before we're done?

"I'll ride with you!" "And I!" "And I!"
Why care if Death is lurking by?
If the number's up, why it's just "Good Night!"
A glorious ride and a top-hole fight.

But should luck hold for the pair of us,
Thrusting us through and helping the bus,
We'll be ready again for another such ride,
Though the gates of Hell are opened wide.
A man doesn't grouse, whatever the odds.
His life is his Country's, his soul his God's.[1]

YOUNG ROGER WEST was not in the pink of health. For more than two weeks he had been in the saddle of his motorcycle, latterly riding day and night, putting hundreds of miles under his skinny tyres, repairing punctures—once within 150 yards of enemy troops—adjusting the drive belt, and doing the myriad routine things it took to keep a motorised bicycle going in August 1914. Not making his ride any easier was the carpet slipper he was wearing on one foot, but there was no help for this, because the foot had become infected following a flea bite, on the last full night's sleep he'd had, on straw, nine days before, and it was too swollen to fit a boot.

There was no help for any of this, because Roger West, and a hundred-odd other motorcyclists, were just about all that stood between the British Expeditionary Force and annihilation, and every one was needed—sore foot be damned. Nor was West's the only sore foot on that Great Retreat: countless men walked "bloodshod", to borrow a poet's term not yet coined. The soft feet of the recently recalled reservists suffered worst, the skin of the blistered soles sometimes peeling off like socks if a man was foolish enough to remove his boots; but most of the old sweats were too canny to do this, knowing that they could never get swollen feet back into leather, so they squelched along stoically, hungry, parched, their faces grey with strain and fatigue and the dust of the unsealed roads that rose with their passage and stuck to the sweat of their brows.

They were a pitiful five divisions, their numbers depleted by battle, and they were in full-tilt retreat before two German armies. They had fought these to a standstill at Mons, and again at Le Cateau, and every day their rearguard was fighting some delaying action or another. Four years later their younger brothers and cousins and neighbours and sons, along with the few of themselves left alive, would drive the Kaiser's once-invincible armies to defeat; but just now few would give much for them. Their own commander had so little faith in their chances he had wanted to pull them out of the line, and only a stern injunction from the most famous poster-boy in history had prevented this.

They might have turned into a straggling mob, that British Expeditionary Force, and been broken up in the field, for they were spread across many roads, and strung out by miles along those by impediments of one sort and another. To make matters worse, the two corps they constituted had become separated by the River Oise. Radio was in its infancy, heavy, fragile, and necessitating either security leaks if broadcasting was *en clair* or potentially fatal delays if in code; besides, the BEF had only one mobile transmitter and most field sets were with the cavalry. Telegraph infrastructure was spotty and often sabotaged by the retreating French, and of the scanty cable supply sent with the Force, much had had to be abandoned at Mons and more was captured at Le Cateau. Communication effectively had somehow come to be devolved onto perhaps 150 motorcyclists, 90 percent of whom had been civilians less than a month before. Some of these volunteers had had almost three full weeks of training.

Roger West had had three days. Now, almost a month into the war, he was hungry, tired, lame, and fevered by his poisoned foot. In recent days he had been fired upon and once ridden through enemy forces—and now he learned that, with the Germans maybe ten miles behind, charges on the bridge that separated them from the BEF had failed to explode.

Roger West was not in the pink; but his life, whatever his health, was not his own. "It seemed a pity to leave this bridge intact", so he requested his colonel's permission to go back and blow it up. Colonel Ward thought the young man "a fool", but he granted permission. West collected a stone of guncotton from a company of the Royal Engineers, along with an officer who volunteered to go with him on the carrier, carrying the detonators "carefully in his breast pocket, lest they go off with the jolting of the ride". As they rode the eight miles back some stragglers may have raised their jaded heads, widened their eyes in alarm, raised a hand in warning: "Wrong way, chum!"

But Roger West was not going the wrong way; he was going the only way he could. For his worldview was so different from ours that often we must portray, and indeed understand it, only through the lens of irony. Roger West saw the world in the bright-unclouded glass of the Victorian empire into which he had been born. Men of his generation spelled *Duty* as they spelled *God*, *King* and *Country*, with a reverential capital. Roger West, in that absurd and enviable world of his that ended in the year he put on khaki, was doing what was, beyond the very notion of a doubt, his Duty. His life was his Country's, his soul his God's.

God was in Heaven. King George was on the throne. General Alexander von Kluck was marching on Pontoise with the First German Army at his back, but young Roger West was on his way there too, on a rickety motorbike, with guncotton on his back and a carpet slipper on his foot. All was well with the world.

Or at any rate, that world was not yet lost.[2]

British Victory

Examination of the role played by the humble motorcycle in winning the Great War drives one to wonder how that role could have been forgotten, for it truly was a crucial one. Yet today memory of the war motorcyclist, apart perhaps from the despatch rider, has been lost, and the extent of the despatch rider's importance has been overlooked almost from the start. The most obvious reason for this amnesia is that the motorcycle, glamorous at the start of the war, had been relegated by technological developments that saw the tank emerge and the aeroplane mutate from a glorified box kite to a huge and deadly weapon of war, both machines pointing the way to the future while the motorcycle seemed almost of the past—something of an Edwardian relic, unchanged through the four years but for small details that even an engineer might fail to notice at a glance. Another reason may be that larger issues came to dominate the historiography, some of which perennially distract from and even get in the way of exploration of such issues as the role of a relatively primitive and fragile contraption: how important can the motorcycle have been set against the "monstrous misconduct" of the generals? Other reasons may have to do with societal attitudes, and the changes in these, through the war and since, combined with changes in the nature of the war motorcyclist through the years of conflict.

Societal changes certainly mean that perception of the war and British participation in it is viewed very differently today than it was at the time. Of course Britain never could have defeated Germany alone, in either war, but for several decades now a lamentable number of people seem to believe that though we can be proud of "our" victory in 1945, the 1914 – '18 game, even if we did win it, wasn't worth the candle. Yet the hard historic fact is that in 1917 and 1918 the British Army, for the only time in history, bore the main brunt of the main fight against the main enemy in the main theatre of a Continental war. John Terraine claimed for decades that the Hundred Days Campaign that ended that war was the British Army's greatest victory, and many more historians are coming to share his view, albeit some with reservations.[3]

The popular misconception about Britain's record in the Great War has, if one will indulge the pun, many fathers. Quite soon after that war ended people began to question its value—and not unreasonably. CE Montague wrote *Disenchantment* as early as 1922, by which time the "land fit for heroes" promised by Lloyd George had turned out rather to be a land that would take heroes to live in, as disgruntled veterans put it (though Montague almost immediately regretted the tenor and tone of his book, admitting that "he had got the balance wrong").[4] Many veterans had no trade or work experience except that of soldiering, and they were competing for scarce employment in a land that ever since Cromwell had been suspicious, fearful or contemptuous of soldiers. Those "temporary gentlemen" who had taken commissions and become leaders of men found it hard to return to clerking or factory jobs—assuming their jobs still were there—and take orders from men who had, as veterans might see it, "shirked their duty". Many men, veterans of war yet innocents abroad, were taken advantage of by fraudsters on their demobilisation, and tricked out of what little money they had.[5]

For veteran and civilian alike, the post-war boom-and-bust balloon sagged down onto a decade that seemed shabby and bleak compared to the Victorian and Edwardian ages on which an iron gate had slammed, to borrow Barbara Tuchmann's resonant phrase, in 1914. Toward the end of the Twenties came *All Quiet on the Western Front*, as well as memoirs by Siegfried Sassoon, Edmund Blunden and Robert Graves, to name but the best-known Britons, and what they wrote made for bitter reading. The poets had been there from the start of the war, and were entitled to their say; but though they told the truth, and told it vividly and well, they didn't tell it all, because they didn't know it all. In addition, because most came from comfortable middleclass backgrounds, their views on the war would not have been shared by either the old sweats or their proletarian companions in Kitchener's Armies. "Some o' these buggers what come out 'ere now"—Frederic Manning's Private

Martlow would have had men like Owen and Sassoon in mind—"'ave never done anythin' they didn't want to do in their lives before, an' now they're up against somethin' real nasty, they don't 'arf make a song about it".[6] Or at any rate, a poem.

Despite the poets' partial knowledge and their minority views:

> It is possible to argue that [by] the early 1930s, as a result of the "war books boom" … memory of the war was monopolised by a small group of highly literate participants, primarily established writers who had served as junior officers, who created the version of the war still dominant today. In the process, they provided a set of scripts by which other veterans could compose their memories of the war.[7]

To make matters worse, the "Frock Coats"—politicians—then took great care in their memoirs to stake claim to victory, of necessity discounting the actual victory won by the "Brass Hats"—the generals. Winston Churchill was first out of the traps, in 1923: as Arthur Balfour put it, with a wit that Churchill would have admired, "Winston has written a great big book about himself and called it *The World Crisis*". The great big book was dismissed as "Brilliantly written—but too much of an apologia to be of general value", by Lloyd George, no doubt jostling for his own great big position in history,[8] and more enduringly damaging was Lloyd George's own *War Memoirs*, published in six volumes spread out over several years through the Thirties—long after Douglas Haig was able to defend himself. Together these books made "an indelible mark on the historiography and social memory of their era",[9] so that eventually, it's hardly exaggeration to say, these "sacred scripts" came to define the epistemology of the war—at very least, directly and indirectly, much of its historiography. The inevitable consequence was that other narratives, such as the despatch rider's, came to be overlooked.[10]

And then came the Depression, and even worse times. No better account of how the Hungry Thirties hit the British working class can be found than the late William Woodruff's stark yet wonderfully uplifting memoirs. In strife-torn Lancashire, genuinely hungry people "wait[ed] for the revolution to begin…. Perhaps … revolution wasn't in the British workers' blood";[11] but it was in the air, and the seeds sown by Comintern between the wars are still bearing mutated, grotesque fruit in our own time. The Liberals never recovered from the shock of the Great War, and effectively were obliterated by the troubles of the Thirties and the rise of Fascism, their once-proud name filched by the sort who would pretend, or could imagine, that Liberal rights can be permanently secured other than by standing firm by Liberal responsibilities. In addition to the appalling cost of living up to their responsibilities in the Great War—to the nation, to Liberal values, to democracy—which shook their confidence to its foundations, the party had been split by Lloyd George and besides had its proletarian support inevitably slip away to Labour, after salaries were paid to MPs in 1911 and working men could afford to be politicians. Though British Labour sensibly brought a long spoon when it supped with Communism—Ramsay MacDonald warned of the horrors inherent in Bolshevism when Stalin still was a relatively minor apparatchik—rumours of a Marxist utopia in the USSR filtered back to John Bull's Island, sapping the sternness of a hungry bulldog's resolve.

Perhaps most insidious of all in undermining traditional values and beliefs was British intellectualism. As George Orwell, arch-enemy of humbug, wrote: "In left-wing circles it is always felt that there is something slightly disgraceful in being an Englishman and that it is a duty to snigger at every English institution … at patriotism and physical courage [in] the persistent effort to chip away English morale".[12] In no small part as a consequence of this politico-intellectual snobbery, the "small group of highly literate participants" who had "monopolised" the war story was weeded down further on the basis of politics. For instance, today one almost never encounters in anthologies Gilbert Frankau's quite extraordinary poem, "The Other Side", but one does find, very regularly, "The Deserter". The latter is vastly inferior, but it serves to perpetuate the myth of the callous Donkey and the tragic Lion, whereas "The Other Side" explores the moral and emotional complexities of war, and affirms the need to have fought.[13] By the 1970s left-wing intellectual hostility was being formulated as "revolutionary defeatism", the rationale being that my enemy's enemy is my friend and my enemy is my country, so one saw such grotesquery as Tony Benn and Ken Livingstone cuddling up to the Provisional IRA who were bombing to death and disablement their fellow countrymen (and women; and children). History's inertia now has left us with everything from that grim Marxist transplant, political correctness,[14] which seeks to advance an anti-traditionalist agenda, to downright denial of the past: "Marxism has never truly been tried!" its apologists now insist—the airbrush being, after the machinegun emplaced behind the lines, Communism's essential tool. Britain always having been in the van of anti-Communism, denigrating her efforts, and certainly her victory in 1918, has become a core component of the Marxist agenda.

The Hitler War was even more surreptitious in undermining belief in British victory in the Kaiser War. Studs Terkel tags this "the last good war" and as wars go it was indeed a "good" one. It defeated Fascism and the thoroughness of that defeat reconciled Germany and Japan to democracy. Victory was, at first blush, unambiguous, and the butcher's bill, for Britain, was modest—certainly by comparison with that earlier, awful four-year slog through fire, mire and wire. And the moral justification was there on the cinema newsreels for all to see: the death camps that "we" had liberated. The so-called Great War lost its very name for decades; it faded into something like a bad dream—or certainly a bad mistake better glossed over by the more recent glorious victory. In the Sixties the cynicism and flagrant lies of Vietnam undermined the last sense of trust and naiveté that had sent Roger West and other young men off in "greedless and fearless straightness",[15] and helped re-launch the careers of Owen, Sassoon, Rosenburg, and the other Trench Poets, spreading their slanted gospel. The Marxist historian, AJP Taylor, gave us a wonderful summary, *The First World War*, the shrewdly-biased excellence and wit of which seduced so many, as did Joan Littlewood's musical and Richard Attenborough's subsequent film *Oh! What a Lovely War*. The BBC's *The Great War* refuelled interest, but also served to reinforce belief that that war had been all misery and futility, however many veterans strenuously protested at such simplified interpretation. In the years that followed, other historians— or those who flatter themselves as such—added such polemics as *Butchers and Bunglers of the First World War* and *Haig's Command*.[16] Twenty years on from *The Great War* the BBC produced *The Monocled Mutineer*, a piece of dreadful drivel that extended politically-motivated slander from the Donkeys to the very Lions—and by the 1980s there were far fewer veterans left to decry such lies. The layperson's understanding of the Great War became, in Dr John Bourne's words, "vitiated not only by deep levels of prejudice but also by deep levels of ignorance".[17] It sank onto a par with Wild West clichés, brass standing in for black hats, tin for white.

So it takes a lengthier introduction than an author would prefer to justify the sub-title, *British Victory 1914-1918*. John Bourne, Peter Simkins, Gary Sheffield, the late Richard Holmes and Paddy Griffith and other historians have gone a great way to set the record straight, and here is not the place to try to improve on their work, but rather to briefly summarise.

The Great War *was*, to a very great extent, a *British* victory; the war that followed was not. The Soviets defeated Hitler. The Yanks did their bit, and so did the British, and the Free French, and partisans of one sort and another. But the best thing the British did in the Hitler War—and it was no small contribution; far from it—was to keep the flag of defiance flying and provide a base from which to re-open a Western Front when the Americans came in. In one sense Churchill was right when he spoke about the British people's "finest hour" in 1940; but when he said those words he was speaking as a politician, rallying an all-but-defeated nation. The finest hour of the British people rather may have been rung on the eleventh hour of the eleventh day of the eleventh month of the Year of Our Lord MCMXVIII.

At the very outbreak of the Great War, despite the tiny size of its Expeditionary Force, Britain played a crucial role. "Our first battle is a heavy, an unheard of heavy defeat", one battalion commander lamented after Mons, "and against the English, the English we laughed at".[18] Though the defeat he bewails is of his own battalion, his tone reflects overall German dismay. Without the BEF's rearguard actions along the line of the August retreat, notably at Mons and Le Cateau, von Kluck and von Bülow might well have been able to fulfil von Schlieffen's plan.[19] Defeat of the French would have been disastrous for British interests, even were the BEF able to re-embark and return home intact, for part of a victorious Germany's terms would have been dismemberment of Belgium, with Flanders and parts of France annexed to the Reich. This could mean a malevolent presence across the Narrow Seas as far west as the mouth of the Somme, a threat to British shipping and communications with the Empire. French defeat also would have left Britain facing a hostile hegemonic European power, as in the times of Philip of Spain, the Sun King and Napoleon, alone against an attack that probably would have followed. Even had it not, Germany could have strangled Britain slowly, through the customs union she intended to impose on a vanquished Europe—after Napoleon's Continental System—a union that would deny to Britain those markets that were far more important than her Imperial ones, and by picking off her colonies. For part of the price France would have had to pay a victorious Germany was *her* colonies, Morocco at least; and a German naval outpost at Tangiers, and probably another at Djibouti, could have cut Britain's Suez and Cape lines to India.[20]

(Before faux-liberals sneer that such an early loss of Empire would have been good riddance they might consider what subject peoples had to suffer under the Second Reich. Uprisings in German South West Africa and East Africa, in 1904 and 1905-06 respectively, were put down with great barbarity, by "streams of blood and streams of money," and 60,000-80,000 deaths in each colony, as well as up to 300,000 deaths in *Ostafrika* from deliberately induced famine.[21] Imperialism is something for which the West well may hang its head, but it was a mixed curse, as any old Sudanese or Zimbabwean will nostalgically confirm.[22])

If Schlieffen's—or Moltke's—Plan had been terminally upset at the Battle of the Marne, the German armies had not been defeated. Though the BEF played a modest and rather belated role at the Marne, that battle never might have been fought without the BEF's previous delaying actions. In 1914 the BEF was regarded as "certainly the most inadequate [but] possibly the most excellent army in Europe",[23] in the words of an American, but even a German general is alleged to have admitted: "The English infantry is the most magnificent in the world; happily there is but little of it".[24] Even more happily for the rest of Europe there was enough to hold the breach while Kitchener's Armies were raised and trained.

First Ypres was a critical battle, one often literally fought tooth and nail; and the price of Allied victory was the Old Contemptibles, the professional army that had constituted the BEF and now were a spent force. Had they failed, the Channel ports were open to seizure. Such seizure might not have given Germany immediate victory, but strategically and politically it would have been a devastating blow to the Western Alliance. A German advance to the Channel would have made it difficult to supply the army from home and limited its tactical and strategic options. Quite discounting a Dunkirk-1940-type outcome, the blow to morale might have proved fatal, and eventual German victory the result. If the Old Army was all but gone after First Ypres, it had bought time for the New Armies to be raised and reserves to be mobilised, and secured ground for them to fight on.

Though the first day of the Somme is regarded as the greatest defeat of British arms in the field, the Somme battles *in toto* constitute possibly the most critical British victory in the Great War. Despite what some historians argue,[25] Britain's New Armies' contribution to the Allied effort in 1916 was both urgent and essential, however those armies were not fully trained, as Haig protested to Joffre, before conceding to send those poor great young men into the haemorrhaging breach—a blood sacrifice to save the French from going under at Verdun, and thereby to save the Alliance. Tactically its first phase indeed was a defeat and a national tragedy; but operationally and politically the Somme ultimately proved a victory, turning incipient French collapse at Verdun into the Germans' being driven back there and leading to, the following spring, their retreat to the Hindenburg Line, far behind the Somme. Without the British attack in July the French army might well have "ceased to exist" by August, as Joffre angrily insisted to Haig they would, through the latter's protests that his troops were not yet fully trained for such an assault. For all the very concept's political unacceptability even then, attritional wastage, on a heartbreaking scale, was unavoidable in the sort of siege warfare that had congealed out of the glorious hopes of August 1914. As Kapitan von Hentig ruefully remarked, "the Somme was the muddy grave of the German Field Army".[26] By the time that battle played itself out few Germans doubted that to win the war they first would have to "break France's best sword": "Beat the British, and the French would collapse; beat the French, and the British might well fight on"[27]—as they would in 1940.

Assuming that the French somehow had survived being "bled white" at Verdun without British intervention at the Somme, their disastrous defeat in April 1917 must have led to collapse had the BEF not diverted the Germans toward Flanders. Unambiguous victory at Messines reflects how well the BEF was climbing the "learning curve" since the Somme and, though "Passchendaele" possibly was an even more horrendous battle than the Somme, if the British assault at Third Ypres did nothing else it probably saved the Alliance—yet again—by drawing the Germans away from discovering that the French were in mutiny after the Nivelle Offensive. Much criticism has been directed against Haig for his conduct of Third Ypres, especially toward the end, and much of it is justified; yet had he broken off battle within sight of Passchaendale Ridge, would his critics be any kinder to his memory?[28] As General "Duckboard" Fayolle put it, "*Quoi q'on fais, on perd beaucoup de monde*"—and Fayolle was, even more so than Pétain, conscientiously conservative of his men's lives.[29]

In any war, a general loses a lot of men, and all generals' losses were on a colossal scale in 1914-1918—but for reasons that a smugly superior posterity disallows or simply doesn't understand, and disdains to examine. Churchill, no friend of the generals, conceded that the Great War "was quite beyond the compass of anybody".[30] It was not the first modern war—that distinction usually being accorded to the American Civil War—but it was the war that brought warfare into the industrial, mass-production age, and it may lay fair claim to being the first war in which modern communications was a critical factor—if in their failure. The "formula" for winning a war is "C³": Command, Control, Communications; but at the outset of the Great War, and almost to its end, the technology lag between communications on the one hand, and weaponry and munitions on the other, together with the vast scale of the battlefield, created insurmountable problems for command and control, and it was this lag or gap that caused the bulk of the problems that led to such disasters as Loos and the first day of the Somme (though "blurred command" and downright incompetence played their part too). Even champions of the generals would find it hard to number many military geniuses among them, but to call them all stupid is grossly unfair and manifestly absurd. Forty years of European peace had had a Darwinian effect, but the bulk of dolts and duds were ruthlessly culled in the opening weeks. Admitting to "grave shortcomings on the part of commanders", Joffre sacked dozens of his generals,[31] and more heads were to roll up to 1918, his own included, before his erstwhile subordinate Foch coordinated the final Allied counterattack. Clemenceau famously proclaimed that war is too important to be left to generals; less famously, he also observed that the Great War was a series of disasters culminating in victory, and it might prove chastening to remember that it was the generals who managed to gain that victory— sometimes, especially after Lloyd George became prime minister, despite the bungling, however well meaning, interference of politicians.

There seems to be a vague idea that somehow, if they weren't all geniuses, there were fewer German duds; but von Moltke's and von Prittwitz's loss of nerve in August 1914 proves that blunderers did breathe the air of the Fatherland, and by the end of the first year not only Prittwitz but Kluck and Moltke himself were gone: even highborn Prussian Junkers had to measure up or march off. Not just the German high command but more army commanders than Prittwitz failed, sacrificing strategic aims to tactical considerations almost as soon as they made contact with their enemy in the

Battles of the Frontier. Though similar beliefs were to be found everywhere in those years of supreme and sublime confidence in everything Christian (well, Protestant), and European (Anglo-Saxon American *in extremis*), it was in Germany more than anywhere that the "power of the will" was extolled,[32] long before Leni Riefenstahl made a variation on the expression infamous. Faith in triumph of the will reflected Germans' lead in the new science of psychology, Emil Kraeplin and Sigmund Freud being only two such Teutonic leaders in this field.

And perhaps the Germans were right: their generals, Moltke and Prittwitz in 1914 and Ludendorff in 1918, lost their nerve, while Joffre, Foch and Haig kept theirs.[33] Belief in science, and in their position at its cutting edge, may have been, in the ironic ways of war, why the Germans failed to win, for all their—otherwise deservedly—extolled military machinery: they placed their faith in radio and electronic communication, and these, in 1914, turned out to be less suited to mobile warfare than the relatively primitive motorcycle, as will be seen.

Muddling along behind the French and the Germans came the jolly old British, whose less-than-jolly old memories of their own civil war, Interregnum and allegedly Glorious Revolution had left them with a very unjolly view of standing armies: a downright jaundiced view, indeed. Their greatest general had described his own soldiers as the scum of the earth, a diametrically opposed opinion from that in Germany where, as Wellington's ally Blücher put it, "it must be a disgrace to a man not to have served [in the armed forces]". Major Frank Watson, MC, bluntly acknowledged "an ancient prejudice connecting soldiers with immorality and drink",[34] and Kipling well captured the ambivalent attitude a whimsical empire had toward its redcoat defenders:

> It's Tommy this an' Tommy that, an' "Tommy get outside!"
> But it's "Special train for Atkins" when the troopship's on the tide.

After Henry Tudor had ended the Civil War of the Roses, even more so after his granddaughter lost Calais, geographical isolation from the power conflicts of Europe had permitted the English usually to dispense with large standing armies, and after the Elector of Hanover took the United Kingdom throne in 1715, the British could call on German mercenaries to beat a few heads together in emergencies, such as the American War of Independence or the Irish Rebellion of 1798. The island nation of Great Britain—like England before it—rightly had seen that its independence was contingent on no power gaining Continental hegemony and seizing control of the Narrow Seas, thereby strangling British commerce and overwhelming Britain's naval defences. The Royal Navy was very much the Senior Service, Tommy Atkins playing second fiddle to Jack Tar. Rule Britannia, Britannia Rules the Waves—and thus much of the world by the time myriad European kings, despots and emperors had been successively disposed of, and the Continental territory acquired in the process of beating them became increasingly a liability as "wee German lairdies" became focused on kingship of an island nation (notably through George III's long reign). Conquered European territory, after each peace, was swapped for extensive wilderness across the various oceans.

It was to police the colonies that these wildernesses developed into that became the British Army's main role. Long before Victoria's time, the army was essentially a colonial gendarmerie, used from time to time, when necessary, as an expeditionary force that was landed by the Royal Navy in remote theatres of war or for hit-and-run strikes close to shore in the main theatre. The Great War is the only struggle in which Britain has fielded a full-size army in the main theatre of a Continental war and taken on the main enemy as his main antagonist. From holding about 25 miles of front at the outset—some five percent of the Western Front total—British troops had increased their liability fivefold by the end. But against their relatively short front "nearly half the German divisions on the Western Front were facing the British sector"[35]—and that was before Lloyd George imposed an extension of front on an already beleaguered Haig in January 1918, *and* withheld the troops to man this front.

By then Britain was fighting in the role of Western champion for her very life, and that of the Alliance. The French were in mutiny, the Russians and Romanians defeated, the Italians licking their wounds on the Piave, the Belgians and Serbs effectively out of the war almost from the start, the Americans still recruiting and training thousands of miles away, and twenty-odd jackal nations licking their chops before deciding which way to snap their yellow teeth. The BEF had been sorely battered by losses at the Somme and Third Ypres, and its ranks now were dangerously depleted further by Lloyd George's withholding of replacement troops to defend the line he himself had extended; yet its officers and NCOs kept up a remorseless training regime, and before war's end the German army had ceased to be the best in the world. When Ludendorff launched his offensive in March the British were driven back but their lines did not break, and they led the advance in the last Hundred Days, capturing territory, guns and prisoners out of all proportion to the size of their sector. It's probably not exaggeration to say that no army in the world was better than the BEF by that stage, and though victory was an Allied one, without the British contribution, through every year of war, it most likely would have been German.

For helmets must come off to those magnificent men who went to war in field-grey in 1914 and slogged it out against what ultimately proved insurmountable odds. For years they had been perceived, far beyond Europe, as "without equal in the world; a fine, strong, hardy, self-respecting, uniform body of men":[36] worthy foes. They defeated Belgium in 1914, Serbia in 1915, Romania in 1916 and Russia in 1917. They came close to defeating Italy in 1917 too, after Caporetto, and but for luck and tight security, which kept the French mutinies secret, they might have forced France to the table in that same year. What stopped them, to a very great extent, was the spirit of San Fairy Ann.

San Fairy Ann

In the course of the Great War many French expressions were wrenched and contorted to fit the less energetic—or more supercilious—British larynx, tongue and lips. The best known is *Ypres*, which of course became "Wipers", but there were countless others: the town of *Hinges* became, predictably, "Hinges", to the extent that eventually locals just shrugged and gave up, resigned to pronouncing the name as atrociously as Tommy Atkins did. "San Fairy Ann" was *Ca ne fait rien*—"that doesn't matter"—until Tommy got his teeth into it; by war's end even the French were saying "Sanfairyann".[37] But Tommy subtly changed the expression's meaning as well as its pronunciation. It came to have ironic or bitter connotations, a capturing of grotesquery in a phrase, sometimes expressed with "dark, sardonic mirth".[38] It could convey acceptance or even fatalism—or the very opposite. There was humour in the bizarre expression itself, especially to a better-read generation who could see Jabberwocky logic in the semantic nonsense—something of a metaphor for the whole war, that aspect.

Perhaps the most accessible interpretation of San Fairy Ann comes from the war that followed the expression's coining: "Who do you think you are kidding, Mr Hitler, / If you think Old England's done?" *Dad's Army* might be a comedy, but the lyrics of its theme song capture the alloy of courtesy and defiance that made Britain first indulge, but eventually challenge, German intransigence—and the sometimes-gallows humour that helped sustain morale through both world wars. For more than anything "San Fairy Ann" connoted determination and conviction, quietly sincere, comically understated, or defiantly aggressive, in the teeth of it all—it was *it all* that didn't matter. Before there was the "spirit of the Blitz" there was the "San Fairy Ann spirit", and this in turn was a restatement by the New Army volunteers of the Old Army's motto, "We'll do it; what is it?"—*ca ne fait rien*.

That spirit is thin on the ground today. So much has Britain changed in the interval that it can be difficult to imagine how society withstood the hardships of the war years; the 1914-18 generation likewise would be baffled and probably outraged by the society for which it sacrificed so much. Recently a school principal applied for, and was granted, a term's leave of absence because of "trauma" he had suffered from the drowning of one of his pupils, something that had occurred during the summer holidays, far away in France. Contrast such sad behaviour with the response of Harry Lauder to the loss of his only son, who also died in France, in very different circumstances.[39] Lauder's reaction was to get right back on stage in order to help keep up morale at home, to "do his duty", however daunting it must have been to sing cheerful songs even as his heart was breaking: "There was so much sorrow and grief in the land that it was the duty of all who could dispel it, if even for a little space, to do what they could". Later Lauder brought his act to entertain the troops in the front lines, the first artist to do so.[40] His determination to "keep right on to the end of the road" helped inspire his countrymen, and women, to do the same.[41]

San Fairy Ann: there was little self-indulgence, then. In the course of the retreat from Mons two artillery officers discuss an abandoned gun:

> "We must get back for it," said the captain.
> "We shall never return," replied the subaltern, gravely.
> "It doesn't matter," said the captain.
> "It doesn't matter," echoed the subaltern.

There is heroism and tragedy in those simple, commonplace words.[42]

Far from feeling sorry for themselves, people back then were more likely to be humbly grateful that things weren't worse. Alice Hackett's only son had taken his New Army father's place as family breadwinner and lost a leg in a mining accident at age fourteen, a few months before his father was killed in the war; yet thanking her late husband's chums for a whip-round they'd made (out of their shilling-a-day wage), Mrs Hackett wrote: "I don't know how to thank my kind friends that God has raised up for me in my trouble".[43]

To what extent this spirit of San Fairy Ann was truly felt, or rather feigned, is something that never can be gauged. "Keep the Home Fires Burning" expresses the San Fairy Ann spirit, yet it acknowledges the effort this takes:

> Let not tears add to their hardship as the soldiers march along,
> And although your heart is breaking let it sing this cheerful song.

While it's safe to say that to some extent at least people were putting a brave face on their fears, for whatever reasons, there can be no doubting the ingenuous sincerity of Mrs Hackett, and she was by no means alone. Her husband—the only man in the Tunnelling Companies to win a VC (posthumously)—could have saved himself from a gallery that had been blasted by a German *camouflet*, but he refused to leave a wounded companion behind; both men were buried alive.[44]

If in a different way, many of the music-hall songs of the time, not just "Home Fires", convey that spirit too. "Oh it's a Lovely War" was so successful in this regard that one suspects Joan Littlewood's hijacking of its title for her Marxist musical was a strategic decision, one designed to undercut, by poking fun at it, the spirit that had defied Fascism and Communism alike, and turned soldiers' notorious grumbling into constructive channels: if you can't make 'em listen, Tommy Atkins reckoned, make 'em laugh:

> When does a soldier grumble, when does he make a fuss?
> No one is quite contented in all the world as us.
> Oh it's a cushy life, boys; really we love it so.
> Once a fellow was sent on leave and simply refused to go.

This is the spirit that animated Bruce Bairnsfather's Old Bill. That there is no better 'ole to go to is San Fairy Ann, but making a laugh of such a glum reality is San Fairy Ann too. There was damn all in the front line to cheer any soldier, so *The Wipers Times* gravely warned its readers to watch out for signs that they might be "suffering from cheerfulness"—which they very often were: from the front line one officer wrote to his wife, "I wish you could come and have a look around here & see how everyone takes things, it would fairly astonish you. Even right up in the front people treat it rather as a huge joke, not that I mean that the actual business isn't taken seriously, but that the lighter side is given considerable prominence". Despite "Mud over your boot-tops everywhere", this officer and his men "seem to live in a constant state of uproarious laughter".[45] *The Wipers Times* exhorted, more seriously yet never succumbing wholly to gravity:

> As someone said, there's no road yet
> But has an end, your grinders set
> On this one thing, that if you grin
> And carry on, we're sure to win—
> "Stick it".[46]

Stick it—yes. But the greatest fear, among men at any rate, in those years, was of fear itself. "I was very frightened about myself as I didn't at all relish the idea of my nerve not standing the strain & was simply delighted when I found my fears to be groundless so far".[47] So men kept a brave face in order to keep their own fears in check, as well as to assure their wives or mothers; women did it to assure their children; soldiers did it for each other or for those whose lives it was their duty to defend. Yet one must not be cynical. If San Fairy Ann was affected betimes, its very affectation was manifestation of the spirit itself. Lieutenant Coningsby Dawson sounds preposterously naïve today, but his very naiveté makes it impossible to doubt the sincerity of his testimony in *The Glory of the Trenches: An Interpretation*: "'Guts' or courage is an attitude of mind towards calamity—an attitude of mind which makes the honourable accomplishing of duty more permanently satisfying than the preservation of self". Dawson remarks how in war men could "grow so accustomed to a brave way of living that they sincerely believed they were quite ordinary persons. That's courage at its finest—when it becomes unconscious and instinctive". In the stern spirit of the time, he's blunt—"Fear, in its final analysis, is nothing but selfishness"—yet fair and honest when he acknowledges a man who confesses to the fear of funking under fire as "the bravest man in the tap-room". Elsewhere he paints a bleak yet affecting image of the San Fairy Ann spirit when he describes the leave-taking of an Old Contemptible and his wife:

> He laid his clumsy hand on the woman's arm; she set down on the pavement the parcel she had been carrying. There they stood for a full minute gazing at each other dumbly. She wasn't pleasing to look at.... Stooping awkwardly for the burden which she had carried for him, in a shame-faced kind of way he kissed her, then broke from her to follow his companions. She watched him forlornly, her hands hanging empty. Never once did he look back.... [Eventually] she wandered off as one who had no purpose.[48]

There is no case made here that the war motorcyclist epitomised the San Fairy Ann spirit through the war; if anyone did this, it was the Poor Bloody Infantryman in the trenches, alongside whose lot the despatch rider—"Don R"—had it very cushy indeed. Indeed, the relative cushiness of his number is part of the reason why Don's story has been overlooked by posterity, as the endurance and heroism of the PBI, and the alleged callousness and incompetence of the Officer Class, came to dominate discussion of the Great War. But in overlooking the despatch rider posterity may have lost sight of the man who, though he never could have won the war, may well have prevented it from being lost.

For Roger West, blowing a bridge in the teeth of the German advance, with a carpet slipper on one foot, personified the San Fairy Ann spirit before the term was coined—as did other despatch riders of the early days. Don R was worked just as hard as the footsore infantryman, though the spirit that saw him through the fraught weeks of the "Great Retreat" of August-September 1914 was of a different sort. As Chapter Four describes, in the early stage of the war many despatch riders were more than comfortably off: among Roger West's colleagues were Lord B Blackwood and Sir M Monson.[49] Innumerable contemporary accounts testify, approvingly, to the high caste of early DRs, something that helps account for the extraordinary self-confidence that enabled them to accomplish what they did: after all, their fathers and uncles did run an empire, on which the sun smiled round the clock and which they would run in their turn; and if we of a more egalitarian age sneer at privilege, part of the reason we are able to sneer is that German militarism was defeated in no small measure by the mindset at which we sneer. One DR of the early days, WH Tait, describes in a single sentence, with almost comical sangfroid, his emergency roadside amputation of a dog's leg; it simply had to be done, just as for Roger West, "It seemed a pity to leave this bridge intact". (For all his modesty, West's adventure made the Official History, and he received the DSO.[50]) In that era privilege implied responsibility as well as self-confidence; those born to rule also were born to serve. One man is appalled by his younger brother's refusal to enlist, and his wife shares the sense of shame: "As you say it would be a sad day for us if Bobbo [their son] was his age and wasn't straining every nerve to go".[51] Creighton Richard Storey felt "as if we were fighting to save the world, and to die in such a cause we consider an honour".

Storey, a despatch rider, was killed in action.[52] Another DR, who survived, testified, "Despite the hardships of that War I do not regret one moment of my Service to my Country and being OHMS".[53] Such a sense of responsibility, coupled to an unshakeable faith in the superiority of British blood and mettle, led of course to disproportionate losses within that class,[54] and the socially elite nature of early DRs may be part of the reason why their importance came to be overlooked as egalitarianism replaced earlier values, a factor that will be examined later.

So Don did his bit, and an important bit his was, especially but not exclusively in the opening weeks of the war. As more than one officer testified: "Quite calmly and without depreciating our wonderful infantry (to whom I take off my hat), no one has put in harder work and got less recognition than artillery drivers and motor cycle orderlies";[55] but down the years the war motorcyclist's vital contribution to winning the war, notably during the Great Retreat, has been forgotten. "I wonder if those despatches really mattered"— at least one despatch rider frankly admitted his doubts about the need to have risked his life, so many times. "But when all is said and done, I did what I was told and that is all that matters, isn't it?"—the off-hand tone and the rhetorical nature of the question both so reflective of the difference between Don's world and ours; the self-deprecation of that generation and its attitude to duty. "It is easy to do things if a man simply obeys orders and defies the rest of creation to stop him".[56]

Easy? Perhaps if you believe in the doctrine that It Doesn't Matter, whatever *It* throws at you, you well may be able to defy the rest of creation in the course of doing your duty.

And there's something of San Fairy Ann in the fact that the name of that despatch rider who wondered if his work had made a difference has been lost: after all, we won the war; so does it matter, who he was?

San Fairy Ann?

What would Don R think?

And what should we think of Don?

Endnotes

1 Published anonymously in *Motor Cycling*, 27 November 1917, p. 49. The poem may have been published elsewhere prior to this, however, so its author's identity may not be lost. Any English scholar who might suggest that in charity it better remain lost ought to read on further only at great risk to all the prejudices his readings of the Trench Poets likely have substituted for understanding of the complexity that was and remains the Great War. "Bus" was a contemporary term for motorcycle.

2 Roger Rollaston West, "Diary of the War: Retreat from Mons to the Battle of the Aisne".

3 And some with no reservations at all—see, e.g., Peter Hart's *1918: A Very British Victory*.

4 Brian Bond, "*Disenchantment* Revisited", in *A Part of History: Aspects of the British Experience of the First World War*, p. 117.

5 See, e.g., Lyn Macdonald, *Ordeal By Fire: Witnesses to the Great War*, p. 308.

6 Frederic Manning, *Her Privates We*, pp. 114-15.

7 Dan Todman, *The Great War: Myth and Memory*, p. 26.

8 Richard Toye, *Churchill and Lloyd George*, p. 334.

9 Toye, ibid, p. 291.

10 Truth kept fighting back, though: an excellent example of this is Sidney Rogerson's *Twelve Days*, published in 1933 as what Malcolm Brown, in his introduction to a 2006 reissue (*Twelve Days on the Somme: A Memoir of the Trenches, 1916*), describes as "a determined attempt to hold back what by then had become an immensely powerful tide" (p. xiii).

11 William Woodruff, *The Road to Nab End*, pp. 250, 388.

12 George Orwell, *The Lion and the Unicorn: Socialism and the English Genius*, p. 48.

13 As if this were not enough, by the 1930s Frankau was a Fascist sympathiser; notoriously, he wrote "As a Jew I am not against Hitler", for the *Daily Express* in 1933 (to the amazement of no one, he later retracted his sentiments).

14 The humourless Puritanism of PC, the haunting fear that someone, somewhere, may be laughing at a racist or sexist joke—or perhaps just laughing—brings to mind Eduard Bernstein's observation that Marxism is Calvinism without God.

15 CE Montague, *Disenchantment*, p. 12.

16 John Laffin, *Butchers and Bunglers of the First World War*; Denis Winter, *Haig's Command*. The latter has often been described as a less than balanced view — see www.johndclare.net/wwi3_winter_thesis.htm.

17 GD Sheffield, *Leadership & Command: The Anglo-American Military Experience Since 1861*, pp. 93-84.

18 Robin Neillands, *The Old Contemptibles: The British Expeditionary Force, 1914*, p. 125.

19 The very existence of a "Schlieffen Plan" has been called into doubt by Terence Zuber in recent years. Dr Zuber's thesis is still being as stoutly defended as it

is contested, but even he would concede that by the time the BEF engaged the German First Army what history has termed the Schlieffen Plan had been put in train.

20 After the Second World War, a rueful Field Marshal Keitel acknowledged that, rather than invading Russia in order to deprive Britain of her "last hope" (part of Operation Barbarossa's strategy), the Reich should have put its energy and resources toward seizing Gibraltar, Malta and Suez, and thus to "strangle" the British Empire. His testimony supports the idea that a victorious Second Reich would have done the same.

21 Hartmut Pogge von Strandman, "Germans in Africa 1900-14: A Place in the Sun", p. 335; Thomas Pakenham, *The Scramble for Africa, 1876-1912*, p. 622.

22 Evidence that many Africans, ignorant of political correctness as of so much else since their liberation from Western oppression, look back on imperialism as a sort of golden age, may be found in Ritu Verma, *Gender, Land and Livelihoods in East Africa: Through Farmers' Eyes*, p. 186; Alan Little, "A frontier between civilisations"; Paul Salopek, "Shattered Sudan", p. 53 (to pick from a surprisingly lengthy list of sources).

23 George H Allen, Henry C Whitehead and FE Chadwick, *The Great War, Second Volume: The Mobilisation of the Moral and Military Forces*, p. 294.

24 *The Times History of the War*, Vol. I. p. 455.

25 Elizabeth Greenhalgh, "Why the British were on the Somme", for instance, as well as Denis Winter, John Laffin, and others.

26 Cited in Gary Sheffield, *The Somme*, p. 155.

27 Hart, ibid, p. 33.

28 So polarised has the Lions –v – Donkeys argument become that, as John Bourne puts it, any historian seeking to redress the imbalance "nearly always becomes[s] far more strident in Haig's defence than is proper and more than the evidence permits"—Brian Bond & Nigel Cave, *Haig: A Reappraisal 80 Years On*, p. 1.

29 He was known as General Duckboard because of the frequency of his visits to the trenches.

30 Toye, ibid, p. 293.

31 Barbara Tuchman, *The Guns of August*, p. 294. At least one, Lanrezac, was unfairly scapegoated.

32 David Lewis, *The Man Who Invented Hitler: The Making of the Führer*, Chapters Eight and Nine, and passim.

33 One could argue that German defeat at First Ypres was caused by failure of von Falkenhayn's nerve as well.

34 Watson, Frank, "A Territorial in the Salient". p. 33.

35 Hart, ibid, p. 26.

36 Allen *at al*, ibid, p. 226.

37 Lyn Macdonald, *Ordeal by Fire: Witnesses to the Great War*, p. 290. Such linguistic horrors had occurred as early as 1915: "You would be awfully amused how the language is being corrupted by contact with Tommy Atkins"—Anne Nason (ed), *For Love and Courage: The Letters of Lieutenant Colonel EW Hermon From the Western Front*, p. 114.

38 OH Davis, PP/MCR180, p. 194.

39 These two events in juxtaposition suggest another—highly speculative—way to account for latter-day hostility toward the Great War and anything to do with it: Oedipal envy for the courage and stoicism of those who had endured it, something that latter-day, softer generations well may doubt they could match;

discounting the value of this stoicism and courage reduces the internal dissonance such envy induces.

40 Harry Lauder, *A Minstrel in France*, pp. 111-12.

41 Gerald J DeGroot, *Blighty: British Society in the Era of the Great War*, p. 282.

42 *Motor Cycling*, 11 May 1915, p. 15.

43 Peter Barton, Peter Doyle and Johann Vandewalle, *Beneath Flanders Fields: The Tunnellers' War*, pp. 292-93.

44 Sapper Hackett could have avoided not just death but war service in the first place by virtue of both his age and reserved occupation, but his evident sense of duty was such that, at 42, he enlisted—on his fifth attempt. See Barton *et al*, ibid, 290-91.

45 Nason, ibid, pp. 15, 28.

46 *Suffering From Cheerfulness: The Best Bits From The Wipers Times*, p. 170.

47 Nason, ibid, p. 106.

48 Coningsby Dawson, *The Glory of the Trenches: A Manifestation*, pp. 62-63, 137, 77, 69. Some would call this reserve evidence of "stunted affect"; they might well be right, but is histrionics better for either individuals or collectives? (To say nothing of dignity.)

49 Roger West, ibid, pp 8, 46.

50 James Edmonds, *History of the Great War: Military Operations, France and Belgium 1914*, p. 243.

51 Nason, ibid, p. 96.

52 *Motorcycle and Bicycle Illustrated* (New York), 19 July 1917, p 34.

53 W George Mead, "Forty Thousand Hours of War", Introduction.

54 Andrew Marr, *The Making of Modern Britain: From Queen Victoria to VE Day*, p 207: "In the ten years after the war 29,000 small country estates were sold off, often simply because there was no heir to inherit them".

55 *The Motor Cycle*, 20 December 1917, p. 593. Artillery drivers, mounted on the near-side horses of every team, were exposed to both enemy fire and the weather, and the iron boot they had to wear on their right foot added to the chilling misery in cold weather.

56 *Motor Cycling*, 13 June 1916, p. 116.

1

Iron Men, Steel Machines

LIKE MUCH ELSE that characterised the Great War—in scale if not in novelty—the motorcycle was a product of the Second Industrial Revolution, the greatest beneficiaries of which were the USA and Germany. The latter new Great Power had emerged after the defeat of France in 1871, when Wilhelm, King of Prussia, was crowned German Kaiser in the Hall of Mirrors at Versailles, thus inaugurating the Second Reich. Otto von Bismarck, the Iron Chancellor of Prussia and now of the Reich, had used the anvil of war to weld Germany's 39 states into an empire under Prussian overlordship. Prussia, the Iron Kingdom, hatched from a cannonball, in Clemenceau's memorable phrase, was to impose its own martial vision onto all of Germany, which became more and more chauvinistic, xenophobic and belligerent under the last kaiser, until its militarism led its people to defeat.

Though he notoriously had declared that great issues of state would be determined not by democratic debate but by "iron and blood", Bismarck knew that the new Reich, surrounded by actual and potential enemies, needed peace to prosper, and he devoted the rest of his political life to maintaining the delicate new balance of power in Europe by a series of treaties—which also served the essential purpose of keeping France isolated, and thereby impotent to recover the lost provinces of Alsace-Lorraine, confiscated by the victor in 1871. These treaties served their purpose during Bismarck's time, but in the longer term they polarised Europe and made war probably inevitable; certainly there can be no doubt that the Second Reich struck fear into other powers, including, eventually, Great Britain, traditional ally of Prussia.[1] Apart from her military strength, Germany quickly became an economic giant, eventually surpassing Britain in industrial output. This need not have incurred the enmity of a trading nation, but when Wilhelm II inaugurated a naval race with the Island Empire, Britain's position in the world, and even her territorial integrity, was threatened. It was this factor that drove her into Entente with ancient enemies France and Russia.

What made Germany great after 1870 was not war but industry. If Bismarck renounced blood, he never renounced iron—but he did beat his swords into ploughshares. The Second Industrial Revolution significantly coincides with the years of the Second Reich: though that revolution is usually dated 1870-1914, the Great War gave it a final impetus, notably in the metallurgical advances driven by the war in the air. The Second Industrial Revolution, unlike the First, was marked by advancements in the science that underlay the technology; better understanding of natural laws and processes made advancement much more rapid, because technology now was more scientific and therefore advanced less by learning from mistakes. Germany had a long intellectual tradition (in 1914 only one in 5,000 army recruits was illiterate),[2] and Bismarck was quick to channel this toward polytechnic education in order to increase the new Reich's economic power. Polytechnic institutions served to disseminate scientific discoveries into myriad fields of technology so that overall gain was all the greater.

The Second Industrial Revolution also saw growth in the importance of economies of scale and throughput, and the emergence of technological *systems*, notably railway systems and electrical and telegraphic networks. As early as 1835 Carl Steinheil saw the advantage of running railway and telegraphic services together, and that of earth return in electrical circuits, something that was to feature in subsequent years in field telegraphy and motorcycle electrics, and prove problematic in both. Such systems were critical in the Great War and the need for standardisation in them saw the sort of governmental "interference" that both traditional liberals and conservatives hated, and that was to grow remorselessly through the war years—and stay with us ever since.

The Second was in great contrast to the First Industrial Revolution, which had been very much pragmatic, opportunistic, and all but confined to Great Britain. The First Industrial Revolution had been an age of iron, cast and wrought; but the limitations of iron were long apparent. Cast iron was brittle and therefore unsuitable for many purposes, while wrought iron, though it had many of the qualities of steel, needed to be forged from white-hot lumps taken from the furnace and thus was labour-intensive and very expensive. Steel, an alloy of iron and carbon and perhaps other elements, could be much harder, tougher and versatile, but it was even more expensive than wrought iron to manufacture.

Then, in 1856, Henry Bessemer discovered that by blasting compressed air through molten pig iron, carbon impurities combined with oxygen in this air and served as a source of heat that helped keep the iron molten until impurities were oxidised and blown out of the "converter". Cheap steel was on its way. Soon afterward, Charles Siemens developed the open-hearth process of steel manufacture. In 1878 Percy Gilchrist and Sidney Thomas discovered that if the hearth was lined with dolomite, phosphorus and other harmful contaminants separated out from the molten metal to form slag, which could be drawn off. Steel now was not merely a fifth or less of its previous cost, but it could be made in vastly greater volume—and economies of scale meant that cost was further reduced.

It was Germany that benefited from these inventions because she had no large-scale factory-industrial infrastructure whose very existence militated against replacement with new technology. So Britain soldiered on with blast furnaces and crucible steel and lost ground to German Bessemer converters and open hearths (just as, a century later, British motor and motorcycle industries were to struggle with outdated designs and machinery against superior products from the Continent and Japan). Gilchrist and Thomas's invention was a particularly welcome development in Germany, because iron ores from the newly acquired province of Lorraine were rich in phosphorous, something that had impeded their exploitation previously. In the first twenty years of the Reich, Germany's annual steel output went from 126,000 tons to 17.6 million tons; that of Britain, still working with older technology, had a much more modest increase, from 334,000 tons to 7.7 million tons. By 1914 Britain was importing steel from Germany, whose industrial economy was now about six times that of Britain.

The Lorraine ore fields in themselves significantly account for Germany's expansion in industrial output, and the reparations demanded from defeated France provided a capital reserve that had helped fund new German industry and expand the railway system. Another factor was Germany's increase in population (from fifty million in 1890 to sixty-seven million in 1914), which provided both a workforce and a market for consumer goods. The cartel system that was adopted by German industry maximised profit and ensured widest dissemination of up-to-date technology; it therefore gave Germany a significant international advantage during the Long Depression (mid-1870s to mid 1890s), and enabled her to emerge early (about 1887) out of that.

The cartels' dissemination of up-to-date technology, coupled to German advantage in electronics, help to account for a somewhat odd fact. Before the war, though Britain imported steel from Germany, the German firm of Goldschmidt had imported 150,000 tons of used tin cans from Britain every year; for in addition to her advances in steel manufacturing, Germany was world leader in steel recycling, something that was of inestimable value after the Royal Navy's blockade was laid down, when the Germans began an active campaign to source and import scrap from adjacent neutrals, and vigorously scavenged the battlefields. Goldschmidt melted the solder from cans, and used electrolysis to recover tin-plating from the steel. The lead in the solder was of course needed for bullets, and tin also was vital for any industrial economy, but most important was the salvaged steel, which was rammed into hundredweight bales and despatched to the steelworks for reuse. Pre-war British attempts to recycle tin cans had been unsuccessful, in part because the country's comparatively primitive electronics industry was unable to strip tin-plating on the scale necessary, and tin and lead contamination compromised the quality of the steel when whole cans were melted down.[3]

Vitally important to German economic growth was the standardisation and extension of railway systems, a reflection of the Prussian spirit. It was strategic use of railways that had enabled the concentration of forces that had won the battles of 1870, and though there is no reason to doubt Bismarck's commitment to pacifism after the Reich had been secured, the threat of French *revanche* demanded further development of a strategic railway system. After Bismarck's dismissal the Kaiser took an increasingly belligerent approach, and after 1898 the programme of naval expansion provided a massive increase in demand for steel. (Curiously, though in later years more advanced technology meant that ships of the Third Reich had welded hulls, stronger and lighter than the riveted hulls of Royal Navy ships, thereby improving speed and allowing more tonnage to be given to guns and shells, the first welded hull was that of HMS *Fulagar*, in 1917.[4])

Apart from her long strides in steel technology, Germany had made further technological advances that gave her a sharper edge. Her chemists realised that the slag produced by the lime-rich dolomite and waste phosphorus of Lorraine ore was an excellent fertilizer, and thereby turned the "waste" of the new steelworks to an asset. Justus von Liebig already had proved the value of chemicals in agriculture, and the salt deposits of the Rhine valley, as well as by-products of the coalfields of the Ruhr and Alsace, furthered Germany's lead in the field of industrial chemistry. At the start of the new century Fritz Haber and Carl Bosch developed a process that synthesised ammonia from atmospheric nitrogen and hydrogen. Ammonia then was incorporated into artificial fertilisers, Liebig having proved that nitrogen is an essential component for plant growth, and these fertilisers boosted agricultural output and helped Germany withstand the naval blockade through the subsequent war. But of greater importance, ammonia also was an essential component in explosives manufacture, and during the war, initially from ammonia, Haber developed various poison gasses.[5]

Germany's lead in the field of chemistry, coupled to her steel advantage, clearly was of huge benefit to her armaments industry. Long before Haber-Bosch, in 1845 Christian Friedrich Schönbein had used his wife's apron to mop up spilled nitric and sulphuric acids; when he spread the apron before the stove to dry, it combusted so thoroughly that it seemed to disappear. From this chance event Schönbein developed nitrocellulose, or guncotton, fine cotton wool immersed in the two acids and then further treated. By almost uncanny coincidence, something that might seem to portend the dismal future, not one but two other German chemists, Rudolf Böttger and FJ Otto, simultaneously discovered guncotton that same year. Guncotton was about six times as powerful as black powder, produced less waste heat and was virtually smokeless, so it could make an excellent artillery propellant. It was dangerously unstable, but in 1891 James Dewar and Sir Frederick Abel discovered how to combine it with equally unstable nitroglycerine in long cords that made a powerful explosive that was safe to handle: cordite.

By contrast to Germany's, in 1914 Britain's capacity for ammunition manufacture was poor: there were ten or fewer shells provided per gun per day at First Ypres. Early bottlenecks were due to propellant shortages, the British chemical industry lagging far behind the German, with ante-bellum dependence for propellant on Germany and Austria. Later ammonal (a compound of ammonium nitrate, trinitrotoluene, coarse aluminium powder and charcoal) was substituted for trinitrotoluene (TNT)-proper; ammonal contained only fifteen percent TNT. Fuses likewise caused problems: the 106 percussion "fuze" (in the spelling of the time), which was to become essential as artillery became more and more sophisticated and important, was copied from a German design.

Britain's petrochemical industry was tiny and her optics industry all but non-existent, so that through the war she had to trade with Zeiss through Switzerland;[6] but a more critical problem, especially for communications, was the lag in electronics technology. Germany was a world leader here as well: Siemens had developed gutta-percha insulation back in 1847, Felten and Guilleaume produced submarine cable seven years later, Thames watercraft were using Siemens electric motors by 1882 and, as has been seen, British industry was unable to deal with electrolytic stripping of scrap tin cans in the way that German industry was.

But irony is an intrinsic aspect of war: it was in part because of her very lead in electronic communications that Germany failed to win the war in the West in 1914. And her failure there and then boded ill for victory later: for all her calculations, given a two-front war, were mooted on a rapid victory against France and Britain, followed by leisurely defeat of the ponderous Russian Empire.

The irony becomes more impressive when we examine why Germany failed at the outset. The strutting Kaiser had made himself a cipher for the new Reich, a vain *parvenu* that looked down on the has-been British Empire, and sought to elbow the older empire aside in its race to the future. It is possible that at the outbreak of war the Second Reich had over 20,000 motorcycles serving its armies,[7] but their usefulness seems to have been underestimated— certainly underrated *vis-à-vis* more up to date technology. The bumbling older empire, by contrast, starved of resources by well-intentioned Liberals, was glad to grasp at anything—specifically a hundred-odd second-hand motorbikes, the products of an industry that many of the scions of empire scorned.

And one whose most successful product owed its existence to a couple of *émigré* Krauts and an Englander. It was called, significantly enough perhaps, Triumph—though many other marques were to feature in the eventual Allied triumph.

Another product of the Second Industrial Revolution was to loom large and airy in the Great War, though this one came from the land of the Johnny-come-lately Doughboy. Cheap steel and efficiencies of modern manufacturing meant that, twenty years after its invention in 1874, it cost a tenth of what it had then. At 45 cents a pound, barbed wire was cheap.[8] It was to be cheaper by 1914, and to make human life cheaper still.

The Mighty Bicycle

When asked what he thought of the French Revolution, Chou Enlai famously replied, "It's too early to tell". This reply often is presented as evidence for profound Oriental wisdom; an insistence on long-term contemplation and evaluation before presuming to venture an opinion on the past. Such flattering representation of Mr Chou and his culture rather reflects on the faux-liberalism of Western hacks who fawningly reported his remarks, and it exposes the danger to any society of following any "intelligentsia" that thinks with its ideology. For what Mr Chou was doing was nothing more profound than kicking to touch: had he ventured any *real* opinion on the French Revolution—i.e. had he made a *substantial* answer—a potentially dangerous question on the *Chinese* Revolution might have followed, the answer to which could have seen Mr Chou end his days in a re-education camp.

If it's so easy to miss the obvious in our own time, how much harder is it to spot the subtle in the past? Who knows now that it was the bicyclist, and not the pioneer motorist, who led to the first modern road maps being drafted?[9] Who now remembers Susan B Anthony's assertion that the development of the open-frame bicycle "had done more to emancipate women than anything else in the world"?[10] Who could believe that the harmless bicycle did more than any gun to initiate the dissolution of the British Empire?

This is no farfetched notion. The bicycle became available to the rural masses of Ireland in the 1890s, when the Fenian Brotherhood was diverting its considerable energies and impressive organisational skills into those movements that were emerging out of the political stagnation that Tory hegemony meant for the Irish Parliamentary Party and constitutional Irish nationalism. In particular the GAA (Gaelic Athletic Association) was organising combative sporting events across the country, and the bicycle enabled the masses to travel to participate in and support local competition, while national competition was made possible by an alliance of the bicycle and the railway. Thus the bicycle broadened ordinary people's horizons, which in turn left them more exposed to radical ideas, and strengthened their sense of national identity, even as competition in very robust games honed their competitive, quasi-martial skills. The militant Fenians subverted GAA sporting clubs and turned them toward their own ends, and subverted the bicycle too.

In short, the bicycle was one of the most revolutionary products of the Second Industrial Revolution. Its origins lie in the First, and by 1839 the design was established, notably in France. In that year a Scottish blacksmith called Kirkpatrick MacMillan built a heavy, clumsy two-wheeler made of wood and with iron-shod compression-spoke wheels. It weighed 57 pounds and was an unpromising revolutionary, but on it Mr MacMillan could cover the fourteen miles between his home at Keir Mill and Dumfries in less than an hour, and in 1842 he rode it 68 miles to Glasgow (where he was fined five shillings for speeding—at eight miles an hour).[11] The MacMillan machine differed from earlier French and German designs in that drive was not to the front wheel, but by a pair of treadles and rods to a crank on the rear-wheel spindle. This arrangement allowed for improving leverage between pedal-crank and driven wheel, while the connecting-rod arrangement anticipated the "slow speed engines" that were used in early motorcycles like the German Hildebrand and Wolfmüller or the British Holden (the connecting rods of these motorcycles ran directly from the pistons to cranked rear wheel spindles).

The MacMillan also marked the shift of bicycle development from the Continent to Great Britain, though the significance of its rear wheel drive was lost sight of for a while. In 1871 James Starley constructed an all-metal-framed machine that since has become known as the penny farthing—though this name was not conferred until later, and disparagingly. The wheels of Starley's bicycle used steel rims shod with solid rubber tyres, and thin steel spokes acting in tension, so it was much closer to the modern bicycle than anything that had been built before. It marked an important threshold in development because it was manufactured, not from iron and wood but from steel, by now increasingly affordable. However, it still cost about half a working man's annual income, so the bicycle remained a wealthy man's curiosity, and the very large front wheel, which was necessary to give enough leverage to the spindle crank to enable worthwhile speed to be generated, made the machine unwieldy, difficult to mount, and all but bereft of brakes, as inertia would pitch the rider, mounted high above the centre of the contraption's gravity, over the handlebars were he so rash as to decelerate hard.

Nevertheless, "the horse that never says neigh", if still a rich man's indulgence, was now a potentially useful vehicle. Thomas Stevens set off from

California on one in 1884 and covered more than 13,000 miles on it. By the time he returned, almost two years later, problems of height and braking had been addressed by John Kemp Starley, James's nephew, who developed the "safety bicycle", which relegated his uncle's design to the "ordinary bicycle", and eventually, dismissively, the "penny farthing". The new "diamond" frame combined structural integrity, low weight and compactness, and is with us still. Advances in steel technology, in scientific insight and—perhaps most importantly—in mass manufacturing, were essential to his bicycle's development. Cheap steel had made light rims and tension-spokes possible; tangential spokes, which spread the load across a far wider arc of the wheel rim than the original radial spokes, had been incorporated into the "ordinary" back in 1874, making for a much stronger wheel.

The safety bicycle depended for its revolutionary success on cheapness, reliability and low maintenance requirements. Cheapness was a product of the Second Industrial Revolution, reliability and low maintenance on developments of this, and each was predicated on both harder steel than hitherto had been available, and much more precise mass-manufacturing techniques. Ball bearings allowed a higher loading to be applied to a lighter rolling assembly, so made possible stronger, lighter wheels. Ball bearings also were fitted to the pedal-crank housing of the new bicycle, to take the thrust loading of the rider's whole body weight.

The second of these tertiary developments enabled efficient transmission of the rider's weight and leg-power from the pedals to the back wheel while facilitating increased leverage to a relatively small wheel by means of different sized sprockets. British resident Swiss engineer Hans Reynold had invented the roller chain in 1880, and a chain running over sprockets was lighter and more efficient in transmitting power than crank-and-rod drive. But a drive chain was—and remains—an assembly of very precisely manufactured pins, bushings, rollers and side-plates. Each of these components calls for different qualities than the others—toughness, tensile strength and shear resistance in varying measures—so the roller chain is a quite sophisticated assembly, something whose invention was predicated on the Second Industrial Revolution. It was regarded by the conservative British Army as so new-fangled that it had to be replaced by the proven belt in most British war motorcycles.

The safety bicycle still is on the road, however refined since Starkey's time. One of the most significant early developments to affect it was John Dunlop's invention of the pneumatic tyre; two years later the bicycle wheel was modified to take a beaded tyre that would mount an inflatable tube, rather than the solid rubber tyre that had been used up until then. Another invention, one that took the bicycle off down a separate avenue of development entirely, was the internal combustion engine.

The motorised bicycle, like the bicycle itself, was developed on the Continent but perfected in Great Britain. The first successful petrol-engined vehicle was fitted to Gottlieb Daimler and Wilhelm Maybach's test-bed motorised bicycle, the *einspur*, in 1885. An obscure British inventor called Edward Butler had beaten them on paper by a year, but his tricycle was not built until 1887, and his design languished in a land that was to retain the Red Flag for almost ten more years.[12] The first successful motorcycle was built in 1889 when Henry and Wilhelm Hildebrand, Alois Wolfmüller, and their (since overlooked) mechanic Hans Geisenhof, fitted a light steam engine into a safety bicycle. This drove the rear wheel directly by rod-and-crank, as on Blacksmith MacMillan's bicycle, and soon it was replaced by an internal combustion engine—first a two-stroke, then a four-stroke. There was no clutch to disconnect the drive, and the only speed control was a thumbscrew mounted on the handlebar, a crude device that adjusted the supply of fuel from an equally crude surface-vaporiser carburettor. Ignition was by "hot tube" protruding into the combustion chamber, heated by external flame. The new invention was demonstrated at the first Paris Motor Show in 1895 (where it was presented as La Petrolette in deference to anti-German feelings). So crude was it in operation, however, so clearly a rich man's curiosity (like the velocipede of eighty years before) that by 1897 Hildebrand and Wolfmüller were out of business.

But two years earlier one Maurice Schulte had brought a demonstrator model to England, where he settled down and began to tinker with his baggage. By now the French concerns of Peugeot and De Dion Bouton had developed "high speed engines" that used enclosed crankcases and "make-and-break" electrical circuits to generate a spark, in place of external crank and con-rod linkages and hot-tube ignition.[13] More than one Englishman already was making engines and fitting them into bicycles, but it took Herr Schulte's Teutonic thoroughness and scientific application to make the first reliable, everyman motorcycle. In the ironic way of war, Herr Schulte's Triumph was soon to play a critical part in defeating his homeland Reich.

For if the bicycle was instrumental in initiating the dismemberment of the British Empire in 1916, the motorcycle may have saved that Empire from military defeat two years earlier.

Endnotes

1 In 1873, in the anarchy that characterised the First Spanish Republic, the British and German navies together captured two frigates of the Cartagena canton, the ships being effectively pirate vessels. This cooperation was in utter contrast to the naval rivalry that brought Britain into the anti-German Entente thirty years later; but even as Prussia's war with France was being fought many Englishmen were coming to believe that their country had been outflanked by a cunning and dangerous foe. See George Tomkyns Chesney's *The Battle of Dorking* and IF Clarke's introduction to the OUP's 1997 combination edition of that book and Saki's *When William Came.*

2 George H Allen, Henry C Whitehead and FE Chadwick, *The Great War, Second Volume: The Mobilisation of the Moral and Military Forces,* p. 210. Germany's was a conscript army, incorporating all classes, and evaluation of standards of literacy may have been less demanding than today's, but the statistic remains impressive.

3 "Autolycus of the Battlefield", *War Illustrated*, Volume 9, pp. 3172-73; Edward Wright, "The Great Work of Salving War Material", www.greatwardifferent.com/Great_War/Garbage_of_War/Garbage_of_War_01.htm.

4 Alexander and Street, *Metals in the Service of Man,* p. 260.

5 During the next war Zyklon B, which also was Haber's invention, was used to murder most of his extended family, for Haber was a Jew.

6 The morality of such inter-belligerent trade is questionable at best. As will be seen, such trade in motorcycle parts also occurred, at least in the early years of the war.

7 "The German military authorities, according to a German technical journal, possessed at the outbreak of war no fewer than 20,335 motor cycles"—*The Motor Cycle*, 27 September 1917, p. 304.

8 Olivier Razac, *Barbed Wire: A History,* p. 14.

9 I'm obliged to Mr David Minton for bringing this to my attention. Road maps had been drawn up at least as early as the 18th century, but they were not designed for ordinary road users, but for ordnance and other governmental purposes.

10 Nelly Bly, "Champion of her Sex", p. 10.

11 The sentencing magistrate is said to have personally paid the fine, so impressed was he by Blacksmith MacMillan and his wondrous invention.

12 See Ixion, ibid, pp. 13-14, and David Burgess Wise, "Pioneers: How It All Began", pp, 1288-90. "The Red Flag" here refers to the requirement for a pedestrian to bear a warning red flag in advance of all cars up until 1895.

13 "Make-and-break" was the term of the time for contact-breaker ignition. Initially an "accumulator"—a battery—supplied low-tension DC current to a high-tension ignition coil, which discharged its magnetically-induced energy to a spark plug. Soon afterward the self-contained AC magneto, a German invention, took over, and was to give yeoman service to the motorcycle industry for sixty years; to the aero industry for even longer.

A "high speed engine" might, on the test bench, hit a dizzy 3000 rpm, about ten times that of a "low speed engine"; but a radial aero-engine of the Great War typically "revved out" at 1250 rpm; even the most impressive Mercedes straight-six produced maximum power at 1750 rpm—and this by the end of the war, after it had undergone great development.

2

To War on Two Wheels

Not in the Fighting Line

Hussars, Dragoons and Lancers, Horse Guards and Fusiliers,
At the enemy fling, and they leave their sting, while the watching Empire
    cheers.
Devons, Gloucesters and Yorkshires, Black Watch and the old Scots Guard,
Get in their blows, and the German knows that the British boys hit hard.
Artillery, field and siege guns, and the sapper who lays the mine,
Each writes his name on the Roll of Fame as a man of the fighting line.

But as you acclaim each honoured name from the land of Thames and Tyne,
Remember our sons behind the guns who are not in the fighting line.

Transport, ambulance, convoys, men of the Motor Corps—
These are the boys who, without any noise, are doing the grim work of war.
Cyclist and motorcyclist, the Mercury of today,
Who carries the news that the Generals use to help them to govern the fray.
Men of the same old spirit, men who our race refine—
Men who were taught in the world of sport how to ride to the fighting line.

When you shout "Hurrah" for the proud Hussar, remember this ditty of
    mine—
The man in the strife who may risk his life, though he's not in the fighting
    line.

PB[1]

THE BEF IN Europe, originally a holding force of four divisions, had by the
end of the war, become five armies. The changes it underwent in four years
were extraordinary, going far beyond mere expansion. Compared to artillery
or the aeroplane the war motorcycle changed very little, yet it made an essential
contribution to victory. By contrast and ironically—given that it had been

invented in Germany—the Kaiser's armies underrated the motorcycle, being so Teutonically technocratic that they relegated motorcycles to a position of tertiary importance and placing their faith in telegraph and wireless, with critical consequences in August 1914. Further irony lies in the fact that a great bulk of British DRs were mounted on Triumph motorcycles, and the Triumph factory had been founded, and still was managed then, by Herr Maurice Schulte.[2]

Though tiny by Continental standards, the British Army was the most mechanised in the world—something that gives the lie to popular notions of hidebound, hippophile generals, especially when one considers that for years British politicians, unlike the Germans, were loath to invest in motorising their army, rather irresponsibly depending on the volunteer spirit of private motorists should war break out. These did, like the rest of the nation, live up to expectations in August 1914, but by then the government also had taken action. The value of the motorcycle, like that of the car, was appreciated by the military early on, one officer reporting back in 1909 that despatch riders were "most useful" on manoeuvres. The same officer, addressing the Royal Automobile Club, acknowledged that in a lecture on "The Use of Motor Vehicles in War" he had, apart from a couple of brief references, "not dealt with motor cycles because they were so important as to demand a Paper to themselves".[3] During the war motorcycles were "regarded as an inseparable part of a modern army"[4]—in the words of one officer, "as much a fixture as the machine gun"[5]—and "the motor cyclist and his machine [were] probably the most popular unit in the British Army".[6] An American war correspondent writes admiringly of "motor-cycle despatch riders, leather-jacketed and mud-bespattered, the light-horsemen of modern war".[7] Britons heartily agreed. A correspondent of the *Daily Mail* proclaimed: "Every General Staff Officer to whom I have spoken is enthusiastic about the work [the 'motor cyclist corps'] is doing, and as a corps, it certainly has not its equal in any army in the field".[8] "For sheer excitement the life of the motor-cyclist despatch rider beats everything", proclaimed *The Graphic*. In a later edition it elaborated:

> There are no more enterprising and ingenious persons in our armies in France than the master despatch riders. The way these lads career about the roads, which are badly cut up by the enormous amount of horse and motor transport, through clouds of blinding dust, between lanes of horses and guns, dodging restive animals or big holes ploughed out by long range shells, is extraordinary.[9]

All contemporary accounts seem to concur: "the motor-cycle for the quick conveyance of despatches was unequalled".[10] "When the full history of the European war is written there will be many tales of valour and devotion to duty by 'the Signals', as despatch riders are called in the army";[11] testified yet another correspondent: "No men are braver, and very few render more important service, than the motor cycle scouts."[12]

Endorsement by commercial interests proves popularity. The motorcycle was found on the cigarette cards so popular then, and for decades afterward: Gallagher's *The Great War* series of 1916 includes a despatch rider on a Douglas with the caption: "A great feature of the modern British Army is the motor-cyclist despatch rider. These carriers have superceded horsemen for speedily carrying messages from point to point of the firing-line....".[13] No 42 card in Wills Cigarettes' 1915 series *War Incidents* depicts two DRs racing along a heavily-shelled road. A 1930s series by Wills portrays not merely the more dashing war-zone motorcyclist but "Air raid wardens and civilian volunteer despatch rider", showing that the war motorcycle had not quite been eclipsed in the public mind by more radical machinery even twenty years later. Horlicks was advertised as being "especially useful to Army Motor Cyclists",[14] the target audience doubtless including DR wannabes, and one factory set up in Birmingham to manufacture the "Despatch Rider" motorcycle. This

The ubiquitous —
— Despatch rider.
They have a lively time
on the damaged roads.

The Motor Machine-
guns are famous
for their mobility —

At the time, motorcycles and their riders were perceived as glamorous and exciting, in direct combat or in support.[15]

was, one suspects, a cheap-and-nasty assemblage of generic components, among them a proprietary two-stroke engine, which the army by then had set its face against. The machine probably never went into production, as civilian motorcycle manufacture was stopped shortly afterward, but its very conception proves the marketable popularity of the despatch rider.

As well as being championed in the popular press, Don R featured in ripping yarns of the time, e.g. Percy Westerman's *The Dispatch-Riders*, Captain Charles Gilson's *Motor Scout in Flanders*, and Max Pemberton's "Battle of the Great High Road and How the Despatch Rider Came Home".[16] When the USA embarked on war in 1917 the visceral appeal of the DR still was strong, his self-sufficiency and initiative appropriated as American virtues when Frederick Jackson Turner's Frontier Hypothesis of American greatness was approaching the zenith of its popularity.[17] Before and through the war Lieutenant Howard Payson published a *Motor Cycle Chums* series of books about boy scouts and young American motorcyclists on high adventure.

The fictive popularity of DRs was well founded in their factual value, which was evident even before war broke out. The Ulster Volunteers' gunrunning operation was so successful partly because of them; in a contemporary report they are mentioned many times, always in admiring tones, e.g.: "Splendid service was rendered during the operations by the Ulster Despatch Riders and Signalling Corps [who] were charged with the duty of establishing communications throughout the province…. The despatch riders were in the saddle all night, and covered a vast amount of ground".[18] Some of these Ulster Volunteer DRs were women, and GA Birmingham wrote an amusing short story, set against the Ulster Crisis, about an Irish Nationalist MP accidentally running down and then rescuing one.[19] Clair Wallace Hayes included motorcyclists in her *Boy Allies* adventure series—though her motorcyclists tended to be German Baddies, which may say something about the genders' respective perceptions but more likely was inspired by a myth from the early days of "spy mania" that had a motorcycle-mounted German saboteur and assassin riding rampant across England.[20] Before Captain WE Johns there was Colonel James Fiske, who wrote about youthful motorcyclists in the *World's War Series*. In Volume 2 of this series two boy scouts, working for the War Office at home, break a spy ring by tracking a chain of heliograph stations across England on their motorcycles; in Volume 5 another pair of youthful motorcycling chums have moved closer to the front line.[21]

Fiske's heroes are in the Biggles mode, even younger, but his accounts may be less far-fetched than our cosseted times may credit, for boys as well as men back then were affected by the spirit of San Fairy Ann.[22] Hoping to enlist as a DR alongside Captain Watson was a "phenomenally grave small boy".[23] Corporal F Raymond was three months short of sixteen when he enlisted at the outbreak of hostilities; he served as a despatch rider in Mesopotamia.[24]

More than half of the men who broke the Hindenburg Line were under twenty, little more than boys, and boy scouts were included with riflemen, Guardsmen and hussars in the risqué music hall song, "I'll Make a Man of You". The scout movement had been founded during one of the invasion scares that preceded the war, and among the boys' envisaged roles was watching the seas for the German fleet. Boy scouts were rated highly by Kitchener himself, who refused to allow General Lord Baden-Powell to return to active service, on the grounds that his work with the Boy Scout movement was more important. It's tempting to suspect this as being charitable camouflage for "Stellenbosching" the elderly Baden-Powell,[25] but we should not be too dismissive: on the home front boy scouts served as orderlies, despatch riders and motorists, as well as in more humble roles, with the energy and enthusiasm of youth and the Muscular Christian confidence of the time imbued in them. "Scouts alone could be relied upon to carry dispatches from anywhere to anywhere else in the same county in the shortest possible time," thanks to their local knowledge, and Lloyd George acknowledged their "most energetic and intelligent help in all kinds of service".[26] Belgian boy scouts, albeit some of military age, played an active part in civilian resistance,[27] while back in Blighty one general proclaimed, "Whenever I go to a new place I always look first for a Boy Scout to act as guide".[28] Other officers also found them

> most reliable and useful.... A day or two after joining [the WO] I wanted to make the acquaintance of a colonel ... whose apartment nobody in the place could indicate. A War Office messenger despatched to find him came back empty-handed. Another War Office messenger sent on the same errand on the morrow proved no more successful. On the third day I summoned a boy scout into my presence—a very small one—and commanded him to find that colonel and not to come back without him. In about ten minutes' time the door of my room was flung open, and in walked the scout, followed by one of the biggest sort of colonels. "I did not know what I had done or where I was being taken," remarked the colonel, "but the boy made it quite clear that he wasn't going to have any nonsense; so I thought it best to come quietly."[29]

In the years since then, though, Colonel Fiske has been forgotten, and no other popular writer, any more than military theorist or historian, has emerged to champion the war motorcyclist. The fact that Captain Johns displaced Colonel Fiske reflects the relegation of the motorcycle, in the military mind and in the popular imagination, by the aeroplane and, later, the tank. In Colonel JFC Fuller's words, "without the petrol engine the war would have been pronouncedly different";[30] but, like everyone else, "Boney" ignores the value of the motorcycle, focused, as he was, on tanks. The motorcycle did far more to win the war than the tank did,[31] but in addition to its being eclipsed by more exciting, more futuristic machinery, "post-war culture came to focus on the soldier in the trench as the iconic experience of the real war",[32] so memory of the war motorcyclist and his importance was whittled away at both ends.

Relegation of the motorcycle is understandable—certainly more so than today's absurd and infantilising Health and Safety regulations, which forbid boy scouts to light campfires, far less help win wars.[33] Though the motorcycle was invaluable, perhaps literally essential to victory, its limitations *vis-à-vis* the plane and the tank are obvious. It was a key component in communications, which are vital to army effectiveness, but so too was the plane, which became more important as the war went on and both aero- and camera-technology became more sophisticated. Depending on the weather, thousands of aerial photographs could be taken every day—how much vital information did these photographs convey?[34] Add to the value of reconnaissance and communication the fact that a plane also could be used as a combat weapon and thereby, like the tank, directly boost the morale of harassed infantry as their guns blazed in support.

All that acknowledged, one should bear in mind that it was the despatch rider who collected film from reconnaissance planes and later delivered developed photographs to the trenches;[35] and certainly the DRLS motorcyclist's delivery of mail boosted morale too, and on a constant basis. But it did not do so at such emotionally critical moments.

Another factor is that the DRLS's low-profile regularity tended to undercut its importance—or at any rate render its importance transparent to both soldier and historian, as the ubiquity of the motorcycle led it too to be overlooked.

The motorcycle, despite a few attempts to make it serve directly in combat—some of them bizarre (see below)—remained through the war what it had been at the start. Improvements were minor; they could not possibly have measured against the extraordinary rate of development of the aeroplane, or of the tank. The difference in performance between the mechanised box kites and *eindekker* Taubes of 1914, and the Camel and the *Dreidekker*, the Gotha and the Vimy, were all but revolutionary. The Mark V tank might not have been much faster than the Mark I, but its reliability had been greatly improved, and if the Whippet was no Panzer it could outpace the infantry.

This admitted, a survey of contemporary sources cannot fail to reveal the importance with which the motorcycle was regarded then—and rightly so. And if it never developed as the plane and tank did, it sustained its usefulness through the war, and that usefulness remained essential to waging war. Its rider, too, was often discounted.

But if it was treated with a certain complacency, the motorcycle was not humble fare; and given that the motorcyclist, antebellum, almost by definition was well to do, the prejudice against him (or of course her, the Baroness de T'Serclaes and Mairi Chisholm, "the Madonnas of Pervyse" being only two of countless "motorcyclistes", in the term of the time) seems explicable only in terms of perennial resentment of the young by the old—for motorcycling in the pioneer days was exclusively a vigorous young person's activity—and the perceived threat posed by independently motor-propelled individuals to shareholders in the various railways. These shareholders included magistrates, who certainly seem to have been all too ready to impose swingeing penalties even on men on furlough from the Front. The general speed limit in those days was 20 mph, and this was sternly enforced by both army and civil authorities. Even in the field, a despatch rider might exceed the limit only if specifically authorised by an officer above the rank of captain[36]—though one suspects that if battle was raging a few miles off, no MP would stop a speeding rider to ask for this authorisation.

When at the front, for all the value of the service they provided, and even if they stuck to the limit, motorcyclists sometimes had to endure commanding officers' hostility. Corporal "Bill" Foster complains of one commander who "required the despatch riders to push their bikes a distance of 200 yards or so before starting their engines so that he was not disturbed by the noise". Bill once met General Haig, whose only words to him were, "Take your bloody motor cycle away. It is upsetting my horse".[37] For some fussy commanders, even 20 mph was too fast: "The generals in the 1st Army took exception to any motorcyclist travelling at more than 15 mph. If they caught you exceeding that, you risked the indignity of having your motorcycle taken away and a push bike substituted".[38] Colonel Fuller's direct experiences of motorcyclists through the war may have become unconsciously contaminated by his class's prejudices, as well as eclipsed by his excitement at the potential of the tank, hence his failure to remark on motorcycles' importance. The fact that post-war, ex-WO motorcycles were dumped on the market and the plebs picked them up, would not have helped to elicit favourable mention in the *RUSI Journal*.

The best evidence indicates that, despite some prejudice, DRs were highly regarded by both officers and men, but indulgence varied from command to command.

> In some places the very strictest supervision is exercised over DRs and their machines and their work, and there is no such thing as "joy riding"[;] it is impossible to get permission to use a motor cycle for one's own personal pleasure. DRs are liable to be halted any time by the military police and asked to produce some authority for their journey.... But, on

the other hand, in other parts [of the war theatre] a DR is practically his own master.[39]

Whatever the suspicion and prejudice that motorcyclists suffered, a variety of sources show that they served in very many roles. In one of these, despatch riding, they may have been critical in winning the war, or at any rate preventing it being lost (as Chapters Four and Seven seek to demonstrate). Despatch riders also were responsible for delivering pigeons to the trenches,[40] and, at a pinch, cable laying,[41] foraging and billeting[42]— two specialist motorcyclists usually were attached to divisional billeting parties,[43] but sometimes the despatch rider was seconded to this task. Motorcycles also were used in the sidecar ambulance service and with Motor Machine Gun units, and for carrying Forward Observation Officers and other personnel,[44] sometimes reducing the need for staff cars. CEW Bean, the Australian Official Historian, claimed that "the only way possible of covering the ... distances [from front line to rest area] is by motor-car or motor-cycle"[45]—though his context makes it clear that he was speaking of officers; poor old Tommy Atkins had to walk.

Motorcycles could be pressed into service as materiel carriers. Here, as for carrying personnel, sidecars were obviously more effective, but solos could go where sidecars could not, and more quickly, so they might be of particular value in bringing up rations (they sometimes could travel along communication trenches), emergency fuses to an artillery unit, aeroplane spares, artificers' kits, officers' gramophones, officers' cigarettes,[46] officers' forgotten watches,[47] leeches ("like newts without legs"),[48] "newspapers, bootlaces or tinned delicacies from the nearest town"[49]—clearly of value in maintaining morale as well as sustaining belligerence, though not necessarily Don's morale: one unfortunate DR was sent out on a "wet and shivery night" to deliver a general's hot water bottle, "as the nights were chilly".[50] Indeed, so valuable were solos as materiel carriers that subsequent to the war a prototype single-track motor tricycle—all three wheels in tandem, the rear pair both driven—was developed. This had a payload capacity of 250 lbs, capable of carrying some 3,000 rounds of ammunition or rations for 40-50 men. Steering such a motorcycle would seem a challenge, as indeed it was. The weight, along with an intrinsically enormous wheelbase, made the machine ponderous at very best, and riders quickly tired. The fact that the prototype was powered by the poor little Triumph 3½ HP engine could hardly have allowed it to make a promising impression (though it reflects well on the "Trusty" Triumph).[51]

Sidecars hauled mobile wireless sets. Though the value of these sets was relatively low right to the end of the war (see Chapter Seven), in further recognition of the importance of the motorcycle at the time, the incorporated dynamo of some wirelesses—which gave them a transmission radius of up to 100 miles—was specifically designed to be driven by a worm-drive off the motorcycle's jacked-up rear wheel.[52] Later a 12lb wireless telephone designed to mount on the carrier of a solo motorcycle was developed; though invented by a captain of the US Marine Corps, this device was first used in the field by the British Signals Corps. But really wireless of the time was too fragile to withstand the harsh treatment such transport meted out.[53] Solo motorcycles were more useful, as far as wireless transmission was concerned, when they were jacked up and their belt drives used to power more robust field dynamos.[54] Their engines might be plundered to do this on a more permanent basis, or for use in a variety of tasks: to drive bayonet cleaning and sharpening machines;[55] to power a railway trolley;[56] to drive air compressors.[57] The Wall Autowheel was an after-market engine that clamped onto the rear wheel of a bicycle (it used a modified cylinder taken from an FN four), and the Royal Naval Division, and perhaps other units, used these engines to power trench pumps, an essential tool on the British front, especially in the Ypres salient.[58] Trench pumps were also powered by ABC motorcycle engines. Motorcycles were used by the "turd burglars" of the RAMC Sanitary Sections, a service that was vital to maintaining the health of an army in the field.[59] In addition to sidecar ambulances, solo ambulance trailers were in service,[60] and solos also were used to tow broken-down vehicles,[61] handcarts,[62] "small calibre artillery pieces",[63] and even a heavily-laden waggon after the horse "gave out".[64] Experimentally, they were sent up in planes to provide downed pilots with a means of escape in enemy territory.[65] (These were standard P&M motorcycles, not lightweight specialities like the Royal Enfield 125cc "Flying Flea" or the tiny collapsible 98cc Excelsior "Welbikes" that were dropped in Normandy in 1944, in order to provide paratroops with a means of rapid dispersal or concentration.) Motorcycles also were used by ground staff to get to downed planes rapidly, and rescue the airmen.[66]

Remarkably, there were at least two proposed designs of armoured motorcycle, and two armoured sidecar outfits, one with a machinegun protruding forward, which actually made it to the prototype stage.[67] One FM Goddard of Brooklyn patented an armoured tricycle, which almost certainly never got far past the back of the envelope it likely was designed upon, for it had the rider protected only partially by frontal armour plate and two riflemen in a fully enclosed armoured cab behind, engaging the enemy through rifle-slits cut in the side of the machine.[68] These slits imply shooting at an enemy, who not unreasonably might be shooting back, from an angle that leaves the rider fully exposed, and shooting the rider would of course leave the riflemen stranded in enemy territory. All such designs surely were a triumph of enthusiasm over common sense, as, apart from direct combat considerations, it was hard enough to drive an ordinary motorcycle over the roads of the time, far less a heavily armoured one across a cratered No Man's Land, which presumably was the inventors' intentions. Besides, apart from overwhelming the modest power of even an 8 HP engine—the strongest in service—the motorcycle's manoeuvrability as well as its speed would be lost when weighed down with armour.[69]

It's easy to overlook the value of the motorcycle on the home front. Motorcycles were relatively plentiful, and cheap by comparison to cars, and in August 1914 motorcyclists responded to the national crisis. An appeal by the Automobile Association resulted in about 20,000 men, out of a total of 92,000 members, volunteering their services on the home front, mostly in guarding telegraph and telephone lines, while sidecarists assisted enlistment by bringing volunteers to recruitment centres.[70] With horses commandeered for war work the sidecar came into its own. It was "quite reliable and incomparably cheaper to run than horseflesh" and used in a wide variety of businesses: baking; chimney sweeping; delivering poultry to market, for example. One farmer claimed that his sidecar gave him access to a wider and farther-flung market than his horse, requisitioned by the army, had done.[71] The war hastened the demise of the working horse, and enforced use of the motorcycle may have been a contributory factor. The Edwardian fore-car reappeared on solos, though in stouter form, to carry freight rather than fair ladies. Sidecars also were used for transporting munitions from factories, and with petrol becoming scarcer as the U-boat campaign tightened, they became increasingly valuable as military personnel carriers, and displaced cars for providing air raid warnings, while press photographers appreciated their speed and manoeuvrability in getting pictures to the newsroom; in this regard one may remember that the despatch rider was incidentally the war correspondent's link with the battlefield, and to some extent with the editorial team at home.

The rate of enlistment in "Kitchener's Armies" was on such a scale that it overwhelmed the resources available, volunteers often being housed in inadequate tent camps the turf of which quickly degenerated so that lorries could not be permitted to enter, because they both cut the ground up further and were liable to be bogged down in the mud. Sidecar outfits therefore often were used to deliver supplies, the sidecar having peculiar advantages: it had a substantial payload but was far lighter than a lorry, so didn't "poach" the turf, and—much more importantly after the damage had been done—its asymmetric wheel-print meant that it could stay upright (where a single-track vehicle might fall over) and retain traction where a four-wheeler's differential drive would immobilise it when one driven wheel began to slip. Furthermore, it could be steered "on the throttle" in slippery conditions—opening the throttle moves the outfit away from the sidecar, closing it in the opposite direction—so control was further enhanced.

Sidecars were used on the home front, as in France, as ambulances, and almost from the start until petrol shortages shut the scheme down, they were used to bring convalescent soldiers on outings, an all-volunteer effort that was hugely appreciated and was important to sustaining the morale of both convalescents and civilians: "Admirable work … in enabling limbless, paralytic and wounded soldiers to get away from the hospitals for a change in the town and open country". Equally important to morale were those volunteer drivers of both cars and sidecars who met soldiers home on leave at London railway stations, and "were invaluable" in bringing them to their homes or to other railway stations around the city.[72] With the outbreak of Spanish Flu Disinfecting Superintendents used motorcycles on their rounds.

Some of these superintendents were women. The war had provided the opportunity for women to prove the truth of suffragettes' claims that women were the equal of men; and women's rising to a sense of duty that was deeply ingrained in all back then, and galvanised by threat from outside, helped break down divisions in society and bestowed a sense of solidarity to the nation. "Wrens" of the Women's Royal Naval Service became despatch riders providing an essential service around and among naval bases at home, and discharged their often-difficult duties well—their most constant hazard was the sett-stones that paved harbour areas and were usually wet and slippery. Similarly many of the DRs at home bases of the RNAS, RFC, and later RAF were women; and as the air services became more important at the front, mileage for their motorcycles within the UK increased, from 234,308 in November 1916, to 491,192 in November 1917—an increase of almost 110 percent.[73] One may assume that most of these miles were covered by despatch riders and mobile mechanics. Women DRs were serving the air services on the Western Front by the end, albeit in the rear of the combat zone.

Women unable or unwilling to serve directly made contributions nevertheless. Upper-class ladies organised knitting-clubs to provide socks and warmers for the troops, volunteered for the VAD and other services; one even undertook to act as nanny for any widowed man so that he could "do his duty" in uniform.[74] Joining in the San Fairy Ann spirit, suffragettes suspended their various campaigns, and though Sylvia Pankhurst broke ranks and led the socialist Women's Suffrage Federation into opposition to the war, her mother and sister urged women to "Let us show ourselves to be worthy of citizenship whether our claim to it be recognised or not",[75] an unselfish expression of duty, typical of the time, and yet another reflection of San Fairy Ann. In the very first days of the war Mairi Chisholm, later to become famous as one of the "Madonnas of Pervyse", joined the Women's Emergency Corps in London as a despatch rider.[76] She and her companion Elsie Knocker, the future Baroness de T'Serclaes, seem to have been spotted on their way to the front by an American journalist: "two handsome young Englishwomen of the very modern aviatrix type—coming over to drive motor-cycle ambulances".[77] Remarkable women and extraordinary human beings, these two deservedly have become feminist icons and universal heroines, admired by the enemy who spared them the worst of war as best they could, though the best wishes of local Germans could not prevent them suffering shelling and gas poisoning. Both women were awarded the MM "for bravery in the field".[78] Other women took their place back home, as they filled the many gaps left by men called off to serve abroad. The British sense of fair play did, of course, recognise women's contribution in 1918: their labour had kept the country going; without it the demands of maintaining in the field a continental-sized army and the pressure this placed on an economy geared for total war could never have been met.

Overseeing all the social and economic change that the war had wrought were an increasing number of policewomen, and Margaret Damer Dawson, founder of the Women Police Service, provided them with motorcycles.[79] The Women's Legion also recruited women despatch riders "with the prime object of training women to take the place of male drivers in various military corps". Women had been used as despatch riders in the Ulster Volunteer Force during the "Ulster Crisis",[80] but now they were better organised. Training took a month to six weeks, and covered solo- and sidecar-, as well as car driving. The first week's training took place at Putney Vale, and then the women did two weeks' traffic work on London streets. Convoy work over country roads followed, with great emphasis being laid on "the importance of observing all road courtesies to the greatest possible degree".[81] Some were sent to the Aeronautical Inspection Department. These women rode sidecar outfits, "mostly 5-6 HP Clynos", as one would expect, given the department's connection to the air services, but some Triumphs and Douglases too; "Their duties are to take officers and men to the various works for inspection purposes. Their journeys are mostly in London ... and they usually amount to ten or twelve miles in length, while in the course of their duties they average from 150 to 200 miles per week".[82] The Auto Cycle Union Motor Messenger Detachment performed somewhat similar duties, providing "fifteen minute service" between various departments. These riders—not all women—were paid a penny a mile,[83] far more than what Tommy Atkins in the trenches, or even the luckier Don R, might be earning (something that caused resentment, as Chapter Four explains). They and other volunteer despatch riders were used by "certain important administrative departments" in London; they worked a minimum of four continuous hours a week.[84]

Clearly the motorcycle was invaluable to sustaining a war economy. In the war theatre it was of even greater value. At the outset it was recognised that in reconnaissance and despatch riding the motorcycle had more potential than the horse. As early as 1901, cars and motor tricycles had been used on French

Army manoeuvres as personnel carriers and for scouting; two years later they were to be found on British manoeuvres, "supplied by members of the Motor Volunteer Corps", indicative of the partly-amateur nature of the British Army, and the volunteer spirit that was to become so important in 1914. On these manoeuvres the motorcycles, approximately thirty in total, "behaved on the whole splendidly".[85] It was believed by many that the motorcycle would replace the galloper completely, "especially in a European conflict, where the roads are plentiful"[86]—though the roads were to prove a DR's nightmare, and the "despised horse", as one *avant garde* DR put it, had to be used when mud was unusually dire.[87] Yet despite the proven value of motorcycles on manoeuvres, the BEF had a mere fifteen on the outbreak of war, though this was increased perhaps tenfold within a few days, thanks to civilian volunteers.

Some visionaries saw the machine's potential as greater than it was to prove. Years before the war broke out Captain Cecil Battine, for one, had realised that "for the rapid conveyance of small detachments [of troops, motorcycles] will be invaluable, and of course, for despatch riding", and for scouting.[88] By 1914 some military minds had seen the motorcycle's potential as even greater, and as the July Crisis deepened the War Office advertised for "several" motorcyclists "to act as despatch riders on 28th July to 8th August next".[89] The date on which this appeal was issued, 9 July, might suggest either that the Great Powers were taking the Sarajevo assassination more seriously than some historians suggest, or that the British Army was less obtuse than many maintain, but manoeuvres were held at that time every year so one should not make too much of it; nevertheless the appeal was timely. Major Gordon Casserly advocated special units of motorcyclists specially trained as guerrillas and used as "Motor Mobile Infantry" in support of conventional forces. Major Casserly, of the Indian Army, was already the author of *Manual of Training for Jungle and River Warfare* and other publications, and he is thorough in his proposed training regime, clearly having given his topic much thought.[90] Though conceding that they cannot go everywhere that horses can, he nevertheless sees motorcycles as largely replacing horses, and motorcyclists as rapidly mobile infantrymen. Such a force, in Casserly's view, could do all that cavalry traditionally has done, and offer several advantages besides: each cycle could carry two or three soldiers (three in the case of a sidecar); all soldiers could be deployed (no horse-holders required, whereas one in four troopers was needed for this job); and "wastage of machines is little or nothing, compared with that of horseflesh". In addition to these immediate advantages, the motorcycle's "speed, range of action, and endurance are far greater" than a horse's, allowing motorcyclists "to scout far ahead of their own cavalry in search of information and act as a screen preventing the enemy from obtaining information".[91] Though to some extent Major Casserly's proposals were out of date by the time they appeared in print—thanks to trenchlock—they were far from irrelevant, and motorcyclists indeed were employed as he envisaged, notably in East Africa. To vindicate his ideas, a decade after the war it was acknowledged that "A road cross-country motor bicycle is becoming more and more a necessity. Without such a vehicle we may get guns and transport inextricably mixed up";[92] there also was perceived a need for "motor cyclists for march protection" of a proposed mobile light division.[93]

In 1914 motorcyclists indeed were deployed as de-facto guerrillas. The Belgian Army had a Volunteer Motorcycle Corps, one of whose members was George Suetens, admirer of Elsie Knocker—later the Baroness de T'Serclaes—one of the "Madonnas of Pervyse". You wouldn't like George to catch you winking at Elsie: "His role was to go out on his motorbike at night and shoot as many Germans as he could, and in the last week he had killed forty-eight".[94] Well done, that man! On an embarrassingly modest scale by comparison, Corporal WH Tait and two companions were attached to GHQ during the August retreat officially as "advance cyclists", scouts by another name, and many motorcyclists were in the thick of the action at times, some being killed in action.[95] Paul Maze was so close behind the retreating Uhlans in September that at Balleuil "the dung of their horses was smoking".[96] The state of flux in the lines through the Great Retreat, and in the subsequent "race to the sea", and again during the war of movement in 1918, made it easy to get fatally lost: one motorcyclist, Pugh by name, drove right through the German lines, past what he imagined to be unescorted prisoners of war, and was lucky to be able to turn his bike and make his escape when he came on a village full of *pikelhauben*.[97] Roger West was another who rode through German forces in the course of the Great Retreat of August 1914.[98] Another DR was less fortunate: he was shot on 7 September on the advance from the Marne, when he mistakenly entered a house in La Ferté, one that still was occupied by Germans.[99] Tait was fired on twice on 24 August, chased by Uhlans two days later and fired on again; the same occurred on 1 September.[100] Roger West's determination to destroy the bridge at Pontoise was carried out in the teeth of the German advance—his own commander "considered this further attempt to lay charges to be 'suicidal'"[101]—made the Official History, and it seems exciting enough to quote from that account:

> The motor bicycle was loaded up with a box of 14 guncotton slabs, and Lieut. Pennycuick [an explosives expert of the RE, who had volunteered to help] sat on top, his pockets filled with fuze, detonators and primers. The two officers then rode back the eight miles, passing first infantry and then through the cavalry rear guard. They climbed up one of the suspension cables and placed 13 slabs on the cables on top of the pier, the fourteenth falling into the river. The first detonator failed, only powdering

the primer; a second attempt was made and was successful: the top of the pier was blown off and the cables cut, and the bridge crashed down into the river. The two officers returned safely, after breakfasting at a farm *en route*. They both received the Distinguished Service Order.[102]

The use of solo machines for communications and scouting duties, as proposed by Casserly, proved critical not only in the war of movement in 1914, and again in 1918, but beyond Europe throughout. Motor Cycle Infantry was important to the East African campaigns, and here and in the Middle East motorcycles in the Motor Machine Gun Service were about to vindicate many of Casserly's ideas for Motor Mobile Troops and Infantry (though Casserly envisaged riflemen rather than machine gunners in these roles, perhaps sceptical of the need for them, but more likely just making use of what was available).[103]

The motorcycle served in more modest roles, right from the outbreak of war. The Army Service Corps had "a considerable number of motor bicycles" allocated for supply column management years in advance of mobilisation,[104] and the machine became increasingly important to another service that well may have been essential to victory yet long has slipped the public mind, if it ever entered it—for the Army Printing and Stationery Services was hardly the most dashing branch of the armed forces. Through the war, though, it expanded from three officers and seven other ranks to battalion size, and was crucial to the famed "Learning Curve" that began its climb during the Somme battles. Eventually the Services held over a thousand items in stock, including 750 manuals and pamphlets written by that well-known nincompoop, the British Army officer, and performance gave the lie to any idea that the Army was a hidebound, inefficient organisation. In one instance 15,000 copies of a text that was received at 5:30 PM had been run off by the following morning. Before war's end "the service was despatching 393,950 separate packets per week", and "a 120-page volume detailing an 'order of battle' could be printed and issued in 36 hours". With such an output the printing presses (located at Abbeville, Boulogne and Le Havre, as well as over twenty in the UK) were under severe strain, yet could not be allowed to "go down", so they were kept going by rapidly-deployable motorcycle-mounted mechanics.[105]

Significant though the motorcycle was in very many branches of the services, and in other roles, it was in the hands of the despatch rider that it rendered its most iconic and important service, as will be seen.

The Machines

It is impossible to give a definitive list of the motorcycles used through the war. But however many tens or hundreds of thousands that was, the enormous increase in motorcycle numbers is emblematic of how the war changed British industry, when one considers that only a hundred-odd motorcycles went to war in August 1914. Captain JC Dunn speaks of "about 150" motorcycles being with the BEF on 20 August,[106] but his tone is casual, and there may well have been fewer—certainly far fewer by the time the Great Retreat had reached the Marne. Four divisions of the BEF landed in France in the third week of August and a fifth soon afterward, each supplied with sixteen motorcycles—in theory. In fact some divisions were under strength in motorcycles, and the 4th Division had no DRs at all when its infantry reached the line on the 24th,[107] a deficit that placed an extra burden on the DRs of the other four divisions. Strength was quickly depleted further by mechanical failures and losses to enemy action. One DR reports: "When the war was young ... our newly formed Signal Company's equipment consisted of eight motorcycles and a few old drums of cable".[108] From such remarks we may compute that there were 80 or fewer despatch riders serving the BEF in Europe at the outset; but to this figure must be added the 42 "Scout Officers" of the Intelligence Corps, all of whom were motorcycle mounted, and though Scout Officer Roger West's account is unclear on this point, the thirteen senior officers of the Intelligence Corps also may have been motorcycle mounted.[109] In addition, some motorcycles were available as personnel carriers, possibly officers' own machines, and there was also, for instance, Anglo-Frenchman Paul Maze, who enlisted in the French army but immediately was seconded to Hubert Gough's cavalry as an interpreter (eventually much more besides), and who bought his own motorcycle—a Triumph—for personal mobility.[110] The cavalry possibly did not have any motorcyclist other than Maze attached just then, but the RFC did. Best estimates indicate that between 100 and 150 motorcyclists were attached to the BEF when battle was joined at Mons; but this number was rapidly depleted.

In the course of the retreat from Mons, broken-down motorcycles, though they might have been stopped by nothing but a fouled plug, were burned to deprive the enemy of an asset.[111] Through position warfare a motorcycle normally would be collected for repair by an artificer if the rider could not fix the problem on the spot,[112] but in the Great Retreat there simply might not be time even to change a plug, so desperate was the pace, and the threat from the enemy, so many motorcycles may have been lost to this quaint form of friendly fire. In early 1915 the Douglas 2¾ HP and the Triumph 3½ HP became the official DR mounts on the Western Front, but the RFC/RAF specified P&M, and BSA gave excellent service to the Motor Cyclist Corps in East Africa (as well as to Allied armies);[113] but in the first months just about any motorcycle was accepted as long as it was under a suitable recruit, and in 1916 a privately owned two-stroke Levis was pressed into service in Ireland, in the emergency of the Easter Rising.[114] The Scott, another two-stroke, was used by the Motor Machine Gun units, but otherwise, by early 1915, the army specified four-stroke singes and flat-twins for its DRs,[115] singles and V-twins for all other work, all machines of side-valve (SV) operation.

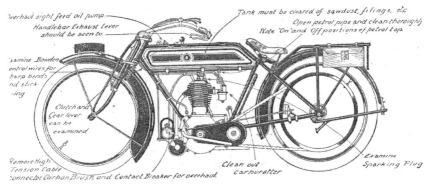

A typical single-cylinder motorcycle of the war years, with areas of routine maintenance indicated. Note enclosed primary transmission to gearbox; belt final-drive; rear brake bearing on pulley-rim; front stirrup-brake; girder-type front forks; close-fitting mudguards; and rigid frame, opened at the bottom to accommodate engine.[116]

This rationalisation was an early manifestation of the Learning Curve, for insistence on side-valves made sense. In the Second World War overhead valve (OHV) motorcycles were admitted, notably the Matchless 350 G3L, but, though this often is lauded as the DR's favourite mount in that struggle, some old Dons claim the BSA M20, a SV, was the all-round best,[117] and eventually "the Fighting Vehicle Development Establishment ... decided that ohv engines were too complicated and inflexible and in the main were unnecessarily fast".[118] Perhaps more important than distrust of new-fangled OHVs was the desire to standardise army vehicles as much as possible. Though staff limousines—and later, tanks—used the superb sleeve-valve Daimler, all other road vehicles used SV engines.[119] The same drive toward standardisation, and the convenience of stocking a single type of fuel, is to be found in the current development of a diesel engine motorcycle, based on the Kawasaki 650 single, for use by all NATO forces.

The light weight of the two-stroke offered theoretical advantages over four-strokes in muddy and sandy conditions, and there were frequent calls for its adoption by the War Office;[120] but the two-stroke was a utility engine, built down to a price (the Scott always the honourable exception), and reliable only in the hands of a fastidious owner (even the Scott included).[121] In the 1960s and '70s the Japanese revolutionised the two-stroke engine, making two-stroke motorcycles reliable, everyman machines; but the performance and reliability of their engines was gained through development of the Schnürle loop-scavenging system, automatic pump-lubrication and excellent engineering, factors that hardly existed in 1914-18. Adolph Schnürle only developed his scavenging system in the 1930s, and though the always-eccentric Veloce had a precocious pump-lubricated two-stroke before 1914 (and Triumph was experimenting with one by 1916, for its Junior model, before all civilian production was stopped "for the duration"), Veloce was never an everyman's machine (I can trace none in the BEF through the Great War, though almost certainly some could have been found, and the Belgian army used them);[122] and though British engineering and metallurgy were of a superb order at the time, they could hardly compare to those of Japan in the 1960s-70s. Besides, even Japanese two-strokes were liable to engine-seizure if persistently driven hard, something that also induced in them dipsomanic thirst. The War Office was wise to discount "stinkwheels".

Overhead-valve and even overhead-camshaft (OHC) motorcycles were available by 1914, but they were much more expensive and perceived as temperamental and less reliable than side-valves. Improvements in metallurgy and cam design recently had rendered valve breakage relatively rare, but to aid marginal metallurgy overhead valves were exposed to the cooling breeze, and the ubiquitous dust quickly infiltrated between valve stem and guide leading to rapid wear. Besides, the war broke out less than 20 years after one local newspaper called on its readers to marvel at a car that could climb a hill "at a faster pace than a pedestrian can walk";[123] caution remained the watchword for many, and the army is a cautious institution. A broken valve could ruin an OHV or OHC engine; such failure on an SV likely would do little further harm and the valve was easily replaced by the roadside. The stem of a broken side valve remained in its guide and the valve head usually did no more than "chatter" damage to the cylinder head and piston-skull, if any at all. The head of a broken overhead valve, on the other hand, was certain to damage piston, cylinder head and the other valve. If the stem subsequently slipped out of the guide, which it almost always did, it could penetrate both piston and cylinder head, and after punching through the piston could do all sorts of mischief "downstairs", a broken crankshaft and burst crankcase being entirely possible outcomes. A real San Fairy Ann scenario.

As an unflattering reflection on the army's recruitment policy, but more so on the level of reliability generally expected at the time, one writer to the motorcycle press caustically describes coming on army motorcyclists stopped by burned-out exhaust valves;[124] the writer's disgust is directed not at the mechanical failure, but that any rider could be so careless or naïve as to travel without a spare valve in his toolkit.[125]

Objectors to the War Office's insistence on side-valves will point to the aeroplane, where the SV had long since been relegated; and certainly when one compares it to the aero engine the primitiveness of the contemporary motorcycle engine becomes apparent. Radials, so popular with the Allies, all used air cooled OHV operation;[126] the Allies also used liquid-cooled OHV and sleeve-valve in-line engines—Daimler, Rolls Royce, Sunbeam and Napier, for instance—and the German Mercedes liquid-cooled straight-six aero-engine used OHC, the tower-shaft connecting crank- and camshafts having the armatures of the twin magnetos wound around it; this shaft also drove the water pump. The Mercedes piston comprised a steel skull screwed-and-pinned into a cast iron skirt,[127] a combination that was heavy but coupled the toughness of steel with the better lubricating qualities of cast iron (cast iron contains a lot of free graphite, a natural lubricant that also improves thermal conductivity), so that each material's best qualities were exploited. The design also facilitated increases in compression as the engine was developed to give more power, a different skull, rather than a whole piston, needing to be designed and manufactured. Seven main bearings supported the Mercedes crankshaft and these, and the big- and small-end con-rod bearings, were supplied with oil drawn from an external tank and delivered at high pressure, a separate oil pump lubricating the camshaft and its bearings. Radial aero engines used two spark plugs and four, five and even six valves per cylinder.

Contrast all this mechanical sophistication with the motorcycle engine, with its SV operation and hand oil pump.

Contrast, also, improvements in performance: for instance, merely in the first two years of war, the Sunbeam-Coatalen aero engine improved its brake mean effective pressure from 106 to 134 lbs/square inch, allowing an improvement in power to weight from 4.3 lbs/HP to 2.6 lbs/HP.[128]

But in an aero engine power development was critical, and war was to make it even more so, and money was far less a limiting factor to the aero manufacturer than it was to the motorcycle manufacturer. Besides, many OHV and OHC motorcycle engines were experimental or exotic designs, which had not proven their reliability or durability, and—most importantly—were unavailable en masse. Whereas performance and reliability were paramount in an aero engine, the motorcycle, prior to 1914, though still something of a rich man's toy, had become more utilitarian and was being built down to a price in order to secure a mass market. A war economy that was struggling to produce enough shells simply could not design and produce a motorcycle that compared in specifications with a Rolls Royce or a Mercedes Benz. Besides, what would have been the point? In the air there were no impediments to increased performance, whereas a motorcycle could hardly have gone any faster over the roads of the time; therefore there was no need to improve its performance. A motorcycle was restricted by military regulation to 20mph in normal circumstances; an aeroplane that could go faster or carry a heavier payload offered huge advantage, so the war in the air saw a new generation of plane emerge more frequently than annually, so that by 1918 those that had taken to the sky four years previously seemed primitive in the extreme. The motorcycle had changed only in detail, in part because of War Office strictures against deviation from standard, in the interests of reliability.[129] The industry accepted the necessity of this state of affairs: "development of aircraft engines is proceeding at an extraordinary rate, whereas by reason of the war motor cycle design is at a standstill, or comparatively so".[130] The motorcycle was serving its purpose—that will be all, Corporal!

In the longer term the motorcycle did gain from the trickle-down of technology from aero-engine development. The erratic genius Granville Bradshaw, of ABC Motorcycles before and after the war, gained great insight into air-cooling principles when he worked on radials for Sopwith; for example, parallel-cut fins were replaced by more efficient tapered fins.[131] Roller bearings and plain bearings were improved, the latter by Ettore Bugatti among others. Carburetion, too, "received a vast amount of deep scientific consideration", which promised a post-war motorcycle carburettor "that will cause some astonishment".[132]

One last consideration here: it would have been relatively easy to redesign an engine to drive a mechanical oil pump, and to drop an OHV top end onto it.[133] Similarly, a spring frame was no great engineering challenge: experimental spring frames had been designed as early as 1906 and Bat used a "semi-sprung" design that spring-mounted the seatpost and footrests. An amateur engineer, despatch rider EW Morley, privately designed and developed a rear suspension system for a Douglas, one that maintained constant belt tension.[134] But such improvements would have necessitated investment of time and resources that were at a premium, and involved increased weight and incorporation of points of potential failure. At what point does "necessary improvement" degenerate into "unnecessary complication"? At the start of the next war the Messerschmitt Bf109 was about the best fighter in the sky, but by 1944 it had gained so much weight and power in keeping up with Allied development that torque reaction of the Gustav model had become dangerous in the way that the Sopwith Camel had been years before, causing many a Nazi novice to flip the plane at takeoff. In the Great War, mechanically "improved" motorcycles were available, notably the Harley Davidson and the Indian. But these were in no way *better* bikes than the Douglas and the Triumph; rather, worse in many ways, as will be shown.

In addition to its proven reliability advantage, the SV was better suited to the total-loss lubrication system employed by British motorcycles. That such a system still existed would seem, like the SV design itself, more indictment then anything to crow about. By 1914 not merely aero- but car engines used pumps for pressure lubrication and to recirculate oil from a reservoir, yet out of 277 "standard pattern motor cycles" on the British market, only 26 used at least partially mechanical lubrication[135]—and these would have been exotic or experimental designs. As a contemporary work (originally published in 1914) puts it: "The simplest lubrication method is to keep oil standing in the crank case, to be splashed to all parts of the mechanism as the crank shaft revolves; the oil feed [from the tank] will supply the number of drops per minute that are necessary to compensate for the oil that is used up"[136]—oil scraper rings were not fitted to pistons at the time. This was the method used by almost all British motorcycles. Indian was to introduce automatic oiling on the Powerplus in 1916, and the German Wanderer featured both mechanical and hand-pump lubrication. The British Veloce, a highly individualistic firm of naturalised Germans (like Triumph) had pressure lubrication for both two- and four-stroke engines, but these models failed commercially, in part because motorcyclists, to this day a conservative bunch, distrusted "unnecessary complication". Of far greater importance than advanced specification was a proven record of reliability and durability. It was not until 1922 that Triumph fitted pressure lubrication, and even some years later Matchless could jauntily boast: "Don't starve your engine, or feed it in lumps— / Matchless machines have mechanical pumps". Douglas and several other firms saw out the 'Twenties with drip-feed lubrication. Yet Britons need not blush: if American motorcycle manufacturers (Indian and Flying Merkel) had been among the first successfully to dispense with total-loss lubrication, another, Harley Davidson, used total-loss until 1936, and the Japanese Rikuo (a Harley copy) only fitted a mechanical oil pump in 1958.[137]

Though the system, like the SV, was primitive, engines with total-loss lubrication could last longer than those using recirculated oil. Owners of the latter type could be tempted to "economise" by skipping oil changes, especially in the Hungry Thirties. Oil back then was essentially just that, mineral oil, with few additives, and it quickly degenerated in service. For this reason, Matchless and other manufacturers deliberately modified their engines to consume more oil, thereby ensuring that fresh oil was added between changes, in effect reverting to partial-loss lubrication.

The true total-loss lubrication system, as Don R found it, called on the rider to depress a syringe-type plunger attached to the oil tank (which sat alongside the fuel tank), at regular intervals. The spring-loaded plunger then bled drops of oil into the crankcase, and crankshaft and con-rod movement, along with crankcase pressure, infiltrated this oil or its mist into the crankshaft- and connecting rod bearings and valve-gear. On an SV engine, all of the mechanism is below the level of the piston crown, so crankcase pressure ensured that there was no danger of local oil starvation, as there might have been with an OHV or OHC design.[138] The system worked well, even in a longitudinally-oriented horizontally-opposed twin which should, in theory, have suffered both oil starvation on the front cylinder and over-oiling—

leading to plug-fouling—on the rear; in practise, the flat-twin Douglas gained as great a reputation for reliability as the Trusty Triumph.

It is at least possible that this primitive lubrication system was actually better suited to the conditions of the Great War than oil recirculation. Oil delivery by a mechanically driven pump is determined purely by engine speed, and depending on conditions this might have proved either inadequate—some early pressure-lubricated motorcycles retained an auxiliary hand-pump for this reason—or overwhelming. An aero engine is designed to run most effectively at or close to full-throttle operation, so optimum oil delivery rate is easy to compute;[139] but there was no optimum speed for a motorcycle in the road conditions of the Great War (and it's fair to point out that radial aero engines also used total-loss lubrication). On a dry day, and over *pavé*, and with an urgent despatch in Don R's pocket, full throttle would be called for; but under sluicing rain, through thick mud, and with a dozen pigeons fluttering and squawking in a top-heavy basket on Don's back, progress could only be possible at the lowest possible speed in the highest possible gear, riding conditions which, if constrained by constant-speed oil delivery, might overcome the marginal metallurgy of the piston rings, foul the plug, and stop the bike.

More significantly, the quality and the very availability of oil could vary alarmingly under war conditions; even toward the end, when enormous improvements in logistics and quality control had been made, oil's consistency "may vary from that of water to pudding", as a three-year veteran testifies.[140] In cold weather it might be too thick to flow dependably and have to be warmed up. Detachable caps from over the valves survived from when cylinder head and barrel had been cast in a single block, and dropping a hot valve cap into the oil tank was a favourite trick. Frequently these caps had to be opened even in moderate temperatures to allow paraffin to be poured into the cylinder in order to release the piston, "as the vile lubricant [had] gummed it up very firmly in the cylinder".[141] When hot, oil might deteriorate to the "consistency of paraffin, with a feeling not unlike the gritty nature of the latter oil.... It is this paraffin-like nature that plays havoc with the engine internally".[142] Problems of supply meant that rifle-oil might have to be pressed into service.[143]

Given this vast range of conditions and availability of oil, a hand pump could be a veritable asset: with it, a knowledgeable rider with a sympathetic ear could adjust lubrication to suit conditions, temperature and quality of the oil. One might note in this regard that just prior to the war the Flying Merkel had reverted from a mechanical to a hand pump, and the Jawa 500, still a dominant force in speedway racing, retains total-loss lubrication to this day. Phil Vincent, a now almost legendary motorcycle engineer, while acknowledging its shortcomings, points out, "the [manual lubrication] system did work much better than one would expect", in large part because "the rider could give the engine more or less oil as he thought fit, according to the work which it was doing. This is a valuable feature for a lubrication system to possess".[144] It must have been especially valuable when the quality of lubricant was so variable.

The Army's insistence on SVs furthermore might be viewed in light of the design's survival into the present day. The Spanish manufacturer Gas-Gas in 2009 announced a new SV motorcycle engine, and Russian and Chinese 750 SVs, both copies of the Wehrmacht BMW R71, still are available new (though old stock), as are Briggs & Stratton utility engines. The design might be dated, but it remains viable (the Gas-Gas reportedly hits 10,500 RPM). Essentially the same Norton SV engine was used in both world wars, though with a mechanical oil pump added to the 16H/Big Four by the Second, and the SV BSA M20 was the Dobbin of the British Army in that latter struggle— over 126,000 were produced. The British industry produced SV-engined civilian motorcycles into the late 1950s, and indeed the Triumph 500 TRW was supplied to armed forces far beyond this—the Irish Defence Forces used it up to the late 1970s and it may have survived even longer elsewhere. The Velocette LE lasted until 1970, and a year or so earlier Floyd Clymer invested a quarter of a million dollars in an updated Indian SV (a lovely-looking motorbike that never got past the prototype stage). Harley Davidson aficionados hold that the "flat head" KH 45/55 proto-Sportster of 1952-56 was the best Harley of all time—no great boast, perhaps, yet acknowledgment of the side-valve's viability—and Harley produced a 750 flat head until 1976 (for the Servicar) and until 1969 actually *raced* one (the KR 750). Just before developing a new OHV racer, Harley race chief Dick O'Brien had designed a new SV engine—its valves were inclined, a feature used by AJS in their transverse V-twin S3 in 1931—that seems to have attained competitive volumetric and thermodynamic efficiency both. Prior to this stillborn design, there always had been a trade-off with side-valves, which is why by the 1920s designers had seen the OHV design as the only way for the poppet-valve engine to go in the long term; but the Ford Anglia 100E was manufactured until 1962 and Anglias, Prefects and Populars, and split-windscreen Morris Minors, all fitted with SV engines, would not have turned many heads into the 1970s. So let pre-revisionists not sneer at the British Army's insistence on side-valves more than half a century before such engines still were chuffing around our roads.

Most importantly to the war motorcycle, though the SV design restricted high-speed gas-flow, it improved gas *velocity* at low engine speeds (part of the rationale in today's Gas-Gas), and it was at low engine speeds that Great War motorcycles needed to give their best performance. This could be far more impressive than raw horsepower figures might suggest: in one test a 4

HP Triumph single, with four men aboard and "so abnormally loaded that the back tyre was almost flat ... made a magnificent ascent" of a 1:8 hill.[145] In addition to being of simpler design, the SV was lighter than OHV or OHC engines, and had a lower centre of gravity, other important factors in the mud and dust of the Great War.

All that said, though, it must be admitted that back in 1914 British motorcycle engines remained primitive, quite apart from their valve gear. Len Setright, that most eloquent and intellectual of motoring journalists, is not impressed:

> [Early motorcycle engines] were metallurgical horrors and tribological nightmares. The lubrication of such few and exiguous bearings as they possessed was commonly achieved as much by accident as design, on the basis that if the oil was splashed around inside the crankcase, some of it at least would arrive in the right places. The delivery of the oil to the crankcase [from the oil tank] was almost as careless, its descent assisted by gravity and impeded by an adjustable metering valve that reduced a steady flow to a periodically repeated drip. Alternatively it might be delivered by a plunger pump, hand operated by the rider whenever he remembered.[146]

Often, if the rider was forgetful—and assuming the engine had not seized—he would overcompensate. Over-oiling often occurred during night riding, when the drip sight-glass could not be seen, and it resulted in excess oil finding its way past the piston rings, to carbonise on the piston and valves and perhaps cause drag between the crankcase and snugly-fitting flywheels (though some engines, like the Douglas, used an outside flywheel, which eliminated the latter problem). In hot weather, even on a standing motorcycle, oil might leak past the pump and flood the crankcase, then oil-foul the spark plug when the engine was started.[147]

Setright's criticisms need to be read in light of the fact that they were made from the vantage point of many decades later (and elsewhere he is no less remorseless in his evaluation of aero-engines of the time). This is not to say that he is wrong in any objective sense. Carburettors were crude—in part because of vicious fighting in patent-law court—and could not provide reliable tickover. (Advice from a slower-paced age advises tilting the machine away from the carburettor float-bowl in order to raise the level of fuel and improve reliability of engine tickover, a "very useful [stratagem] when stopping to light a pipe when one's hands are not free to open the throttle slightly".[148]) The Triumph, though in other respects possibly the best British motorcycle in 1914, used a primitive tandem-barrel carburettor, each barrel housing a separate slide, one to control the air supply, the other the fuel, and the rider had to juggle two handlebar-mounted levers to match the mixture to conditions, his other hand meanwhile twiddling a third lever to adjust the ignition timing to suit—and all the while trying to negotiate deep mud or sand or greasy *pavé*.

In practise it's much easier than it sounds, though, and in the previous decade motorcycle development had made enormous strides, and development was ongoing rapidly. All but as the war broke out, BSA fitted a caged roller-bearing big-end, something that, compared to plain bushings or crowded-rollers, was "unusual".[149] But the greatest improvement had occurred years earlier: adoption of magneto ignition. The fact that Bosch made the best magneto and that the German electrical industry supplied almost all of the British motorcycle industry was to prove embarrassing after war broke out. Before the turn of the century a magneto design had been patented by a quite remarkable Englishman, Frederick Simms, but by the outbreak of war Bosch had developed the magneto to a point which was not to be surpassed until the invention of microprocessors. British- and American-made substitutes such as CAV, ML, Runbaken, Spildorf and Dixie were very inferior,[150] though one has to read between the lines of contemporary patriotic reports to decipher this—admission that the British Boulton and Runbaken "somewhat resembles the Bosch" rather gives the game away. At the outbreak of war "about nine-tenths of the magnetos used in England came from Stuttgart", but by mid-1915—i.e. before Britain fully got onto a war footing—CAV were manufacturing about 600 magnetos a week, EIC about 300, and ML 200. All these factories had the potential to increase their output considerably—ML calculated it was capable of 500 units a week with existing facilities, and planned to expand in order to reach 1,000 a week—but manpower was scarce then, due to the rush to the colours, so the potential for expansion was constrained.[151] Furthermore, projections for expansion probably were postulated on the output of skilled workers, but semi-skilled workers were likely the best that could be found through the war, so magnetos were to remain in short supply.

So scarce were they, indeed, that apocryphal tales of enemy DRs surreptitiously meeting in No Man's Land to swap British tyres for German magnetos should not be dismissed as fantastic: illicit trade between belligerents in such things as optical glass for telescopic sights is well known, and the Triumph factory traded tyres for Bosch magnetos through Holland, at least in the early part of the war.[152] So precious were magnetos that an appeal went out in 1914 for motorcyclists to surrender theirs to the war effort, and many did so, both appeal and response telling us much about the nation's unpreparedness for war and the people's sense of duty.[153] In early 1915 Douglas secured a reliable supply of American magnetos,[154] and in 1916 suspension of patent law and rationalisation resulted in Joseph Lucas being given effectively a monopoly on

British magneto manufacture, and this probably ended such rascality as illicit bartering.[155] Frederick Simms had for years been manufacturing magnetos under licence from Bosch, and in partnership with Lucas he now brought his considerable energy and ingenuity to the problem. But these radical changes to both patent law and manufacturing were driven by the need to optimise aircraft performance and reliability; motorcycles benefited incidentally, as they did from other advances that were driven by the aero industry.

That Simms and Lucas did not quite meet national expectations is indicated by a member of the Institute of Automobile Engineers, one AG Pendrell, who as late as 1918

> suggested that after the war we should in all probability have to return to German magnetos [because] while British magnetos are excellent mechanically, they are not quite perfect as regards insulating compound used for the mouldings, and such foreign magnetos as are now available may at the best of times only be regarded as third-rate substitutes for the German article.

The acknowledged problems with "insulating compound" reflect German superiority in chemical as well as electrical engineering, but Mr Pendrell also acknowledges problems with output quantity as well as quality.[156] Such shortcomings really more than anything reflect the fact that the entire British industry was being stretched to its very limits to meet the war effort.

Thanks to the German magneto, but also to excellent design and "superb, conscientious workmanship",[157] the Triumph 3½ HP was a landmark motorcycle, known as the "Trusty Triumph" to admiring DRs. Columnist Ixion, normally "a trifle jaundiced" toward singles, "must admit that the WD Triumph is a rare slogger". One, fitted with "a very heavy sidecar and two big men ... slogged away on top gear ... all day at a 27 or 28 mph gross average".[158] As already observed, the Triumph owed its success in large part to Teutonic thoroughness and engineering quality: it had been founded and was managed, right through the Teutonophobic war years, by Germans—though the "Trusty" model was designed by (English) Works Manager Charles Hathaway.[159] With the Triumph 3½, for the first time motorcycles were not rich men's toys but viable means of transport. In 1911 one Triumph rider, a travelling salesman, was covering 12,000 miles a year,[160] about the average annual mileage covered by the modern car, and that over roads that often were little more than tracks and all of which lacked a sealed surface. In an endurance test that same year businessman Albert Catt of Northampton rode a similar single-speed Triumph 2,500 miles in six days—over 400 miles a day. In 1915 an ABC rider could cover 300 miles in ten hours, race the ABC, and then return home "with no engine trouble of any sort".[161]

A motorcyclist of today could be quite proud of this sort of performance, and though one may reasonably suspect that marketing strategy or owners' bragging may have inflated some such claims, many are too well documented or accounted for in convincing detail: Albert Catt's, for instance, and that of three motorcyclists who immediately before the war covered 1,500 miles around France in fifteen days;[162] as early as 1906 a motorcyclist covered 1,200 miles in six days, a remarkable feat at the time,[163] but as he was a clergyman (Canon Basil Davies, alias Ixion), one is inclined to believe his claim. Alfred Angas Scott had designed and produced a remarkable two-stroke twin, the descendants of which were hard to catch into the 1960s, and George Silk put an updated version on the market in 1975.[164] Scott sidecars were used by the Motor Machine Gun units (though they seem not to have been able to withstand the rigours of the Front, none remaining in service by 1918— see Appendix 1), and some solos slipped through for DR work too, where their light, soft power delivery gave them a welcome resistance to skidding on loose surfaces.[165] The Douglas 2¾ HP flat twin was down on power but it also had a smooth delivery of what power it had, a consequence of its two small pistons and low compression—the pistons' reciprocal movement incidentally gave the engine perfect primary balance—and its heavy outside flywheel. The small displacement of each piston, with the low compression and heavy flywheel, made the Douglas easy to "paddle-start", a significant advantage when falls tended to break off pedals, kickstart levers, etc, leaving machines "flattened out both sides".[166]

Nevertheless, British motorcycles, if more reliable than in previous years, still were motorised bicycles, their frames being weakened, in many instances, by the lower "diamond" being opened to fit the engine, this being bolted in front and rear, to serve like an inverted keystone,[167] except that this "keystone" created weakness rather than strength. Bradbury tried to overcome this weakness by use of a three-piece crankcase, the cast iron centre section brazed into the frame, with the rest of the engine assembled about it.[168] But such a design complicated repairs in the field because the frame remained that of a bicycle, however strengthened (apart from the Scott which was designed about the engine, rather than modified to fit this), and the stress of rough going fractured frame members. So often did the front down-tube break that in-field repair kits were distributed, apparently factory-made; rather like splints on each side of the down-tube, these were clamped to the upper end of the tube and bolted to the front engine mounting-lug.[169] Stress failure also occurred around the steering head, as early as August 1914.

Frame production, as well as design, was less than it might have been. In those days before cheap welding, Victorian engineering meant that frames comprised cast lugs for the steering head, other junction points and rear wheel mountings, with tubes inserted into these lugs and drilled and pinned in place, then hearth-brazed around the joints.[170] This was a stout enough arrangement, if heavy, but most British manufacturers used malleable iron rather than stronger cast steel for frame lugs. One DR claims that Rudge frames and forks were less likely to break than those of other marques, and he wonders whether this might be because of Rudge's use of steel stampings rather than malleable iron,[171] resulting in lugs that were both lighter and stronger (as well as being more economical of material). Far more a problem than lug failure was that poor workmanship, an inevitable consequence of wartime expansion and use of unskilled labour, could result in a tube being "burnt"—weakened through overheating on the forge-hearth[172]—and some motorcycles reached the front with unbrazed lugs, the tubes being "only held together by the enamel and the dowel pin".[173]

A damning indictment comes from one "who had considerable experience in France". In this man's opinion—and he seems a thoughtful, intelligent judge—the motorcycle frame was

> of hopelessly unscientific design, depending for its strength and rigidity on stout gauge tubes and heavy lugs, rather then on correct proportions and a scientific distribution of frame material.... There are far too many lugs, and each lug involves a separately brazed joint. Any of these joints may be defective or the tube may have had its strength seriously impaired by overheating, and these defects will probably remain latent [until the frame fails in service]. The abrupt changes in cross-sectional area of the frame members, due to the use of lugs, tend to localise the stresses and concentrate them.... Long before the engine required a complete overhaul the frame would crack or break.... Some machines lasted for as long as eighteen months but ... six to eight months' running was usually the life of a frame, and ... frames got worse rather than better towards the end of the campaign.[174]

The last remark supports the idea that the necessary use of semi- or unskilled labour caused problems in production.

This critic is no mere grumbler: he has had 40-50 motorcycles under his control "and a week seldom passed without one or two having to be exchanged through frame breakage". Furthermore, he clearly has engineering expertise, as he shows in his proposal to replace the lug-and-tube frame with steel stampings welded together, as used many years later in the most successful motorcycle ever, the Honda Fifty. His complaints are supported by an artificer sergeant whose DRs suffered thirteen frame breakages in one month—though this man attributes failures not to faulty design but to "the worst possible material [and] bad workmanship".[175] A "Three Year Artificer Corporal" bitterly endorses this sergeant: "some of the workmanship was scandalous".[176]

This may well be so; but the power of *pavé* to punish frames cannot be underestimated. Artificer Corporal Alfred Wade attributes frame failures to the "constant 'hammering' vibration set up by *pavé*",[177] and evidence that he was right could be found more than half a century later when Norton was developing a new motorcycle, the Commando. One of the challenges was to produce a frame that combined lightness with adequate strength, and the various prototypes were tested to breaking point over "Belgian *pavé*" at the MIRA test track[178]. If modern suspension could go only so far in preventing frame failure no wonder rigid frames broke through the Great War. Unsurprisingly, perhaps, given their weight, "combinations are unquestioningly the worst offenders", but solos suffered almost as badly. Typically the steering head-lug cracked behind the steering-stem, and the front down tube above the engine mount. So common was the latter failure that a forged bracket was designed to effectively replace the down-tube in the field, and an 8 HP Royal Ruby, destined for Russia, where conditions could be even worse than on the Western Front, was fitted with outrigger down-tubes in the factory.[179] The Douglas used two widely-splayed front down-tubes, and this design, coupled to the bike's low weight, probably reduced the incidence of frame breakage, but Douglas frames still broke.

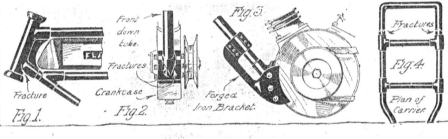

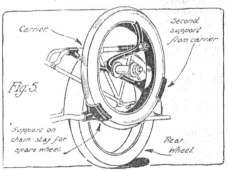 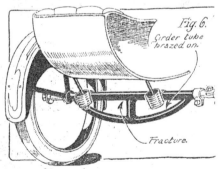

Figs. 1, 2 and 4.—Typical fractures under war conditions. Fig. 3.—Shows an extempore repair of a common fracture of the down tube. Fig. 5.—A suggested form of spare wheel carrier. Fig. 6.—A girder tube brazed on as shown to prevent breakages of the sidecar axle.

Frame breakage was endemic on both solos and sidecars. The main weak points are illustrated.[180]

Complaints about workmanship and materials were aired after the war had ended, and there can be no doubt at all that but for the Defence of the Realm Act there would have been many more complaints published through the war itself—indeed, some criticisms did reach expression in ink. To put it at its mildest, there is serious question as to whether machines disimproved through the war. Major SR Axford of the RAF pointed out at the war's conclusion that developments in aero engineering had driven a pace that affected motorcycle technology too, and that government experimentations in metallurgy, and attendant stipulations in material supply contracts, benefited motorcycle manufacture as everything else. Also, government regulations forced manufacturers to amalgamate their trade secrets in order to optimise overall output.[181] In May 1916 the Engineering Standards Commission issued a report regarding specifications for steels used in the auto industry, as well as standards in steel treatment.

But however true all this may have been, competition for scarce materials, overwhelming demand, and scarcity of skilled labour at home would seem to have countered much of such advances as were, in theory, made. Despite persistent appeals,[182] improvements to motorcycles were minimal, so that by war's end one disgruntled enthusiast complained: "My firm opinion is that few makers have anything new to show excepting a few comparatively unimportant details".[183]

Army motorcycles in 1915, i.e. Triumph and Douglas, incorporated the stronger Colonial Model frame, strengthened rear wheel mountings, stronger belt-rim attachment,[184] and larger hubs with seals outboard of the wheel bearing; prior to this modification wheel bearings were cup-and-cone, and not dust- or waterproof, so dust and mud could clog bearings to the extent that wheels might seize solid.[185] The American *Motorcycle and Bicycle Illustrated* reports on improvements: "War Affects Hub Design: Conditions Encountered by Machines at Front Force British Makers to give Problems Serious Attention: Some Methods Evolved for Better Bearing Protection". Taper-roller wheel bearings, adjustable and designed to take axial as well as radial thrust, were particularly suited to sidecar outfits, with their side-loadings. Felt washers were fitted to seal against ingression of dust and mud, and to contain oil supplied to the centre of the hub by an oil-gun.[186]

But demand for further improvements persisted, and in 1916 Corporal Sproston was calling for larger diameter wheels, increased ground clearance, "a totally enclosed kick-starter [with] folding crank", and handlebar-mounted clutch control, something he considered "absolutely essential".[187] Roger West describes how the frequent falls quickly wipe off every protuberance;[188] the elegant footboards that were so popular before the war gave way to in-field manufactured foot-pegs (West turned up his own on a lathe in a wayside workshop),[189] fixtures that were both less vulnerable and easier to repair, but a broken kickstart shaft or lever could not easily be fixed in the field, so we can understand Sproston's request for a crank-pedal that folded in out of harm's way.

Yet apart from adoption of the countershaft gearbox, somewhat stronger frames and forks, and 28-inch wheels, little more was done.[190] Triumph and many other makers did fit handlebar-mounted clutch levers, and DRs shortened the gear-change levers and bent them to suit foot control, allowing riders to keep both hands on the bars at all time. There was no "positive stop" mechanism in the gearboxes of the time (the hand-change "gate" provided the stop between gears), so such a modification meant that selecting second gear called for sensitive application of a mud-encrusted hob-nailed boot. The modification probably meant that the little Douglas, with its two-speed transmission, was equal in this regard to the three-speed Triumph, whose second gear was likely stamped past. Almost from the start, DRs showed individual initiative that anticipated the "official" Learning Curve.

Some improvements certainly were incorporated, both in manufacture and remanufacture of machines sent back to the factories for overhaul. In 1915 Douglas introduced a special WD model incorporating many minor modifications, all of which would seem to be retrospectively adaptable to earlier models, and probably were when those eventually were returned to the factory for overhaul. The 1915 Douglas had larger induction and exhaust ports, and these, combined with a re-profiled camshaft, allowed better gas flow and more power to be developed; strengthened pistons and more generous cylinder finning ensured this power could be harnessed and its extra waste heat dissipated. Perhaps more important than these engine modifications, the Colonial Model frame was strengthened: there were wider and larger diameter wheel rims, with stronger spokes and stronger belt-rim attachment; larger, waterproof hubs; new forks; a stout carrier box was provided for spares, tools and equipment; and the rear brake pedal was mounted on a separate pivot rather than on the footrest bracket—previously, a bent footrest could have incapacitated the rear brake. The mudguards were larger and sturdier, with greater clearance—though they continued to clog.[191]

Late that same year representatives of all motorcycle factories supplying the armed forces—Triumph, Douglas, P&M and Clyno—visited the front in an attempt to gauge the real-world conditions their motorcycles had to deal with and eradicate shortcomings, the most urgent concerns being "weak forks and fork links, inadequate mudguarding ... touring handlebars, [non-weatherproof] hubs"; they made further slight improvements in light of their discoveries. P&M simplified the design of their front forks and fitted larger bearings to the lower spring shackles, but "otherwise the P&M machines will be practically the same as in 1914".[192]

Corporal Best's replacement Douglas, issued in March 1915, was "much improved both in fittings and design"—or so he feels initially. It "is much heavier [thanks to the Colonial frame], but it has sufficient power, and the alterations all make for comfort and reliability." Best opines: "I should imagine the makers must have studied the machines returned disabled, for the improvements are all to the point and much as we have altered the old design of machine where possible"—an example of Don R setting the standard, and of the factories responding. However, Best's initial enthusiasm does not last; later he opines that pre-war motorcycles were better machines, and other DRs agree. For all its "improvements", Best's new Douglas is slower than the one it replaced in December 1914, and "is not quite as nice in some respects as the old one". Five months later this motorcycle breaks its frame and its replacement "needed a lot of adjustment which took time and it stranded me with a puncture and no repair outfit, so I had to push it a mile home as the rim was cracked and would not stand the cobbles deflated". A cracked rim certainly suggests poor materials, and later Best is more forthright: "bikes made up to 1915 ... were of better workmanship than for some years to come". In early 1917 Corporal Grice is issued with a—presumably remanufactured—1914 Triumph,[193] suggesting shortage of new machines but also the greater durability of older ones.

Ex-Corporal Sproston, a competition rider, disagrees: "I was never more convinced of the excellence of the present motor cycle.... Since those anxious days of Mons, I have seen fewer breakdowns directly traceable to faulty design or construction".[194] But by that time Sproston was in the RFC, not the DR corps, so was out of touch with motorcycles; besides, his status as an officer might have persuaded him that his duty was to raise morale, even if he had to stretch the truth to do so.

It is reasonable to imagine that shortage of both materials and skilled workmanship as the war advanced did lead to a reduction in quality, even as designs were improved (in minor detail): if the high-profile Tank Corps had to fight with the Navy for steel, and never get the thousand tanks that General Haig ordered in 1916, humble motorcycle factories must needs put up with even worse problems. The artillery, the single most critical branch of the armed services in this, "the war of the guns", suffered from sub-standard material, at least in the early years—buffer springs, for instance, failed under repeated firing—and if cynical profiteers supplied sub-standard Brodie helmets, on which a man's life might depend, can a motorcycle manufacturer be too harshly blamed for cutting corners in order to meet the War Office's remorseless demands? Through the war demand for all vehicles far exceeded supply.[195]

What is beyond doubt is that motorcycles, as supplied to Don R, had to have several hours spent in setting them up. Corporal Best observes:

It is rather curious that, though motor bikes are supposed to be turned out ready for the road yet they are always in need of a good examination. The new bike has taken some three or four hours in re-arranging things such as lamps, control leads [cables] etc which are wrongly fitted, whilst the nuts persistently work loose at first.[196]

Evidently the factories were under too much pressure to carry out pre-delivery inspection of machines, and unskilled labour was incapable of working to optimum standards.

In addition to metallurgical and production problems, all frames were unsprung, and this both caused discomfort to the rider and meant that road-shocks had to be absorbed by the frame alone. The result could be more than discomfort: one DR suffered blood poisoning, apparently from haemorrhoids that had been burst by the pounding over rough roads on a rigid frame.[197] Frame breakages were regular. An artificer sergeant reported thirteen such failures in a single month (albeit at Salonika, where roads were essentially non-existent;[198] "It was more like trick riding than motorcycling"[199]) and "The DRs of the 21st Division" averaged about one frame breakage per month in France and Belgium through the war, mostly due to "sheer failure of the metal to stand up to the strain".[200] Another artificer sergeant suggests that despatch riders of the artillery suffered more machine breakages than those of the air arms or the Army because those of the artillery have to "work up to the firing line", where conditions were worst.[201] Gas welding was available, but far from commonplace, so brazing was the only way, other than splinting, to repair broken frame tubes in the field—Corporal Tait reports such a repair as early as 7 October 1914[202]—and brazing is a hard-soldering process that sticks metal to metal rather than fusing the two together, so such brazed repairs, though better than steel splints, could only be less temporary, not permanent.

By 1914 all motorcycles had rudimentary suspension by girder forks in front, movement being limited to a couple of inches. For all its other virtues, the Triumph had particularly weak suspension,[203] with a spring cantilevered at right angles to the axis of movement.[204] Spring breakages were frequent—Corporal Tait broke one after three weeks' riding[205]—but a broken spring would not stop a bike, and bolts, rubber wedges and D5, "the strongest type of telegraph wire obtainable",[206] were used as in-field repairs.[207] These repairs, however, *could* stop a bike: by transmitting further road shocks to an already over-stressed frame.[208] Braking was primitive, typically stirrup-blocks on the front rim and a V-block or shoe bearing against the rear pulley,[209] and possibly because it aided and abetted the mudguards in clogging the wheel with mud, Don often threw his front brake away: it was "more trouble than its existence warrants".[210] The best brake was the engine. This was stopped by "lifting" the exhaust valve—i.e. levering it off its seat so as to interrupt the combustion cycle. The engine then acted as a drag on the back wheel, and a very gentle and progressive brake, particularly valuable on slippery surfaces. Breaking the valve-lifter cable could be a significant problem, as Corporal West discovered when it happened to him on the Great Retreat—effectively he found himself without a brake.[211]

Wheels were far larger in diameter and narrower in section than those of modern motorcycles, yet their diameter was not large enough for war conditions—later 28-inch rims were adapted (up from 26-inch) and these rolled more easily over ruts and potholes. Beaded-edge tyres were held in place by small rubber protrusions that tucked into a curled-over rim, these "beads" conforming themselves into position as the tyre was inflated. Secure location of the tyre was therefore dependant on tyre pressure, which collapsed when punctures were suffered, and these were frequent: often several a day over the broken surface, scraps of barbed wire, shell fragments, cast horseshoe- and hobnails.

Transmissions also were primitive, though by 1914 direct drive to the rear wheel was giving way to multi-speed transmissions with clutches to disengage the engine, and there were few direct-geared machines by 1918.[212] Early multi-speed transmissions were by hub gear, similar to that found on three-speed bicycles, and this could not be durable or reliable in the long term without the sort of attention that was hard to provide at the Front.[213] The typical hub was maybe four inches in diameter and perhaps a little less in width. Up to half the space was taken up by a clutch that contained some 40 razor-thin plates, which called for painstaking adjustment and left little room for the epicyclic gears, which therefore had insufficient bearing surface to transmit more than very modest power. Moreover, the assembly's clutch was fragile, and the sensitivity of its controls complicated wheel removal.[214] Sturmey-Archer, manufacturers of probably all epicyclic hubs fitted to British bikes, recommended "Relyabull" oil; this was whale oil, thinner and more consistent than the mineral oils available, and securing such specialist lubrication was another headache for the "quarter bloke" because, for all the preponderance of water, the trenches suffered no great infestations of cetaceans. Some manufacturers had gone over to the far more robust and reliable countershaft gearbox, and by 1915 Triumph had done this with their WO model; yet as a measure of the soundness of the Triumph overall, in October 1916 one signals unit still had "three 1914 hub gear Triumphs in commission [which] do not show any signs of giving out".[215]

Chain drive was common by 1914, but many motorcycles retained belt final drive, and in 1915 this was insisted upon by the War Office for all DR work—on the Western Front at least. Sunbeam was justly famed for its superb oil-bath rear chain enclosure, yet the factory was forced to fit belts to a small War Office order of fifty bikes, if Sunbeam wished to get the contract.[216]

By 1915 the standard DR bike (for the BEF, to whom the "standard" DR belonged) was either the 2¾ HP Douglas or the 3½ HP Triumph, each of which was fitted with a countershaft gearbox, chain primary- and belt final-drive. As with the side-valve, one should not shout "Luddite!" too loudly at "belt". The belt was proven,[217] and if it was subject to slippage in wet conditions, there is practically no complaint about this in service. Perhaps as it clogged mudguards, the mud of France and Flanders clogged pulleys sufficiently to overcome slippage—though it also might clog them so thickly as to dislodge the belt.[218] Corporal Watson complains of belt-slip only once, and that on 21 August 1914—i.e. before battle had been joined, over roads that were dry and dusty.[219] In typical muddy conditions a belt would long outlast the hundreds of small bearing surfaces of an exposed chain: chain breakage occurred as early as 6 September 1914, 24 days after the bike was issued, and over roads that were relatively benign,[220] so what chance had chain in the muddy conditions of the Western Front? Not the least of belt's advantages was its ease of in-field repair and replacement, and allied to this was the ease of remanufacturing belts in the field, from recycled horse harness.[221]

Rubber-impregnated canvas had previously replaced leather as best belt material, leather being slimy and elastic when wet, but "needs must…", and recycling was in keeping with the war footing onto which the economy had been placed by 1916.

> Nothing is thrown away out there; nothing is wasted…. Men go about, behind the front, and after a battle, picking up everything that has been thrown away. Everything is sorted and gone over with the utmost care … everything is saved. Reclamation is the order of the day. There is waste enough in war that cannot be avoided; the British army sees to it that there is none that is avoidable.[222]

"Indeed you cannot, with the greatest ingenuity in the world, make anything altogether useless in this war".[223] Even cast horseshoe- and hobnails were collected and recycled, a practise that incidentally reduced the rate of punctures. "Waste not, want not" might have been a slogan of the times, but the deliberate and well-organised policy of recycling was another manifestation of the British Army's Learning Curve (and in contrast to British industrial practice before the war, as Chapter One has shown).

That conditions favoured the relatively primitive belt- over chain-drive seems clear. Full enclosure could obviate chain wear, but such enclosure would need to fit snugly or it might become a reservoir for abrasive mud, exacerbating the very problem it was designed to overcome, and this did occur in some instances;[224] and when a chain broke it could lead to "paper [thin] chain cases wrapped in the back wheel *as usual*".[225] Sidecar outfits did use chain drive, but the load these carried would have overwhelmed a belt's limited friction grip, sidecars were far more limited in use and their employment was more judicious, and they therefore could be more regularly maintained, so their chains' enclosures were less likely to be damaged, and their chains replaced before they failed in the field. The Motor Machine Gun Service's Clyno sidecar outfit had a chain case that was, allegedly, dust-proof, and certainly was very well made.[226] BSA's (enclosed) chain drive on their African solo machines may be justified by the far smaller number employed (400) in combination with the enormous distances over remote territory the bikes had to cover—one campaign called for a journey of 2,800 miles "over roads that were mere bush tracks"[227]—where an enclosed chain offered advantage.[228] These bikes, besides, were weighed down with 140 lbs of equipment, as well as a rider,[229] a load that would strain the friction drive of a belt. BSAs supplied to French and Russian forces for service in Europe used chain primary- and belt final drive.[230]

Given constant outcry from DRs, what baffles most is failure to fit effective mudguards. By the end of the first year of war it was "a well-known fact that despatch riders were in some districts unable to progress more than three or four miles at a time without stopping to remove the thick mud which had caused the wheels to clog, due to the close-fitting guards".[231] Indeed, clogging might occur within mere hundreds of yards. *The Motor Cycle* fulminated: "Guards made to the curvature of the tyre are a mistake, as they cause accumulated mud to jam", and the writer specified that front mudguards be doubled in width and made to a larger radius than the wheel, rear mudguards made "flat, or nearly so".[232] One reader put forward an idea for a tyre-scraper to prevent clogging[233]—though the device appears too flimsy to have lasted long; indeed it looks as though it might have folded under pressure and jammed the wheel more effectively, and dangerously suddenly, than mud ever could. (Curiously, no one seems to have suggested a strong wire stretched across the bottom of the mudguard as a mud peeler, though such a device was used in the 1920s, if not before, to pluck nails out of tyres before they caused punctures. A similar device at least would have slowed the rate of clogging.)

It seems amazing, given the persistent screams of outrage, that the manufacturers never seriously modified their mudguards. Triumph replaced its front mudguard with an earlier type that was less valanced, and incorporated a broad flare at the bottom, steeply-raked rearward to deflect mud and water from engine and rider, but the continued howls of protest say that this didn't make much difference. Douglas added a mud-shield in front of the engine in about January 1915,[234] but though such a shield served to keep some mud off the bike and rider, it did not solve the problem of mudguards clogging. Don R improvised, often simply throwing the 'guards away; some fitted homemade leg-shields in their stead,[235] and in late 1915 *The Motor Cycle* devoted a two-page article to this potential solution, all but proof of the gravity of the problem.[236] The casual tone of some reports suggests that such modifications had long become commonplace in the field. Again, we have an example of individual initiative and the Learning Curve. Captain Watson claims that his Blackburne,[237] "the finest and most even-running of all motorcycles, ran with unswerving regularity," unlike his companion's Douglas, the front mudguard of which "choked up with a lamentable frequency".[238] It would be exhausting to list the number of complaints made about mudguards clogging; suffice it to say that they were being made to the end.[239]

And the almost amusing thing is that Don R had jerry-rigged better solutions than the factories ever explored. Apart from homemade leg-shields, riders had adapted old tyres, suitably cut and mounted, which shed mud by their flexibility.[240] These anticipated by several decades the plastic mudguards of motocrossers and shows again Tommy and Don on the Learning Curve, belying the clichéd image of soldiers as the automatons of mindless generals.

Watson goes so far as to claim that if all DRs were Blackburne-mounted "the percentage ... of messages undelivered owing to mechanical breakdowns or the badness of the roads would have been reduced to zero",[241] in large part, it seems implied, because of the Blackburne's superior mudguarding. But closer inspection exposes Watson's swan as a humble goose: another Blackburne-mounted DR had "to remove the front mudguard, which ... so collected the mud as almost to lock the front wheel",[242] and elsewhere in his account Watson admits to "clogging up".[243] His evaluation would have been coloured by the fact that two of his colleagues, Alec and Cecil Burney, were the actual manufacturers of the Blackburne.[244] It's difficult to comparatively evaluate the various machines used, as inevitably there is a subjective quality to users' accounts, but apart from Watson's criticism, there is little directed against the little Douglas, or the Triumph, other than the generic problems already noted, and the Letters pages in the press are full of praise for these machines—though the frequent paeans for them need to be read in the light that these two were by far the most numerous motorcycles in service, as well as the all-too-human tendency to see our geese as swans.

The Triumph and the Douglas do seem to have been unusually excellent motorcycles, vindication of the War Office's choice of them for use by the DRs of the Royal Engineers. Virtually all other bikes draw praise, and the fairest evaluation seems to be that most motorcycles of the time, given the conditions they had to work in, and admitting to various shortcomings, reflected well on the British industry (in contrast to the sad and shameful junk cynically churned out in the Seventies, before the once-great British motorcycle industry crashed and burned).[245] As one DR put it after two and a half years' service, "the motor bicycles stand up to the terrific gruelling to a degree which is little less than marvellous".[246] This evaluation is supported by a logged list of repairs carried out to a Triumph over nine months: a clutch cable; a throttle cable; two broken footrests (due to falls, an occupational hazard); a broken fork spring (the Triumph's Achilles' heel); new rear wheel bearings—a remarkably modest maintenance bill, though hardly typical.[247] West claims that in the early days the life expectancy of a motorcycle could be "only a matter of weeks",[248] and Sproston had wondered by 13 September 1914 how long the division's motorcycles could "put up with such daily treatment";[249] but it was not until 5 October that these were replaced, having advanced to Mons, retreated to the Marne, and advanced again to Ypres: "Hundreds of miles without a falter, bad treatment at all times and little attention".[250] Watson speaks of the "utter damnable waste of *everything* out here";[251] for not just bikes suffered: the *British Medical Journal* reports that "Ambulance Bodies Last Only Two Months" on the Western Front.[252]

The sort of maintenance that was possible in other less frantic theatres perhaps gives a better measure of the quality of British motorcycles: George Frost reports that all 400 BSAs supplied to the South African Motor Cyclist Corps "came through successfully",[253] despite incredibly tough going. In one instance fifty miles were covered in six hours, through sand that sometimes bogged the BSAs up to the crankcases. So deep was this sand that crankcase breathers had to be modified to prevent the sand from getting into the engines, and homemade washers made from canvas had to be cut to protect the wheel bearings.[254] There is much supportive testimony for the BSAs' endurance, as will be seen in Chapter Seven.[255]

Old and New World Motorcycles

British motorcycles of the time were primitive compared to American machines. Twist-grip throttle control and automatic carburettors on the latter relegated a lot of lever-juggling and made riding a more effortless affair. The 1000cc Cyclone used an OHC V-twin engine that could speed it up to 100mph, and though this was an exotic machine, its speed unobtainable on the open roads of the time, American bikes offered all-chain drive—even cardan shaft in the case of the Militaire—and larger wheels and tyres. Though Harley Davidson eventually was to exemplify engineering conservatism, in 1913 Indian had a sprung frame, electric lighting and high-tension coil ignition, the engine-driven dynamo doubling as electric starter (on the Hendee Special model) when power was fed back to it from the battery. This was two world wars before rear suspension, and more than half a century before self-starting was to become even optional extras on everyman motorcycles,[256] and it's sobering to realise that the Indian's electric starter antedated the kickstarter on some British motorcycles. The Flying Merkel, and the 1916 Indian Powerplus, came with mechanical oiling as well.

But Indians and Harley Davidsons still used foot-clutches, which could present problems of control over war-torn ground and—much more significantly—the weight of their power and refinements made them all but useless as solos in such conditions. Electric lighting and battery-powered ignition might seem advanced, but when batteries were fragile and heavy, and road shocks likely to both shake battery plates asunder and fracture battery cases and bulb elements, magneto ignition and acetylene lighting were likely to prove more reliable; and, as has been seen, a belt might offer subtle advantages over chain final-drive. The Triumph and Douglas, notably, were great little bikes, and other British motorcycles provided excellent service with other Allied armies. The Belgians used mostly the 3½ HP James (with three speeds and chain final drive) and a few Veloces, the French a wide variety: "Triumphs, Rovers, BSAs, Sunbeams, New Hudsons, Douglases and Indians",[257] the last probably supplied by Britain from Indian's Canadian branch—early in the war 50 Indians had been supplied by the Hendee Manufacturing Co from its Toronto branch to the Canadian Expeditionary Force. Early in the war, too, the Russians had considered several British makes—James, Premier, Sunbeam and Chater-Lea—and tested them mercilessly, including running sidecar outfits loaded with five men uphill and through deep sand. In the end the Russians went for three-speed 3½ HP Humbers, Rovers and Triumphs, and AJS and Matchless V-twin sidecar outfits, and all models seem to have given creditable service.[258]

Before the war all-chain-drive American machines had seemed to date other motorcycles, and toward the end of it the American Expeditionary Force even had the shaft-drive Militaire; but this was a dreadful turkey, which served to highlight the virtues of "primitive" British bikes. A 1300cc longitudinal straight four, the Militaire used timber-spoked wheels like those on Blacksmith MacMillan's treadle bicycle almost 80 years before, and the front wheel moved in an arc along a curved spindle to effect steering, the ends of this spindle being mounted on a suspension system that looks heavy enough to find a place on a suspension bridge, and gave all of maybe an inch of wheel movement. The front end appears to have weighed as much as an entire Douglas, and as a solo the bike was so cumbersome it needed outrigger wheels to give its rider any chance at all of keeping it upright. It was so heavy it was completely useless off *pave* and unreliable besides (warranty claims eventually closed the factory). It was loathed by anyone who had anything to do with it, and Indians and Harleys weren't much better. Corporal Tait dismisses such motorcycles as "no good for these roads".[259] "Three RAF motor cyclists" concur:

In this neighbourhood we see a large number of Yankee motor cyclists and they present an appearance of extreme clumsiness compared with the British DR. They seem very far from being at ease and show a great lack of skill in handling their heavy Harleys and Indians on bad roads. We think the fact that many of them are now mounted on Douglases is a great tribute to the British machine for active service conditions.[260]

A Canadian Don was more forthright: American motorcycles "were just no damn good. You couldn't keep them on the road";[261] and though weight was the major factor here, one Yankee DR was forced to concede that "Chain-cum-belt drive is comfortable", and that the Douglas could "hold to a wet road [pulley-] rim deep in mud at 30 per. Damn!"[262]

One three-year veteran makes a detailed critique of American and British motorcycles:

> the American machine will be useless except in the fine weather…. Apart from the fact that the American 7-9 [HP] machine will be an awkward proposition to ride, its mechanical construction for use as a military machine is entirely unsuitable for the purpose…. For Army use the keynote of the successful machine is simplicity. [Supposed improvements] add weight and complication not only to the machine itself but also to the supply column people who have to stock these spares.

This man dismisses spring frames because wear in the linkages is bound to be very rapid in the muddy, gritty conditions, so that "unless they are renewed frequently that rigidity so necessary for winter riding will be absent". The system of levers and Bowden cables used on British bikes might look less robust than the twistgrips and rod-linkages on American ones, but they were more easily repaired in the field: for instance, an ignition-retard cable might be substituted for a broken throttle cable, and the ignition timing temporarily locked in place; similarly, levers might be swapped about. As already noted, automatic oiling might be less efficient than hand-lubrication in conditions of war.

Similar criticism came from the Eastern Front: "There are a great number of American machines in the Russian army, but they show signs of rough usage and damage, generally caused by skids as the machines are very heavy and have exceedingly high gear ratios".[263]

In fairness, it must be acknowledged that "Three AFC [Australian] motor cyclists" refuted the three RAF motorcyclists' above criticisms: "The Yank machine has a decent saddle and a more decent spring fork";[264] and the push-pull piano-wire controls that the Americans used—along with rod linkages—was more robust than British Bowden. On *pavé* the 7HP Indian was "excellent, owing to its spring frame and ... its weight", which tended to steady it, but in slippery conditions "it is a fair devil, and you can't stop it".[265]

It also must be admitted that patriotism no doubt coloured the testimonies of many; but as both Canadians and Americans conceded the virtues of the British motorcycle, and as the British industry supplied to American forces "over 1,000 each of motor-bicycles and sidecars",[266] one is forced to conclude that British bikes were by far the more suitable for war conditions.

English veteran CK Shepherd seems to confirm this when, after his demobilisation, he rode a motorcycle across America on what were for the most part "nothing better than our fifth-rate country roads", yet hardly worse than those in a war theatre. His mount was a brand-new Henderson 1200 Four, probably the highest-specification motorcycle made, and Shepherd had "nothing but praise for its smooth running" and the "luxurious travel" that its sophistication made possible. But over three months and less than 5,000 miles necessary repairs came to more than the purchase cost of the motorcycle! They included:

> Five new cylinders; three pistons; five gudgeon pins; three complete sets of bearings; two connecting rods, and eleven sparking plugs. The machine was entirely overhauled on four occasions [and the] engine cut-out switch was the only part of the machine that did not break, come loose, or go wrong.

The spirit of San Fairy Ann served Captain Shepherd well: "Apart from that I had no trouble".[267]

Maintenance and Remanufacture

However good the machine, "The life of a motorcycle at this work is only a matter of weeks", Roger West laments.[268] Another DR and an officer independently estimate the average life as two months;[269] interestingly, this is the same as that of motor ambulances.[270] The failure rate certainly was high at the frantic pace set by the retreat from Mons, when "field workshops were not very accessible to most of us and if anything went wrong which one could not repair on the road it just somehow had to run without repairs".[271]

Such was the rate of damage that in-field bases for overhaul were established in October 1914, if not even earlier,[272] but this did not solve the problem, for repairs even here required "much patience and ingenuity, according to one DR, "owing to the lack of sundry tools or materials", and the administrative red tape that militated against replacement—though genuine shortages were at least as important. Bikes were "inspected periodically, say three or four times a year, by the Inspector of Mechanical Transport", but his inspection was likely to be cursory, because inspectors "often were ignorant of motorcycles". The wise DR cultivated a good personal relationship with the artificers.[273] By 1916 large Motor Transport Base Heavy Repair Workshops were set up at St Omer;[274] later up to five such workshops were located closer to the front. At least one of these was over-run during the Spring Offensive of 1918, something that "seriously affected the mechanical transport repair organisation and the output of repaired vehicles was considerably reduced at a time when the wastage in mechanical transport was exceptionally high".[275]

Quickly it was realised that the system of overhauling motorcycles in the field was ineffective and wasteful. Possibly because of the relative ease of transporting them, significantly damaged motorcycles soon began to be shipped back to their respective factories for comprehensive overhauls that incorporated any improvements—an early manifestation of the Learning Curve. The rate of turnover was such that in August 1918 one mechanical staff sergeant recognised a Douglas undergoing a factory overhaul, "at least the second time this machine has been 'invalided home'" in eight months,[276] and "the average rider has two or three machines issued to him in a year".[277]

We get an impressive picture of the Douglas factory toward the end of the war from *Motor Cycling*. With its "red-and-black tiled floor, the kitchen whiteness of the walls", the Douglas test shop, which by then was run by women, struck the reporter as more like a scientific laboratory. Engines were run for 30 minutes—on coal gas rather than on petrol, because of oil shortage—and top speed and power output measured and recorded. If the engines met expectations they were fitted with new valves and their valve-spring tension was checked before they were installed in new or remanufactured frames.[278]

Not all factories could overhaul their worn out machines, because they had converted to munitions manufacture, so repair depots were established in the UK to deal with such motorcycles—though they also dealt with Douglases and Triumphs, P&Ms and Clynos, augmenting the factories' efforts. These depots could cover several acres and were in full operation by the time the Battle of the Somme opened.[279] *The Motor Cycle* describes one depot that employed 250 workers and overhauled about 60 motorcycles a week; it was so busy that it had outgrown its premises. One Triumph here "was hardly distinguishable from new.... Its fine condition marked it for work abroad, as those machines which are not quite in such good order are 'for home service only'.... Machines for use abroad are given new accessories, while those employed at home are equipped with ... fittings which have been repaired". Repair—using acetylene welding, an advanced method in British engineering then—was necessary in part because those factories now producing munitions might be unable to supply spares, and improvisation was the order of the day: "it has been discovered that a New Hudson cylinder will fit a Premier", for instance. Because many industries used proprietary engines—notably the JAP—such substitution could be relatively easy. But part of the need to make and mend was the critical dearth of material, steel being needed to replace ships sunk by German U-boats and, after 1916, to build tanks. In repair workshops "waste is not only discountenanced but is actually non-existent".[280] "Quite ninety percent of these war- and weather-worn rusty derelicts ... would eventually be restored to a state almost like new".[281] Total wrecks were cannibalised: "The strictest economy is exercised, and, no matter how badly wrecked a machine may be, every sound part is taken from it and placed in a big stores [in order to] replace faulty parts of other machines". Even damaged drive chains were dismantled and new components fitted.[282]

Other depots carried out only minor repairs, but assessed machines for comprehensive attention, delivered them to either factory or overhaul depot, and acted to coordinate delivery of reconditioned motorcycles to wherever they were needed. One such depot housed over 2,000 motorcycles, so many that some had to be stored outside, "carefully protected by tarpaulins". They included such "non-military makes as Scott, James, Premier, Harley Davidson, NUT, AJS, Humber, Thresher-JAP, Chater Lea, New Hudson, Ariel, Bat-JAP, Bradbury and Connaught", all dating from the frantic early days, when anything with an engine and wheels was whipped up.[283] Such non-WO marques obviously were destined for home service, but their number and variety, so late in the war (1917), is a measure of how essential and ubiquitous the motorcycle was right through those fraught years.

Numbers

It is impossible to say how many motorcycles were used throughout the war. At the very outset the BEF had fifteen,[284] though in the first few days this number was increased approximately tenfold by recruitment of despatch riders with their own motorcycles, thanks in part to the foresight of the army in advertising for volunteers almost a month before war broke out.[285] Appendix 1 lists those in service at the time of the Armistice, but these cannot include those wasted, and wastage was enormous. The appendix indicates that some 48,000 units survived by 1918, out of over 750,000, which *Motor Cycling* estimates was the total number supplied;[286] this would give a figure of over 96 percent wastage. But *Motor Cycling*'s figure seems absurdly high: best estimates indicate that about 30,000 Triumphs and 25,000 Douglases, the most common bikes, were produced through the war.[287] If *Motor Cycling*'s figure was inadvertently increased tenfold by a misprint the wastage becomes less than ten percent. *The Motor Cycle's* figures, by contrast, give 13,854 solos and 2,459 sidecar outfits.[288]

These numbers cannot all be right; *Motor Cycle's* is certainly wrong. Part of the confusion—the San Fairy Ann factor—may lie in the method of computation, and the fact that most machines were returned to their respective factories for comprehensive overhaul, often many times. If one includes those re-manufactured in the total number of motorcycles supplied, *Motor Cycling*'s figure begins to seem perhaps less a product of brain fever.

Bringing the figure still closer to actuality is the statistical confusion that may have arisen from the fact that some motorcycle factories supplied engines to the war effort for other purposes, and these engines may have been included in statistics of "units" delivered. Douglas in particular produced an unknown number of stationary generating engines but so too did other manufacturers, and others supplied engines for trench-pumps, notably ABC and Wall. And there is a "colonial" factor that may help account for *Motor Cycling*'s remarkable figure: through most of Asquith's war ministry there was a pretence of "business as usual", and in this period it seems than an inordinate number of motorcycles, sometimes in kit form, as well as separate engines, transmissions and myriad components, were exported to South Africa and the Antipodes. The Precision was manufactured as a complete motorcycle only in Australia, the parent British Precision firm focusing on production of engines for supply to other manufacturers at home. Today there are far more Precisions in Australia than in the "Mother Country"—they were manufactured in both Adelaide and Melbourne—as well as more Suns (which mostly used Precision engines). [289] Another interesting, or at least intriguingly named Australian motorcycle from that time was the Swastika, which, like them all, used a British engine, the JAP in the Swastika's case (the conjunction of names weirdly anticipating the unholy alliance of the next war). It seems that these motorcycle components and kits were used to back-load the endless troop- and cargo-ships that were delivering men and meat to Britain in those fraught years, and *Motor Cycling* may have included such motorcycles or partial-motorcycles in its statistics.

Doing the mathematics as best we can: by 1918 there were 67 British divisions engaged in all war theatres, as well as nine retained for home defence and for training new formations.[290] Each of these 76 divisions had a nominal despatch rider strength of sixteen motorcycles, a total of 1,216. But this is only the start; despatch riders of the Royal Engineers also were attached to Armies, Corps and GHQ. Besides, while each Corps Signal Unit had six despatch riders, it also had at least fifteen other functionaries who were motorcycle-mounted. Each Army Signal Unit had at least sixteen motorcycle-mounted functionaries in addition to its DRs. Each Royal Field Artillery brigade had two DRs as did each sub-section of Heavy Artillery. Also, some DRs of the Royal Engineers were seconded to the "Arty": Corporal WL Anderson had been seconded from the RE to divisional artillery HQ when he won his DCM; Corporal RR Read had been seconded to the Heavy Artillery when he won his.[291] Such overlapping complicates the computations.

GHQ had at least 162 motorcyclists attached, not including the five Telegraph Construction Companies that were raised in the final year of the war, each of which had fifteen motorcycle-mounted sappers, whose job was to speedily repair any "dis"—disconnection or disablement—in the lines. Either five or six Railway Telegraph Companies also had been raised between 1915 and 1918, and each of these had eighteen motorcycle-mounted personnel. The Cavalry Corps Signals Squadron had 25 motorcyclists attached, each Cavalry Division had thirteen, and each Cavalry Brigade had three.[292] The Intelligence Corps had 31 motorcycles attached to headquarters, plus ten to each of its five Army Companies, seventeen to its Intelligence Police, seven each to four Corps Sections, and one attached to "every Cavalry and Infantry Division and Tank Brigade Headquarters". "All Intelligence Corps officers, other than those at GHQ, were provided with a motor cycle for their work".[293]

The maths is far from finished, the computation more confusing. Motorcycles also were used by a great variety of functionaries, from the mobile mechanics of the Army Printing and Stationery Services to the "turd burglars" of the RAMC Sanitary Sections—and there were the sidecars of the MMGS and of the British Ambulance Committee to the *Service de Santé Militaire* (though these were not with the BEF or under army command, of course), and the DRs and other motorcycle-mounted personnel attached to the air arms and the Royal Navy. Though most Army despatch riders were attached to the RE, not all were: the Artillery, Army Service Corps and Royal Army Medical Corps all had their own. "The Field Ambulance maintains constant communication with the regimental aid-post in front and the clearing hospital in rear",[294] and sometimes such communication called for a DR such as Jack Rennick, a former racer.[295] Both A Shaw and JJ Hawker were DRs with the Army Service Corps when they were awarded the DCM.[296] By 1918 this vast organisation—the ASC—numbered more than 10,000 officers and 315,000 other ranks, in addition to thousands of non-British labourers, and its *monthly* delivery to the two million British soldiers in the field by then included 90 million pounds of bread, 32.25 million pounds of forage and 13 million gallons of petrol—to say nothing of other food, equipment and ammunition.[297] Ensuring delivery of these supplies all over the British sector called for the most intricate and excellent coordination and communication—by the much-reviled staff—which in turn, given the technology of the time, called for despatch riders. According to the Director of Transportation: "They are primarily for use in connection with the supervision and control of MT [Mechanical Transport] transport".[298] Like the DRs of the RE, those of the RAMC or ASC could be seconded elsewhere: F Bunce, ASC, won his DCM when attached to the Royal Garrison Artillery.[299] And to complicate matters further, Captain William Dane Wallis, who was not a DR but a

Divisional Trench Mortar Officer, was motorcycle mounted when he won his MM at the Battle of the Selle in October 1918:

> in the attack from the Selle river, information as to the situation of the attacking troops was unobtainable. This officer was sent forward on a motor-cycle from divisional artillery headquarters with orders to get in touch. This he did, and brought back the most important information.[300]

Again that conjunction of words, even in the last days of the war, when electronic communication had improved almost out of recognition since the start of it: "information", "unobtainable" and "motor-cycle". It bears repeating: the motorcycle was essential to managing the Great War. It was ubiquitous.

To return to the matter of numbers: the War Office's *Statistics of the Military Effort of the British Empire during the Great War 1914-1919* claims that in January 1918 there were 9,552 motorcycles (solos and sidecar combinations) in France, plus 2,788 "available in shops or depots", most of these, probably, being on their way to or from being remanufactured. However, the figure of 13,516 is also given for the total in France. These figures include 675 actually in use "On lines of communication"; 192 "En route for the front"; and 309 "Employed at bases". But contradictions abound: up to 1 March 1919 there had been, "Despatched to the BEF in France", 26,375 motorcycles and 15,920 "cycle cars"—presumably sidecar outfits; to "Salonica, Egypt, Mesopotamia, &c" there had been despatched 158 motorcycles; to Italy, 331 motorcycles. These figures add up to 26,864 motorcycle solos, plus 15,920 "cycle cars", a total of 42,784.

Other figures include:

Theatre	Returns 11 Nov 1918	Returns 16 Nov 1918
France	14,464	14,328
Italy	765	solo 615 s/car 150
Salonica (includes those with Serbian Army	628	solo 658 s/car 5
North Russia (with White Army)		28
Malta and Gibraltar	16	16
Egypt	1,486	solo 1,349 s/car 88
East Africa	830	897
Mesopotamia	1,233	solo 1,132 s/car 30
India	135	

This gives a total of: 19,557 or 19,296

These figures in turn fit into a larger pattern:

	19,557	19,296
Total overseas		
Total in home service	5,391	solo 2,978 s/car 1,654
Total in home depots	9,917	solo 9,286 s/car 631
Grand total	34,865	33,845

Elsewhere, though, we find the following figures:

11 November 1918: 34,711;

15 March 1919: 35,805.[301]

It would seem that there were about 35,000 motorcycles in the various theatres at the end of the war. But the above statistics do not include machines serving with the RFC/RAF, or the Royal Navy; this may explain the 42,784 figure given earlier.

Statistics for the enemy are hard to find, but there is evidence that at the outset of war the Reichswehr had 4,000 motorcycles,[302] though up to 48,000 may have been "under military control"—perhaps subject to being commandeered from the civilian population.[303] This compares to fifteen in the BEF! The Germans used mainly the 3½ HP NSU and the Wanderer V-twin, the latter a very sophisticated machine with suspension front and rear and engine and transmission built in unit; one captured at Salonika made a favourable impression on a British DR.[304] The Germans also used (as with tanks) captured British motorcycles, and this suggests that their supplies were running low as the demand for armaments increased through the war. It seems that Germany was down to about 5,400 motorcycles in 1918 and the other Central Powers combined probably had even fewer.[305] There may be significance in one German DR's observation that "the moving parts of the motor were very worn". This man, named Voight, was a contributor to the *German Despatch Rider's Monthly Magazine*, and despite wear in its engine he reports "excellent" service from his pre-war NSU 3½ HP V-twin. "Never have I been left by the bike. In sunshine and rain, on the perfect French roads and on the Russian sandy ones, it was my truest companion, on whom I could always rely". Herr Voight's description of French roads as "perfect" may be taken as a relative reflection on those of the Eastern Front. It appears from his account that the German DR suffered similar problems and performed similar duties to his British counterpart, but in addition had to commandeer and herd to the local butcher cattle and horses in occupied territories.[306]

Exactly what use Germany made of her motorcycles through the war would make for interesting reading. Even less is known about the other Central Powers; at the outbreak of war at least four, possibly more, Austrian

Jäger battalions used companies of cyclists, each company including two motorcyclists,[307] but any motorcycles in the Turkish or Bulgarian forces must have been supplied by either Germany (Wanderer, NSU) or Austria (Puch), and they would have been hard to come by as the war went on. Clearly the Germans had huge numbers at the outset by comparison with the BEF, but a large proportion of them were used as sidecar personnel carriers (as in the next war), and materiel carriers,[308] and in the early years at least, security patrols in occupied territories were motorcycle mounted.[309] Like the British, the Germans also appreciated the motorcycle-sidecar's potential as a machinegun-mount and -delivery system.[310] But they may have underestimated the value of the motorcycle despatch rider at the outset (see Chapter Seven), and in the early phase of the Somme battles a captured report written by General Sixt von Arnim admitted: "The establishment of motor cycles proved insufficient for the heavy fighting; the deficiency was painfully in evidence".[311]

If motorcycles were of such importance in position warfare, they were far more so during the opening war of movement, when the British despatch rider quite literally may have saved the Allies from defeat, as will be seen. However primitive, the British motorcycle did a tremendous job. As a subsequent *Motor Cycling* editorial put it, "British motor cycling services are to be congratulated as ... being at least one branch of the Services whose superiority the Germans have never challenged".[312]

Certainly the British motorcycle industry rose to the challenge from the outset. Two weeks into the war an order for 100 Triumphs was filled in 48 hours, and through the remainder of 1914 Douglas produced 300 motorcycles a week for the war effort (as well as an unknown number of stationary engines). Through the first year of "business as usual", the Board of Trade advocated the "capture of enemy trade"—however remarkable that advocation may seem today, in its implication of warped priorities—and British industry was happy to oblige. All industries had to struggle against the loss of skilled workers to Kitchener's recruitment campaign, and after "reserved occupations" were recognised, industry suffered increasingly from material shortages, as artillery, munitions and tanks all clamoured for such steel as was available after shipping lost to the U-boat campaigns (up to 900,000 tons a month) was replaced.[313] In 1916 all civilian production stopped, but the motorcycle industry went from strength to strength supplying armed forces and Allies.

This need not give great comfort today. In 1918 Humber paid a 6 percent dividend on ordinary shares, while Rudge-Whitworth paid a remarkable 20 percent, after having averaged ten percent through the first three years of war.[314] When soldiers were dying for a shilling a day, these figures make for uncomfortable reading, and reinforce faux-liberals' cynical views on the Great War.

Endnotes

1 *Motor Cycling*, 8 September 1914, p. 539.
2 David Minton, *The Triumph Story: Racing and production models from 1902 to the present day*, p.10.
3 *The Royal Automobile Club Journal*, 9 December 1909, p. 410-12. Antebellum, government neglect of the motorcar and motorcycle was something that greatly exercised champions of the motorcar. Considerable progress had been made by 1914.
4 *The Motor Cycle*, 22 February 1917, front page.
5 *The Motor Cycle*, 31 May 1917, p. 498.
6 *The Motor Cycle*, 22 February 1917, ibid. Certainly this is a partisan view, but it cannot have been entirely wide of the mark.
7 E Alexander Powell, *Italy at War and the Allies in the West*, p. 76.
8 *The Motor Cycle*, 22 October 1914, p. 408.
9 *The Graphic*, 19 December 1914, front page; 2 October 1915, p. 430.
10 *The War Illustrated*, Vol. II, p. 681.
11 Herbert Strang, *The British Army in War* (unpaginated).
12 William E Sellers, *With our Fighting Men*, p. 76.
13 No 92 in a series of 100.
14 *The Motor Cycle*, 2 September 1915, p. 19.
15 *Motor Cycling*, 2 May 1916, p. 647.
16 Max Pemberton, "Battle of the Great High Road and How the Despatch Rider Came Home, *The War Illustrated*, 6 January 1917 www.greatwardifferent.com/ Great_War/Despatch_Rider/Despatch_Rider_01.htm.
17 See Percy K Fitzhugh, *Tom Slade: Motorcycle Dispatch Bearer*.
18 *The Belfast Evening Telegraph*, 25 April 1914.
19 GA Birmingham, "The Despatch Rider", in *Minnie's Bishop and Other Stories*, p. 180.
20 James Hayward, *Myths & Legends of the First World War*, pp. 11, 20.
21 James Fiske, *Facing the German Foe; The Belgians to the Front*.
22 Fiske was not the only novelist to feature boy scouts in his work, many fictive accounts confirming that these young lads were an everyday component of the war effort; see, for instance, Gilbert Frankau, *Peter Jackson, Cigar Merchant*, p. 65.
23 WHL Watson, *Adventures of a Despatch Rider*, p. 4.
24 *The Motor Cycle*, 30 August 1917, p. 209.
25 Stellenbosching: a South African War term for sidelining.
26 *The Times History of the War*, Vol. XVII, pp. 166, 145. For a comprehensive account of boy scouts' work see Chapter CCLIII of this work, "The Boy Scouts".
27 Hayward, ibid, p. 73.
28 *The Times History of the War*, Vol. XVII, p. 164.
29 Charles Edward Callwell, *Experiences of a Dug-out, 1914-1918*, p. 28.
30 Col. JFC Fuller, "Progress in the Mechanicalisation of Modern Armies", p. 74. So fixated on mechanical warfare was Boney that he once remarked that when he died the words "spare Parts" would be found engraved on his heart—Charles Carrington, *Soldier From the Wars Returning*, p. 206.
31 By contrast, the importance of tanks was inflated over the years, especially when "the Donkeys" school began to portray tanks as having had the potential to save many lives had the doltish generals only been less hostile to innovation. In fact Haig ordered a thousand tanks only three days after this "wonder weapon" made a very inauspicious appearance on the battlefield, an order that was never filled

through no fault of the generals (or, indeed, anyone else, given the more urgent need for shells and—more critical still to an island nation beset by U-boats—ships).

32 Dan Todman, *The Great War: Myth and Memory*, p. 26.

33 The insane diktat on lighting campfires was issued at the 2008 International Boy Scout Jamboree in Ireland—which, to underline the insanity, was held in possibly the wettest August since Third Ypres.

34 Before the end of the war the Allies' map of entire front line, from the Channel to Switzerland, was being revised at least once daily, by analysis of aerial photography.

35 R Chevenix-Trench, "Signal Communications in War", p. 303.

36 OH Davis, IWM document PP/MCR/180, p. 10.

37 Lieutenant WH Foster, "Distant Guns", p. 8. In fairness to Haig, horses, never blessed with good nerves at the best of times, were skittish under war conditions, and motorcycles didn't help their condition. Riders complain of the danger from kicks—e.g. *Motor Cycling*, 6 July 1915, p. 218—and in his fictive account of his own war, Gilbert Frankau accounts how "an occasional despatch rider, phutting past, disturbed the horses"—*Peter Jackson, Cigar Merchant*, p. 150.

38 Foster, ibid, p. 10.

39 *The Motor Cycle*, 23 August 1917, p. 183.

40 *Motor Cycling*, 5 March 1918, p. 334; Imperial War Museum folder PP/MCR/180.

41 Watson, ibid, p. 212; Tait, passim; TW Grice, passim.

42 WH Tait, 21 November 1914.

43 Stephen Bull, *An Officer's Manual of the Western Front 1914-1918*, p. 59.

44 WHL Watson, ibid, p. 159; Roger West, *Diary of the War: Retreat from Mons to the Battle of the Aisne*, pp. 66, 73, 95, 96; Herbert A Stewart, *From Mons to Loos*, p. 43.

45 CEW Bean, *Letters From France*, p. 34.

46 E Van Isacker, "The Diary of a Dispatch Rider Attached to the Belgian General Staff", www.greatwardifferent.com/Great_War_Dispatch_Rider/Dispatch_Rider_02.htm.

47 Watson, ibid, p. 100.

48 Davis, ibid, p. 213.

49 *The Motor Cycle*, 27 January 1916, p. 71; 16 November 1916, pp. 424-25.

50 HP Bonser, "A Sapper in Palestine", in *On the Front Line: True World War I Stories*, p. 329.

51 Lt Col GCG Blunt, "Mechanised Transport in Small Wars", p. 563, and Bart H Vanderveen, *Onyslager Auto Library: Motorcycles to 1945*, p. 39. The tandem three-wheeler was not new: a strange machine, the Singer, had appeared briefly at the turn of the century in prototype form; its *front* end comprised two tandem-coupled wheels mounted on a bogey. The Singer possibly survives. Between the wars, as well as the Triumph, there were prototype tandem three-wheelers from the British OEC and the French-Swiss Mercier, and possibly from other manufacturers. Some designs allowed the two rear wheels to mount a caterpillar track. The design has reappeared occasionally since, most recently in 2009 with Julien Rondino's French-manufactured A3W Motiv.

52 *The Motor Cycle*, 31 May 1917, p. 496; *Motor Cycling*, 8 January 1918, p. 155.

53 Burns and Messenger, *The Winged Wheel Patch*, p. 15.

54 *The Motor Cycle*, 2 March 1916, p. 214.

55 *The Motor Cycle*, 15 June 1916, p. 561.

56 *The Motor Cycle*, 5 April 1917, p. 308
57 *The Motor Cycle*, 23 August 1917, p. 181.
58 *The Bulletin*, October/November 2007, Number 79, p. 24.
59 *The Motor Cycle*, 30 July 1916, p. 68.
60 *The Motor Cycle*, 10 February 1916, p. 136. Ambulance trailers were reasonably common before the war, though normally towed by four-wheelers—The *British Medical Journal*, 2 January 1915, p. 44.
61 *The Motor Cycle*, 3 February 1916, p. 116B.
62 *The Motor Cycle*, 31 October 1918, p. 386.
63 Burns and Messenger, ibid, p. 13.
64 *Motor Cycling*, 13 November 1917, p. 12.
65 *The Motor Cycle*, 26 April 1917, p. 375; 10 May 1917, p. 419.
66 Louis A Strange, *Recollections of an Airman*, p. 89.
67 David Fletcher, *War Cars: British Armoured Cars in the First World War*, pp. 59-60; *The Motor Cycle*, 9 May 1918, p. 448; *The Great War in a Different Light*, www.greatwardifferent.com/Great_War/Gizmo/Gizmo_03.htm
68 *The Motor Cycle*, 9 May 1918, p. 448.
69 Note that "8 HP" refers to the RAC rating of the time, something that related to engine capacity rather than brake-measured horsepower output.
70 Horace G Wyatt, *Motor Transport in War,* p. 184-85.
71 *The Motor Cycle*, 16 March 1916, p. 254.
72 *The Times History of the War*, Vol. XX, pp. 375-76.
73 War Office, *Statistics of the Military Effort of the British Empire during the Great War 1914-1919* p. 503.
74 Gerald DeGroot, *Blighty: British Society in the Era of the Great War*, pp. 67-68.
75 DeGroot, ibid, p. 66.
76 Malcolm Brown, *The Imperial War Museum Book of the First World War*, p. 185.
77 Arthur Ruhl, *Antwerp to Gallipoli: A Year of the War on Many Fronts—and Behind them*, p. 71.
78 *Motor Cycling*, 4 December 1917, p. 66.
79 Chris Willis, *Motorcycles, Murder and Misogyny*, www.chriswillis.freeserve.co.uk/Sayersbikes.htm; (London Metropolitan Police motorcycle patrols were not established until 1930).
80 Keith Jeffery, "Nationalisms and gender: Ireland in the time of the Great War 1914-1918", p. 5.
81 *Motor Cycling*, 7 May 1918, p. 492; 15 October 1918, pp. 406-07.
82 *The Motor Cycle*, 2 May 1918, p. 431.
83 *The Motor Cycle*, 6 December 1917, p. 546.
84 *The Motor Cycle*, 15 November 1917, p. 472.
85 Wyatt, ibid, pp. 41, 44-45
86 *Motor Cycling*, 11 August 1914, p. 453.
87 Watson, ibid, p. 160.
88 *The Royal Automobile Club Journal*, 2 December 1909, p. 396; 9 December 1909, p. 410.
89 *The Motor Cycle*, 9 July 1914, p. 56.
90 *Motor Cycling*, 22 June 1915, p. 172, 29 June 1915, p. 197; 13 July 1915, p. 251; 20 July 1915, p. 257.
91 *Motor Cycling*, 15 June 1915, p. 146.
92 General Percy Hanbro, "The Horse and the Machine in War", p. 95.
93 Major HCH Eden, "A Mobile Light Division", p. 57.

94 Diane Atkinson, *Elsie and Mairi Go to War*, p. 44.

95 Sproston, ibid, 15 December 1914; *Motor Cycling*, 6 October 1914, p. 624; 27 October 1914, p. 700. It would be unwise to believe all the lurid accounts in the motorcycle press, however: see Watson, ibid, p. 78; *The Motor Cycle*, 11 May 1916, p. 445.

96 Paul Maze, *A Frenchman in Khaki*, p. 76.

97 Charles Wadsworth Camp, *History of the 305th Field Artillery*.

98 West, ibid, p. 20.

99 JH Morgan, *Leaves from a Field Note-Book* p. 185.

100 Tait, ibid, 24 August, 26 August, 1 September 1914.

101 Anthony Clayton, *Forearmed: A History of the Intelligence Corps*, p. 18.

102 James Edmonds, *History of the Great War: Military Operations France and Belgium, 1914*, p. 243.

103 *Motor Cycling*, 15 June 1915, p. 146. There was no hostility to machineguns in the British Army, rather a recognition that in the frantic scramble for men and materiel they had their proper place; Haig's "infamous" remark that two machineguns per battalion was adequate was made at a time when the German Armies, the best in the world then, used … two machineguns per battalion. In 1909 Haig had requested six per battalion but was turned down by Lloyd George, who in later years sneered at the alleged admission that two were adequate.

104 M Young, *Army Service Corps, 1902-1918*, p. 37. This "considerable number" may have been the fifteen motorcycles that the BEF had acquired by 1914, and which, one may presume, were allocated to despatch riding duties in August.

105 Stephen Bull, *An Officer's Manual of the Western Front 1914-1918*, pp. 6-7.

106 JC Dunn, *The War the Infantry Knew, 1914-1919*, p. 15.

107 *The Long, Long Trail*, http://www.1914-1918.net/4div.htm.

108 *Motor Cycling*, 2 May 1916, p. 646.

109 Roger West, ibid, pp. 8-9.

110 Maze, ibid, p. 60.

111 Sproston, ibid, 14 December 1914. See also West, ibid, p. 38, for instances of destruction of broken down lorries. In the light of all this, and of similar destruction at Dunquerque in 1940, we may assume that the same occurred during the Spring Offensive of 1918.

112 Watson, ibid, p. 79.

113 George H Frost, *Munitions of War: A record of the work of the BSA and Daimler Companies during the world war 1914-1918*, p. 57. Perhaps the BSA, as good a bike as any, and the mainstay in World War Two, was excluded from supplying the Western Front because the factory was so involved in other war work that it could not dependably meet the demand for machines, given the huge wastage in that theatre. Only 400 BSAs were supplied to the African campaigns and, though BSA did supply French and Russian forces, presumably these markets could be regarded as dispensable if necessary.

114 CA Brett, *Recollections*, p. 9.

115 *Motor Cycling*, 25 May 1915, p. 66.

116 *Motor Cycling*, 1 May 1917, p. 583.

117 CE Allen, *Titch: The Founder's Tale*, p. 94; another former DR, identifying himself only as "Ex 2337318", claims that while "I had several rides on other machines, I think that the BSA M20 was just about the best for the job"— "Motorcyclist at War", p. 316.

118 Bert Hopwood, *Whatever Happened to the British Motorcycle Industry*, p. 53.

119 Soon after the war a sleeve-valve engined motorcycle, the Grindlay-Peerless, was manufactured; though streets ahead of almost everything else, notably in terms of oil-tightness and mechanical silence, its cost of manufacture consigned it to commercial failure.

120 E.g. *The Motor Cycle*, 10 February 1916, p. 130.

121 It will be noted from Appendix 1 that Scotts were absent from overseas service by 1918.

122 *Motor Cycling*, 29 December 1914, p. 204.

123 William J Claxron, *The Mastery of the Air*, p. 110.

124 *The Motor Cycle*, 1 October 1914, p. 402; earlier, a ruddy "motorcycliste" had come to the rescue of a DR in distress—*The Motor Cycle*, 3 September 1914, p. 296. Damn world's going to the dogs, harrumph

125 This writer once travelled some 650 miles in the company of a friend mounted on an SV BSA M20, which burned out two exhaust valves over three days; all were replaced by the roadside, the second by one plundered from an ancient tractor, and modified to fit with hacksaw and file, and fine sandpaper (the rider optimistically had packed only one spare valve). These minor vexations failed to spoil a splendid weekend, way back in 1975.

126 One of the first radials, perhaps the very first, was a five-cylinder built into the front wheel of a bicycle by Frenchman Félix Millet in 1892. This design reappeared after the war in the Megola.

127 *The Motor Cycle*, 17 January 1918, pp. 52-53.

128 *The Motor Cycle*, 24 May 1917, p. 484; 14 June 1917, p. 546.

129 *The Motor Cycle*, 27 June 1918, p. 610.

130 *The Motor Cycle*, 24 May 1917, editorial.

131 Parallel-cut fins were reintroduced by the Japanese in the 1970s, but in the interest of style, not efficiency. The RD series Yamaha counter-pointed a matt-black engine with polished-edge cooling fins, the better heat-dissipating qualities of the matt-black surface going some way to counter the less efficient fin cross-section.

132 *Motor Cycling*, 19 November 1918, p. 25.

133 As an indication of how easy: after the Second World War a number of enterprising Italians, operating from small workshops, designed bolt-on OHV conversions for the many British SV motorcycles left behind.

134 *The Motor Cycle*, 13 September 1917, p. 253; *Motor Cycling*, 26 October 1915, p. 622.

135 *The Motor Cycle*, 19 November 1914, p. 566.

136 Roger B Whitman, *Motor-Cycle Principles and the Light Car*, pp. 70-71.

137 This was the last year of Rikuo production—and the first of the Honda Cub, the fabled "Fifty".

138 Thirty years later BSA introduced its superb parallel twin, which boasted "no external oil lines"; but these quickly were added to prevent rapid wear in the OHV assembly.

139 To cope with the high stresses of full-throttle operation, aero engines ran on castor oil, whose lubricating qualities were incomparably greater than that of even top-quality mineral oil, and of an entirely different order than the dodgy stuff Don R had to make do with.

140 *Motor Cycling*, 6 August 1918, pp. 232-33.

141 Ixion, *Motor Cycle Cavalcade*, p. 37.

142 *Motor Cycling*, 28 August 1917, p. 318.

143 *The Motor Cycle*, 24 October 1918, p. 374.

144 *Motor Cycling*, 3 March 1937, p. 562.

145 *The Motor Cycle*, 23 August 1917, pp. 180-82.

146 LJK Setright, "Oil to All Parts", p. 1243.

147 Davis, ibid, p. 60. "Wet-sumping" was to afflict British motorcycles into the 1970s, at least those that used gear-, rather than-plunger-driven, oil pumps.

148 *The Motor Cycle*, 25 April 1918, p. 409.

149 *The Motor Cycle*, 19 November 1914, p. 555.

150 *The Motor Cycle*, 21 September 1916, p. 244; Burns and Messenger, ibid, p. 20.

151 *Motor Cycling*, 19 January 1915, p. 279; *The Motor Cycle*, 1 July 1915, pp. 7-9..

152 Burns and Messenger, ibid, p. 20.

153 David Fletcher, *War Cars: British Armoured Cars in the First World War*, p.54.

154 *The Motor Cycle*, 28 January 1915, p. 83.

155 The Lucas monopoly has ironic overtones it would take a motorcyclist of advancing years to appreciate: Joseph Lucas had got into the cycle game with his "King of the Road" bicycle lamp, and the dreadful quality of Lucas electrics, toward the end of British motorcycle manufacture, meant that the "King of the Road" had become the "Prince of Darkness". (In fairness, many of the problems had more to do with rider neglect or ill-maintenance than with the quality of Lucas products, prior to the 1960s at any rate.)

156 *The Motor Cycle*, 21 February 1918, p. 181. Long after the war the Bosch had "never been beaten ... being as near perfection as it is possible for a magneto"—E Charles Vivian, *A History of Aeronautics*, p. 260.

157 Ixion, *Motorcycle Cavalcade*, p. 54.

158 *The Motor Cycle*, 4 October 1917, p. 319.

159 David Minton, *The Triumph Story*, p.12.

160 Minton, ibid, p. 19. See also *The Motor Cycle*, 9 December 1915, p. 591, for an instance of a motorcycle doing "approximately 1,000 miles per month".

161 *The Motor Cycle*, 30 September 1915, p. 337.

162 *Motor Cycling*, 27 October 1914, pp. 687-89, through 29 December 1914, pp. 202-04.

163 Minton, ibid, p. 15.

164 Though not commercially successful, this was a wonderful motorcycle that retained many of Scott's original design features yet could hold its own against larger multi-cylinder machines from Japan—at least on twisty roads, where its superb handling could overwhelm the limitations of its top speed (which, though, at 115mph, was pretty good for the time).

165 *The Motor Cycle*, 27 April 1916, p. 395.

166 West, p. 107.

167 The now Indian-made (erstwhile Royal) Enfield retains this design to the present day.

168 I'm obliged to Mr Richard Rosenthal for this information.

169 *Motor Cycling*, 4 March 1919, pp. 339-340.

170 Acetylene welding was displacing hearth brazing to some extent—see *The Motor Cycle*, 4 March 1915, p. 224—but frame lugs were to survive the Hitler War and even into the 1990s, in the case of the antediluvian Harley Davidson and—surprisingly—BMW, who reverted to lug mounting for its rear suspension when it went over to single-shock operation. Despite its shortcomings, a brazed-lug frame absorbs vibration better than a welded-tube frame, in part because of the extra mass, but also because resonance is dampened by the lug-joints.

171 *Motor Cycling*, 6 February 1917, p. 330.
172 *Motor Cycling*, 4 March 1919, p. 339.
173 *Motor Cycling*, 25 March 1919, p. 444.
174 *Motor Cycling*, 4 March 1919, pp. 339-40.
175 *Motor Cycling*, 11 March 1919, p. 379.
176 *Motor Cycling*, 25 March 1919, p. 444.
177 *The Motor Cycle*, 2 December 1915, p. 559.
178 I am obliged to Mr Steve Wilson for this information.
179 *Motor Cycling*, 22 May 1917, p. 43; 18 September 1917, p. 380.
180 *Motor Cycling*, 13 September 1917, p. 330.
181 *Motor Cycling*, 19 November 1918, p. 25. Such practises, it will be remembered from Chapter Two, were part of the Second Reich's industrial success.
182 E.g. *The Motor Cycle*, 24 September 1914, pp. 377-78, 8 July 1915, p. 29; 5 August 1915, p. 141, 26 August 1915, p. 141, front page; *Motor Cycling*, 13 September 1917, pp. 380-81, 27 November 1917, p. 40, 4 December 1917, p. 66.
183 *Motor Cycling*, 11 February 1919, p. 279.
184 *The Motor Cycle*, 15 July 1915, p. 66.
185 West, ibid, p. 99.
186 *Motorcycle and Bicycle Illustrated*, 5 July 1917, p. 10.
187 *The Motor Cycle*, 27 July 1916, p. 70. .
188 West, ibid, p. 107.
189 West, ibid, p. 110.
190 *Motor Cycling*, 23 July 1918, p. 183. (Folding kickstarts were not fitted to British bikes until the 1950s.)
191 *The Motor Cycle*, 15 July 1915, p. 66; 23 November 1915, pp. 63-64.
192 *The Motor Cycle*, 10 February 1916, front page; p. 136.
193 Grice, ibid, 9 December 1914; 25 March 1915; 16 July 1916; 14/16 May 1916; 4 January 1917.
194 *The Motor Cycle*, 27 July, 1916, p. 70.
195 War Office, *Statistics of the Military Effort of the British Empire during the Great War 1914-1919*, p. 852.
196 Best, ibid, 25 March 1915.
197 Watson, ibid, p. 205.
198 *Motor Cycling*, 11 March 1919, p. 379—though some improvements had been effected by early 1916: *The Motor Cycle*, 6 April 1916, p. 325.
199 *The Motor Cycle*, 3 February 1916, p. 116B.
200 *Motor Cycling*, 8 April 1919, p. 494.
201 *The Motor Cycle*, 27 June 1918, p. 613.
202 Tait, ibid, 7 October 1914.
203 *The Motor Cycle*, 31 August 1916, p. 181.
204 See the American Schwinn bicycle for a similar design. The design meant that suspension movement altered the wheelbase and therefore the steering geometry, but at the modest speeds the motorcycles reached this is unlikely to have caused handling problems.
205 Tait, ibid, 7 October 1914.
206 E.g. *The Motor Cycle*, 16 November 1916, p. 424-25; Burns and Messenger, ibid, p. 16.
207 Triumphs of this era, when ridden in vintage events today, often have a leather strap gusseting the spring. If this precaution is deemed wise over modern roads…?
208 *Motor Cycling*, 4 March 1919, p. 339.

209 The shoe bore against the back of the pulley, the block into the V of the front of the pulley; the former was progressive but weak, the latter was effective but "could jamb most perilously"—Ixion, ibid, p. 49.

210 *The Motor Cycle*, 23 September 1915, p. 299.

211 West, ibid, p. 80.

212 *The Motor Cycle*, 9 May 1918, p. 447.

213 *The Motor Cycle*, 8 July 1915, p. 29.

214 See, for instance, *Motor Cycling*, 4 May 1915, p. 630 and 19 October 1915, p. 590.

215 *The Motor Cycle*, 12 October 1916, p. 322.

216 James Sheldon, *Veteran and Vintage Motorcycles*, pp. 112-13.

217 Burns and Messenger, ibid, p. 11.

218 *The Motor Cycle*, 31 December 1914, p. 731.

219 Watson, ibid, p. 22. One must acknowledge that after battle had been joined Don might have worse things to complain about than slipping belts.

220 West, ibid, p. 90.

221 I'm obliged to Rob Thompson for this information.

222 Lauder, *A Minstrel in France*, p. 151. See also "From Scrap Heap to Complete Motorcycle: How War-time Wrecks are Rejuvenated", *The Motor Cycle*, 23 August 1917, pp. 180-82.

223 *The Illustrated War News*, 2 August 1916, p. 28.

224 *The Motor Cycle*, 7 February 1918, p. 125.

225 *The Motor Cycle*, 23 May 1918, p. 505. Emphasis added to illustrate the likelihood of problems with anything but a truly effective enclosure case.

226 See Chapter Five.

227 Frost, ibid, p. 58.

228 Post-war BSA Colonial Models used marvellous cast aluminium chaincases for both primary and secondary drive; was this in part a consequence of experience gained in East Africa?

229 *The Motor Cycle*, 12 October 1916, p. 324; Frost, ibid, p. 60.

230 Frost, ibid, p. 57.

231 *The Motor Cycle*, 23 September 1915, front page.

232 *The Motor Cycle*, 18 February 1915, p. 144.

233 *Motor Cycling*, 19 February 1918, p. 299.

234 *The Motor Cycle*, 28 January 1915, p. 82.

235 E.g. *Motor Cycling*, 23 September 1915, front page; 25 December 1917, p. 124.

236 "Shields Instead of Mudguards for Military Machines: Suggestions for a Much-needed Improvement", *The Motor Cycle*, 23 September 1915, pp. 299-300.

237 Alick and Cecil Burney, founders of the Blackburne were, incidentally, in "the first detachment of motor cycle despatch riders in France"—Ixion, ibid, p. 208.

238 Watson, ibid, p. 115.

239 For a very incomplete list of instances see, apart from those references already made, *The Motor Cycle*, 13 January 1916; 17 February 1916, p. 158; 13 April 1916, p. 354; 24 August 1916, p. 160; 5 April 1917, p. 308; *Motor Cycling*, 18 September 1917, p. 381.

240 *Motor Cycling*, 23 July 1918, p. 194.

241 Watson, ibid, p. 160.

242 *Motor Cycling*, 15 December 1915, p. 171. The DR in question, Lionel A Dashwood, was the son of Sir George Dashwood, further evidence of the class from which many early despatch riders came.

243 Watson, ibid, p. 207.
244 I am obliged to Nick and Martin Shelley for this information.
245 The nadir was probably plumbed by the 1972-'73 Norton Combat Commando, which could wear out its main bearings in less than 2,000 miles, one tenth of the life expectancy of 1903 Triumph mains—Minton, ibid, p. 13.
246 *The Motor Cycle*, 6 December 1917, p. 547,
247 *The Motor Cycle*, 5 April 1917, p. 308.
248 West, ibid, p. 117.
249 Sproston, ibid, 15 December 1914.
250 Sproston, ibid, 17 December 1914.
251 Watson, ibid, p. 176. Emphasis added.
252 *The British Medical Journal*, 14 November 1914, p. 843.
253 Frost, ibid p. 58.
254 *Motor Cycling*, 31 August 1915, p. 412.
255 See also, e.g. *Motor Cycling*, 29 May 1917, front page.
256 Buzz Kanter, *Indian Motorcycles*, pp. 10-12.
257 *Motor Cycling*, 10 October 1916, p. 502, 518.
258 *The Motor Cycle*, 1 October 1914, pp. 391-93; 15 October 1914, p. 448.
259 WH Tait, 3 September 1914.
260 *Motor Cycling*, 30 July 1918, p. 216.
261 Burns and Messenger, ibid, p. 27.
262 *The Motor Cycle*, 12 December 1918, p. 521.
263 *Motor Cycling*, 24 April 1917, p. 566.
264 *Motor Cycling*, 20 August 1918, p. 270.
265 *The Motor Cycle*, 13 April 1916, p. 354.
266 *The Times History of the War*, Vol. XXI, p. 190.
267 CK Shepherd, *Across America by Motor-Cycle*, pp. 9, 227, vi-vii.
268 West, ibid, p. 117.
269 *The Motor Cycle*, 11 February 1915, pp. 130, 134.
270 *The British Medical Journal*, 14 November 1914, p. 843.
271 West, ibid, p. 117.
272 Sproston, ibid, 17 December 1914.
273 *The Motor Cycle*, 23 August 1917, p. 183.
274 Vanderveen, ibid, p. 23.
275 War Office, *Statistics of the Military Effort of the British Empire during the Great War 1914-1919*, p. 856.
276 *Motor Cycling*, 6 August 1918, p. 220.
277 *Motor Cycling*, 27 November 1917, p. 40.
278 *Motor Cycling*, 17 September 1918, pp. 322-23.
279 *The Motor Cycle*, 10 February 1916, p. 130.
280 *The Motor Cycle*, 23 August 1917, pp. 180-82.
281 *The Motor Cycle*, 14 June 1917, p. 547.
282 *The Motor Cycle*, 28 March 1918, p. 303.
283 *The Motor Cycle*, 19 July 1917, p. 63.
284 Corelli Barnett, *Britain and Her Army 1509-1970*, p. 391.
285 *The Motor Cycle*, 9 July 1914, p. 56.
286 *Motor Cycling*, 13 August 1918, p. 243.
287 Frank Glendinning, "Triumph: Living on Former Glory" p. 1850 and "Douglas: Diverse, innovative and successful" p. 463 respectively.
288 *The Motor Cycle*, 26 June 1919.

289 I am obliged to Mr John Quirke for this information.
290 "The British Divisions of 1914-1918" www.1914-1918.net/britdivs.htm
291 Supplement to *The London Gazette*, 3 September 1919, p. 11093, 11 March 1920, p. 3087.
292 Priestley, ibid, pp. 334-351.
293 Clayton, ibid, p. 27, 29.
294 Douglas P Winnifrith, *The Church in the Fighting Line*, p. 14.
295 *Motorcycle and Bicycle Illustrated*, 30 August 1917, p. 42.
296 Supplement to *The London Gazette*, 21 October 1918, pp. 12346, 12369.
297 *The Long, Long Trail*, www.1914-1918.net/asc.htm
298 Initially the ASC had been sceptical of motorcycles, at least for convoy work, fearing that "if they take it into their heads to run well, one gets miles ahead", while mechanical failure could mean that "one is soon left behind"—almost as if the motorcycle was a wilful thing. After the 1911 Olympia Show the ASC bought ten motorcycles of six different makes and soon changed its mind. See Young, ibid, p. 37.
299 Supplement to *The London Gazette*, 2 September 1919, p. 11103.
300 Supplement to *The London Gazette*, 30 July 1918, p. 9804.
301 War Office, *Statistics of the Military Effort of the British Empire during the Great War 1914-1919*, p. 518, 519, 521, 594, 595, 855, 877.
302 *The Motor Cycle*, 27 September 1917, p. 304.
303 David Ansell, *The Illustrated History of Military Motorcycles*, p. 13
304 *The Motor Cycle*, 22 August 1918, p. 172.
305 Pat Ware, *The Illustrated Guide to Military Motorcycles*, p. 18.
306 *Motor Cycling*, 21 November 1916, pp. 47-48, 62.
307 *The Times History of the War*, Vol. II, p. 229.
308 Ansell, ibid, p. 13.
309 Malcolm Brown, *The Imperial War Museum Book of the Western Front*, p. 28.
310 Ansell, ibid, p. 13.
311 *Motor Cycling*, October 1916, p.502
312 *Motor Cycling*, ibid.
313 *The Motor Cycle*, 6 January 1916, pp. 1-2.
314 *Motor Cycling*, 19 November 1918, p. 23. Rudge-Whitworth's main contribution to the war effort was in supplying wheels, in particular to the RFC/RNS/RAF, so as early as this, Rudge wheels and wheel-lacers were recognised as the best in the world, a reputation they were to maintain long after they went out of business in 1939. Daniel Rudge had invented adjustable wheel bearings for bicycles in 1878, and today aftermarket wheels for such cars as Porsches bear the name Rudge.

3

You Could Get Killed Out There

The Despatch Rider

It isn't a thing of beauty and
It's caked with mud and mire.
A bullet's been through the petrol tank,
And the levers are held with wire.
But it's all that there is, and it's got to serve
For a ride through the gates of hell
To save the lives of a hundred men
On a road that is swept by shell.

Drop the exhaust! Will she never fire?
Hurrah! she is off at last.
Bend low, bend low on the tank, dear lad,
As the shells come screaming fast.
It's only a mile, but they've got the range,
Now open the throttle wide.
'Tis a race with Death through the reeking hail
Of shrapnel on every side.

Dear God! that was close. See, his leg hangs limp,
But the half of the journey's done.
There's a humpbacked bridge that spans the stream,
Once over—the goal is won.
They're shelling the bridge, it's tottering now,
At the crest it is rent in twain.
You have taken the leap at Ballig Bridge,
Dear lad, can you do it again?

As the arrow speeds from the quivering bow
So straight for the gap he flies.
The engine screams as it races free
As he leaps for the further side.
We hold our breath as he takes the leap—
Oh! bravely, bravely done!
He is speeding safe on the further side,
And the race with death is won.

C. Hubert Turner[1]

IT GOES WITHOUT saying that war can be bad for your health, and insurance companies insist that motorcycling is a risky way of travelling, however enjoyable. Riding a motorbike through a war zone undoubtedly is a dangerous thing to do, but back in the Great War there were hazards unknown to the modern motorcyclist, even before a man got off the troopship in France.

It is not easy for today's motorist to appreciate the road conditions of a century ago. The "well-metalled high roads" of Edwardian England, on which Kenneth Grahame's road-hog Toad was "so happy, disporting himself" at dizzying speeds of maybe 50 mph maximum, would horrify the modern road user. According to Canon Basil Davies, "There was not one square yard of either tarmac or concrete on British roads in 1900";[2] the good clergyman means outside of cities and towns, where cobblestones or setts had been laid since the eighteenth century; but these were treacherously greasy in wet weather and frequently displaced by heavy industrial traffic, and even more treacherous in the wet were the wooden blocks lain in place of cobbles outside hospitals or wherever there was a perceived need to quiet the passage of traffic. Horse dung was ubiquitous, and slippery too, as were tramlines, which were hazardous to cross, especially when wet. Rural roads might be "no more than a barely visible grass-grown moraine of three ply formation (two wheel ruts with a central hoof-devastated strip)".[3]

Such had been the railway's success that roads had deteriorated since the age of the stagecoach: the first car journey from Dublin to Belfast, in 1898, took two days, longer than the fast stagecoach had taken more than a century before;[4] while Stephenson was perfecting his Rocket a fast stagecoach could cover the 409 miles from London to Edinburgh in just over 42 hours, but a pioneer motorcyclist essaying the much more modest distance from Reading to Bristol on the Great West Road (now the A4) on his Triumph a couple of years before the Great War "lost his way as the westward highway, abandoned by traffic since the advent of the railways, simply petered out over the Marlborough Downs".[5] In the mid-eighteenth century Pierre Tresaguet had used pitch as a surface binder in France, and Nottingham had experimented with tar in 1845,[6] but dropped the material due to cost, and roads everywhere were "sealed" with a thin slurry of mud. Though that newfangled thing, asphalt, first laid down on the streets of Louis Napoleon's reconstructed Paris in the 1860s, was making an appearance in Britain, it still was rare by the Great War: ninety years on, centenarian veteran Bill Stone recalls "driving a water cart [spraying] water over the surface, making a muddy cement, which we then rolled flat with a steam roller".[7] Almost before the roller was out of sight, the graded surface began to break down under the iron tyres of waggons and carts, and drippings from tree foliage along the sides.

On such roads the ever-present hazards were dust in summer and mud in winter, each bringing its own problems. It was possible to track a car's progress for miles by the cloud of dust it dragged behind.[8] In his classic account of pioneer motoring, Charles Jarrott alludes repeatedly to this problem; dust presented particular dangers to the racing motorist, who could be more or less driving blind when trying to overtake.[9] Long before the war the Royal Automobile Club speaks of "the dust difficulty", and a Major Creagh points out: "In regard to sending despatches from point to point [in pre-war exercises], the motor cyclist had proved most useful in all manoeuvres, but the dust problem detracted from his usefulness".[10] Canon Davies describes his appearance after a long trip by motorcycle: "I was in an indescribable condition of filth, filmed deep from head to foot in the loathsome powder, of which pulverised animal droppings were a substantial ingredient. My eyes, ears and nose were full of it".[11]

Such dust was unpleasant for marching men but no less so for a motorcyclist, especially one in column or on escort duty. "The dust when everyone moved was appalling," reports DR Corporal Lamb, and he has to endure being almost "choked" by the cloud raised by the car of General Shaw, to whom he acts as motorcyclist orderly on manoeuvres at Camberly.[12] On convoy work in particular, and despite the goggles that all despatch riders wore, dust irritated the eyes, something that the rider might not be aware of until he dismounted and lost the cooling effect of movement. "Now before the war a motor-cyclist would consider himself ill-used if he were forced to take a car's dust for a mile or so," writes Corporal Watson. "Your despatch rider was compelled to follow in the wake of a large and fast Daimler for twenty-five miles, and at the end of it he did not know which was him and which dust".[13]

But dust could be more than just unpleasant. A French captive, forced to march with the invading Germans, reports that "The road lay inches thick of chalky dust".[14] Such a depth of dust could provide a treacherous surface as well as obscure vision: DR Davis on the Somme reports: "Dust blinding and in Sausage Valley 6 [inches] deep so that you skidded in it worse than in mud". In exotic theatres it could rise in blinding storms that might cause a rider to lose his way.[15] Dust of course turned to mud after rain, something that was even more treacherous, as Davis admits when he has to walk and catch lifts on lorries.[16] Even at home roads could become "liquid swamps of mud", as Corporal Lamb reports, making it "no joy riding motorcycles",[17] and at the front it was much worse. AJ Sproston, a competition rider, once was brought down four times within a mile by the mud of Ypres,[18] and Corporal Best reports:

> I had to spend the night on the road last night. I went out to find some Territorials reserve, and an ambulance, and had a broken chain [this was before belt was specified for final drive] which I replaced with a spare one, the cover of my carburettor [got] lost, which I replaced by the lid of a tin, mud in the float chamber [how bad must it be for mud to get in *there*?], which I had to clean out, a lack of carbide, which I could not replace, and above all three inches of mud on the road were just drying, and clogged the wheels every hundred yards or so. A spring on the contact breaker also broke in the magneto…. However one takes things very calmly, as nothing seems to matter very much.

Indeed—San Fairy Ann. Best goes on: "It is snowing slightly today, and the roads when one is pushed off the pavement are from 6["] to 1'0 in thick glutinous mud, so that the circumstances are not ideal for riding".[19] The clogging of wheels by such mud has been dealt with already, and though this was more an aggravation than a hazard, it did not make Don's life any cushier.

And British and French roads were good, by the standard of the time, Napoleon having provided the French with the best roads in the world. The Official History remarks: "Belgian roads [were] paved only for the width of one vehicle, and with deep mud on either side".[20] In 1915 they were widened and improved, but remained unloved by motorcyclists. "The *pavé* in the centre is not so bad, but the excessive camber is very troublesome to solo riders. At the side there is any quantity of mud, which would make the most experienced rider quake".[21] In France there was extensive *pavé*, "without which there would have been a complete breakdown in mechanical transport of supplies".[22] Such roads were built of large square stone setts "for a breadth of about twenty feet … outside which on both sides was grass churned into deep mud".[23] They had been designed or adapted to speed Napoleon's *Grand Armée* on its way—as the autostrada, autobahnen and interstate highways of later years had mobilisation value—and endured the war remarkably well. Rudyard Kipling is impressed with how they withstood the "incessant traffic" of war in 1915: "My impression—after some seven hundred miles printed off at between 60 and 70 kilometres [an hour]—was of uniform excellence".[24] Right through the war some roads survived amazingly well: an officer who fought at Ypres reports that even the Menin Road, which must have seen more war than any other, was "so strongly built that, except where trenches were cut across it, it withstood the withering rain of shells to which it was subjected for four years without showing very great signs of wear".[25] (Though obviously no road could withstand a direct hit by a large shell.) One DR agrees that "*Pavé* appears to wear remarkably well, and wears gradually, not going into pot-holes as do other roads".[26]

Pavé, however, brought problems for motorcyclists. Another DR, after two years in France, reports:

> *pavé* is undoubtedly the worst sort [of road]. The average road of this type is usually from ten to fifteen yards wide, with a strip of *pavé* (six to eight yards) in the centre, each side of which is made up of [road] metal, which is worn down very soon by heavy and slow-moving traffic which, as the rule of the road requires, keeps to the side. The metal, of course, is worn away first … and thus the *pavé* in some cases is left four inches above the metal. The junctions of metal and *pavé* are invariably allowed to remain thus as a constant menace to DRs who have frequently to pass from one side of the road to the other through traffic.[27]

Even without having to dodge other traffic, riding *pave*, given its pronounced camber, "is like riding on the top of a drainpipe and the whole of the time skidding from one side to the other".[28] *Pavé* remained hated by despatch riders in the Second World War as well.[29]

On *pavé* or off it, punctures were commonplace; several might be suffered in the course of a day. They probably became less of a nuisance in the later years of the war as the Army Salvage Branch scrupulously recycled everything possible, including nails,[30] and they were not, in any event, likely to delay a rider long. The beaded-edge tyres were easy to remove and butt-ended tubes, long curved cylinders rather than annular inserts, which were very popular at the time, could be stripped out without need to detach the wheel, so a proficient rider could be on his way in minutes.[31] Reflecting how commonplace punctures were at the time, some firms converted "endless" tubes to butt-ended,[32] and the Thames Rubber Company marketed a split tube whose ends were spliced together over a ribbed insert, the joint reinforced by snapping a rolled-back outer sleeve over it, special lubricant both easing assembly and aiding air-tightness—which all seems like a lot of work.[33] But sometimes the urgency of the despatch—or the proximity of Old Jerry—might preclude repairing the puncture and Don might have to proceed on a flat tyre, "slipping all over the road", to quote Corporal Watson.[34] More dangerous was a ripped tyre or concussion-burst on *pavé*: the immediate loss of pressure inevitably dislodged the bead from the rim and caused the tyre to separate from the still-rolling wheel; in the case of a front-wheel blow-out the rider could be pitched over the bars and with no crash helmet—the Brodie was useless in this regard, though German motorcyclists did have crash-helmets of a sort—the consequence could be fatal:[35] as Lieutenant Best puts it, "a hundred skids are not to be compared to a burst tyre on front wheel".[36] The prevalence of falls is indicated by DR Eric Williams's being "always specially padded" for the usual tosses on greasy *pavé*.[37] Security bolts could keep the tyre on the rim, but they complicated puncture repairs so were seldom if ever fitted. Beaded edge tyres also had to be inflated to very high pressure, 50 psi or more, in order to secure them to the rims, and this high pressure, coupled to lack of frame suspension, made for a very hard ride. Tyres also could be weakened or destroyed by the ubiquitous rats' gnawing, making failure more likely.[38]

A car driver confirmed the worst:

> The roads were awful. How motor-cyclists stayed on them no one knew. Often enough they failed to do so, but the cheerful dispatch-riders always "showed up smiling" sooner or later, save now and again when one of them "ran into" a shell. Heroic work, that dispatch carrying over roads that never knew complete freedom from shell fire.[39]

So dangerous had the roads become as early as the winter of 1914-15 that some DRs were calling for replacement of the motorcycle by a car or sidecar outfit. And of course it was not just the roads, but what a rider might find in them, that were hazardous. In particular, lorry convoys posed a deadly risk to riders. They were "perilous things to pass" on the slippery, narrow *pavé*, with churned up mud and deep drainage ditches on either side,[40] and they were to remain a constant hazard: "There was far more danger from lorries and motor ambulances than from shells", reports Watson;[41] for while in theory Don had priority—"My blue and white [arm] band carries me everywhere and gives me preference over all traffic"[42]—the reality was that lorries could not leave the *pavé* without getting stuck; on corduroy roads a raised plank divider prevented them from sliding into each other,[43] but this was little aid to Don R overtaking on the inside were a lorry to slip sideways. An 8 mph top speed on lorries was rigidly enforced, and most travelled at closer to 5 mph,[44] but usually they travelled in convoy, and for one to fall out could cause all sorts of traffic and logistical problems, so often Don had to give way, which could mean sliding off into the morass along each side of the road. Corporal Davis reports how "trying to pass transport on the narrow track, I had to spill down 8 ft of trench"; later he gets "knocked over by lorry.... Pitched me into ditch. Lucky ... that it didn't knock me under wheels and smash me".[45]

Another rider reports: "What DR will ever forget trying to pass a convoy of lorries? The column seems never-ending, and as each lorry is passed one hears a sigh of relief that nothing appeared through the blinding dust 'head on'". With a lorry on the road ahead "I must either crawl behind it or plough through a foot of rutty mud at the side [and] last time I tried this it was a toss-up whether the back wheel of the lorry passed over me or the machine; I only just won and the machine was 'evacuated', or sent to the base for repair".[46] A colleague of Corporal Etherington was struck by a lorry, though not fatally, but many such collisions must have been.[47] One surreptitious risk of overtaking lorries was dangling rope entangling with the handlebars; the fact that handlebar levers were inverted back then made the risk greater. An Army Service Corps member remarks: "It is marvellous that more of them [DRs] are not run over".[48]

In much of the war theatre hardwearing *pavé* was unknown, and roads were poor to terrible. In the Somme sector they were particularly bad, with a mere three inches of metal laid on the soft chalk in the case of *main* roads. *All* Somme roads were particularly vulnerable to rain, of which plenty fell toward the end of the 1916 campaign. Through those battles roads had to be repaired and maintained even as they were being used, and were in a constant state of disrepair, because the logistical support required was on an overwhelming scale. As the battles intensified roads all but collapsed and the frost heaves of that terrible winter caused them to "turn completely over [so that] the chalk that is usually found a foot underneath has now climbed to the surface, and lies in big lumps, making it almost impossible to ride". One DR measured a pothole at eighteen inches.[49]

Then, of course, there were the battles. "A Night on the Somme: A DR's Exciting Experience" gives a vivid portrayal of what despatch riding in an active battle zone was like:

> Lines and lines of lorries, all heavily laden, were crawling toward the Front, whilst on the opposite side of the road an equally unending stream was returning. Between the two lines of traffic I floundered along in the awful mud, knowing that the lorry drivers could not see me, and might run me down without being any the wiser. The din was terrific enough, but soon Fritz started his night strafe and I felt very small indeed, wallowing along among the wheels of the heavy lorries whilst shells howled overhead.... I found it no joy-ride wearing a gas mask and a tin hat, and trying to dodge between those heavy vehicles, which, like myself, were skidding about on the slimy mud in an appalling manner.[50]

An officer paid tribute:

> the motor cyclist on the Somme and on the Arras side has exhibited a fortitude, a courage, daring and marvellous quickness of action and

decision a hundred times a day.... He is an opportunist with nerves of iron, a clear head and eye, and a knowledge of space and pace.... I have seen [DRs] riding between two columns of traffic—both miles long, travelling in opposite directions, on narrow roads, a bog everywhere and punctuated with shell holes. I have watched them wriggle through, pass restive or exhausted and fallen horses, and great heaving, rolling motor lorries and wondered. I have watched them when hail was driving in their faces and they could hardly look up, when they have had to ride in a gutter almost knee deep in mud for two or three hundred yards, and I have thought, "My God! You are among the heroes of the war".[51]

In addition to road hazards, there remained the hazards of the battlefield. Captain Dunn recounts how one DR was decapitated by a shell,[52] and the whimsically named George Coward, a feisty Old Contemptible, describes how another lost a leg to shellfire on the Somme.[53] Graham Walker also got a Blighty wound from shellfire, though he suffered no lasting consequences. There must have been many, many other DRs who suffered thus through the four years of war.

In the Great Retreat the main problem, as for everyone, was exhaustion. Corporal Tait reports being "nearly 48 hours in the saddle and that following a two hour night", with "Boots not off for 5 days". So used does he get to snatching sleep wherever he can that a couple of weeks later he remarks, "I don't believe I could sleep in a bed now".[54] Exhaustion could make it easier to get lost, but even a fresh man could find that directions "may be wrong and are probably misleading", because the target unit is likely to have moved from its coordinates even before the despatch was written. Watson reports men falling asleep in the saddle from exhaustion[55]—who knows how many injuries or even fatalities this may have caused?

Right through the war, some hazards were routine, notably falls and swollen hands from the pounding of rigid frames over rough roads. Shell holes became deeper and more ubiquitous as the war congealed,[56] and were camouflaged by the Germans on the retreat to the Hindenburg line, "with wire netting and a thin layer of earth [to] form ... traps for British motorcyclists" over the old Somme battlefield.[57] Not unusual in the early war of movement was direct attack by enemy troops,[58] with death or capture the result.[59] Don also could be mistaken for a spy, especially during the confusion and panic of the Great Retreat: West was arrested by a Scottish regiment on 28 August and held overnight before his identity could be confirmed (he didn't assuage his captors' suspicions by engaging in long and apparently amiable conversation with another prisoner, in German);[60] Paul Maze was actually being led out to be shot by the French when a passing British officer fortuitously recognised him.[61]

Jumpy sentries with sharp bayonets were a constant source of complaint, especially in the early days: Watson and West suffered from them,[62] and Tait was "mistaken for a German and nearly bayoneted before I managed to prove my nationality".[63] Best points out that driving without lights, which was mandatory close to the front lines,

> meant that every sentry thought I was trying to escape him.... They [sentries] are more or less alone, and their nerves get shaky, and they try to avoid risks by halting everyone a long distance off. One does not hear their challenge, they [consequently] think their fears are well grounded, and try to shoot or bayonet one. It takes some time to reassure them.

Even after things settled down "the sentry system though necessary is intensely irritating, and I have been stopped and my passport [sic] has been demanded as many as twenty times in a night".[64] A despatch rider in the Second "once heard that in the First World War more DRs were killed coming into the camp than the numbers killed by the Germans on their runs".[65] Given the many complaints about sentries, this may not have been a great exaggeration.

A particularly dreaded hazard was "running into telephone wire strung about four feet high across a road by the enemy"[66]—Germans used disposable "thin enamelled ... fine black wire", which they abandoned on their retreat to the Aisne,[67] in contrast to the British who, when they did manage to string wire, recovered as much as possible before retreating farther.[68] This "clothes-lining" of despatch riders, which could have decapitated men, inspired great fear and anger. During the Irish War of Independence CA Brett, a former despatch rider, now a motorcycle-mounted ex-serviceman, was very wary of the danger,[69] and memory of it, like that of jumpy sentries, survived into the next war and fomented dark rumours among despatch riders during the Battle of France.[70] Back in the Great War, some DRs were captured,[71] others killed in action.[72] Graham Oates lost the sight of one eye to poison gas, as well as suffering lasting respiratory damage (he was asthmatic to start with, but that was San Fairy Ann when it came to enlisting);[73] Eric Simpson Morrison, of the Canadian Division, also was gassed and severely wounded.[74] In the course of the Great Retreat Joseph Graves was knocked off his motorcycle by a shell blast, captured by the Germans and—briefly—abused in an effort to elicit information,[75] and an anonymous despatch rider allegedly was found with lance wounds to his palms and his body partially burned;[76] this yarn smells like a variation on the crucified Canadian myth, but many British POWs complained of rough treatment during this phase of the war.

From the outset, "the despatch carrier is under fire, and he seems to attract his full share of attention from enemy aeroplanes",[77] a danger that was exacerbated as the air war became more sophisticated, and especially after Fokker's interrupter-gear was adopted. Motorcycles could be camouflaged by faggots and foliage against this danger; two might be parked side by side and "roofed over" by such camouflaging, the riders hiding underneath.[78] Strafing, surprisingly, could occur by night: Corporal Grice reports such night flying twice, and as the dates he gives are almost exactly eight weeks apart, one suspects that night flights occurred under what came to be called in the next war a "bomber's moon";[79] in fact, the moon was only half-full on the dates in question, a reflection of the progress in flight control through the war.[80]

Road accidents accounted for some despatch riders, as one might expect; one of George Mead's colleagues was killed when his and another motorcycle collided head on in training,[81] and of course fatal collisions, notably with lorries and such hazards as dead horses after dark, were more common in the field.[82] Semi-feral dogs, abandoned by their owners in 1914, were not uncommon in the war zone of the Western Front; large ones could be quite dangerous and, as dogs do, they chased motorcycles and could bring a rider down.[83] Graham Oates was in painful collision with a deer—which came off much worse, ending up on the table of the officers' mess.[84] One of the most unusual hazards was septicaemia that followed "fundamental soreness", a euphemism, presumably, for ruptured piles, resulting from rough roads and rigid frames.[85] And Don was no more immune to nervous breakdown under pressure than the man in the trenches: Corporal Best reports on two of his companions going "dotty" and being sent home as early as October 1914.[86]

At night the rider might have to ride in pitch darkness in order to avoid giving away his position. The trick of flashing on the light momentarily, to show the way without providing a target, was not an option, for auto-electric lights were in their infancy and almost every vehicle used gas: water from a hopper dripped onto powdered calcium carbide in a reservoir below, producing acetylene gas that was piped through rubber tubing to lamps front and rear, where it was lit by a match after the lens of each lamp was hinged open. At the time, though, rear lamps were not required so usually the front lamp incorporated the hopper and reservoir and made a self-contained lighting system. For the speed Don R was likely to be doing, the light was adequate—if the delicate system was in perfect order, and the water in the hopper hadn't frozen. But if the drip-rate was wrong, say, or the tubing got nipped, or had perished, the light could be reduced to a "feeble glimmer".[87] If a spill broke the lens the front lamp could not stay lit, and if the rear lamp failed for any reason the rider would not know. (A remedy for loss of light from momentary failure of gas to the rear lamp, if fitted, was to stretch a wire through the flame: this got red hot and the incandescence would re-light the gas after the "blip" in gas delivery.) Close to the lines Don often had to ride without lights even in quiet sectors: he might be out of range of enemy fire, but his lights could enable the enemy to track radial paths and thus locate Divisional HQ or Signals centres.[88] Even by day, if there were any danger of observation and no driving urgency, DRs would "leave their bikes at a convenient distance, hidden under a hedge for preference, and slip up to HQ shyly and on foot".[89]

Night riding, even with lights, had its own hazards. Corporal Davis calls it "agonising",[90] and Paul Maze describes:

> Bent over the handle-bars, I rode in the darkness, my eyes staring on the V-shaped ray of light of my head-lamp which edged both sides of the road with a silver streak.... My lamp would suddenly light up a marching battalion, and in a cinematic motion it would slip past, oaths and curses rising from the ranks because my lamp blinded them.

Maze suffers eyestrain from the "brilliance" of his own light beam, and worse from that of other vehicles: "almost blinded [by the lights of an oncoming car] I found myself in the ditch off the road, as the car drove past me like the wind.... Striking match after match I looked for the scattered bits of my lamp which had tinkled on the road".[91] Frederic Coleman, driver to General de Lisle, gives a sanguine account of another such nighttime accident:

> In passing a motor-cyclist at good speed, the back part of a car in front of us brushed him off his machine. He slid thirty feet, coming to rest in front of my car and in the full glare of my headlights as I skidded sideways to avoid passing over him. We picked him up, straightened his handlebars, and bent a pedal into place. Finding him by no means incapacitated, we mounted him and started him off again. I was surprised he was able to ride.[92]

Another DR describes a long run behind the lines on a moonless, rainy night. "No lights on private vehicles; glaring lights on official cars, and only two hours in which to cover 60 miles of convoy-cut-up roads, with the chance of meeting several convoys at that". Five miles into the journey his headlamp lens is broken by a stone tossed up by a car wheel, but resourceful Don stretches his handkerchief across the aperture, secures it with a rubber band taken from his despatches, re-lights the gas and proceeds in the dim light. He meets three convoys of lorries: "sometimes they stretch over a mile and number over 50. It is best to dismount and wait till they have passed".[93] Frankly, it is impossible to believe that a machine with a top speed of 40-45 mph and effectively no lights could possibly average 30 mph on such a journey, but Don is entitled to stretch things, and to brag a little.

In the Middle East and Africa sand replaced mud as the ubiquitous riding problem, but in Palestine at least netting-wire roads were constructed across

Dispatch riding at night. This is the work in which motorcyclists are most useful.

... or so it was thought in 1914. In fact, night riding was a DR's nightmare.[94]

sandy stretches,[95] three three-foot rolls of netting wire, wired together in a nine-foot span, providing enough stability for safe passage (and, of course, evidence of the unimaginative military mind at work again). In these exotic theatres there were more alarming hazards than bad roads, lions and charging rhinos among them,[96] as will be seen in Chapter Seven.

The extent to which despatch riders were exposed to direct hit by bullet or bomb was overall low, though in the early months many were killed, and they were similarly exposed in the war of movement in 1918. Their importance was recognised by the enemy, as by their own: "The Huns have a short way and bloody with British ... despatch-riders", reports one observer.[97] Dr Crowther, who had been in charge of an asylum in Surrey but had "done his duty" and become a DR, was killed by shellfire near Ploegstreet Wood, during the Race to the Sea. Two motorcyclists were killed by the same shell during First Ypres,[98] a desperate fight in which every hand had to hold a rifle. Corporal Best reports: "We as despatch riders had rather a bad time as the enemy kept the three towns, Ypres, Zonnebec and Zillebec humming with shells, and there was no way of getting past them, without going through [the shellfire]".[99] One rider reports that "during the first three months of the war ... five of his colleagues were killed by enemy fire".[100] Countless more were wounded, like Max Cremetti at the Marne (where he won the DCM).[101] "Friendly fire" too claimed victims, as in every war.[102]

Position warfare to a good extent distanced Don from the sharp end, but not entirely.

> The motor cyclist despatch rider's work had to a great extent lost the romance which made it one of the most interesting aspects of the Signal Service during the 1914 campaigns. The danger of his work had markedly decreased, though the new German practice of putting down shell storms on the main roads behind our front was once more adding a considerable element of excitement to his routine journeys.[103]

Don was under scrutiny by observers in balloons, who might call up artillery against him, but he learned tricks to cope. Where observation was a serious threat, roads were screened by artificial hedges or curtains of brushwood hung across them.[104] When exposed, one veteran reports: "the cute DR can sometimes from a comparatively safe place estimate the time between each shell coming over and take advantage of an interval for a dash across the danger zone";[105] Watson already had discovered this ruse in 1914.[106] Occasionally, Don might take similar advantage of an enemy machine gunner changing belts; alternatively, he might suddenly increase and reduce his speed in order to throw off the gunners' aim. But many fell victim to enemy fire even through the war of position, notably shellfire.[107]

Some French DRs used camouflage to break up the outline of the rider, and, to some extent, that of the machine: "The coat [a very long 'duster' type] is painted a mixture of colours, so that the rider of a quiet machine would not be easily detected".[108] Paint also aided waterproofing and, as will be seen in the next chapter, Don's "uniform" was so individual during the first year and more that some British DRs may have copied the French example.

After Ludendorff's breakout in 1918, mobile warfare returned, bringing a return of many of the hazards encountered during the Great Retreat. Chapter Seven elaborates on these.

Endnotes

1 *Motor Cycling*, 8 December 1914, p. 131. The exhaust valve was mechanically opened, or "lifted", then "dropped" as part of the starting procedure. "Ballig Bridge"—nowadays usually spelled "Ballaugh"—is part of the Isle of Man racing circuit; its mention is a reminder that many despatch riders at the outset of the war were competition riders.

2 Ixion, *Motor Cycle Cavalcade*, p. 39.

3 Ixion, ibid, p. 162.

4 Arnold Horner, "Ireland's Time-Space Revolution: improvements to pre-Famine travel", pp. 23, 27.

5 David Minton interviewed the man, an early AA patrolman and then the oldest one surviving, for an AA publication, though the interview never was published. I am grateful to Mr Minton for this and much more help.

6 Ixion, ibid, p. 181.

7 Max Arthur, *Last Post*, p. 257.

8 The insouciant way in which Kenneth Grahame refers to dust in Chapter Two of that Edwardian classic, *The Wind in the Willows*, illustrates the point.

9 Charles Jarrott, *Ten Years of Motors and Motor Racing, 1896-1906*, passim.

10 *The Royal Automobile Club Journal*, 9 December 1908, p. 410.

11 Ixion, ibid, p. 180.

12 HAJ Lamb, IWM documents PP/MCR/187, pp. 14-15.

13 WHL Watson, *Adventures of a Despatch Rider*, pp. 152.

14 *The Times History of the World*, Vol I, p. 456.

15 Lamb, ibid, p. 47.

16 OH Davis, IWM document PP/MCR/180, pp. 65, 81.

17 Lamb, ibid, p. 13.

18 AJ Sproston, "Four Months Under Fire: A Despatch-Rider's Adventures", 19 December 1914.

19 OH Best, IWM document 87/56/1, 25 October 1914.

20 James E Edmonds, *Military Operations: France and Belgium, 1914*, p. 261; Edmonds and GC Wynne, *Military Operations: France and Belgium, 1915*, p. 6.

21 *The Motor Cycle*, 10 February 1916, p. 129.

22 Brevet Lieutenant Colonel WD Croft, "The Application of Recent Developments in Mechanics and other Scientific Knowledge to Preparation and Training for Future War on Land", p. 454.

23 CA Brett, "Recollections", p. 48.

24 Rudyard Kipling, *France at War: On the Frontier of Civilisation*, p. 51.

25 TA Lowe, *The Western Battlefields: A Guide to the British Line*, p. 21.

26 *The Motor Cycle*, 2 May 1918, p. 433.

27 *The Motor Cycle*, 29 August 1918, p. 199.

28 *The Motor Cycle*, 18 February 1915, p. 160.

29 DH Chisholm, *Memories: the wartime recollections of a Royal Signals despatch rider*.

30 To ensure that Tommy Atkins played his part in the vital business of salvaging all possible resources, down to cast horseshoe nails in the dust, the Army offered incentives in the form of extra leave.

31 One DR, however, dismisses butt-ended tubes as "an endless nuisance", though he does not explain—*The Motor Cycle*, 28 March 1918, p. 309.

32 *The Motor Cycle*, 16 May 1918, p. 483.

33 *The Motor Cycle*, 29 July 1915, p. 116.

34 Watson, ibid, p. 37.

35 Watson, ibid, p. 29. It was the extensiveness of head injuries to despatch riders in the next war that prompted Australian neurosurgeon Sir Hugh Cairns to develop the first true crash helmet.

36 Lieutenant O H Best, 2 May 1916.

37 *The Motor Cycle*, 18 March 1915, p. 250.

38 *The Times History of the War*, Vol VII, p. 285.

39 Frederic Coleman, *From Mons to Ypres with French*, p. 205.

40 Roger R West, IWM document 67/122/1, pp. 11, 54.

41 Watson, ibid, p. 248.

42 *Motor Cycling*, 31 October 1916, p. 577.

43 I am obliged to Dr Rob Thompson for this information.

44 *The Motor Cycle*, 21 June 1917, p. 565.

45 Davis, ibid, 27 July 1916, 20 June 1917.

46 *Motor Cycling*, 31 October 1916, p. 577.

47 HE Etherington, IWM 81/23/1, 23 May 1915.

48 *The Motor Cycle*, 7 January 1915, p. 21.

49 *The Motor Cycle*, 8 March 1917, p. 210;19 April 1917, p. 362.

50 *Motor Cycling*, 30 July 1916, p. 201.

51 *The Motor Cycle*, 30 August 1917, p. 206.

52 JC Dunn, *The War the Infantry Knew, 1914-1919*, p. 175.

53 George Coward, *Coward's War*, p. 102.

54 Tait, ibid, 24 August 1914, 26 August 1914, 6 September 1914.

55 Watson, ibid, pp. 75.

56 Corcoran, *The Daredevil of the Army: Experiences as a "Buzzer" and Despatch Rider*, pp. 37, 72.

57 *Motor Cycling*, 14 August 1917, p. 277.

58 West, ibid, pp. 25, 43.

59 John Ferris claims that this was relatively unusual—*The British Army and Signals Intelligence During the First World War*, p. 4—but during the phases of movement it was anything but.

60 West, ibid, pp. 51-53.

61 Paul Maze, *A Frenchman in Khaki*, p. 45.

62 Watson, ibid, p. 70; West, ibid, p. 69. Sometimes, though, sentries could be more lax, possibly due to exhaustion—see West, p. 19.

63 Tait, ibid, 25 August 1914.

64 Best, ibid, 7 October 1914; 18 December 1914.

65 ES Nicholson, *Adventures of a Royal Signals Despatch Rider*, p. 201.

66 Burns and Messenger, ibid, p. 23; *Motor Cycling*, 5 October 1915, p. 554.

67 West, ibid, p. 102.

68 Corcoran, ibid, p. 32.

69 Personal communication with Mr Brett's grandson.

70 Chisholm, ibid. In 1940 this fear may have been inspired by both memories of the earlier war and "the 'Fifth Column' paranoia which pervaded the experience of retreat" (and substituted for the "spy mania" of 1914), as a recent scholar puts it—Glyn Prysor, "The 'Fifth Column' and the British Experience of Retreat, 1940", in *War in History* 2005, 12 (4), p. 419.

71 West, ibid, p. 42.

72 Corcoran, ibid, pp. 52, 76; West, ibid, p. 93.

73 Bill Snelling: *Aurora to Ariel: The Motorcycling Exploits of J Graham Oates*, pp. 9, 10, 29.

74 *Memorial of the Great War, 1914-1918: A Record of Service*, p. 75.

75 *The War Illustrated*, Vol V, p. 1561.

76 Coleman, ibid, p. 85.

77 HC Lafone, "The Motor's Place in War", p. 102.

78 *The War Illustrated*, 1915, p. 1320.

79 Grice, ibid, 19 September 1916, 16 November 1916; 12/13 October 1916.

80 The Germans had put much thought and practise into night flying even before the war.

81 Mead, ibid, p. 21.

82 Watson, ibid, p. 117.

83 *Divisional Signals Company Royal Engineers*, http://www.fairmile.fsbusiness. co.uk/signals.htm.

84 Snelling, ibid, p. 10.

85 Watson, ibid, p. 205.

86 Best, ibid, 11 October 1914.

87 Watson, ibid, p. 36.

88 In like fashion, after the "deep bury" system was adopted in 1915, the convergence of buried cables could betray a Signals centre to enemy aircraft; camouflage was necessary.

89 *The Illustrated War News*, 26 November 1916, pp. 26-27.

90 OH Davis, IWM document PP/MCR/180, p. 67.

91 Paul Maze, ibid, pp. 268-69.

92 Coleman, ibid, pp. 15-16.

93 *Motor Cycling*, 13 June 1916, pp. 115-16.

94 *Motor Cycling*, 11 August 1914, p. 455.

95 GCG Blunt, "Mechanised Transport in Small Wars", p. 561.

96 *The Motor Cycle*, 23 November 1916, p. 452; *Motor Cycling*, 22 August 1916, p. 325.

97 JH Morgan, *Leaves from a Field Note-Book*, p. 122.

98 Coleman, ibid, pp. 201, 238.

99 Best, ibid, 20 November 1914.

100 *The Motor Cycle*, 24 October 1918, p. 374.

101 *The War Illustrated*, Vol. X, p. 3588.

102 *The Motor Cycle*, 24 May 1917, p. 465.

103 RE Priestley, *The Signal Service in the European War of 1914 to 1918 (France)*, p. 207.

104 *Motor Cycling*, 10 October 1916, p. 518.

105 *The Motor Cycle*, 16 August 1917, p. 159.

106 Watson, ibid, p. 114.

107 See for instance *The Illustrated War News*, 16 October 1916, p. 26.

108 *The Motor Cycle*, 13 April 1916, p. 339.

4

Meet Don R

Despatches

Swift as a bullet out of a gun
He passed me by with an inch to spare,
Raising a dust cloud thick and dun
While the stench of his lubricant filled the air.
I must admit that I did not like
The undergrad on his motor bike.

I have seen him, too, at the wayside inn,
A strapping lad scarce out of his teens,
Grimy, but wearing a cheerful grin;
A young enthusiast, full of beans.
While his conversation was little better
Than pure magneto and carburettor.

Now he has got the chance of his life,
The chance of earning glorious scars,
And I picture him scouring a land of strife,
Crouching over his handle-bars,
His open exhaust, with its roar and stench,
Like a Maxim gun in a British trench.

Lad, when we met in that country lane
Neither foresaw the days to come,
But I know that if ever we meet again
My heart will throb to your engine's hum,
And today, as I read, I catch my breath
At the thought of your ride through the hail of death!

But to you it is just a glorious lark;
Scorn of danger is still your creed.
As you open her out and advance your spark
And humour the throttle to get more speed,
Life has only one end for you,
To carry your priceless message through!

"Touchstone"[1]

BEFORE THE AGE of electronic communications, the despatch rider, whether galloper or motorcyclist, was starkly essential to maintaining an army in the field, and never was this truer than in the Great War. But Don R also did essential work at home where, as has been seen, the Women's Legion and ACU Motor Messenger Detachment provided riders in the London area. The Royal Navy used despatch riders within and among their home bases. Many of these riders, more as the war went on, were WRENS, members of the Women's Royal Naval Service, and Donna R's work was not without risk. Much of it was around dockyards, where slippery cobblestones could lead all

Despatch riding was glamorous, exciting, dangerous work in 1914. Airships were seen as the main menace from above back then, aeroplanes still perceived as flimsy motorised kites, the whimsical indulgence of "knuts" (and God, of course, was still an Englishman).[2]

too easily to hard falls, and longer distance rides between bases might have to be covered at speed, perhaps in the dark, over roads that might be better than those in the war zone, but nevertheless were poorly surfaced, as has been seen.

Despatch riders also were attached to the nine Home Divisions that were retained to resist any invasion attempt, as well as to train new formations for the BEF. These DRs maintained patrols aimed at what now might be called homeland security, patrols aimed more at deterring spies than actually hunting them down. They were maintained

> generally along the sea shore or in view of the sea, to report on any unusual lights or signalling, and to halt and enquire the business of any stranger....
> [The despatch rider] rides without lights, and so can see without being seen. He varies the times and routes of his journeys ... so that no one actually knows where he is at any particular time.[3]

Spy mania was more a feature of Belgium and France, and Roger West and Paul Maze were only two despatch riders who would discover this to their discomfiture (see last chapter); but folk in Blighty were not immune. Colonel Fiske's ripping yarn, already mentioned, has two boy scouts break a spy ring by tracking a chain of heliograph stations across England on their motorcycles.[4] But however important Don's work at home may have appeared, it was in the war theatre that he played his critical role.

The Great War is the one in which technology of weaponry, combined with the unprecedented scale of war, had so overtaken technology of communication that battlefield control often was poor and frequently was lost. Colonel JFC Fuller, one of the most important military thinkers of the interwar years, had learned this lesson in the course of his own war: "Information is the evidence upon which judgments are made.... Information of the enemy and our own troops comprises the most important conditions under which war is waged".[5] Perhaps nowhere was this so critical, potentially disastrous even, than during the August retreat, which brought the BEF from Mons to the Marne, a movement that "would have seemed incredible and impossible to military experts, who know ... the frightful difficulty of keeping an army together in such circumstances", as war correspondent Philip Gibbs reported.[6]

Detailed examination of the despatch rider's role in the Great Retreat and in the various theatres of war will be made in Chapter Seven.

Organisation and Training

DRs were used in all theatres and in all of the services—home ministries, the Royal Navy, the RNAS and RFC (and, when those two services were

amalgamated, the RAF), the cavalry, the artillery and—by no means least—
the ASC and RAMC. The air services' motorcyclists "are not, for some
reason, known as DRs"[7]—motorcyclists in all other branches of the services
but the Signals Corps were officially "motorcycle orderlies"—but were a rose
by any other name, and those of the air arms performed more onerous tasks
as the war progressed and the aeroplane became of increasing importance.
These riders had to bring film from aerial cameras to be processed, and then
the photographs from the field lab to staff headquarters and perhaps from
there, if an Army despatch rider was unavailable, farther forward. They
also handled despatches between the air services and the Army, and these
increased enormously in number and importance as strategy evolved. By the
time of the Somme battles planes were incorporated into ground attacks, and
by 1918 air support had become an intrinsic part of the all-arms offensives
that eventually defeated the German armies. Before the first year of war
was out cable and wireless telegraphy was in place, but the DR still was
needed to carry film and photographs and anything else unsuitable to wire
transmission, as well as field messages when the wires were "dis"—disabled
of disconnected—as they often were by shellfire.

Even more important than air support to the all-arms offensives of 1917-
18 was artillery. The contemporary expression, "artillery conquers, infantry
occupies", is a little over-simplistic but not inaccurate, and the effectiveness
of artillery was a reflection of the immense changes war had wrought. In
1914 artillery had consisted largely of field guns acting in direct support of
the infantry, right up at the front line. By 1917 industrial support of the war
was in full swing, and field guns had been relegated to a minor role, their
place taken by other weapons better suited to trench warfare, from Stokes
mortars in the front line to howitzers miles behind it, shooting to coordinates
on detailed maps that had been built up from aerial photographs. The main
target of these big guns might be enemy artillery far out of sight, their
location registered by "flash spotting" and "sound ranging", and subsequent
triangulation. Telegraphic communication between artillery and infantry was
usual, but always there remained a need for despatch riders, and there may
have been some rivalry between those of the artillery and those of the Army,
until the RE subsumed the artillery in this regard, in 1916.[8] RE men conceded
that DRs attached to the artillery "often [had] a rotten job".[9]

Most DRs belonged to the Motor Cycle Despatch Corps, which was
attached to the Army, part of the Signals Section of the Royal Engineers, a
section that one Don called the "nerves of the modern army".[10] This accurate
metaphor was employed by many. The Signals office was "the nerve centre
of the Army in the field, for into it radiate the tentacles along which flash
messages from every part of the field of operations, from the base and
from England."[11] "[O]ne liaison officer described the army as: 'A giant with

a quick and brilliant brain, but whose nervous system is slow, lethargic and inadequate'".[12] The brain was the signals office; the sensors and effectors included cable and airwaves as well as despatch riders.

> Every telegraph office, large or small, is under the control of the senior telegraphist, termed in the case of a soldier the "telegraph master", and in the case of an officer the superintendent.... Telegraph offices in the field form part of the signal office, which controls all methods of communication, and may, if in a town, have several telegraph offices under it.[13]

The signals office to which DRs reported contained as well "buzzers"—telegraph operators—and this office was ultimately in communication with the trenches in one direction and the War Office in the other.[14] It is no exaggeration to claim that without the "nerves" that Signals provided the army would have been "paralysed, and might well be dead".[15] This is the estimate of a despatch rider, but officers agreed: "The Signals companies ... had only been completely organised a month or two before the war, and what we should have done without them passes my imagination, for they were quite invaluable, and most excellently organised and trained".[16]

"Reorganised" the officer should have said, for the Royal Corps of Signals had its antecedents as far back as 1870, when a Telegraph Troop was formed under Captain Montague Lambert, its responsibility being to provide in-field communication by means of visual signalling—heliograph, semaphore, etc—telegraph and despatch rider (then a galloper, of course). Over the years telephone and wireless were added to the unit's resources, the bicycle and eventually the motorcycle augmented the horse, the Telegraph Troop became the Telegraph Battalion, Royal Engineers, in 1884, and the Royal Engineers Signal Service in 1908, but the role remained the same: to ensure effective communications for the army in the field in order to provide command with control.

Signals companies were attached to divisions, and DRs came to form the same loyalty to their division as other soldiers felt toward their regiments.[17] Don's tasks encompassed a wide variety beyond despatch riding, as outlined in Chapter Two, notably delivering pigeons to the trenches (see Chapter Seven), cable laying in emergencies,[18] and, when called upon, foraging and billeting. Despatch riders of the RNAS/RFC/RAF had the urgent job of bringing aerial reconnaissance photographs to staff and field officers who might need the information for planning or implementing an attack. Less urgent was the Despatch Rider Letter Service (DRLS), established in October 1914 and which, reports Corporal Mead, "in reality became a glorified post office or letter carrying 'fetch and take' service. In truth, however, "The operation of the military postal system was another triumph"; "the Army post service had the efficiency of a Swiss clock and the Persistence of the Pony Express".[19]

The items carried were not just personal mail, but everyday routine orders, invoices, receipts, etc, between respective Staff Officers".[20] The service operated at fixed times, twice a day—the latter bringing in mail from home—leaving "only the very urgent stuff to be sent out by a special despatch rider". The DRLS was slightly different from the Field Postal Service, which was for private and non-urgent official correspondence, but also was operated by the DR.[21] Though the DRLS and Field Postal Service do seem unglamorous and tame, certainly compared to the desperate, frequently heroic actions of the Great Retreat (see Chapter Seven), each was essential—the latter most important in sustaining morale—and besides DRs performed other duties incidentally, "bringing ambulances for wounded, and guiding officers here and there. We were looked upon as a sort of encyclopaedia of the district, and supposed to know where everyone and every place of importance was for miles around".[22] DRs' encyclopaedic knowledge stemmed in part from their having to know the contents of their despatches in case of loss or premature destruction of the written copy, and their pooling of their knowledge—not in a gossipy way, but toward improving the chances of all getting their despatches through, and indeed surviving.

Don saw his "real work" as delivering "special" despatches from one officer to another—signed authorisations for action could only be delivered by DR or runner. In training recruits were urged "to forget that there was such a word as 'cannot' in our vocabulary, and that it must be our first duty to get our despatches 'through'"[23]—in the best San Fairy Ann spirit. Sometimes these despatches were in code—George Mead carried such messages in the Middle East,[24] and on the Western Front encrypted telegrams might be delivered too[25]—but usually they were uncoded, written in triplicate, with all material signed for by the Signals office, the DR and the recipient, to ensure full accountability.[26] Don's copy was on "slim tissue paper that would almost melt in the mouth", so that it could be swallowed in case of capture by the enemy, and in particularly "warm" zones he might secure the despatch to a forefinger to facilitate this in case he was wounded; should the message be so destroyed and he evaded capture or escaped, the DR memorised his despatches.[27] (IRA despatch riders also swallowed their despatches when captured in the Irish War of Independence, prompting one to suspect that some Irish DR veterans of the Great War brought the practise back.) Military historian Martin Van Crefeld "has calculated that a single British Army on the Western Front generated daily 10,000 telegrams, 20,000 phone calls and 5,000 messages delivered by despatch riders".[28] These messages, though, would have included non-urgent items of the DRLS and the Field Postal Service.[29]

It was in the nerve centre of the Signals Office that all was coordinated "so that each [medium] by its special capabilities makes good the weak points in the others".[30]

[I]n the field of operations, the lines of communication were kept open between the respective Army-, Corps-, Division- and Brigade HQs by Air [overhead] line, [ground] cable, wireless and despatch rider of which the Signal office unit was of paramount importance. The one or two "pipper" Signal Officers controlled each of three daily shifts, but it was the NCO and sapper telegraphists who were the mainstay of the Signals unit.[31]

All media were important, but through the war the "indispensable" DR was able to "often go where all other means have failed".[32] "Field wire was good only for about twenty-five miles, and ... the radio was frequently overcrowded with messages or not functioning."[33] Some phone calls seem to have been indulgence: one army "allowed 140 subscribers to accumulate on its exchanges, with an average of 20,000 calls a day",[34] neat confirmation of Mr Crefeld's calculations but suggestive of a lot of fat. Fat or otherwise, though, Signals provided a critical service to the BEF, especially through the Great Retreat: many authorities believe that German defeat at the Marne stemmed from communications failure.[35] This possibility will be examined further in Chapter Seven.

A Divisional Signals Company, to which despatch riders were attached, comprised "five sections, headquarters [and] Nos 1, 2, 3, and 4. Headquarters and No 1 are attached to the headquarters staff of the division; 2, 3, and 4 being attached to the first, second and third brigades respectively".[36] Headquarters and No 1 sections "include three cable detachments with thirty miles of telephone cable and nine vibrator offices, as well as four mounted men, eight cyclists and nine motor cyclists for flag signalling and despatch riding".[37] But it should always be borne in mind that fixed practises and precise numbers could not be applied to all situations and all stages of the war: Corcoran claims that in the course of the August 1914 retreat Motor Cycle Sections comprised about six DRs apiece,[38] and Best's account concurs: "There are fifteen motor-cyclists now", he reports in early October, "and all telegraph lines are laid out, so that things are different from the absolute inferno of the retreat, when we were only six".[39] Captain JC Dunn speaks of "about 150 youthful enthusiasts with motor bicycles" on 20 August,[40] serving four, and a couple of days later five, divisions. Each section was in charge of a sergeant,[41] and though attached to Divisional HQ, they all operated from GHQ and Corps HQ down to Battalion HQ. "Three quarters of us rode between the divisional and the brigade headquarters. The rest were attached to the brigades, and either used for miscellaneous work or held in reserve so that communication might not be broken if the wires were cut or smashed by shells".[42] After the war of movement gave way to positional warfare, those DRs working from GHQ and Corps HQ had a much easier time of it than those working from Divisional and Brigade HQ, thanks not only to greater distance from enemy activity, but much more so to the far better state of the roads.[43]

Behind the front, all the way to the Channel and Paris, along myriad routes, relay stations were provided, normally at 20-mile intervals, and marked by flags, with lights at night.[44]

> Signals, like any other branch of war, are subject to the principles of concentration, economy of force, security and co-operation [best effected by] a system of *signal centres*, connected from front to rear and laterally, so as to cover the theatre of operations with a grid of signal communications. Each link of the grid is made as secure as possible by employing on it not one method only but as many ... as are available.

Thus, from DHQ "the *divisional main artery*" connected forward to the Divisional Signal Centre, and from here a hierarchy of radial links were made with Brigade HQ, then with Brigade Signal Centres and farther forward to Battalion HQ; artillery batteries as well as infantry battalions were so served by the DR. Don also communicated backward from DHQ to the Corps Signal Centre and from there farther back along the Corps Main Artery to Corps HQ; laterally between Corps, Divisional and Brigade Signal Centres; and obliquely with the RFC/RAF.[45]

It is impossible to overstate the importance of communications in any war, but in the Great War communications were more essential than ever before, yet never so problematic. During the position phase, signals offices often were located deep down to avoid disruption from shellfire. During an assault, of course, surface lines were damaged, but they were augmented by flares, heliographs, semaphore ("flag-wagging"), pigeons and of course Don R, and the signals office remained "the nerve centre of the whole complicated system of defence, with a switchboard larger than those in the 'central office' of many an American city", one American correspondent, Alexander Powell, claims. Field telephone lines were strung out in

> no haphazard and hastily improvised system either, but [one] as good in every respect as you will find in American cities.... [A]s the armies advance the telephones go with them, the wires and portable instruments being transported by the motor-cycle despatch riders of the Army Signal Corps, so that frequently within thirty minutes after a battalion has captured a German position its commander will be in telephonic communications with Advanced GHQ.... I have seen an officer at General Headquarters establish communication with the Provost Marshal's office in Paris in three minutes and with the War Office in London in ten.[46]

Powell paints a picture that was no doubt accurate after the war settled down—it is supported by incidents such as that of an artillery observer who "absent-mindedly gave his own private telephone number, and about a quarter of an hour later was speaking to his wife in North London"[47]—but was not typical of the war of movement phases. Once the war congealed it might be "Only when the telegraph wires become 'dis' is it that 'DRs' are called upon to take field 'telegrams' from one spot to another and in justice to the Signal Service it must be said that this is an event which very seldom, if ever, occurs".[48] This up-beat account is more propagandistic than strictly accurate, for although electronic communication made enormous advances, it remained vulnerable, and the need for DRs remained to the hard-fought end. American forces, in 1918, found that "motorcyclists and horse-mounted orderlies served a crucial role of passing information from one headquarters to the next when wire communications were interrupted".[49]

It took little time for the army to set up a signal station. As early as September 1914 Tait reports:

> It rarely takes an hour for us to have a dozen telegraph links at work connecting up to Havre, Rouen, London etc. Where possible existing wires are used and where not air or earth cables are run out. The latter can be put down at 6 mph and form a decent permanent job. I have seen them, though, putting down at 12 mph.[50]

Presumably the difference in speed in laying reflects the use of horse waggons and motor lorries respectively—though sidecar outfits could be pressed into cable laying, and a long belt from the motorcycle's engine pulley might be used to spool the cable in or out.[51] (And one should certainly note that long before 1914 was out such cables as Tait describes would not be regarded as either "decent" or "permanent".)

DRs carried all messages that could not be sent over wire, because of bulk or for security reasons, each rider rostered in turn. Before the Fullerphone, telephonic and electronic security was so lax as to "border upon the criminal".[52] It meant that the Germans knew about General French's plans on the August Retreat,[53] and though the leak was excusable on this occasion, given the frantic circumstances, and was hardly critical, it illustrates the importance of the DR. Another instance of wireless leaks, a less forgivable one, is that intercepted by German intelligence at 0245 on the eve of the Somme: a "Good Luck" message from Rawlinson to his commanders.[54] How many lives did that laxity cost?

Apart from all other factors, therefore, security risks over wire or wireless made the despatch rider essential. And not just in what we think of as the "war theatre": because the rebels had seized the General Post Office and could tap into phone lines, DRs had to be used in Dublin during the Easter Rising. In high-risk situations, such as often were found back in the main theatre, several might be sent with the same despatch, each taking a separate route, to improve the chances of the message getting through,[55] and to ensure this, they could commandeer any vehicle: apocryphal stories of outraged generals being bundled out of Daimlers by lowly Dons may have a basis in fact.

> Sometimes there came a warning shriek from behind, and everything drew to one side to make room for a dispatch rider on a motor cycle. These had the right of way. Sir Douglas Haig himself, were he driving along, would see his driver turn out to make way for one of those shrieking motor bikes![56]

Don held the rank of corporal, a quaint consequence of privates being forbidden to approach an officer without being accompanied by an NCO coupled to the strict requirement that despatches be delivered in person—always to an officer—and signed for.[57] The rank of corporal was, according to an Old Army sergeant anyway, considered "a great privilege … in the RE. In peace time, men have to work many years to gain that position",[58] so the DRs of 1914 should count their bleedin' blessings. Those in the Intelligence Corps were even more privileged, being appointed as second lieutenants—but, "though we had received commissions, we were never under any circumstances to consider ourselves officers"; these men were "virtually … despatch riders", and eventually "despatch riders pure and simple";[59] though their other duties became more important after the frantic retreat of August 1914. The war broke down many protocols, though. Men whom the Old Army would have refused a commission became "temporary gentlemen", as diehards disparagingly referred to them, and privates who could ride a bike might be temporarily assigned to do DR duties.

A threefold breakdown of tasks can be distinguished: column riding, "work parallel to the front" and "work radial to the general staff's in a frontal sector".[60] The column rider was utterly essential on the retreat from Mons, maintaining contact between battalions, brigades, divisions and corps, and rounding up stragglers, constant work that was exhausting on the rider.[61] Acting as "the eyes, ears and lips" of the convoy officer, his task was to maintain smooth uninterrupted movement along the route, advising on breakdowns and obstructions and organising their clearance.[62] Road space was at a premium in France and Flanders and convoy work and traffic management was critical;[63] Don R was vital to retreating in good order and holding the army together.

The size of an army on the march, the amount of traffic it involves, is something that can be difficult to envisage, and the farther the retreat went the more congested grew the roads. West describes them as "blocked for miles with English troops, transport, both horse and mechanical, guns and limbers all inextricably mixed up ... a mess of mixed transport standing wheel to wheel and facing in all directions".[64] War correspondent Alexander Powell followed the German advance through Belgium. "For twenty miles every road was jammed with clattering cavalry, plodding infantry, and rumbling batteries, the guns, limbers, and caissons".[65] He motored for five hours through the German First Army without ever coming to the end of "that mighty column":

> We passed regiment after regiment, brigade after brigade of infantry; then hussars, cuirassiers, Uhlans, field batteries, more infantry, more field-guns, ambulances with staring red crosses painted on their canvas tops, then gigantic siege-guns, their grim muzzles pointing skyward, each drawn by thirty straining horses; engineers, sappers and miners with picks and spades, pontoon-wagons, carts piled high with what looked like masses of yellow silk but which proved to be balloons, bicyclists with carbines slung upon their backs hunter-fashion, aeroplane outfits, bearded and spectacled doctors of the medical corps, armoured motor-cars ... battery after battery of pom-poms (as the quick-firers are descriptively called), and after them more batteries of spidery-looking, lean-barrelled machine-guns, more Uhlans—the sunlight gleaming on their lance-tips and the breeze fluttering their pennons into a black-and-white cloud above them, and then infantry in spiked and linen-covered helmets, more infantry and still more infantry—all sweeping by, irresistibly as a mighty river, with their faces turned towards France.[66]

Keeping even the far more modest masses of men in the BEF on the move, preventing regimented order from collapsing into chaos, was largely down to Don R and his motorcycle, and his conduct during the Great Retreat may well have saved the day. Then, and again in 1918, any

> elaborate system of cable and aerial communication collapses more or less according to the speed of the movement and the effectiveness of enemy fire.... For when an army is in motion or under a fierce barrage or [sic] artillery fire, only individual effort will maintain communications, and that is supplied mainly by the Motor Cycle Despatch Corps.[67]

Even after the war settled down traffic conditions remained hectic in the battle zone.

> Never was Piccadilly or Fifth Avenue more crowded with motors at the busiest hour of the day than was that road. As we passed through villages

or came to cross roads we saw military police, directing traffic, precisely as they do at busy intersections of crowded streets in London or New York.[68]

Harry Lauder is describing the road from Boulogne toward Vimy, but all along the front, and especially when an offensive was either under way or in the offing, traffic was similarly congested, making the motorcycle, as it is in today's crowded streets, the most efficient and effective way to get about.

One of the many remarkable facts about despatch riders is that, in the early days, when their services were so vital, they received the most rudimentary training—a couple of weeks at most. Barely a month into the war Corporal Vernon Busby reports: "Everything was done in a terrible hurry, and there was only time for a few drills. An officer addressed the section and told them that they would be engaged in the most dangerous work, and if half of them reached England again they would be lucky." The work involved "all day long laying telegraph wires, hunting for faults, carrying despatches when the telegraphs failed, and going in search of lost transport columns, etc."[69] Corporal Watson joined up the day the war broke out, was posted to Ireland to do some vague training, and then to France on or about the opening of the Battle of Mons—i.e. within three weeks of enlistment.[70] Lieutenant West was in action even quicker: he enlisted on 10 August and landed in France *three days* later.[71] The potential for catastrophe in the face of the German advance was such that DRs were "so urgently required that refinements of training had to be dispensed with", as one officer in the Royal Engineers admitted,[72] but the consequence of this was that otherwise-suitable men knew little or nothing about army organisation and officer personnel, as well as other things that were essential to their doing a good job. Early volunteers learned on the job, but soon a six-week training course for suitable recruits was established by Signals Service Training Centre. This emphasised riding and maintenance of motorcycles, use of maps and "points" work—essentially a timed trial in map reading—field operations, office work, and horse and stable management.[73] The retention of horse management in the training regime was not just Old Army inertia, as Watson is forced to admit the value of the "despised horse" in the heavy mud of winter.[74] Not everyone is such a hippophobe as Watson: from October 1916 the remarkable Corporal Grice is grateful for a horse to ride when the dreadful mud of the Somme renders his motorcycle useless: "Road conditions of the very worst sort. Horses, motors and bikes stuck in the mud. Many horses dead as a result of exposure".[75]

After the war settled down there was time for more rigorous training. George Mead signed up on 31 August 1914 and unlike Watson and West, received ten months training at home before being posted abroad.[76] Mead, however, was very young—seventeen—and a mere junior draftsman rather than a university graduate or undergraduate, so this may account in part for his being seen to need the sort of training Oxbridge men like Watson evidently did not; and indeed snobbery need not have been the main reason for such discrimination, for most if not all public school and university men would have been in the Officer Training Corps. Mead reports being trained in marksmanship and "schemes" (a widely used foreshortening of "training schemes"), "rally riding, hill climbing, map reading, journeys coupled with an against the clock competition!",[77] as well as acting as motorcycle orderly to officers. At an advanced stage of training "we would join in Army manoeuvres around the country. These 'stunts' as they were called lasted several days. HQ movements took place at least daily—the idea being to simulate speedy movements in attack or retreat. For the first time we DRs were engaged in night time operations".[78] Elsewhere he reports: "Night schemes are very hard work, apart from other troubles such as filling the lamp container with a mixture of lemonade and water [to generate acetylene gas from the carbide] when we were short and getting very little sleep".[79]

Corporal—later Lieutenant—TW Grice joined up on 20 March 1916, by which time "the test applied to candidates is much more stringent than formerly".[80] Grice was a remarkable character, and his journal, which gives a great insight into the world of the despatch rider, includes the following entries on training:

> 5 April 1916: "… revolver practise in the afternoon".
> 11 April 1916: "One of a party of 50 despatch riders detailed off to help repair telegraph wires some 13 miles from Birmingham".
> 13 April 1916: "Busy putting up poles and wiring"

Similar work follows on succeeding days.

> 17 April 1916: "Wire pulling from one to eight poles in morning. Up a pole fixing wires most of the afternoon".
> 18 April 1916: "Up pole most of the time and got wet through".[81]

Such disheartening work was all part of the training regime, a reminder that riding motorcycles was only one of Don R's duties, and that he was subject to strict military discipline, with drilling and square-bashing all in a day's work. A regular fatigue duty, even in the field, was cleaning one's motorcycle or staff cars, down to the underside of the engine. Most do not seem to have minded, taking things in the San Fairy Ann Spirit. Corporal Davis summarises his first three weeks' training as "enjoyment robust. The drills to me are never monotonous, because of their being so frequently broken into by breathers and breaks and by the variety of other duties we had to perform.... Day by day I and others have enjoyed what we thought [would] be onerous.... Nothing was actually irksome".[82]

Grice gives details of map-reading and machine maintenance tasks, a mixture of practical lessons and lectures, and the fact that it's not all grim: "On an eight point [training] scheme all day. Covered about 80 miles in beautiful country".[83] After his transfer to France on 15 July, training continues, "schemes" and "Continentals", as he calls them, occurring on an almost daily basis. The Somme battles are raging, and Grice is on the very foot of the Learning Curve. By September he has been fully trained and in the thick of the third phase of the Somme. "Very busy in office. Working most of night. Our runs now through towns and woods captured during the week". DRs have telegraphic and/or administrative tasks: Grice refers to orderly duties elsewhere as well as here,[84] so the responsibility of early despatch riders has been sustained through the change from Oxbridge men to skilled artisans, one of which Grice had been in civilian life.

Motor Cycling gives a good description of the training regime that was installed after it became clear that this was going to be a long war. Recruits were given a test on their riding ability and an oral examination on how the motorcycle works. After foot drill with the Royal Engineers they graduated as pioneers and entered upon their "real" training, which lasted three or four weeks. They usually spent one week in workshop, where they were lectured on army organisation and the structure and maintenance of the motorcycle, and the next week given rider training on old hacks of various makes. "It is not all beer and skittles running these training machines, which have been used over and over again by different recruits since the beginning of the war, or scrapped by one authority and rebuilt to provide recruits with experience". Such was the ignorance of some of these recruits, for all the screening and initial training, that one severely overheated a Douglas by running it hard in low gear, being unaware that a higher gear was available.[85]

At the end of this phase of training each recruit was issued with his own personal motorcycle, a new Douglas or Triumph, for which he became responsible. He usually had to make what now would be called a pre-delivery inspection of the bike, making minor adjustments and tailoring it to suit himself, before more detailed training.

"Point schemes" were held on Tuesdays and Thursdays. On these schemes up to 200 riders were provided with a map and a "scheme paper", which had eight or ten "points"—specified locations—all some 20 miles apart, out of which each man would be expected to visit probably six in total, covering 100-120 miles, depending on the weather and the season. The riders were required to average 18 mph, with an extra two minutes allowed between points; their times were entered on their scheme papers and any breakdowns were detailed on a special section of this. Because of the large number involved, they were despatched to the first pre-arranged spot with 30 yards between them; after the first spot, they were sent to different points. "It is made a point of honour to find the way between points entirely by way of the map and not to inquire the way from anybody or to look at signposts".

On Thursday was held the "36 hour scheme". This commenced at 8:30 AM, and involved the setting up of various field headquarters, in an imitation of actual war zone organisation. All the recruits carried rations and camped out to get what little sleep they might. They rode 20 or 30 miles to a point where General Headquarters was set up, with a signal office equipped as such an office would be in the field. Two Corps Headquarters were then set up at some distance, and usually two despatch riders were attached to each of these. At a further distance, and in fan-like arrangement, were set up perhaps four Divisional Headquarters, each of which had four DRs attached. Messages then were sent across this network for the rest of the day and far into the night until at 1:30 AM on Friday the various HQs were dismantled and the recruits set off for home, no doubt tired out, as all headquarters would have been moved at least twice during the exercise, and in addition to assisting with these moves, each despatch rider would have carried at least eight despatches; he also would have manned the signals office, and sent telegraphic messages in code. To heighten his joy, he might find that his motorcycle had been deliberately interfered with, in order to test his initiative, ingenuity and repair skills. Each Saturday there was a written exam, three of which had to be passed before the recruit progressed to sapper, after which he got six days leave and then returned to a trained squad, where he waited to be called upon to serve as either a signaller or despatch rider.[86] Further training closer to the war zone took place in France: while recovering from gunshot wounds, Corcoran acted as an instructor at the Signals Depot at Abbeville.[87]

DR training schemes reflect how the BEF went from "muddling through" to being a professional force, young men at first going from civilian life to the front line literally in a few days, training schemes being implemented as it became clear that this war was not going to be over by Christmas. Much has been made of the "Learning Curve" that allegedly the British began to climb after the disaster of the first phase of the Somme, perhaps too much, for all armies were learning lessons from this utterly novel war, often from each other. Training schemes at home accordingly became more rigorous. *The Graphic* was enthusiastic and patriotic, but oddly ingenuous in admitting to prior shortcomings in army training:

> Thanks to ... official foresight the Lake Country mountains and the snowy wilds of the Pennines have given these men [trainee DRs] practice under the very conditions in which they may shortly have to work. The

strange thing is that until quite recently the advantage of training troops in similar country to that in which they will fight has not been recognised.

"Quite recently" was not entirely correct. From early 1915 some trainee despatch riders had been sent to the Western Mounted Brigade, stationed in Kendall, and trained in the rugged terrain and often-severe conditions of Cumbria. George Braithwaite, a well-known local competitions rider, helped in their training. Clearly not all trainees were sent to Cumbria, as many diaries and personal accounts do not mention the place, but the scheme did find official favour, it being concluded "that the experience gained on [training] runs such as this would be very valuable to riders when they go on foreign service, as they find their way over all sorts of by-paths". So rugged was the terrain that even Braithwaite could be beaten by the snowdrifts often encountered in winter, and by the time *The Graphic*'s reporter followed one group of trainees up Dent Hill in Cumbria, across steep icy slopes and through deep snowdrifts, cooperation was necessary. In some places an accompanying sidecar outfit could be used as a sort of slow-plough to clear a way for the solos, but machines sometimes had to be bodily carried through.

> Eventually, under man-power rather than horse-power, five official machines reached the crest of the hill. One arrived minus the tread of the back tyre, and with the engine hot enough to burn a hole in the driver's overcoat … a remarkable exhibition of pluck and determination which augers well for the future of the despatch riders.[88]

The Men

More mechanised—relatively if not absolutely—than any of the other belligerents, nevertheless in 1914 the British Army proved to be inadequately provided and a call for motorised volunteers had to go out: "Hundreds of motor cycle [AA] members volunteered for dispatch-carrying work"; AA patrolmen "were evidently ideal recruits … for scouting work", and more than 250 enlisted or rejoined the colours, about half the total number of patrolmen.[89] But

> To ensure good service in this important branch during mobile warfare, men of exceptional intelligence, endurance and courage, and, especially, men possessing initiative of a high order, were required [and] the University Officers' Training Corps came to the rescue with a particularly good type of men for the purpose.[90]

DRs "are, many of them, students from Oxford and Cambridge. Their intelligence, knowledge of languages, and general resource are a great asset to the British Army."[91] Captain Dunn describes them as being, "for the most part, University students and young schoolmasters, with a sprinkling of young businessmen".[92] "University undergraduates [are] just the type of man the War Office wanted",[93] and Corporal—later Captain—WHL Watson was an Oxford man. There was a rush to become a DR, and Watson found himself in a throng of "all sorts and conditions of men" when he enlisted.[94] "The streets in all directions … were packed with motor cyclists and motor cycles of all descriptions" outside one recruiting office on 6 August.[95] The volunteer spirit was such that months into the war an intriguing article appeared in *The Motor Cycle* proclaiming the need for 50 despatch riders for a "privately raised force", one that would be attached to a battalion; all volunteers would have to "provide their own kit, which will cost in each case about £5".[96]

Though at the start "any motorcyclist almost who was willing to go was taken",[97] not all volunteers were suitable. The ideal DR had "native ability … keenness … initiative … readiness to meet an emergency", and was physically robust.[98]

> It will be seen that very special qualifications are required of a despatch rider. He should in the first place be fit and in hard training, ready at a moment's notice to undertake any mission that may be given him. He should be a good horseman, a cyclist, and something of a mechanic; be able to find his way by day or night, with the aid of the sun, stars or compass; know the names and ranks of all generals, staff officers and commanders of units; possess a good knowledge of scouting, to enable him to pass safely through hostile territory; and—perhaps most difficult of all—be qualified to deliver a verbal message word for word as he receives it.[99]

The Motor Cycle summarised what was required: "a mere rider is of little service as a despatch rider, he must be part and parcel of his mount, alert, ready for emergencies, and quick to diagnose a fault in his machine and equally smart in effecting the necessary adjustment".[100] An ability to leap tall buildings at a single bound is not specified, but it does seem rather implied. There's something of almost comic *sangfroid* in Corporal Tait's casual mention of his emergency amputation of a dog's leg, which had been "run over by a lorry. Don't know if it will do".[101] (Another DR, Dr Crowther, might have been able to give a more accurate prognosis, Crowther being a middle-aged doctor who had sacrificed practice and security to duty and excitement; he was killed at First Ypres.)[102] Oddly, only a couple of days after Watson had enlisted, West, an eminently suitable man—a Cambridge-educated engineer—had to visit several recruiting offices before he was finally "[given] something", accepted as "the last of five men for the Intelligence Corps".[103]

This was an interesting unit. Back in the South African War the Field Intelligence Department had done useful work and though it had been disbanded since, it formed a precedent for subsequent intelligence units in both British and Indian Armies. In 1911 the government accepted "the need for an Intelligence Corps of Scout officers, Guides, Interpreters and Intelligence Police for any European expeditionary force ... selected for expertise, linguistic" notably. Included was "a Motor-Cycle Section using Douglas, Premier, Rudge and Triumph motor cycles". Like the first DRs, these men, who had been selected for their civilian skills, got only hasty training in military matters before being despatched to France, and as lack of suitability had eventually sidelined more than a third of the 81 provided for, men like West were recruited at the last moment. They often were discounted by the Old Army officers, "misused as ordinary soldiers, and under-valued", but soon they proved their worth, "distant reconnaissance by car or motor cycle around the German outer flank acquiring information on enveloping movements". Even as "mere" despatch riders their knowledge of French was of enormous value during the war of movement, and in "Sir John French's first BEF Honours List 26 names appear under the heading 'Intelligence Corps'";[104] it's worth noting that only fifty had been attached to the BEF at the outset so more than half distinguished themselves.

In August 1914, when men were going frantic to get into the war before it drew to its expected speedy close, those wealthy enough to be able to afford the luxury of a motorcycle were privileged as the need for motorcyclists became evident. Purchasing one's own bike actually meant nothing financially except in the immediate-term—Watson and Paul Maze step in off the street and buy new motorcycles almost as casually as other men might buy a packet of cigarettes—because despatch riders, before the army supplied machines, were remunerated for the value of their motorcycles as well as earning a £10 enrolment bonus.[105] Bill Foster found that the War Office "would give him only £62.50 [£62.10.00 in the currency of the time] for his bike but that 'I would not have got that if I sold it so I won't grumble'".[106] Such rewarding of the rich may seem outrageous in our more egalitarian age, but such a view is anachronistic: the vast bulk of people then felt confident in the ability of their "betters" and more comfortable in their "own place" as followers, and antebellum elites often assumed leadership and power out of a sense of duty (until 1911 MPs had been unpaid), and most discharged those duties conscientiously if not always well.

Besides needing the wherewithal to purchase their own motorcycles, some knowledge of French and German was looked for in the aspiring DR, and this implied post-primary education, which only the well off could afford or see the need for. Senior NCOs of the Old Army, the terror of other ranks, instinctively recognised in the plum-toned graduates their "betters", and gave them respectful treatment and glowing tributes before long;[107] but this need not imply fawning on the NCOs' part, and Watson's—and presumably many of his peers'—feelings toward what he had previously regarded as "a crowd of slavish wastrels and empty-headed slackers" soon became reciprocal.[108] Already aware of the need to expand the armed forces, and the need to "grow" leaders, the army (and senior NCOs are among the most professional of soldiers) would have seen the value of public schoolboys' and university men's sense of duty and initiative, essential to DR work, and the potential that DR work had to develop riders into sorely-needed officers. Though almost all were inexperienced then, with mere weeks or even days of service, they were trusted to use their initiative on the Great Retreat, "with instructions to get the stuff [artillery, in this instance] wherever [they] could lay hands on it".[109]

Not merely NCOs, but officers, up to the level of general, had a high regard for Don R. Off duty on Sundays during training, George Mead and his friends "used to 'borrow' our motor cycles and disappear to our homes in London, all against regulations." Once they were apprehended by their Senior Signals Officer who turned a blind eye to their escapade—the fact that he had been on a similar jape and needed their help in recovering his broken-down motorcycle was perhaps a factor that time.[110] "The General and all the Staff Officers are most awfully nice to us, and are very interested in our machines and ask endless questions", reports a clearly flattered Corporal—later Lieutenant—Lamb.[111] If Bill Foster's encounter with Haig was unimpressive (see Chapter Two), he describes Rawlinson as "a right sport". All the DRs seem to have liked "Rawly", and "were assured of good food whenever they were on duty at the chateau".[112] The plain-speaking "Wully" Robertson, who had been an instructor in signalling, was forthright in his praise:

> The despatch riders ... performed invaluable service.... Most of [them] were boys under twenty years of age who had joined on the outbreak of war ... and the manner in which they carried out their duties in the face of great hardships and dangers confirmed me in the opinion that the English boy has no superior.[113]

In Fortunino Matania's illustration, *Notes from the trenches: British despatch rider arrives at headquarters in an old French chateau with reports from the front*, we see Don R clearly at ease at the general's own desk.[114]

The other sort of man the army looked for was the competition rider, whose ability and initiative—and daring—were proven, these traits being limpidly of value in DR work. Eric Williams was an Isle of Man TT winner,[115] and Vernon Busby, Sergeant Healy and AJ Sproston were among the very many competition riders who wore on their sleeves the blue-and-white brassard of the Signals Corps. The fact that these men owned motorcycles, and—more tellingly—could afford the time and money to race them, suggests that they came from a comfortable background.[116] The discovery that Sproston was "in the habit of daily dining" at "the Corner House Restaurant in London" confirms the financial security of his position, and like Corcoran and Watson, Sproston later went for a commission, ending up in the RFC.

Though most DRs in the early days came from the upper or upper-middle classes, social standing was not in itself enough: Stanley Casson, another Oxford man, though proficient in French and German, was rejected when he betrayed that he never had ridden a motorcycle.[117] Neither had George Mead, but he lied through his teeth and his engineering experience got him through the oral examination, and he became a proficient despatch rider.[118] Other bluffers proved less successful in the field. Letters to the motorcycle press indignantly criticise the mechanical abilities of many DRs,[119] and editorials concur. Captain Dunn believed that "a large percentage" of the initial draft of DRs "had no idea how to manage their mounts".[120] A "large percentage" may be exaggeration, but inevitably some mechanical duds must have slipped through in the frantic early days. The historian of the Intelligence Corps tactfully admits to "varying degrees of skill",[121] but Roger West is more forthright: one of his colleagues, "Blenner West, whose efforts on a motor cycle had been the standing joke of the army … was constantly coming off, but was always game to take another try".[122] Vernon Busby, a former competition rider and therefore probably a stiff critic, complains that "most" of the DRs in his company, though "thoroughly good fellows … lacked riding experience, showing that they were chosen in somewhat of a hurry".[123] "At the time there was little attempt made to ascertain whether the recruits were experts or the merest novices", another veteran admits. "Consequently some terrible 'wash-outs' were engaged".[124] Though he later makes lieutenant, HE Etherington comes across as something of a blithely incompetent, callous toff who could walk straight into a Blackadder or Monty Python skit: "Hit a Frenchman. Small damage to bike but plenty to victim", he reports pithily in August 1915; next month: "Run over boy".[125] (Davis too knocks down a child who runs out from behind a lorry but he is sympathetic—"poor little mite"—even though the collision fetches him off; both rider and child are uninjured.)[126]

That there were "terrible wash-outs" in the first draft of DRs, which quite probably saved the BEF from defeat in August 1914, must imply that an even greater burden was carried by those men who truly were able—or that the wash-outs quickly upped their game—but to go by the many decorations and mentions in despatches they gained, despatch riders, overall, did a fine job. They were brave, determined, resourceful and intelligent. Of the 42 Scout Officers who went to France with Roger West in August 1914, four were killed in action or died of wounds, another was wounded, three were taken prisoner, 26 were mentioned in Sir John French's Honours List, as has been noted, and

West was awarded the DSO and two of his colleagues the *Légion d'Honneur*. Their casualty rate comes close to that of the junior officer corps during the worst battles, though after the war of movement turned to trenchlock the risk to despatch riders declined. In addition to their faith in men of "good quality" (two of West's companions were titled),[127] the "hidebound" military believed that "there is some magical quality in the motor engine which develops the intelligence of the man used to grappling with the problems it presents him"[128]—a different sort of magic from the witchcraft that many at the time probably suspected was involved in engine maintenance and repair, an intelligence that could be put to "growing" officers or promoting suitable men to artificers. Roger West's blowing up the bridge at Pontoise shows initiative, courage and a sense of duty, and Captain Dunn tells another story of a DR's initiative during First Ypres when he called—in German—on a group of attackers to halt, and then directed British machineguns and rifles on the Germans.[129] This does sound rather like a "trench legend", but it may well be true.

In the first year of the war "All Classes [were] Represented Among Despatch Riders at the Front", but "Most of them are undergraduates or public-school boys";[130] as many as eighteen out of twenty in one group were Oxbridge men, the other two "professional men of high standing";[131] one DR was a middle-aged doctor who had been in charge of a hospital before enlisting.[132] Such men would, in the main, likely have held the sort of lofty but understated sense of duty expressed by another anonymous volunteer: "there was no credit in coming to fight, but merely disgrace if you did not".[133] In the ignominious retreat with which the BEF began the war, Corporal Watson feels so humiliated that the banter of the men trying to keep up their spirits seems "Blasphemous".[134] Bragging about one's exploits while on leave was very definitely "bad form" for these men: Corporal Enstone wrote to *The Motor Cycle* to disown a very favourable account about his "alleged adventures" that had been published earlier, and his colleagues, perhaps doubting his resolve to do so, wrote too to refute the account—which it would appear he did in fact supply to the paper's correspondent (though the correspondent may have embellished what he was actually told).[135] Corporal—later Lieutenant—Best is more grim: speaking of a colleague who supplied a self-serving account to a Colchester newspaper he writes, "There will be a hot time in store for him should he return here, whilst Cambridge will be untenable for him should I by chance get back and find a few men I know still up at Clare [College]".[136] Davis describes one of his colleagues, another self-serving braggart, as "an absolute shit", likely to need the protection of a personal MP against his own colleagues.[137]

As the war wore on, the socially elite quality of DRs, like that of the officer corps, was eroded, though probably the need for experience would have continued to favour those wealthy enough to have owned a motorcycle, until the glamour of despatch riding became dulled, and meritocracy promoted the best to officer (a good number seem to have gone to the RFC—which does seem understandable of young thrill-seekers, which motorcyclists to a good extent remain, long beyond youth). Before the war was over, however, the upper crust likes of Watson and West were all in the officer corps, and Don R might be much more proletarian—George Mead had been a junior draughtsman and Gordon Wood a trainee metallurgist chemist.[138] Though as late as 1917 "The Best Type of DR" was still "a gentleman and a true sport",[139] one DR sergeant in the Fifth Army was a "quadroon",[140] by definition not a "gentleman" in those insouciantly racist times. One veteran complains that after the Lord Derby scheme was introduced in 1915, and more so after conscription, applicants to the DR Corps included "the funk who wished only to evade the trenches".[141] By the last year of the war FW Hopps is of a very different stripe to the "typical" DR of the early days (he appears to be a relief despatch rider), perhaps a cipher for how despatch riding becomes debased through the war of position.[142] Hopps's education is relatively poor, as his English usage betrays, and he seems to be an example of the sort of man who makes Lieutenant Best feel "sick of the private soldier as a companion". The scruples of Watson and West seem to have faded, too—in 1916 Corporal Davis observes that "DRs pinched things as easy as you like"[143]—though posing is still frowned on: one Don complains that some of his colleagues "exaggerate in the press the difficulties of the DR's work [, some] taking quite unnecessary rides over the very roughest tracks and having their photographs taken in places where they never have any actual duty".[144]

In the next war a somewhat similar change in the DR corps occurred. There was nothing elite in the social sense about the DRs of 1939, but they were of a "good sort": "We were fortunate in that in the early days most of us were ex-clubmen who had volunteered for the job, liked the job and were self-motivated. Later on when the Army had a go at selecting DRs from conscripts the motivation was not always there". Furthermore, "If the DRs did their duties well … we would be left pretty well to our own devices. The result was that we always did more than was expected of us". As in the Great War DRs "gradually developed a resourcefulness which was part of their way of life and came eventually to be appreciated by their superiors."[145] The huge difference was that in the Second War, while he remained important, Don R never was so essential as he had been in the earlier struggle.

Pay and Conditions

Conditions often were atrocious. Corporal Davis reports: "Sleeping quarters, a dark, ugly loft over stinking stable … with rats running all around the floor"; later, on the Somme, he and his colleagues sleep in "minute shacks made of scratch wood and felt ... two rats scuppering about kept me awake".[146] Such, and cleaned-out henhouses and the like, often were Don's accommodation. Through the August Retreat, and in position warfare if he was serving the artillery, he might have to bivouac in the open, even in hostile weather.[147] But overall the despatch rider's accommodation was infinitely better than conditions endured by the Poor Bloody Infantry, and it could be quite palatial, depending on the sector and whether the front locally was active. In the San Fairy Ann spirit, Don didn't grumble, whatever the conditions.

He did grumble, though, about pay, right through the war. Pay varied greatly, often with no evident logic, across the services for many skilled jobs, and it's hard to blame the men for sometimes being bitter. Before the war motorcyclists on manoeuvres were paid up to sixteen shillings a day, an exceptional rate even for exceptional work.[148] Also before the war, a special reserve of mechanical transport personnel had been established, and skilled drivers and mechanics were paid six shillings a day on being mobilised.[149] Despatch riders were covered under this scheme initially, but later a lower rate was introduced, and after conscription the six-shilling rate was dropped. Motorcyclists' pay was as low as 1/2½ a day on enlistment in the Motor Machine Gun Service and the Army Service Corps,[150] but the RE, to which most DRs were attached, were paid 3/- (three shillings) per day—strictly 2/6 as a DR plus sixpence "engineer's rate" after training.[151] However, the first 120 DRs who went to France were paid five shillings a day, plus a £10 enrolment bonus.[152] Some earned six shillings a day after training, "depending upon the section", but all car drivers got this rate whatever their section; the discrepancy was particularly egregious in the Motor Machine Gun Service, where car drivers earned five times the rate of sidecar drivers in the very same section (though of course these were not DRs, but still motorcyclists). However, sidecar drivers in the Naval Section (Armoured Cars) were paid six shillings a day plus 2/6 billeting allowance, a total of 8/6 a day, over *seven times* what their opposite numbers in the Army were paid.[153] No wonder motorcyclists grumbled: more dangerous work, in more arduous conditions, for far less remuneration than car drivers! By 1916 a DR's pay had been established at two shillings and sixpence a day, "plus 6d [sixpence] on passing the engineers' test".[154] This could cause real hardship: one DR's rate of pay dropped from five to three shillings a day, but with "the reduction applying retrospectively, and so far affecting his remuneration that it was found [he] owed the government a matter of £84 odd for overpay"—all but unbelievable today.

But even worse examples of unfairness could be found back then. In Mesopotamia DRs were randomly allocated to the British Army and the Indian Army, and paid respectively three rupees two annas, and three shillings per day, a several-fold disadvantage for those allocated to the *British* Army.[155]

Those serving in the South African forces earned ten shillings a day—three shillings "ordinary Army pay" plus seven for despatch riding, "plus Imperial separation allowance".[156]

In the air services inconsistency and resentment was also to be found. DRs in the RFC and RNAS, prior to these services' incorporation in the RAF, were paid between two and four shillings a day if they were "skilled", 1/3 if "unskilled". But qualified artificers in the same unit were paid seven shillings a day plus eight more separation allowance.[157] RFC motorcyclists bitterly resented reclassification as "*non-technical* under the new RAF", because of the reduction in pay and opportunities for promotion such reclassification meant. This was seen as "injustice to motor cyclists", given that "a petrol or steam car driver remains technical at considerably advantageous rates".

Reduction in pay is perhaps evidence of old prejudice re-emerging—one may speculate that as despatch riders were decreasingly drawn from the social elite, it was easier for such prejudice to assert itself. But in some cases at least, what was resented more than loss of pay was the blow to professional pride: "The matter of pay and promotion, although of some importance, is outdone by the degradation of being called 'non-technical privates', and not being allowed to keep the honourable title of (air) mechanics".[158]

The blatant unfairness of pay rates is highlighted when one considers that civilian volunteers in the Motor Messenger Detachment in Blighty were paid a penny a mile while on duty or while proceeding to and from HQ, up to a ten mile radius[159]—just reporting for duty could earn a man more than Tommy, or even Don in some units, might be paid for a day's hard, dangerous work. Before conscription was introduced, there was a quaint "civilian military" category of DR attached to home-based units, and these were paid five shillings a day.[160] Volunteers in the Sidecar Ambulance Service (see Chapter Six) were paid £2-0-0 per week—i.e. almost six shillings a day—as well as travel expenses.[161]

What must have galled more than anything, in those patriarchal days, was what women could earn as despatch riders in the Women's Legion: £1-15-0 a week, for an eight-and-a-half-hour day, plus five pence an hour overtime.[162] Superintendents in the Women's Auxiliary Army Corps or Auxiliary Motor Transport Service (albeit in France) earned between £2-6-0 and £2-12-6 a week; "head drivers" earned £2-0-0; "qualified driver mechanics" £1-15-0; even "washers" earned a full pound a week.[163] In addition, overtime might be paid after eight and a half hours' work in a day. "*Overtime!*"—one can imagine the outrage among men exhausted from riding round the clock as they tried to stem the Spring Offensive, for as little as ten bob a week or even less. To say nothing of those in the trenches dying for a shilling a day.

Again, one cannot wonder that disillusionment set in.

Clobber and Gear

Still so new was motorcycling in 1914 that the concept of specific clothing to suit had not quite been grasped. Walking and golfing garb, snug and as windproof as, until recently, had been called for, were commonly used, with various over-clothes to turn the rain. In 1824 Charles Macintosh had developed a rubberised fabric that was reasonably waterproof[164]— at least until the raw rubber perished. Later in the nineteenth century the product was improved by vulcanising the rubber, and with modern, synthetic material sandwiched between two layers of thick cloth, the design survives in today's mackintosh. Canon Basil Davies was, in 1904, garbed in a mackintosh derivative, "a special Hoare motor cycle outfit, constructed of thick Harris tweed, interlined with the finest sheet rubber to render it stormproof".[165]

Muddling through as usual, the British Army had made no provisions to provide its despatch riders with the sort of clothing that half a minute's thought would have determined to be desirable, if not essential, for the all-weather work that despatch riders did. As the first winter began to close in *The Motor Cycle*, drawing on the volunteer spirit that famously had Sister Susie Sewing Shirts for Soldiers, opened a "Shilling Fund" by which readers could contribute toward "purchasing useful Christmas presents for motor cyclists on active service ... articles such as gloves, mufflers, handle-bar muffs, warm socks and abdominal belts".[166] Everyone in the services was affected by shortages at the beginning, one correspondent noting "The strange diversity of active service garb[;] the British soldier cannot be particular about appearances". (The same observation was made by a DR early in the next war: "Oh! What a motley crew we were".[167]) Corporal Davis, in January 1915, notes "the varying qualities of tunics and greatcoats and caps and knickers dished out during our kit distribution".[168] Among non-standard equipment were "Jack-boots, jerseys and fur coats", as well as rubber boots and waders— remarkably, soldiers had to pay for non-standard footwear by instalment deductions from their pay.[169] According to Corporal Davis, by 1916 at any rate, "posh black artillery boots and laced leggings combined [were] much affected by DRs".[170]

Through most of the war the kit supplied was inadequate, and Don often must have been as thoroughly soaked as Tommy was in the waterlogged trenches. Lieutenant Foster's son remembers that his father "was constantly writing home for various oilskins, leggings, Burberrys, etc, often made to his own design, to be sent out to him in his efforts to keep warm and dry".[171] Others had the same fixation on clothing: in late November 1914, Corporal Best is wearing a "furcoat", obtained from a non-Army but non-specified source, apparently back home, a coat that he fears may be stolen by envious people. This may refer to other DRs, and if so it's an eloquent testimony to the deficiency of the gear that they were wearing, as at this time in the war despatch riders still were predominantly public school types with a high regard for "good form". Soon, Best reports, "We are going to be served out with long leather overcoats".[172] In January 1915 he writes to his father asking if he could "send out a racing helmet? It is a thing like a sleeping helmet only is waterproof, more or less, and usually made of soft leather and has small holes so that one can hear things".[173] This serves some purpose, but Best remains—understandably—fixated on the weather:

> We wear no end of clothes when we are out on our runs, and manage to keep warm tho' not dry [woollen army clothing would explain this remark, wool retaining its insulation even when damp]. The problem of keeping dry is almost impossible to solve as the liquid mud splashes onto the boots and then drives up thro' the lacing of the boots.
>
> The same sort of thing occurs down the back of my neck owing to the thoughtful ablutions of the back wheel. The hat which I have just received should prevent that.

Unsurprisingly, manufacturers cashed in: Burberry boasted in the motorcycle press—which was avidly read at the front—that their "garments are woven and waterproofed by special processes, and will resist torrential downpours and arctic cold".[174] One discerns a certain legalese in the choice of that word "resists".

In the first winter of the war goatskin jerkins were issued to the troops, and to Don R. Many contemporaries, among them American novelist Edith Wharton (who earned the *Légion d'honneur* from France for services to her adopted country), report on "despatch-bearers on motor-cycles ... goggled officers in goat-skins and woollen helmets,"[175] and goatskins certainly were an improvement over woollen khaki; the best part of a century later a re-enactor could report: "The goatskins were great.... Totally windproof, they were very warm".[176] But how waterproof they would be after being ridden into a rainy headwind at even 20mph for many hours no seasoned motorcyclist of today, spoiled by Gore-Tex, would care to imagine. They must have smelled pretty ripe too, after a few soakings—but then the Western Front was a malodorous place, so the stink of goat hardly caused many nostrils to twitch, and some jerkins survived the war.[177] Leather coats were widely distributed in late 1914,[178] they are to be seen in many photographs through the war years, and Corporal Grice was served with one in 1916, so one may suppose they were regular if not necessarily standard issue; but leather is far from waterproof. Even in 1916 DRs were augmenting their army issue clothing: in January Corporal TE Raw wore non-standard issue Barbour Beacon oilskins, Bullseye boots and woollen helmet under a racing leather helmet,[179] and in November

Grice has a Burberry sent out from home; the following January (1917) he has a fur lining fitted.[180]

On the count of clothing, though, one must not be too hard on the army: it wasn't until the 1930s that waxed cotton was developed, and that was the best of the small selection of allegedly-weatherproof clothing a motorcyclist could buy into the 1980s. And the glum truth is that waxed cotton wasn't much better than the oiled or rubberised linen of a century earlier, and it took a long time for anything better to arrive. In the years preceding the Trade Descriptions Act a variety of synthetic fabrics, masquerading as waterproof, came on the market. Most of them disappeared with some alacrity, and to this day motorcyclists search hard for genuinely, permanently, waterproof clothing. Even Gore-Tex will eventually leak under the harsh usage it gets on a motorcycle, so what chance did Don R have of staying dry ninety years ago? More than Old Bill and Young Bert in a flooded shell-hole did, perhaps, but not by much. No better 'ole was to be found.

Into the 1970s Army and Navy Stores sold military-surplus despatch rider clothing, which outfitted many an impecunious motorcyclist. Stock dated from the Second World War and afterward, but the garb was developed in the latter half of the First War. Those who bought such garments discovered that they were far from completely waterproof: the seams in particular leaked in heavy rain. By the Seventies they had been in storage for decades, so the waterproofing would have perished to some extent, and the glue and taping of the seams certainly had deteriorated, but one Don R of the Hitler War claims that his "waterproofs DR for the use of" were "alright in a shower but in heavy rain soon leaked".[181] It's possible, though, that he and his companions had been issued with Great War surplus, whose waterproofing would have deteriorated. But another Don of the latter war complains that winter motorcycling in particular "with Army type of clothing was a real test of stamina and fortitude";[182] how much greater a test must the Great War have been? As in the earlier war there were many complaints in the Second, with civilian clothing used to augment army issue and even campaigns in the weekly motorcycle papers "to get military motorcyclists some decent wet-weather gear [to replace the] waterproof suits, motorcyclists for the use of, which were a joke costume in rather poor taste … the colour of brown paper and … just about as waterproof"; the plastic oilskin gas cape was far more effective. This particular DR suggests that the poor performance of some garb was due to "crooked contractors" skimping on the material, even leaving out the rubber layer in the mackintosh fabric.[183]

Yet by the standards of 1914 the DR outfits that had been developed by the end of the Great War were all but excellent. The appointment of Sir Eric Geddes to overhaul the BEF's logistics system had been so successful that the allegedly hidebound, xenophobic generals welcomed civilian investigations into other aspects of the armed forces. As a result, supply of army uniforms was improved and designs modified in small details—for instance, pocket pleats were dropped from the Other Ranks' tunic—to streamline production. The despatch rider benefited from a standardised two-piece all-weather suit. The mackintosh fabric comprised two layers of canvas with rubber sandwiched in between. These suits were much simpler in design than those of the later war, whose long coats (introduced in 1942) had a comprehensive wrap-around flap secured by strong steel hooks and a belt, so that there were no zips to burst or buttons to pop off, while the wrap-around ensured that the coats were windproof and as weather-proof as it was possible to get. Great War jackets were shorter, three-quarter length, and double-breasted with an auxiliary flap covering the large buttons. Initially the sleeves had strap-and-buckle cuffs, but later elasticated inner cuffs were fitted. These jackets lacked the later design's large slanting breast pocket for carrying despatches—the Great War despatch rider carried these in a shoulder bag. The trousers ended in spats that flared over the tops of the boots and were secured by straps around the ankles and instep.[184] The improvement in Don's equipment is of a piece with the huge improvements in training and logistics that began in the course of the Somme battles.

Under the waterproofs Don R wore the uniform of the Other Ranks. In the case of the Army this meant, initially, the 1902-issue general services tunic but mounted pattern britches; RFC despatch riders wore the "maternity pattern" smock tunic. Photographs from the time indicate that total uniformity was not the order of the day. Leather leggings were standard wear from the beginning, but well into the war some DRs wore puttees, and others appear in tall lace-up boots—presumably gusseted—with buckle-flap cuff, rather like the pattern that was issued in the Second War though usually taller than these; they may have been private purchases. Interestingly, some photographs show puttees wound from the bottom up rather than from the top down, which was the mounted services pattern, though the britches were mounted pattern, and DRs were trained as horsemen, often having to revert to horseback in very muddy going. Some were issued with infantry greatcoats, but most with the mounted pattern overcoat, which was double-breasted. Woollen vests and drawers were standard issue, but jumpers, cardigans, balaclava helmets, scarves and other clothing were added, often sent out from home. Don also was supplied with goggles and heavy gauntlets, lined or unlined, made of tough leather—though sometimes the gauntlet-flare was of canvas. If lined, the material was strong cotton stitched in with the seams rather than inserted later, so that it could not be dragged out by withdrawing a damp hand. The gloves might be augmented with under gloves, and handlebar muffs provided further insulation; the gloves were more useful to protect the hands in falls than to keep the riders warm. Gas mask and Brodie helmet were added as they became standard issue; the Brodie provided little or no protection in the event of a spill.

Usually two bags were carried, one a map case, with celluloid window, the other for despatches. Both were made from heavy harness-leather, stiff enough to act as a firm backing for signing off on deliveries—trying to discern names ghosting out of the past on old despatch cases can be a fascinating if eerie business. In exotic theatres topees with Puggaree wrapping were added to the list. Corporal Grice, on the Somme in 1916, lists his kit as including two gas helmets, revolver and ammunition, "books, maps and mapcase, inner tube, emergency [puncture repair?] outfit, electric torch, jack knife, goggles and armlets"; also "overcoat, overalls and leggings".

Signals men wore an armband or brassard with a blue and a white band running longitudinally, the white band above the blue. Despatch riders normally wore one on each arm, whereas other Signals staff wore only one. For horseback work and parades, Don wore spurs, which were far more decorative than functional; by the next war, when "talkies" had introduced young men to spurs that go jingle-jangle-jingle, despatch riders drilled out sixpences and fitted these as rowels to their spurs, and no doubt gave excellent John Wayne impersonations.[185]

In the early days, at least in training, some despatch riders were armed with the SMLE Mk3 rifle, either worn over the shoulder on a hunter's sling or carried in a vertical scabbard mounted on the right hand side of the fuel tank, forward of the gear change lever.[186] One of West's companions suffered a bad fall when his rifle fell into the wheel spokes. On this occasion "the rifle barrel was twisted from the stock",[187] the weapon had been rendered useless and it quickly became evident that a rifle was totally unsuited to a despatch rider, the success of whose mission is in part determined by his being unencumbered and who is likely to be an active combatant only in an emergency. That said, though, right to the end Paul Maze was armed with a "carbine"[188]—almost certainly an SMLE—but Maze was hardly a typical despatch rider (though he did serve as such, and as a runner when called upon), being primarily an interpreter and Anglo-French liaison officer.

Don R therefore usually was armed with a handgun. The Webley .455 revolver was standard issue, but in 1914 there was much that was non-standard in the British Army, frantically grasping at whatever it could lay hands on. Corporal OH Davis was supplied with a Colt revolver,[189] Bill Foster with a .38 Webley & Scott nine-shot automatic,[190] and if non-regulation weapons were privately acquired in those more secure days before firearms licences were needed, they may have been purely "optional extras" in the army's view (Ted Rayns claimed that he "never carried a rifle or a revolver").[191] Lieutenant Best writes to his mother for a private weapon in late 1914: "An automatic pistol, Webley & Scott, or something like that would also be useful, if accompanied by cartridges…. I think .320 is about the thing". This weapon was received on 2 November, and on 9 December Best requests more ammunition, having expended his initial supply on target practise: "we have none of us been able to shoot at a German with a revolver and it would be a physical impossibility to draw it and shoot successfully from the bike". He adds, on 11 December, "It is highly improbable that I shall ever have to use the pistol in self defence".[192] Corporal DM Brown admits, "the only time I have used my revolver has been to shoot game",[193] and Watson and his companions likewise get no chance to use their weapons: "not one of us had fired a shot in anger since the war began. We treated our revolvers as unnecessary luggage".[194]

Others, though, were closer to the action. In the desperate campaigns of the initial war of movement, some despatch riders had to go right up to the front lines where they could become casualties of rifle- or shellfire,[195] and through the Great Retreat they remained in danger. "The Germans are very near now and the guns are quite deafening", wrote Corporal Tait on 26 August 1914.

> I have been very busy and am now waiting for a despatch to take up to the 5th Cavalry Division … a very risky job and … I had best leave all my kit behind so that I would have all the speed possible at my disposal. Most exciting. I shall have to crawl along under hedges and things as the Cavalry are almost surrounded.

Subsequently the sanguine Tait was "chased by Uhlan cavalry and fired upon repeatedly". (So was a Belgian despatch rider, Van Isacker by name, attached to the 4th Belgian Brigade; this man crashed heavily in the course of making his escape, fortunately in friendly territory, but had to be invalided out of the army.) On 1 September 1914 Tait had "a narrow squeak" when charged and fired on by enemy cavalry. "I emptied my revolver at them. I don't expect I hit any, though. I got a hole or two in the bike but wasn't hit. I had just got well away and was considering myself safe when I discovered they had shot my petrol pipe and I had lost all my petrol". Tait pillaged tubing and petrol from an abandoned lorry, repaired the bike and continued.[196]

When Divisional HQ was on the move the despatch rider had a difficult task of loading all his equipment and ensuring that the bike was controllable. Roger West describes driving along "with our voluminous kit piled high on the carriers",[197] something that couldn't do much for steering or control; Corporal Tait concedes that it "made riding rather difficult".[198] George Mead details how packing was done:

> On and across our handle-bars was fixed our blanket and great coat. Over the rear wheel carrier a pair of saddle bags (horse type) would be straddled

containing tinned rations and primus stove etc. Upon and over the rear wheel grid carrier fitted a despatch box on top of which was packed the second blanket plus other odds and ends. On the "warrior" himself was strapped to leg a six shooter, around his belted waist ammunition pouch, over each shoulder an aversack [sic], water bottle, map case, and binoculars. Sometimes ... treasures collected [in] a knapsack on the back.[199]

Another account, this time from the Second War describes it thus: "I had on all my equipment, respirator at the 'alert' on my chest, full pack on my back, side haversack, full water-bottle, revolver, ammo, gas cape rolled up fastened to the top of my big pack, kit bag strapped to the rear carrier, and two blankets rolled in a groundsheet on the petrol tank." When thus encumbered, Corporal Chisholm's carburettor catches fire and he is so crowded by his luggage and accoutrements that he is unable to dismount—fortunately he is saved by a colleague. Such incidents likely happened in the Great War too, and must be added to the hazards suffered by Don R.

Evaluation

This will be dealt with in greater detail in Chapter Seven, but all the evidence points to the fact that the despatch rider was invaluable; utterly indispensable. One officer at least was in no doubt:

> After this war the learned in such things will have to write a treatise on the psychology of the motor cyclist, for indeed he does things entirely without parallel, as will be confirmed by those whose lot it has been to control any number of these enthusiasts.... In our case the motor cyclist was so necessary that without him, several of him, we were lost. He fetched the letters daily, going sixty miles to do it, carried reports [and] demands ... traced lost supply columns ... and fetched newspapers, bootlaces or tinned delicacies from the nearest town. Moreover, he lay in ditches [and] slept with the gun crews in ice-cold bivouacs before action, and staggered up shell-pitted roads under a load of ammunition boxes on dark nights when the air was full of bullets.[200]

Reverend Douglas Winnifrith, a padre attached to the 14th Infantry Brigade Field Ambulance, credits Don R with saving the unit after Mons:

> We owed our escape to one of the motor-bicycle despatch-carriers, a Corps, consisting very largely of University men, which has done such valuable service in this campaign.... It transpired that he had been instrumental in saving on this occasion not only ourselves, but an Ammunition Column and a squadron of Cavalry.[201]

In the next war, for all the strides made by electronic communications, Don still offered advantages. In one impromptu test of "the relative merits of various forms of communication" a single DR delivered a series of messages to several depots across England within a day, "a week or more before the teleprinter messages finally got through". It should be borne in mind that this was an unofficial experiment, stemming from a wager between two COs, and probably unfairly biased by an inability to assign electronic priority to the test messages, yet the exercise reflects on the effectiveness of the DR, and in the "real world" of that war the motorcycle retained value to the end, proving the point of at least one Don, "that though the Jeep had taken over most of the DR work there would still be a time and place when a DR on a bike would be the only way of getting a message through, when the pigeons were grounded, the lines were down and secrecy demanded radio silence".[202] These conditions far more often pertained in the previous war, when electronic communication was much more primitive and vulnerable, and an *official* experiment proves the DR's worth years after even the Second World War: a 1953 study showed that the despatch rider was marginally more useful than the telephone in transmitting information at divisional level.[203] He was less than half as valuable as wireless by now, it's true, but given the great strides in radio technology and reliability made in the intervening years this very fact sets in bas-relief how utterly essential the despatch rider was when wireless was "in little more than its infancy"—as one signalman describes it as late as 1918.[204] On 1 September that year, in preparation for the assault on the Drocourt-Queant line, the Canadian corps handled 7,811 messages, of which 2,440 were carried by DR, "the balance by land wires or wireless".[205] Unlike in 1914, cable now was readily available, and with the Germans on the run it was less prone to disruption by shellfire, but it was not until after the war that "tactical radio capable of transmitting voice" became available (usually field wireless was used for radio-telegraphic communication, in part because of background noise),[206] and indeed, as late as the Battle of Britain, wireless might be "unreliable and inadequate" in second-line planes, according to a Blenheim pilot.[207]

How essential was the DR in the years of wireless's "infancy" is perhaps best illustrated by the consequences of failure. On 24 August 1914 three separate instructions to disengage and fall back failed to reach the 1st Cheshires; all but two officers and 200 men, out of a complement of 1,000, were killed or captured.[208] Two days later, after Landrecies, one DR, detailed to instruct several units to fall back, was unable to locate one of his targets, the 2nd Munster Fusiliers.[209] The entire battalion was lost.[210] That same day the most of two companies of the 2nd Connaught Rangers also were lost at Le Grand Fayt, cut off after contact was lost with brigade HQ—"at that juncture nobody knew where anyone else was, or what was happening".[211] If such was the case at brigade and even battalion level, imagine the task of the despatch rider, trying to hold entire divisions together?

It truly is difficult to see how command and control could have been exercised, how the war could have been won, without Don R.

Endnotes

1 *The Motor Cycle*, 8 October 1914 (reprinted from the *Daily Mail*).
2 *Motor Cycling*, 11 August 1914.
3 *The Motor Cycle*, 16 August 1917, p. 159.
4 James Fiske, *Facing the German Foe*.
5 Col. JFC Fuller, "The Application of Recent Developments in Mechanics and other Scientific Knowledge to Preparation and Training for Future War on Land", p. 241.
6 Philip Gibbs, *The Soul of the War*, p. 83.
7 *Motor Cycling*, 2 July 1918, p. 142.
8 See, for instance, letter to *The Motor Cycle*, 27 July 1918, p. 613.
9 OH Davis, IWM document PP/MCR/180, p. 233.
10 Corcoran, *The Daredevil of the Army: Experiences as a "Buzzer" and Despatch Rider*, p. x.
11 *The Times History of the War*, Vol. XVIII, p. 119.
12 Brigadier Peter Young, "The Great Retreat", p. 201.
13 Strang, ibid.
14 Corcoran, ibid, p. 91.
15 Corcoran, ibid, p. 95.
16 Edward Lord Gleichen, *The Doings of the Fifteenth Infantry Brigade August 1914 to March 1915*, p. 93.
17 Watson, *Adventures if a Despatch Rider*, e.g. pp. 129, 266-70.
18 Watson, ibid, p. 212; Tait, passim; Lieutenant T W Grice, IWM document reference P391, passim.
19 Charles Messenger, *Call-to-Arms: The British Army 1914-18*, p. 505; John Lewis-Stempel, *Six Weeks: The Short and Gallant Life of the British Officer in the First World War*, p. 102.
20 WG Mead, "Forty Thousand Hours of War", p. 20.
21 *Motor Cycling*, 11 April 1916, p. 573.
22 John Jackson, *Private 12768*, p. 49.
23 Jackson, ibid, p. 41.
24 George Mead, p. 76.
25 Gleichen, ibid, p. 6.
26 *Motor Cycling*, 11 April 1916, p. 573.
27 Corcoran, ibid, pp. 15, 24.
28 University of Birmingham Centre for First World War Studies, www.firstworldwar.bham.ac.uk/donkey/fowler.htm.
29 Priestley, ibid, p, 51.
30 Major R Chevenix Trench, "Signal Communication in War", p. 296.
31 George Mead, "Forty Thousand Hours of War", p. 67.
32 Chevenix Trench, ibid, p. 296.
33 Myer, ibid, p. 170.
34 FS Morgan, "The Development of Communication and Command", p. 135.

35 Myer, ibid, p. 172.

36 *Motor Cycling*, 6 July 1915, p. 220.

37 Hubert Strang, "The Signallers", in *The British Army in War* (unpaginated).

38 Corcoran, ibid, 21-22.

39 Best, ibid, 5 October 1914.

40 JC Dunn, *The War the Infantry Knew, 1914-1919*, p. 15.

41 Watson, ibid, p. 46.

42 Watson, ibid, p. 158.

43 *Motor Cycling*, 27 June 1916, p. 173.

44 Strang, ibid, "Despatch Riding".

45 Chevenix Trench, ibid, pp. 297, 299-301; emphasis in original.

46 E. Alexander Powell, *Italy at War and the Allies in the West*, p. 227.

47 John S Margerison, "Spotting For The Guns", www.greatwardifferent.com/ Great_War/Balloon/Balloon.htm.

48 *Motor Cycling*, 11 April 1916, p. 573.

49 Douglas J Orsi, "The Effectiveness of the US Army Signal Corps in Support of the American Expeditionary Force Division and Below Manoeuvre Units During World War I", p. 19.

50 Tait, ibid, 7 September 1914. "Air" cable was supported on poles, "earth" laid on the ground. There was a sort of compromise, "comic" cable, mounted on very short makeshift poles; the rationale for this seems to have been in part that cables' contact with damp ground quickly caused gutta-percha insulation to perish.

51 Motor Cycling, 9 May 1916, p. 5.

52 John Ferris, *The British Army and Signals Intelligence During the First World War* p. 13.

53 General von Kuhl, "The Operations of the British Army, August-September 1914", p. 302.

54 Alastair Horne, "Verdun and the Somme," in *Purnell's History of the 20th Century*, p. 568.

55 Corcoran, ibid, pp. 21-24; *Motor Cycling*, 5 January 1915, p. 219.

56 Harry Lauder, *A Minstrel in France*, p. 150.

57 Corcoran, ibid, p. 14, p. 13.

58 Davis, ibid, p. 10.

59 West, ibid, pp. 14-15, p. 46.

60 *Motor Cycling*, 5 January 1915, p. 219.

61 West, ibid, pp. 15-16; pp. 46, 57, 65; Watson, ibid, pp. 21, 38, 77. Convoy work remains an important part of a DR's work today.

62 *Motor Cycling*, 5 January 1915, p. 220.

63 Niall Ferguson argues that Moltke's stripping of the German right wing made no difference to the outcome of Schlieffen's invasion plan: the road network was so choked that even a single extra division could not have made a fighting difference. This may be a controversial claim, but it helps convey the problems a despatch rider had to contend with.

64 West, ibid, pp. 29, 31.

65 E Alexander Powell, *Fighting in Flanders*, p. 149.

66 Powell, ibid, pp. 116-17. Powell describes this army as the Ninth, but it can only have been the First or Second, and would seem more likely to have been von Kluck's First.

67 Corcoran, ibid, pp. xii-xiii.

68 Lauder, ibid, p. 149.

69 *The Motor Cycle*, 10 September 1914, p. 333.
70 Watson, ibid, pp. 8, 14.
71 West, ibid, pp. 3, 6.
72 Priestley, ibid, p. 12.
73 *The Motor Cycle*, "The Work and Training of a Despatch Rider", 24 May 1917, pp. 464-67; "The Training of a Despatch Rider: A Two Days Field Scheme Described", 2 August 1917, pp. 106-08.
74 Watson, ibid, p. 160.
75 Grice, ibid, 11-25 October 1916, 20 November-1 December 1916.
76 W. George Mead, "Forty Thousand Hours of War", Introduction.
77 Mead, ibid, p. 21.
78 Lamb, ibid, p. 22.
79 Lamb, ibid, p. 16.
80 *The Motor Cycle*, 22 June 1916, p. 584.
81 TW Grice, P391.
82 Davis, ibid, p. 28.
83 Grice, ibid, 18 May 1916.
84 Grice, ibid, 13/15 September and 27 September 1916.
85 *The Motor Cycle*, 2 August 1917, p. 108.
86 *Motor Cycling*, 25 September 1917, pp. 585-86.
87 Corcoran, ibid, p.69.
88 *The Graphic*, Christmas Supplement, 1916; *The Classic Motor Cycle*, August 1985, pp. 22-24.
89 Wyatt, ibid, p. 186.
90 Priestley, ibid, p. 16.
91 William E Sellers, *With Our Fighting Men: The Story of their Faith, Courage, Endurance in the Great War*, p. 76-77.
92 Dunn, ibid, p. 15.
93 *The Motor Cycle*, 24 May 1917, p. 464. This article endorses the good relationship between despatch riders and officers.
94 Watson, ibid, p. 4.
95 West, ibid, p. 1.
96 *The Motor Cycle*, 15 October 1914, p. 442.
97 *Motor Cycling*, 8 September 1914, p. 540.
98 Corcoran, ibid, pp. 17-18.
99 Strang, ibid (unpaginated).
100 *The Motor Cycle*, 24 May 1917, p. 464.
101 Tait, ibid, 24 August 1914.
102 Frederic Coleman, *From Mons to Ypres with French*, p. 201.
103 West, ibid, pp. 1-3, 14-15.
104 Anthony Clayton, *Forearmed: A History of the Intelligence Corps*, pp. 16-18, 22..
105 *Motor Cycling*, 25 December 1917, p. 119.
106 Foster, ibid, p. 6.
107 *Motor Cycling*, 8 December 1914, p. 130.
108 Watson, ibid, p. 6.
109 A Corbett-Smith, *The Retreat From Mons: By One Who Shared In It*, p. 164.
110 Mead, ibid, p. 21.
111 Lieutenant HAJ Lamb, "As You Were", p. 13.
112 Foster, ibid, p. 7.
113 Sir William Robertson, *From Private to Field Marshall*, pp. 211-12.

114 Hamilton Fyfe, "At Army Headquarters". Matania is more famous for two other illustrations, "Goodbye Old Man", which depicts a soldier sadly taking leave of a mortally wounded horse, and a painting of Private Henry Tandy evacuating a wounded soldier, an action for which Tandy received the VC. Hitler had a copy of this painting at Berchtesgaden, having recognised Tandy as the man who had had him in his sights, close enough up not to miss, but had spared his life. This extraordinary incident probably occurred at First Ypres rather than in 1918, as has heretofore been believed.

115 *The Motor Cycle*, 24 June 1915, p. 619.

116 Sproston, ibid, 18 December 1914.

117 Stanley Casson, *Steady Drummer*, p. 33.

118 Mead, ibid, p. 19.

119 *The Motor Cycle*, 3 September 1914, p. 296; *Motor Cycling*, 11 May 1915, pp. 27-28;

120 Dunn, ibid, p. 15.

121 Clayton, ibid, p. 17.

122 West, ibid, p. 10.

123 *The Motor Cycle*, 10 September 1914, p. 334.

124 *The Motor Cycle*, 2 August 1917, p. 108.

125 HE Etherington, 81/23/1, August-18 September 1915.

126 Davis, ibid, p. 231.

127 West, ibid, pp. 8, 120

128 *Motor Cycling*, 16 February 1915, p. 350.

129 Dunn, ibid, p. 87.

130 *Motor Cycling*, 27 October, 1914, p. 700. The youngest DR may have been KO Bathgate, who became a despatch rider for the RFC in 1915, aged fifteen years and eight months—*The Motor Cycle*, 16 August 1917, p. 151. Max Pemberton's fictive DR was a public schoolboy who had "got his colours for football": www.greatwardifferent.com/Great_War/Despatch_Rider/Despatch_Rider_01.htm.

    Wars were still seen as being won on the playing fields of Eton.

131 Corcoran, ibid, p. 17.

132 Frederic Coleman, *From Mons to Ypres with French*, p. 201.

133 "Sapper", *The Lieutenant and Others*, p. 7.

134 Watson, ibid, p. 31 .

135 *The Motor Cycle*, 28 January 1915, p. 90.

136 Best, ibid, 28/29 November 1914.

137 Davis, ibid, p. 229.

138 Mead, ibid, p. 1; Wood, ibid, p. 7. "Trade!" Joan Littlewood might satirise this development.

139 *The Motor Cycle*, 26 July 1917, p. 81.

140 Davis, ibid, p. 215.

141 *The Motor Cycle*, 2 August 1917, p. 108.

142 FW Hopps, 06/54/1.

143 Davis, ibid, p. 67.

144 *The Motor Cycle*, 16 August 1917, p. 159.

145 CE Allen, "A Motorcyclist at War", pp. 280-81.

146 Davis, ibid, pp. 60, 68.

147 *The Motor Cycle*, 27 January 1916, p. 71.

148 *Motor Cycling*, 30 June 1914, p. 268.

149 War Office, *Statistics of the Military Effort of the British Empire during the Great War 1914-1919*, p. 853.

150 *Motor Cycling*, 3 November 1914, p. 710; *The Motor Cycle*, 18 March 1915, front page.

151 *The Motor Cycle*, 29 October 1914, p. 482; *Motor Cycling*, 24 November 1914, p. 58.

152 *The Motor Cycle*, 18 March 1915, front page.

153 *The Motor Cycle*, 26 August 1915, front page.

154 *The Motor Cycle*, 22 June 1916, p. 587.

155 *The Motor Cycle*, 12 July 1917, front page.

156 *Motor Cycling*, 22 February 1916, p. 411.

157 *The Motor Cycle*, 3 February 1916, p. 116; 19 April 1917, p. 351.

158 *The Motor Cycle*, 4 April 1918, p. 334; 11 April 1918, p. 360; 18 April 1918, p. 385.

159 *The Motor Cycle*, 6 December 1917, p. 546.

160 *The Motor Cycle*, 15 April 1915, p. 370.

161 *Motor Cycling*, 27 August 1918, p. 274.

162 *The Motor Cycle*, 14 March 1918, p. 254.

163 *Motor Cycling*, 6 March 1917, front page; 27 November 1917, p. 45.

164 Macintosh spelled his name without the *k* that was added to his invention.

165 Ixion, ibid, p. 163.

166 *The Motor Cycle*, 22 October 1914, front page.

167 Ex 2337318, "Motorcyclist at War", p. 307.

168 Davis, ibid, p. 28.

169 FA McKenzie, "Winter in the West", www.greatwardifferent.com/Great_War/Winter_1915?Winter_1915.htm ; *Motor Cycling*, 27 June 1916, p. 159.

170 Davis, ibid, p. 90.

171 Foster, ibid, p. 6.

172 Lieutenant OH Best, 29 November 1914.

173 Best, ibid, 1 January 1915.

174 *The Motor Cycle*, 11 February 1915, p. 140.

175 Edith Wharton, *Fighting France: From Dunquerque to Belport*, pp. 47-48.

176 "Christmas Truce 1914-1999", www.hellfire-corner.demon.co.uk/chums.htm

177 Charles Carrington, *Soldier from the Wars Returning*, p. 156.

178 Watson, ibid, p. 268.

179 *Motor Cycling*, 18 January 1916, p. 300.

180 Grice, ibid, 16 November 1916, 25/27 January 1917.

181 DH Chisholm, *Memories: the wartime recollections of a Royal Signals despatch rider*, http://www.southampton.ac.uk/~mic/Dad/index.htm

182 Ex 2337318, ibid, p. 307.

183 CE Allen, "A Motorcyclist at War", p. 283-84.

184 I am deeply indebted to re-enactor Chris Roberts for sharing his wealth of information on DR apparel, and on much more.

185 Neil Walker, *The King's Shilling*.

186 *The Motor Cycle*, 4 February 1915, p. 98.

187 West, ibid, p. 10.

188 Paul Maze, *A Frenchman in Khaki*, p. 337.

189 Davis, ibid, p. 10.

190 Foster, ibid, p. 10.

191 Max Arthur, *Last Post*, p. 237. No disrespect at all to Mr Rayns, but his

testimony was made many years after the event, and a standard caveat for historians is that memory can fail after a much shorter interval.

192 Best, ibid.

193 *The Motor Cycle*, 18 February 1915, p. 160

194 Watson, ibid, p. 241.

195 JF Lucy, *There's a Devil in the Drum*, p. 113.

196 Tait, ibid, 26 August, 1 September 1914.

197 West, ibid, p. 12.

198 Tait, ibid, 6 September 1914.

199 WG Mead, "Forty Thousand Hours of War", p. 61.

200 *The Motor Cycle*, 27 January 1916, p. 71.

201 Douglas P Winnifrith, *The Church in the Fighting Line*, p. 28.

202 CE Allen, *Titch: The Founder's Tale*, pp. 96-97; "A Motorcyclist at War", p. 116.

203 BD Hankin, "Communication and Control of Military Forces", p. 68.

204 John Jackson, *Private 12768*, p. 205.

205 JFB Livesay, *Canada's Hundred Days*, p. 346.

206 Orsi, ibid, p. 11.

207 Jim Bailey, *The Sky Suspended*, p. 46.

208 Robin Neillands, *The Old Contemptibles: The British Expeditionary Force, 1914*, p. 149.

209 This despatch rider was captured according to *The War Illustrated*, Vol. VII, p. 2494; it seems more likely, though, that he was cut off from the Munsters by enemy forces—see Gary Sheffield and Dan Todman (eds), *Command and Control on the Western Front: The British Army's experience 1914-18*, p. 26.

210 The Munsters sold their lives and freedom dearly, though. For hours they held up an enemy force many times their number, allowing their companions to gain perhaps a dozen miles on enemy pursuers. By the time ammunition ran out there were fewer than 250 men, many of them wounded, left to surrender. They "were warmly congratulated by the Germans on the fine fight they had made". See S McCance, *History of the Royal Munster Fusiliers, Volume II*, pp. 115-19.

211 HFN Jourdain, *The Connaught Rangers, Volume II*, p. 412. Some of the Rangers and Fusiliers escaped, and constituted the bulk of the "Iron Twelve", who operated behind the German lines until captured and executed in February 1915. See Hedley Malloch, "Behind the Lines: The Story of the Iron Twelve", pp. 6-11.

Posed picture of policewomen arresting a "suspect". Women took over more and more formerly male roles through the war, and Margaret Damer Dawson, founder of the Women Police Service, provided the service with motorcycles. © Imperial War Museum (HU 69728).

A clearly posed photograph from very early in the war, of new volunteers and the motorcycles they "enlisted" with themselves. These chaps seem to exude the confidence of the class to which most early DRs belonged, as they study the maps that were sadly missing when they got to France. The bikes include a 3½HP (482cc) Ariel, (left), and 4HP (554cc) Bradbury (right).

By 1915 Triumphs and Douglases were specified for DRs of the Signals Corps, and rigorous training regimes established. British motorcycles stood up very well to the rough handling of war, and the often arduous conditions. On duty, though, DRs seldom carried rifles. © Imperial War Museum (HU 106764).

Outposts of Empire had to make do through the war. Rufus Scampton of the London Scottish Regiment, posted to Shanghai, stands by his Premier—an older model, like the motorcycle beside it, with direct drive from engine to wheel. Transmissions were usual by the time this photograph was taken (1916-18), though direct drive motorcycles were used on the Western Front until at least 1917, and possibly to the end. The voluminous mudguards of the time quickly clogged on the Western Front and were modified or even removed. © Imperial War Museum (HU 70962).

An officer of the RNAS Armoured Car Division, posted to Russia 1916-17. The Caucasus Mountains in the background look dramatic, but the roads took their toll of the motorcycles. The later pattern slim-line front mudguard is in evidence. The rider wears what looks to be a motoring dust-coat and puttees — non-standard items of clothing were widely used by DRs, especially before 1916. © Imperial War Museum (HU 72613).

A DR of the South African Brigade, attached to the 9th Division, 1915-16. Good detail of the Triumph and the DR's kit is evident in the cantilevered front fork spring (a weak point on the Triumph), later-pattern mudguard less prone to clogging, and belt final drive; the rider wears dust-goggles, map case, leather gaiters and gauntlets, and three-quarter-length mackintosh waterproof jacket issued in 1916. © Imperial War Museum (HU 68190).

In addition to despatches, DRs also carried pigeons from their lofts to the front line. More than two dozen birds might be stuffed into baskets on Don R's back, and, as one put it, the weight of "the load pulling and swaying at the straps used to cut into my shoulders so painfully".

A sidecar made the job much easier. American machines, like this Indian, were more sophisticated than British motorcycles, and had more powerful engines, but they were heavy and ungainly and no use off-road. Perhaps this man was bound for a central distribution point from which other DRs collected their pigeons, an arrangement that was put in place during the Somme battles.

Through the war women acted as DRs and drivers of cars and personnel- and freight-sidecar outfits all over the home front, but by 1918 they also were at work behind the front lines in France. The necessity of their adopting such mannish attire as trousers, as well as the sort of work they now did, helped advance the suffragette cause and gain votes for women after the war. This young woman belongs to the Women's Royal Air Force (WRAF), and her sidecar outfit is powered by a P&M 500cc single, the type used by all the air arms, and a solid motorcycle. The engine acts as a stressed member, replacing the front frame downtube, and the forks are noticeably robust. © Imperial War Museum (Q 12291).

Ms Ellen Soall, a modern-day WRAF, on a restored P&M from 1918. (Courtesy Mr Vernon Creek.)

Re-enactor Mr Chris Roberts poses with his restored Triumph in front of the Ulster Tower, Thiepval. He wears the blue-and-white brassard of the Signals Corps on both arms, as DRs did. The havelock he has unrolled from his service cap would have been useful on the famously hot first day of the Somme battles, and on the Great Retreat. (Courtesy Mr Chris Roberts and the Great War Society.)

Mr Roberts poses with his restored Douglas, next to the Triumph the most popular of Army DR mounts. (Courtesy Mr Chris Roberts, "Historic Scotland" and the Great War Society.)

5

Chariots of
Automatic Fire

AS EARLY AS 1888 one GH Waite, a cyclist who worked for the Humber Company, had constructed a three-seat quadricycle that mounted an air-cooled Maxim machinegun. Its suitability for warfare would seem to have been dire, as the angle of traverse was limited by the gunner's fixed position and—much more critically—the heads of the front two tandem-seated soldiers, directly in line of fire. Just before the turn of the century the French firm De Dion mounted their 1½ HP engine to the back of a sturdier quadricycle—think of a Victorian quad bike—a design that was licensed to Coventry cycle manufacturers Beeston, and in 1899 Frederick Simms, already well known for a magneto of his own design (see Chapter Two), demonstrated a Maxim machine gun fitted on a Beeston quadricycle at the Richmond show.[1] This "Motor Scout" had provision for carrying ammunition and a small steel shield and it made an impression, though no sales for Simms.

Other designs emerged, in the ad hoc way that the British Army often developed. In 1908 Sergeant—later Major—Northover of the Canadian Army mounted another Maxim on a Harley Davidson sidecar outfit, and this design was to go to war six years later, though built about a different motorcycle. Before then, by August 1911 at the latest, the 5th East Yorks Cyclists—and other bicycle units—were supported by a machinegun mounted on a light carriage with two wire-spoke cycle-type wheels and towed by a motorcycle.[2] But quadricycles and forecars, popular at the turn of the new hopeful century, were displaced by the sidecar through the first decade, so that by the time the Motor Machine Gun Service was designated as a unit of the Royal Field Artillery by Army Order 480, dated 12 November 1914, it was Sergeant Northover's sidecar design rather than any other that was specified.

Thanks in part to Northover, it is with the Canadian forces that the Motor Machine Gun Service has come to be associated. At the outset of the war

Canada sent a motor machinegun battery of 40 guns, fifteen of them supplied through the generosity of one JC Eaton of Toronto, philanthropy and the volunteer spirit evident here as everywhere in the sudden emergency of war and the popular sense of duty.[3] But it should be noted that at the 1914 Olympia show a prototype Scott solo, mounting a Laird-Menteyne machinegun, had made an appearance, a foretaste of things to come, as Scott was to make an impression in the early part of the war, though as a sidecar outfit and not a solo.[4]

Immediately the new service captured the popular imagination, as tanks were to capture it later. German car-mounted machineguns "did great execution" in the invasion of Belgium,[5] and a British armoured car was deployed with impressive effectiveness against an Uhlan patrol on 16 September,[6] these actions both apparently confirming the value of the mobile machinegun. "Imagine the great possibilities of a small, fast, and easily handled vehicle mounting a quick-firing gun for short range work!" proclaimed one excited leader writer, Geoffrey Smith, editor of *The Motor Cycle*.[7] People got carried away by the new machine's potential: "Protected behind almost impregnable steel armor plate, the driver may dash ahead of the advancing lines and enable the gunner, almost completely protected, to mow down the ranks of the enemy with a sweeping stream of rifle [sic] bullets, played along a line of men much as one would play a stream of water from a fire hose."[8] The ability of the Motor Machine Gun Service to rapidly concentrate forces was highlighted in the propaganda film *Britain Prepared*.[9] But the extent and effectiveness of the Service's use would depend on local circumstances and the tactics these permitted, and trenchlock did not favour it.

Before military limitations were realised, the motorcycle industry had responded in a way that reflected popular enthusiasm. Within weeks of the war's outbreak, 532cc Scott- and 6 HP Enfield sidecar-outfits had been constructed, and soon afterward a Zenith outfit was too.[10] Like the Enfield, the sidecar component of the Zenith incorporated a shield for the gunner and allowed the gun—a Vickers Light Machine Gun—to be fired backward or forward and was "immensely strong", an essential requirement for a mobile gun platform, carrying a very heavy payload of gun, gunner and 2,000 rounds of ammunition.[11] A Matchless outfit likewise provided for firing forward or backward,[12] and by year's end Clynos were added to the stable—it is these that were to become the standard machine. The Australian Imperial Force used the 6 HP New Hudson,[13] while from Canada came an Indian-powered outfit carrying a Colt machinegun.[14] At this time the Indian factory had an assembly plant in Toronto and many Canadians favoured the powerful 1000cc V-twin, though its weight, and difficulty of obtaining spares (after the U-boat campaigns opened), were largely to relegate it later. There was great experimentation, and many detail differences emerged, though all outfits seem to have had quick-release interchangeable wheels, with a spare mounted on the sidecar, to minimise potentially critical delays caused by punctures over broken and iron-splintered ground.

Clearly the vision was of sidecar-outfits going into action with guns blazing in a glorious modern-day chariot-charge; but though the gunner was shielded in either attack or fighting retreat, the driver had no such protection (apart from partial shielding on a prototype Matchless outfit),[15] which rather curtailed the chariot's potential. In the real world of war the weight of heavy shields militated against the sidecar's advantage of speed in the role in which it eventually best served, and also made it harder to camouflage or conceal. The gun's limited arc of traverse, about 90 degrees,[16] was another shortcoming if shooting on the move, and if a wider track could increase the arc without imperilling the driver's brains, it compromised the sidecar's

In the nick of time! A sidecar Maxim, hurried to a favourable height, might hold back the enemy until reinforcements arrived.

Great things were expected of the Motor Machine Guns in 1914; they were not delivered until 1918.[19]

virtues of narrowness and ability to turn in a small circle.[17] Bat Motorcycles patented a sidecar-mounted turntable that increased the arc of fire, but this never saw production, as the Bat factory was soon given over to munitions manufacture.[18]

The Motor Cycle had "no doubt that the armoured sidecar has come to stay",[20] and editor Geoffrey Smith was to use his office as an enlistment centre for the Motor Machine Gun Service until conscription in 1916, and champion the service to the very end. But cooler military heads saw problems early on, realising that, for all the "great execution" carried out by German mobile machineguns in Belgium, such outfits' best "purpose was only to reconnoitre and not to engage in serious battle".[21] The military reflected that sidecars might be better employed as rapid gun delivery systems rather than as mobile gun platforms, with a three- or possibly four-man crew, two on the cycle, the other(s) in the "chair". Though the first Zenith had the sidecar chassis triangulated and "designed thoroughly to resist the recoil of the gun",[22] it also incorporated a "spade", a sidecar stand driven into the ground to steady the outfit, implying that already the sidecar was envisaged as a static rather than a moving gun platform.[23] The Enfield was designed to have two legs of a sidecar-mounted tripod lowered to the ground, providing a stable and more effective static gun.

Reflecting a different way of military thinking, a Premier outfit had all three feet of the tripod secured to sockets in the platform by quick-release spring-locked lugs, enabling tripod and gun to be dismounted in less than ten seconds for use *off* the sidecar;[24] this was one of the most important and enduring features of the system, modest though the change might have seemed when it emerged.

The envisaged role had gone from firing on the move—which could not possibly have been accurate, due to both ground irregularities and recoil on a non-stable gun platform—through fire-and-movement-type tactics, to a gun delivery system pure and simple, the crew carrying gun and tripod into position: in modern parlance, "shoot and scoot" tactics. Further evidence of imaginative military thinking, in the very first months of the war that saw air power become the Third Arm, resulted in a mounting that allowed the gun to be tilted to the vertical for anti-aircraft work, operated by the gunner lying prone beneath the sidecar.[25]

In mid-1916 Joffre was lauding in the *New York Times Tribune* (courting American voters in this election year): "The motor cycle armed with a small *mitrailleuse* is much more useful than the armoured motor car";[26] but that was hardly saying much by then, when position warfare had just about relegated all mobility. More than a year earlier it was plain that the best use of the sidecar was to bring gun and crew as close to the action as possible, the outfit being located nearby and camouflaged by straw or similar. "We never count upon operating a machine gun from the sidecar chassis", Captain Keene of the RFA reported after trenchlock set in.[27] Designs to optimise such tactics turned the sidecar from a massively built gun platform into a spare construction that easily was detached from the cycle, the spare wheel being fitted onto the attachment spindle in order to create a light gun carriage.[28] This had obvious advantages when, by 1917 at the latest, procedure saw the sidecar left 1,500 yards behind the firing line[29]—or so Captain Louis Keene says; but the good Captain elsewhere betrays his testimony as suspect; he sounds more like a PR agent for an army then being pressed hard, his audience America. Perhaps 1,500 yards was an average distance, not a military stipulation—or even an offhand estimate. In the ironic way of war, the spindly-wheeled towed gun carriage of pre-war years had re-emerged, and one can imagine an unreconstructed Old Contemptible crowing, "Told yer so!" But the gun carriage, though narrow, was still an encumbrance in a trench, so most guns and tripods were "humped" into position, and the robust Clyno outfit, the mainstay of the service, was not easily converted into a two-wheeled "light gun carriage".

One must not underestimate the value of propaganda and morale, though. Sidecar-mounted machineguns featured in the 1915 film, *Britain Prepared*, and *The Motor Cycle* announced that after watching this, "Anybody who may have doubted the efficacy of sidecars in modern warfare will quickly change his views".[30]

The Navy's first motor machine gun sidecar outfits were all powered by the unconventional two-stroke Scott twin, the sidecar custom made by Alfred Scott to a design worked out by him and Sir Arthur Dawson of Vickers. The aim was a mobile gun platform, the gunner protected by a steel shield against enemy fire, but the driver exposed. This design was to generalise across the range of machinegun outfits in the early months, as has been seen, and might appear to reveal a puzzling perception of priority; but an effective shield would have "blinded" the driver so he had to trust to luck and the firepower of his passenger to keep enemy heads down. Ammunition was stowed behind the gunner, while the accompanying limber combination carried a lot more (and only one crewman, the rider, to allow for the greater payload).[31]

Such was early enthusiasm that the War Office's order, on top of the Navy's, threatened to overwhelm Scott's output potential; and it was partly for this reason, but also because doubts were emerging about the Scott's robustness and suitability, that other motorcycle factories were approached and invited to tender. Matchless, Premier and Zenith, and some other manufacturers, all of rugged four-strokes, developed prototypes, but it was Clyno, and to a lesser extent Enfield, that supplied production machines to the BEF.

Uniquely, it seems, the Australian Imperial Force specified a 6 HP Hudson combination.[32] Whether any Hudsons took to the field is doubtful, for the factory went over to munitions manufacturing quite early in the war. (It's possible that Australia opted for the Hudson because native son George Pattison had set an ante-bellum speed record on a Hudson.[33])

In 1915, as it did with despatch rider mounts, the Army settled on a standard motorcycle combination for the MMGS, though any other outfits already supplied were retained. Choice of the Clyno is supposed to have been made by Winston Churchill after his observing trials of several contenders for selection. The winning Clyno used a 744cc V-twin rated at 5 – 6 HP with special factory sidecar designed, in consultation with Vickers (as had been Scott's sidecar), specifically for its role. There were six spring clips on the bed of the sidecar, designed to securely engage the tripod feet of the machinegun so that the gun could be mounted facing either backward or forward and—of increasing importance—quickly and easily dismounted in order to be carried into position.

Though the name Clyno had been derived from "inclined pulley", a design patented by Frank and Alwyn Smith to improve belt-drive efficiency, by 1914 the Clyno used all-chain transmission, primary- and final-drive both fully enclosed in allegedly "dustproof" casings—possibly the first use of aluminium chain cases—and with a cush drive to smooth power delivery. It was an extremely advanced machine, with a kickstarter and two-speed epicyclic gear in a housing behind the engine. It was designed as a combination rather than as a solo with sidecar stuck on: when most sidecars used three points of connection to the motorcycle frame, the Clyno used four, all snug, secure socket fittings, an important asset over the rough ground of the battlefield. Another first for the firm was interchangeable, quickly-detachable wheels, and a spare was added, mounted on the offside rear of the sidecar, in the space between it and the motorcycle, while still leaving room for a pillion passenger. The front forks appear uncommonly robust, and the steering head was a heavy casting that extended far down over the front down-tube and back over the parallel upper and lower top-tubes. All told, a machine to compete with the best from America, and through 1915-16 Clyno was building about 100 of these outfits a year, the factory working eighteen hours a day. It also was working on aero engines, and, in 1917, manufacturing an 8 HP JAP-engined combination for the Russian Army; the Russians took some 5 – 6 HP models too. Later the War Office commissioned a larger combination, one with an in-line liquid-cooled four-cylinder engine, but the war ended before this reached production.[34]

Despite being sidelined by Clyno, Scott did not give up on supplying the War Office, and developed an extraordinary prototype in early 1915. Nicknamed the Guncar, this was rather like an open-top car with the nearside front wheel removed and the nearside rear moved a few inches forward of the offside rear (to provide the "lead" necessary for acceptable steering and handling on an asymmetric vehicle). Suspension was car-type, wishbones providing wheel movement along with sturdiness of mounting; the wheels were discs, adding further rigidity. Driver and passenger both sat in the sidecar, and controls were car-type, including steering wheel. Ammunition could be stored behind the seats. The 5 HP liquid-cooled two-stroke twin used rotary induction valves and quickly-detachable separate engine barrels, very high specifications for the time (rotary valves were not fitted to everyman two-strokes until the 1960s). The engine was mounted behind the front wheel, with a three-speed gearbox, a conventional enough arrangement, but it drove the rear wheel by cardan shaft, which ensured low maintenance and long-term reliability. Both seats were hammock-type, made of interlocking leather rings, and the passenger's could be uncoupled at its upper fitment and refitted forward to allow the passenger to face backward; likewise, the gun could be mounted pointing either fore or aft. Scott still was thinking of machineguns firing on the run, but even before position warfare this idea was more dashing than realistic and, though two pre-production models were delivered for evaluation—they were reported to have "extreme stability and the manoeuvrability of a sidecar outfit"—the Guncar never saw production.[35] (After the war, the design was presented as the civilian Sociable, which also never got past the prototype stage.)

At least one other prototype emerged before the limitations of motor machineguns in position warfare became evident. The make so far is unknown, but it had "very large wheels and tyres, a disc wheel for the sidecar, and a four-speed gearbox", and was capable of "nearly 60 mph",[36] which would have been a genuinely impressive speed for any motorcycle combination for many years afterward.

Training and Organisation

The military had seen through popular illusion early on, yet was in no way dismissive of this modern weapon, again giving the lie to any notion of hidebound "donkey-wallopers" being in charge. It was the Royal Navy that initially endorsed the armed sidecar outfit, and sent a Motor Machine Gun Squadron—the service was thus organised at the time—to Gallipoli in March 1915.[37] They also were deployed in support of the Belgian coastal defences at Dixmude, where according to a contemporary report, they gave "proof of great activity and efficiency".[38] The Navy was to maintain its own Armoured Car Division, which included five squadrons of sidecar combinations,[39] but the Army quickly copied. A sidecar, "being small and consequently easy to conceal ... would prove invaluable for scouting work, in covering retreats, and for individual sorties upon the enemy". The ability to turn in a tight circle was seen as a significant asset in mobile warfare, as was ease of concealment.[40] Training commenced at Bisley immediately, and "after but two months' training [recruits] are thoroughly efficient, smart, orderly and disciplined".[41]

At the outset, the Navy's five squadrons each "theoretically comprised twenty-four gun-carrying machines organised into six sections". But all was in a state of flux in the frenzy of a peaceful nation organising for war: within the same account one reads that each section contained "four limber combinations with spare ammunition, four solo machines and one Ford car. The headquarters comprised a lorry and four solo machines while the first section had an extra staff car, section B2 a wireless and C2 an ambulance".[42] Organisation of solos and wireless indicates overlap with the Signals service, whose lorry could be used in recovering machines that had broken down or been damaged in action.

The Army—as distinct from the Navy—had its Motor Machine Gun Service established before December 1914, when *The Motor Cycle* reported:

> Each motor machine gun battery consists of sixty-four men, though six extra men are kept in touch. There are six gun teams, each team having three motorcycles and sidecars—one carrying a gun, another gun mountings (but without a gun) to take the place of the former in case of necessity, and the third carrying ammunition and other necessary impedimenta. There are six riders of solo machines in close attendance, who act mainly as scouts, three mechanics, and nine car drivers with ammunition, etc, making up the total.[43]

Organisation was still plastic, and soon afterward the MMGS battery consisted of three sections and a headquarters. Headquarters comprised two subalterns and three orderlies, each motorcycle-mounted, as well as a commanding officer who travelled in a staff car, accompanied by a driver and an orderly; attached to headquarters was a three-ton lorry carrying two drivers and two privates. Each of the three sections included two armed sidecar outfits, two replacements and two limbers; each was commanded by a solo-mounted sergeant and was accompanied by a one-and-a-half ton lorry, carrying a driver, a corporal, a private and a mechanic.[44] In the final days the MMGS was formed into brigades of four batteries each.

Training comprised a two-month course, including instruction in control and maintenance, which for novices might be preceded by basic instruction in driving a sidecar outfit. In an early exercise in field manoeuvres one of the three sections was ordered forward—led by its solo-mounted scout—while the other two sections covered the flanks, in order to allow infantry to retire and reform,[45] a role endorsed by Major Casserly.[46] This sort of work could not have taken place in the real war that developed but perhaps the exercise suggests the embryo of all-arms cooperation that marked the successful end of the war, in which the sidecars played a sometimes-important role. Like that of despatch riders, the training regime of the MMGS appears to have been pleasant: training finished at four o'clock, after which "we can do what we like until 9:30 PM". "Altogether, we could not wish for a better life; everyone enjoys it [training], and life never once becomes monotonous ... while everyone who can ride a motor cycle will nearly be certain of being at the Front within two months"—the war might not have been over by Christmas, but in 1915 men remained anxious to get out before it finished.[47] By now the awful conditions of trench life were known, so latter-day notions that the voluntary spirit was down to ignorance are simplistic.

The value of machinegun-armed combinations to the sort of guerrilla tactics proposed by Major Casserly is obvious, but position warfare—and the increasing availability of Lewis guns after 1916—meant that "methods of transportation [of machineguns] ceased to be of primary importance", one Captain Jebens subsequently reports—at least on the Western Front.[48] "Elsewhere [though], and most particularly in Egypt, Palestine, East Africa and Mesopotamia, the mobility of the units was of great value, and they saw considerable action in those theatres",[49] some details of which can be found in Chapter Seven.

On the Western Front, by Loos there were eighteen MMGS battalions serving with the BEF, and the War Office's intention was "to provide one battery of the Motor Machine Gun Service to each infantry division, one to each brigade of the Royal Field Artillery and the Royal Horse Artillery".[50] Up until April 1915 seven MMGS batteries were sent to the Western Front, far short of the War Office's target, but by now it was evident that trenchlock had changed the envisaged role, and after creation of the Machine Gun Corps in October that year the MMGS was absorbed as the Machine Gun Corps (Motors)—though confusingly, control of the MMGS (this title will be retained for clarity's sake) was now under the various Army Corps, and not the MGC;[51] previously control had been Divisional. Most MMGS batteries on the Western Front were disbanded through 1916, those retained remaining constituted as batteries of eighteen combinations and either six or eight solos, each battery mustering six Vickers machinegun-mounted sidecars and with other vehicles supplying ammunition and backup.

Performance

Though position warfare had robbed them of their greatest strength, the motor machineguns were sent to the Western Front, where under Corps command they were used as a mobile reserve, deployed to reinforce resistance as required, and often to where separate armies adjoined, always a point of potential vulnerability.[52] A subtle advantage of the outfits' mobility was drawing the enemy's fire and leading to his expending shells as the outfits moved on.[53] This was no small contribution in the early years, when German preponderance in materiel output contrasted with the dearth of shells on the British side. One MMGS team rendered "invaluable service" at Hill 60, during the Battle of Neuve Chapelle,[54] from which an officer's report states:

> These machines were absolutely to be depended upon all through the operations. Their carrying capacities being great; at times the machines were overloaded with wounded infantry, especially [during] the withdrawal from Frémicourt on the 24th when not only did they carry guns, full equipment and ammunition, but as many as four men. Some of the machines which were literally perforated with shrapnel still carried on, great credit being due to the ASC mechanics....

"By the opening of the Battle of Loos on 25 September 1915, there were 18 MMG Batteries with the BEF.... Five of them were engaged at Loos".[55]

However, the machines' limitations in static warfare had become evident. Early in the new year Sergeant Artificer Longfield, of No 1 Motor Machine Gun Battery, had realised that there was no opportunity to use sidecar-mounted machineguns in movement: "we are on the mobile reserve"[56]—though of course as such they were potentially very useful, as they were to show. After they were incorporated into the Machine Gun Corps, some units were reserved to War Office use.

The decision by the Navy to send four of its five squadrons to Gallipoli—keeping one (No 13) at home—is even more puzzling than the Army's decision to send solo motorcycles there, and reflects on the incompetent management of the whole Gallipoli campaign. The sidecars could not be used in the rocky sandy confines and their crews became machine gunners plain and simple. No 10 Squadron subsequently was sent to Egypt and the others, Nos 9, 11 and 12, were broken up.[57] Of those batteries retained by the War Office after formation of the Machine Gun Corps one each went to Italy and Palestine, and they also saw action in Mesopotamia and East Africa, and in India, where at least part of the objective was "to put the fear of God into the native chief and tribesmen",[58] who possibly had been encouraged in their truculence by the Irish Easter Rising.[59] Though in Egypt, Palestine and Mesopotamia traffic often was impeded by sands, pegged-down wire netting could make desert routes passable and "the mobility of the units was of great value". Fortunately, five batteries were retained on the Western Front,[60] for the MMGS was to come into its own in 1918.

The Germans had realised the value of mobile machineguns and seen their value in open warfare in 1914 and later when, in the Caporetto offensive, they used sidecar-mounted machineguns to help breach the Tagliamento defence line.[61] While they seem to have had as much misplaced enthusiasm for the military potential of this new weapon as the British had, they also seem to have been more pragmatic, and confined their output to a simple platform sidecar designed to mount the Maxim heavy machinegun with its iron sled and carry a three-man crew (driver, pillion passenger and gunner in the sidecar). They relied mostly if not entirely on the advanced NSU 7.5 HP 1000cc V-twin, a motorcycle of fabled Germanic excellence, with effective coil spring suspension front and rear and two—later three—speed gearboxes. Less excitable than the British the Germans may have been, yet they were not immune from beguiling dreams of modern-day chariot-charges: they too provided for mounting the machinegun facing either backward or forward on the sidecar, and fitted a small shield for the gunner, at least in the early months.[62]

When Ludendorff launched Operation Michael, on 21 March 1918, the guns of the British MMGS had been dismounted and distributed in the trenches, but the service was still extant. It had been deployed briefly at Cambrai a few months before,[63] after the tanks had broken into the enemy's lines and driven his forces back, offering the tantalising possibility of a breakthrough—which, of course, the MMGS would have been perfectly suited to exploit. The service was far from rusty as a consequence of this action, and units were all armed and mobilised by 5:00 AM on 22 March—a tribute to the organisational skills of the always-maligned Staff. The outfits were used for reconnaissance but chiefly in fighting rearguard actions, in order to buy time to retreat, and "the contribution which some Canadian motor machine-gunners put in was of the greatest value. It saved many British lives. It accounted for many Germans. It tided over a number of difficult moments during the battle". Correspondent Hamilton Fyfe reports spectacular moments of courage and self-sacrifice. When one battery ran out of ammunition some of the gunners charged the advancing Germans, using gun barrels as clubs, in order to allow the precious cars and sidecar outfits to get away.[64] Philip Gibbs describes how

> they fought through ten days and nights, with less than twenty hours' sleep all that time. These cars near Maricourt gathered together 150 men who had been cut off, and held the enemy at bay, covering the withdrawal of some of our heavy guns and Tanks.... One of [three survivors] mounted a motor-cycle and brought back the cars and took back the wounded.... [Apparently Lieutenant John Douglas Seton—see below.] These cars have been in scores of fights, and one day their history must be fully written.[65]

General Currie, in his order of the day on 27 March, acknowledged the service's contribution: "Our Motor Machine Gun Brigade has already played a most gallant part and once again covered itself in glory".[66]

Any commander could have been tempted to overplay the value of any asset in those dark days, but the effectiveness of the MMGS may be gauged from a single page of *The London Gazette*, where no fewer than four of its men appear, two awarded the DCM, two the MM. One of these, Lieutenant John Douglas Seton, was decorated

> For conspicuous gallantry in action. He was severely wounded and burnt by a shell which struck one of the two armoured cars of which he was in charge. In spite of his injuries he helped to turn the car round, under heavy machine-gun fire, and led it on his motor cycle back to our lines. He set a fine example of determination and endurance to his men.[67]

The deployment of the MMGS in this action may not have been widely advertised; possibly kept secret at the time: even the editor of *The Motor Cycle*, who had recruited for the formation, seems to have been ignorant until months later: "To a great many people the use of the motor machine gun batteries on the battle front of France came as a surprise.... The arm ... which up to the present has not had the opportunity of especially distinguishing itself ... made its appearance on August 8th". This date marks the Battle of Amiens, which permanently turned the German tide, and as the editorial says the MMGS played a part in that critical battle. In preparation, a "special mobile force of two motor machine-gun brigades and a Canadian Cyclist Battalion ... was ordered to follow up the success along the line of the Amiens-Roye road", and this they did, "render[ing] most valuable and gallant service.... As the attack progressed, our cavalry and armoured cars and motor machine-guns pushed on ahead and played havoc among the retreating Germans".[68]

So in the end the MMGS played an important role, from helping to stem Ludendorff's rampage through to the end of the Hundred Days, when its soldiers brought their now hard-won experience into play. The official Canadian war correspondent, Roland Hill, reported:

> The Motor Machine Gun Brigade flanked our cavalry and kept the Boche on the right from rallying.... They dashed up side roads and enfiladed the enemy as he tried to dig new machine gun posts and they disgorged crews at every vantage point who made little nests of their own and caught the Boche as he went over the sky-line.[69]

According to Michael Holden, the Canadian Motor Machine Gun Brigade—we may tentatively extrapolate to all such units in the BEF—"are an excellent example of a unit that was able to adapt new tactics and make an immediate and successful transition from trench warfare to open style combat".[70] In the Spring Offensive they provided "defensive-style infantry support", helping to "stabilize the line with firepower in a number of locations". Through the summer the unit's strength was increased and training regimes designed "to teach the men ... to think and operate in open warfare setting"—the importance of training to the Learning Curve again in evidence. The men were drilled in flanking and pincer movement, direct and indirect fire, and collaboration with other units, fitting into the All Arms strategy that characterised the British victory: at Morlancourt they worked successfully with Whippets; elsewhere with cavalry.[71] On 2 September they took part in the decisive action at the Drocourt-Quéany sector of the Hindenburg Line.[72] The Canadian MMGB was incorporated into GHQ Reserve for subsequent secondment to either the British or French armies and at the Battle of Amiens, along with trench mortars, they "provided covering fire while French infantry advanced on German positions", a nice little cipher of unified command and Allied politics in action. Rapid deployment and re-deployment was an intrinsic strength of such mobile units once the advance began, and they proved their worth in reconnaissance, "exploit[ing] success, forming defensive flanks ... holding and consolidating ground, and flanking and overcoming strong points". As the Germans pulled back the speed and manoeuvrability of the sidecar outfits sometimes enabled them to direct enfilade fire.[73] Like the rest of the British Army they were always on the Learning Curve, discovering as they advanced how best to collaborate with artillery, infantry, cavalry and bicycle- and motorcycle-mounted troops: in one instance a motorcycle scout, Private Bebeau, drew the fire of German machine gunners, who then were dealt with by British mortars and machineguns.[74]

Through the war, there were 25 Motor Machine Gun Batteries, as the following table details,[75] but some of these never saw action.

1. Operating on the Western Front by Spring 1915. Absorbed into 1 MMG Brigade, 7 November 1918.
2. Operating on the Western Front by Spring 1915. Disbanded October 1916.
3. Operating on the Western Front by Spring 1915. Attached to 24th Division between 30 October and 23 November 1915. Moved to Italy October 1917. Transferred to 16th Indian Division in India, January 1918.
4. Operating on the Western Front by Spring 1915. Absorbed into 1 MMG Brigade, 7 November 1918.
5. Operating on the Western Front by Spring 1915. Disbanded October 1915.
6. Operating on the Western Front by Spring 1915. Absorbed into 1 MMG Brigade, 7 November 1918.
7. Operating on the Western Front by Spring 1915. Joined 3rd Cavalry Division 30 March 1916, became GHQ Troops 18 July 1917. Attached to 9th Division between 7 October and 8 November 1918.

8. Attached to 14th Division in England, moving with the Division to the Western Front, and left 5 November 1916. Joined 1st Cavalry Division 18 March 1916, became GHQ Troops 23 October 1917.
9. Attached to 12th Division in England, moving with the Division to the Western Front, and left 20 June 1915, to join II ANZAC Corps.
10. (Scotch Battery) Attached to 9th Division between 3 April 1915 and 11 June 1916. Disbanded October 1916.
11. Attached to 11th Division in England, but did not embark with the Division for Gallipoli. Joined 15th Division and moved to the Western Front. Left to join I Corps on 22 July 1916. Joined 1st Division between 19 July and 17 October 1917, then moved to Italy. Returned to Western Front December 1917. Attached to 9th Division between 7 October and 8 November 1918. Absorbed into 1 MMG Brigade, 7 November 1918.
12. Attached to 17th Division in England on 10 July 1915, and moved to the Western Front. Left to join X Corps on 7 May 1916. Joined 1st Division between 19 July and 17 October 1917, then moved to Italy. Returned to Western Front December 1917.
13. Attached to 10th Division in England from 4 May 1915, but did not embark with the Division for Gallipoli. Joined 19th Division and moved to the Western Front. Left on 7 March 1916 to join 33rd Division; left on 9 May 1916 to join VIII Corps. Disbanded November 1916.
14. Attached to 20th Division in England, moving with the Division to the Western Front, and left 22 April 1916. Joined I ANZAC Corps. Attached to 1st Division between 19 July and 17 October 1917. By January 1918, was with 5th (Mhow) Division of Indian Army at Jubbulpore.
15. Attached to 18th Division in England, moving with the Division to the Western Front, and left 9 May 1916. Joined VII Corps. By January 1918, was with 1st (Peshawar) Division of Indian Army in India.
16. Attached to 37th Division in England, moving with the Division to the Western Front, and left 9 May 1916. Joined VII Corps. Disbanded October 1917.
17. Moved to Egypt in January 1917. Was equipped with 5 Studebaker armoured cars, moving into Palestine April 1917. Redesignated 15 Light Armoured Motor Battery in June 1917.
18. In France by February 1916, but transferred to IX Corps in Mediterranean theatre in March 1916. Returned to the Western Front by end of that year, but disbanded around September 1917.
19. Attached to 33rd Division from 9 November 1915, but moved independently to the Western Front. Joined 30th Division 10 February 1916, and moved to 18th Division 6 June 1916. By January 1918, was with 4th (Quetta) Division of Indian Army, in India.

20. Became 13 Light Armoured Motor Battery in England in June 1916.
21. Moved to IX Corps in Mediterranean theatre in March 1916.
22. Formed April 1916 in India and attached to 4th (Rawalpindi) Brigade in 2nd (Rawalpindi) Division.
23. Formed in India
24. Operating on the Western Front by Spring 1916. Disbanded November 1916.
25. Established in India, in May 1917. Moved to Egypt July 1917. Disbanded January 1918.

Despite relative success in 1918, the MMGS had already been seen as redundant, as the following table of personnel shows:

Date	O/Ranks	Officers	Total
Jan 1915	459	37	496
Dec 1915	2,963	169	3,132
Apr 1916	3,578	141	3,719
Mar 1918	1,767	152	1,919
May 1918	2,255	146	2,401

The peak of April 1916, months after the shortcomings of the service in position warfare had been recognised, merely shows the inertia of huge bureaucracies like the British Army. The increase of almost 25 percent after the Spring Offensive may seem modest, but the Army was scraping the barrel for men then, and the real need was for infantry and artillery. After the Spring Offensive figures remain essentially constant to the end of the war—the service had a total of 2,396 personnel in November.[76]

Though the MMGS fell short of expectations of the early days, what didn't, through that entire disenchanting war? It was only in the last months that sidecar machineguns came into their own. Holden's praise for them echoes that of war correspondents Philip Gibbs and Hamilton Fyfe. Yet Fyfe also inadvertently confirms the redundancy of the outfits through most of the war: "The unit had not yet been in action when it was suddenly called upon to take part in fighting some of the rearguard actions required for the protection of our armies as they fell back [in the Spring Offensive]. Its machine-guns were actually in the trench system when the call came".[77] This is a fair comment on a service whose potential could not be realised until the conditions of war changed to suit the strengths of its motorcycle combinations: rapid deployment and localised concentration of firepower.

These strengths at first appear to fall far short of those of the tank, which took the MMGS's place in the popular imagination—as well as their men: the Tank Corps absorbed most of the personnel of disbanded MMGS batteries after 1916. Yet historians have tended to exaggerate the value of the tank (especially those historians fixated on "hidebound" generals), and overlook the Motor Machine Guns. These never could have been war-winning weapons in their own right; but neither were tanks, and, unlike tanks, the Motor Machine Guns had speed and flexibility, which in some instances may have been of more urgent need than tanks' greater firepower in supporting the far more effective firepower of artillery. Certainly, when integrated into an all-arms offensive the sidecars proved their modest worth. Unlike the tank and the aeroplane, though, their belligerent value was unique to a single war, at least as far as Britain was concerned: "In 1922, the Tanks Corps absorbed the MGC(M) completely and the Motor Machine Gun units disappeared from the British army's order of battle".[78] By 1930 the army saw no future role for them.[79]

The German army, however, always more mindful of the lessons of 1918, mounted machineguns on their superb BMW R71 sidecar outfits in the Thirties, when Hitler was rearming. These outfits, which had sidecar-wheel drive through limited-slip-differential to give unrivalled off-road performance, and similarly equipped R75s, played an important role in Blitzkrieg, so it's not quite true to say that motorcycle machineguns were unique to the Great War, nor to discount their tactical value. Long before Hitler did the more-or-less honourable thing, though, Speer had seen to it that the ruinously expensive BMW outfit—and the tracked NSU *Kettenkraftrad*—had been displaced by the *Kubelwagen*, the Nazi Jeep.[80]

Endnotes

1 David Fletcher, *War Cars: British Armoured Cars in the First World War*, pp. 4-5; *The Motor Cycle*, 1 October 1914.
2 Postcard "PB 108", Peter Smith private collection.
3 Logan Marshall, *A History of the Nations and Empires Involved and a Study of the Events Culminating in The Great Conflict*, http://www.gutenberg.org/dirs/etext03/ecigc10.txt.
4 Jeff Clew, "The Sound of Something Special", p. 1535.
5 *The Times History of the War*, Vol. I, 368, 384.
6 *The War Illustrated*, Vol. I, p. 271; Charles Messenger, *Call to Arms: The British Army 1914-18*, p. 176.
7 *The Motor Cycle*, 17 September 1914, front page.
8 Marshall, ibid.
9 *The Motor Cycle*, 6 January 1916, p. 17.
10 *The Motor Cycle*, 24 December 1914, p. 703.
11 *Motor Cycling*, 22 December 1914, p. 176.
12 Ixion, *Motorcycle Cavalcade*, illustration between pages 144 and 145.
13 *The Motor Cycle*, 13 May 1915, p. 469.
14 *The Motor Cycle*, 14 January 1915, p. 29.
15 *The Motor Cycle*, 18 February 1915, p. 154.
16 *The Motor Cycle*, 11 February 1915, p. 124.
17 *The Motor Cycle*, 11 February 1915, p. 124; 24 February 1916, p. 195.

18 *The Motor Cycle*, 24 February 1916, p. 193.

19 *Motor Cycling*, 1 September 1914.

20 *The Motor Cycle*, 14 January 1915, front page.

21 *The Times History of the War*, Vol. I, p. 368. The army brass were far from immune to daft ideas, though, right into the Second World War when Monty came up with a notion "that Sten guns should be mounted on a swivel arrangement on the handlebars of all military motorcycles. The thought of motorcyclists riding into battle with Sten guns blazing must have excited him"—CE Allen, "A Motorcyclist at War", p. 284.

22 *Motor Cycling*, 22 December 1914, p. 176.

23 *The Motor Cycle*, 24 December 1914, p. 703.

24 *The Motor Cycle*, 24 December 1914, p. 710, and 31 December 1914, p. 735.

25 *The Motor Cycle*, 4 February 1915, p. 104; 11 February 1915, p. 125.

26 *The Motor Cycle*, 8 June 1916, front page.

27 *The Motor Cycle*, 31 May 1917, p. 499.

28 *The Motor Cycle*, 17 February 1916, p. 154; 8 June 1916, p. 547.

29 *The Motor Cycle*, 31 May 1917, p. 499.

30 *The Motor Cycle*, 6 January 1916, p. 17.

31 Fletcher, ibid, p. 54.

32 *The Motor Cycle*, 13 May 1915, p. 469.

33 *The Motor Cycle*, 13 May 1915, p. 469; Frank Glendinning, "Engineers Extraordinary", pp. 1176-77.

34 David Burgess Wise, "Churchill's Choice", pp. 292-94.

35 Fletcher, ibid, pp. 58-60; Jeff Clew, "The Sound of Something Special", p. 1537.

36 *The Motor Cycle*, 10 June 1915, p. 561.

37 *The Long, Long Trail*, www.1914-1918.net/mmg.htm.

38 *The Times History of the World*, Vol. XII, pp. 71-72.

39 Fletcher, ibid, pp. 54, 91.

40 *The Motor Cycle*, 31 December 1914, p. 727; 14 January 1915, front page; 11 February 1915, p. 124; 11 March 1915, p. 231.

41 *The Motor Cycle*, 11 March 1915, p. 228.

42 Fletcher, ibid, p. 54.

43 *The Motor Cycle*, 3 December 1914, p. 621.

44 Bruce Gudmundsson, *The British Expeditionary Force 1914-15*, pp. 32-33.

45 *The Motor Cycle*, 30 September 1915, pp. 323-25; 11 March 1915, pp. 228-31.

46 *Motor Cycling*, 16 February, 1915, p. 350.

47 *The Motor Cycle*, 1 June 1915, p. 11; 27 May 1915, p. 512.

48 FH Jebens, "Transport of Infantry Machine Guns", p. 777.

49 *The Long, Long Trail*, www.1914-1918.net/mmg.htm.

50 Fletcher, ibid, p. 57.

51 *The Long, Long Trail*, www.1914-1918.net/mmg.htm.

52 Fletcher, ibid, p. 56.

53 *The Motor Cycle*, 5 August 1915, p. 141.

54 *Motor Cycling*, 27 April 1915, p. 613; *The Motor Cycle*, 13 May 1915, p. 465.

55 Fletcher, ibid, p. 57.

56 *The Motor Cycle*, 4 March 1915, p. 211.

57 Fletcher, ibid, p. 55.

58 *The Motor Cycle*, 13 July 1916, p. 35.

59 The Irish Republican Brotherhood conspired through the war with Indian separatist factions, notably in the USA.

60 Fletcher, ibid, p. 57.
61 David Ansell, *The Illustrated History of Military Motorcycles*, p. 12-13; *Motor Cycling*, 13 November 1917, p. 13.
62 Mick Walker, *NSU: The Complete Story*; p. 50; Pat Ware, *The Illustrated Guide to Military Motorcycles*, p. 138.
63 *The Illustrated War News*, 5 December 1917, pp. 10-11.
64 Hamilton Fyfe, "What Canadian MM Gunners did".
65 Philip Gibbs, The Way to Victory, Volume I, pp. 260-61.
66 JFB Livesay, *Canada's Hundred Days*, p. 296.
67 Supplement to *The London Gazette*, 7 November 1918, p. 13176.
68 *The Times History of the War*, Vol. XIX, pp. 139-41.
69 *The Motor Cycle*, 22 August 1918, p. 166.
70 Michael Holden, "Training, Multi-National Formations, and Tactical Efficiency: The Canadian Motor Machine Gun Brigades in 1918", www.cda-cdai.ca/symposia/2003/holden.htm.
71 *The Motor Cycle*, 22 August 1918, p. 166.
72 *The Times History of the War*, Vol. XIX, pp. 305-06.
73 *The Motor Cycle*, 22 August 1918, p. 166.
74 Holden, ibid.
75 *The Long, Long Trail*, www.1914-1918.net/mmg.htm.
76 War Office, *Statistics of the Military Effort of the British Empire during the Great War 1914-1919*, p. 218
77 Hamilton Fyfe, "What Canadian MM Gunners did".
78 *The Long, Long Trail*, www.1914-1918.net/mmg.htm.
79 Jebens, ibid.
80 Roy Bacon, *Military Motorcycles of World War 2*, pp. 108-09.

6

Frenchmen on the Side

NO ONE KNOWS who invented the sidecar. Alfred Scott is one of those sometimes credited, and a WG Graham hitched one to a motorcycle as early as 1903, but sidecars had been fitted to bicycles years before. We do know who invented the sidecar ambulance, though: one TH Henderson of New South Wales, who registered a patent just in time for the war in which his invention was to play an important, however now-forgotten, role.[1] Unfortunately Mr Henderson did not extend registration of his patent beyond the antipodes and therefore made no significant profit from it, as the Australian Front was quiet through the war. His design was shamelessly copied in Britain, including by one Adolph Timpi, of Urmston, who offered his design to the War Office and was promptly fined two guineas for having it in his possession as an enemy alien, when the authorities realised that the sinister Herr Timpi had been goose-stepping all over his Manchester neighbourhood for 42 years.[2]

As with solo motorcycles, sidecar combinations were much cheaper than motorcars, and they served many purposes. On the home front, sidecar ambulances were used by local authorities,[3] and by mining companies (something that suggests that the expansion in mining, due to the massively increased demands of war, together with the attendant unavoidable use of unskilled labour, led to an increase in accidents).[4] Collieries seem to have depended mainly on Campion motorcycles with Mathieson sidecars.[5] The Campion-Mathieson combination used a 6 or 8 HP JAP engine, Sturmey-Archer three-speed gearbox and all-chain drive, top specifications for the time. The Mathieson was notably well sprung and had a special stretcher that allowed the patient to sit upright, recline or lie down, depending on the nature of his injuries. It was fully weatherproof, but a sliding celluloid window allowed for communication between sidecar and motorcycle, and there even was electric lighting in the sidecar, driven by an engine-powered dynamo. At a time when the motorcycle, in solo or sidecar-combination form, was making a serious challenge to the motorcar, the Campion-Mathieson "makes it almost impossible for the motorcar to hold any balance of superiority".[6]

The Great War saw the motor- take over from the horse-drawn ambulance—though the latter did not vanish, the perception that "the liability to [mechanical] breakdown is much greater in military ... transport" reinforcing conservative views.[7] The *British Medical Journal* prescribed the motor ambulance's role as transferring wounded from clearing stations to nearby railheads, and from town railheads to local hospitals. The *BMJ* initially was suspicious of the sidecar ambulance, in part because of "noise", but it did acknowledge the "need for good suspension and reduction of vibration", and admit that motorcycle sidecars were "often very plangently sprung".[8] As early as September 1914 "Motor cycle ambulances [were] receiving a considerable amount of attention from the War Office".[9] (Curiously, before the war not all "[m]edical experts who have experience in the carriage of wounded men" agreed on the value of ambulance suspension to their charges' comfort—or indeed survival."[10]) Soon afterward, the *BMJ* could find "no fault" with a Zenith outfit, which could take one prone or two sitting patients in the sidecar, and acknowledged, "The notion of well-designed sidecar ambulances is quite a practical one". The *BMJ* did retain reservations about the motorcycle's value on the grounds of exhaust noise, which was likely to cause distress to wounded passengers "who have already experienced sufficient shock from gun-fire".[11] (In January 1915, this constitutes a relatively early recognition of what came to be called shellshock.)

Manufacturers seem to have taken suspension seriously—at least until either war profiteering or (to be fair to some) material constraints imposed on war-production by the U-boats' campaigns sidelined their most conscientious interests. A Norton-Watsonian ambulance, like a Zenith, used "large C-springs at the rear [with] coil buffer springs" in front of the sidecar, and the "full-sized army regulation army stretcher" was further isolated on separate suspension inside; a combination of tilted box-lid and fabric curtain provided "an entirely enclosed, warm and waterproof covering for the patient".[12] Rudge-Whitworth produced a spiral-spring clip that secured the castor wheels of stretchers, combining secure location with speedy release.[13] The Red Cross approved an 8 HP NUT outfit, "to accommodate two recumbent patients on regulation army stretchers borne on very plangent springs".[14] America copied the trend with a two-stretcher (double-deck) Hendee outfit.[15] Baroness T'Serclaes and Mairi Chisholm used an 8 HP Matchless-JAP-Empire outfit at Pervyse.[16]

On the battlefield sidecar ambulances were used to transport wounded men from Regimental Aid Posts back to Advanced Dressing Stations, and sometimes farther back (in the rear zone they might be driven by women volunteers). But for all the good sidecar ambulances did at home and on the battlefield, it was only in the French sector that they made an historic contribution, with the British Ambulance Committee to the *Service de Santé*

Militaire. This operated "about 125 ambulances" in total, including "two sections" of sidecar ambulances, and may have evacuated 400,000 French wounded through the war.[17] The sidecar model most commonly used here was the 6 HP Sunbeam-JAP outfit, kept in repair by a "workshop car attached to the British Ambulance Committee's convoy".[18] Each outfit and driver served three or four casualty clearing stations, bringing to these stations *blessés*—wounded Frenchmen—from wherever in the local sector the fighting might be particularly hard. From those stations, *blessés* were evacuated farther back by car ambulance.

The *Service de Santé Militaire* had been formed on the outbreak of war by one Bradley Payman and some other "friends of France",[19] conscription leaving little room in France for voluntary work; but the *Service's* roots went back to St John's Ambulance's Voluntary Aid Detachments of 1908, so there was an infrastructure on which to build,[20] and it worked under the auspices of the Red Cross. Its practical usefulness cannot have been great in any absolute sense, given the scale of slaughter along the Western Front, and the relative paucity of casualties in the sector served by the sidecars (there were only "several" sidecar ambulances in use at any one time by the *Service de Santé Militaire*);[21] but as a symbol of Allied solidarity the service must have done great good, especially as the British drivers acted as unpaid couriers to the *poilou*,[22] who so often was neglected by his own officers, a factor in the 1917 mutiny.

Such Allied solidarity as the service supplied could do nothing but good in a working coalition that often was marked by mutual suspicion, some French fearing in the early years, as again in 1940, that the British were prepared to fight to the last Frenchman. The scale of the battlefield, stretching 450 miles from the Channel coast to Switzerland, and the size of the opposing forces, meant that the initially tiny BEF could not have an independent strategy; Britain simply had to conform to French plans, even when she had her doubts as to the wisdom of these. Temperaments often clashed and tempers were lost: at the very start of the Allied campaigns, the ill-named Sir John French (he was a Francophobe) resented General Lanrezac's sarcastic response— "Fishing"—to French's puzzled query as to what the Germans were doing on the Meuse (they had not been expected there). Even after Britain had come to be regarded as Germany's main enemy the need for her forces to conform with the French remained, for France still had the larger army and this had to be sustained in belligerency, whatever the cost in British gold and British blood, if British interests were to endure. These demanded that the French be supported in every way possible, so British volunteers driving sidecar ambulances in France made a greater contribution to the war than they could have realised; it went far beyond humanitarian. (In addition to their official duties, they also acted unofficially as stretcher-bearers and personnel carriers, as well as delivering the mail each day.[23])

These volunteers did their bit on the Vosges front. The Vosges is an old block mountain or *horst*, worn down to a series of buttes and valleys, and thickly forested. It presented peculiar challenges in a war fought mostly over level or undulating ground, especially after the Germans seized the buttes in January 1915. French *élan*, and requirements of national morale, demanded that these be attacked *à outrance*. But in this minor sector, starved of guns strong enough to direct plunging fire onto lofty German blockhouses, uphill attacks were bloody. The Germans developed proto-stormtroop bite-and-hold tactics, using flamethrowers, gas and grenades.[24]

The Vosges therefore saw a low-level but constant haemorrhage of French casualties all of whom needed to be evacuated out of territory very difficult of access and egress, "over gradients of [up to] 1 in 4 ... strewn with big boulders", up to heights of 3,000 feet. These roads, with greasy surfaces, hairpin bends, and appalling potholes, rendered the fighting zone inaccessible to car ambulance. Winter storms could make things even worse, and parts of the road were under observation by the enemy—who often showed admirable forbearance.[25]

Sidecars, with their narrow wheelbase and the peculiar advantages asymmetrical wheel distribution confers on traction and control, could go where cars could not and were light enough to be manhandled out of ditches, if necessary. Presenting a small target, they could venture closer to the action,[26] and were, besides, "Generally ... not only cheaper and quicker, but more reliable than the cars",[27] which would have been pounded to pieces. *Les Anglais* could enormously reduce evacuation time, from dressing station to the road, and furthermore could improve any *blessé*'s comfort thanks to "plangent" suspension and the ability of a narrow-track outfit to pick the easiest way. Depending on exactly where in the sector the casualty was sustained, evacuation time might be reduced from the best part of a day by ox cart to "little over an hour"; from 30 hours by ox cart to 100 minutes by sidecar; from over two hours, shouldered by eight men, to twenty-seven minutes by sidecar, driven by one (at most, two).[28] Removal of casualties from road clearing stations by conventional car ambulance provides an example of not alone complementary Allied warfare but integrated evacuation "tactics": car ambulances ran at night, when the sidecars, due to their poor lighting over the dangerous trails, could not operate.[29]

Lieutenant AP Bradley, seconded to the French, though he was a car ambulance driver, was "honestly ... surprised" by the success of the sidecars, to which "several men owe their lives" due to speed of evacuation. Another driver concurred. This man previously had driven a Mercedes ambulance and found that the partition between him and his *blessé* impeded empathy and—more significant—that "a properly sprung sidecar ... is infinitely more comfortable than the average car".[30]

Not all of the outfits in service were as comfortable as might be required, though. Stretchers were spring-mounted in the sidecars, but springing of the sidecar itself was rudimentary, and shackle-bolts on leaf-spring linkages frequently broke. The spare wheel was carried under the stretcher, which meant that a seriously injured man might have to be removed in order to repair a puncture. This design shortcoming seems particularly regrettable as there was room between the sidecar and motorcycle for a spare wheel, and the outfits of the MMGS had been using such a mounting arrangement since 1915 at the latest. The Sunbeams had adequate ground clearance and particularly robust clutches, which were vital, the steep gradients often calling for the clutch to be slipped mercilessly, and the engines were "marvellously reliable", despite hard usage. But unlike the Watsonian with its large C-springs, which had so impressed the *BMJ*, the Gloria sidecar had harsh leaf springing that disimproved patient comfort and transmitted road shocks that could lead to chassis breakage. There was a need for "long, curved [sidecar-chassis] springs" with stout spring shackles to remedy mounting-bolt failure, and larger sidecar wheels, independently sprung, to improve passage over broken roads, as well as separate spring mounting of the stretcher within the sidecar. Early Mills-Fulford and Norton-Watsonian sidecars had had better springing, and it may have been a measure of economising, enforced in an economy geared for total war, that led to more spartan devices replacing them as they inevitably broke up over the awful roads. Various canvas covers were effective to some degree, but the patient remained more exposed than in a car ambulance, and the location of the spare wheel meant that he had to be removed to access it, and remain fully exposed until the wheel was changed.[31] The design of the sidecar meant that collapsible field stretchers could not be used; modification here would have streamlined movement from the battle zone to the motor ambulance (which did accommodate field stretchers, as had the early Zenith).[32] While accepting the need for them in the Vosges, sidecars absorbed manpower, two men, a driver and (sometimes) an assistant, being needed to carry one patient, where a car ambulance driver could carry ten.[33]

Conditions were challenging, to understate the case, for the drivers of these ambulances—and their charges: "Our road … is a mere mule track in the mountains … none too smooth, so that with a '*blessé*' who may have the misfortune to have a broken limb, the pace must become a walking one, whereas with a man suffering only from a flesh wound the speed may be moderate". In the case of a *grand blessé*:

> even with the most perfect suspension road shocks will be transmitted to the suffering passenger unless the greatest care is taken to dodge every stone and rut on the path. Often, if the case is a very serious one, an extra passenger is taken on the carrier to steady the machine behind, and it is

then that we are thankful that our 6 HP engines give every ounce of their power, and that our low gears are really low, for going up a 1 in 6 gradient with three up, including kit, at a speed which must not be much more than walking pace, the machine is indeed tested.

Less seriously-injured men could sit up and act as lookouts, and with these the speed could be much faster, the driver meanwhile being entertained by tales from the "real" war that "make one's hair stand on end".[34]

Roads in the Vosges were pulverised by winter frosts and spring floods, and sidecar drivers had to improvise where they were washed away.[35]

In the winter of 1915-16 roads were under two feet of snow and after the thaw "Raging rivers roared down the valleys, and the evergreen pines shook their heads sadly at the howling wind". One rider found his way blocked by a fallen tree, and the alternative route "contained two appalling hairpin bends and a gradient like the roof of a house". Part of this road was washed away, leaving only a narrow ledge wide enough for a solo, so a plank was lain down for the sidecar wheel. This obstacle crossed, the rider came to where a snowmelt-generated waterfall had broken up the road to the extent that a plunge-pool obstructed the ambulance's path. Risking a full-throttle dash, the rider came through, soaking wet. Farther on the stream, which normally flowed alongside the road, had overflown across it, excavating a deep channel. The resourceful rider built a causeway of large stones—such was the torrent that smaller ones were washed away as they were lain down—and continued. Finally, within sight of the clearing station, the rider was stopped by a bridge that had been washed away; fortunately, *poilus* could be called upon here, and these carried the *blessé* to safety, while the intrepid British volunteer turned his sidecar outfit and headed back into the mountains, to do the same again.[36]

Even at the best of times, Vosges roads were poor, and through the war they were awful, whatever the time of year.

> These so-called roads have been made always under the enemy's direct fire, so that the use of a steam roller was, of course, out of the question, though even in peacetime the severe gradient might also prevent one being used.... But motor cycles are wonderful machines and will traverse such roads, though it can scarcely be considered good for their health.[37]

Of particular importance in traversing such roads, and conveying a *blessé* in comfort, was the handlebar-mounted clutch-lever, a recent innovation much called for by despatch riders; one driver admitted that "one used the clutch to just the same extent as one uses the throttle", admitting further that "the work … is abuse rather than fair use". Despite all abuse the JAP engines were "marvellously reliable", and, for all the hard usage of the transmission in particular, "no more than one or two warped [clutch] plates" needed replacing at service intervals. Such durability was due to the use of all-metal clutch plates, rather than an interleaving of metal and cork-lined plates, the normal arrangement at the time (cork would have burned out in short order), and in turn this arrangement suggests extremely heavy clutch-spring pressure, which had to add to the rider's challenges. Heat generated by almost constant clutch slippage not only wore down and warped the plates, but could render the primary transmission case too hot to touch. Such heat implies distortion of the two case halves, which means that the case could not have been oil-tight, so the primary chain must have needed almost daily greasing or oil replenishment.

" We landed safely on the other side, very wet, but otherwise not much inconvenienced." *(See previous page.)*

Sometimes San Fairy Ann was the only approach to take.[38]

179

Given what we know of the pressure of work, and "deconstructing" several off-hand remarks from the time, it seems that for all the crying need for it, maintenance was of the lick-and-promise variety. "At times they [the sidecar outfits] are caked with mud till hardly recognisable, and long spells of neglect are the common order. All the rider wants is absolute reliability". By and large riders seem to have got that, and the fact that they did reflects again on the quality of British manufacture at the time.

British volunteers were being sought almost to the end. On 27 August 1918 the British Ambulance Committee advertised for twenty motorcyclists, men over 40 or "Grade 2 men over 35".[39] Two days later *The Motor Cycle* echoed the appeal: the French Army "is urgently in need of another twenty motor cyclists.... The pay is £2 a week, while uniform, travelling expenses and rations are provided".[40] Cheap at twice or ten times the price to Allied political interests, for a service whose usefulness was only toward the end being appreciated:

> now that their usefulness is more fully realised they are slowly becoming recognised as a part of the desirable equipment of an army. [Sidecar combinations] are cheap, they are quick, they can negotiate roads which are quite impossible for a heavier vehicle, and owing to the small mark they present, they can venture nearer the lines than can a heavy automobile.[41]

For their services in such dreadful conditions, specifically "for keeping up communications between a '*Poste de Secours*' and the base, when the only road over the mountains had been demolished", Mr R Hannay and the Hon C Hill-Trevor received the *Croix de Guerre* with Silver Star; Messrs J Bower, WD Linsall and E Hartley Hacking the *Croix de Guerre* with Bronze Star.[42] Many other brave men, who for whatever reasons were unable to "do their bit" on the front line, did their duty by Britain's allies.

Endnotes

1   *The Motor Cycle*, 18 March 1915, p. 265.
2   *Motor Cycling*, 7 November 1916, p. 13.
3   *Motor Cycling*, 11 September 1917, p. 301; 1 January 1918, p. 135; 12 February 1918, pp. 268-69.
4   *The Motor Cycle*, 5 December 1918, p. 507. One such casualty was the fourteen-year-old son of William Hackett, VC, referred to in the Introduction. Young Arthur Hackett lost a leg.
5   Campion was a Nottingham-based manufacturer that began production in 1901 and went to the wall in 1926; it used proprietary engines throughout.
6   *Motor Cycling*, 12 February 1918, pp. 268-69.
7   Wyatt, ibid. p. 121.
8   *The British Medical Journal*, 10 October, 1914, pp. 642-43; 14 November 1914, p. 843.
9   *The Motor Cycle*, 10 September 1914.
10 Wyatt, ibid, pp. 80-81.
11 *The British Medical Journal*, 2 January 1915, pp. 44-45. .
12 *The Motor Cycle*, 16 March 1916, p. 253.
13 *The Motor Cycle*, 10 September 1914, p. 325.
14 *The British Medical Journal*, 16 January 1915, p. 133.
15 *The Motor Cycle*, 7 September 1916, p. 203; see *The Motor Cycle*, 5 September 1918, p. 227, for a similar double-deck design.
16 *Motor Cycling*, 13 November 1917, p. 7; *The Motor Cycle*, 15 November 1917, p. 471.
17 *The Illustrated War News*, 30 January 1918, p. 36. The source had propagandistic value at the time, so the 400,000 figure should be treated with caution. That said, British propagandists were clever enough to base their claims on fact.
18 *The Motor Cycle*, 28 December 1916, p. 563,
19 *The British Medical Journal*, 14 November 1914, p. 858; *The Motor Cycle*, 28 December 1916, p. 563.
20 *The British Medical Journal*, 7 December 1918, p. 644.
21 *The Motor Cycle*, 28 December 1916, p. 562.
22 *Motor Cycling*, 23 November 1915, p. 57; 22 February 1916, p. 400; *Motor Cycling*, 11 April 1916, p. 569.
23 *Motor Cycling*, 11 April 1916, pp. 567-69.
24 John Mosier, *The Myth of the Great War*, notably Chapters 7 and 9. Mosier, an American English professor, betrays limited understanding of the complexity of the Great War, but his book does provide a succinct and valuable description of a sector often ignored by British scholarship.
25 *The Motor Cycle*, 11 July 1918, p. 30.
26 *Motor Cycling*, 23 November 1915, p. 58; *The Motor Cycle*, 11 July 1918, p. 28.
27 *The Motor Cycle*, 11 July 1918, p. 28.
28 *Motor Cycling*, 5 December 1916, p. 98; *The Motor Cycle*, 28 December 1916, pp. 562-53
29 *The Motor Cycle*, 11 July 1918, p. 28; *Motor Cycling*, 11 April 1916, p. 567-68.
30 *Motor Cycling*, 23 November 1915, p. 58; 8 August 1916, p. 292.
31 *Motor Cycling*, 23 November 1915, p. 60; *The Motor Cycle*, 11 July 1918, p. 29-30.
32 *Motor Cycling*, 23 November 1915, p. 60; *The Motor Cycle*, 24 October 1918, p. 373.

33 *The Motor Cycle*, 11 July 1918, p. 30; *Motor Cycling*, 23 November 1915, p. 59.
34 *Motor Cycling*, 8 August 1916, pp. 292-93.
35 *Motor Cycling*, 22 February 1916, p. 409.
36 *Motor Cycling*, 22 February 1016, pp. 409-10.
37 *Motor Cycling*, 22 February 1916, pp. 410.
38 *Motor Cycling*, 22 February 1916, pp. 410.
39 *Motor Cycling*, 27 August 1918, p. 274.
40 *The Motor Cycle*, 29 August 1918, p. 189.
41 *The Motor Cycle*, 11 July 1918, p. 30.
42 *Motor Cycling*, 5 February 1918, p. 244.

7

Not the West End

LIKE THAT OF all other personnel engaged in the war, the sort of work that the war motorcyclist did varied from theatre to theatre, and over time. Only in the French sector of the Western Front were the sidecar ambulances of the *Service de Santé Militaire* important; the Motor Machine Gun Service was active in several theatres; but in every theatre the despatch rider performed essential service. Never was this service more critical than during the Great Retreat of August 1914.

The Great Retreat

It's natural to think that the San Fairy Ann spirit is exemplified in the trench phase of the Great War, during which the expression itself was coined. Indeed it is to be found there, but it was manifest long before. Though no one could ever claim that the trenches were cushy, it's worth considering what life would have been like without them: apart from the awful—but untypical—first day of the Somme, the greatest daily death tolls were during the phase of open warfare in 1918.

That other phase of open warfare, in 1914, was marked by horrors of its own. During the retreat from Mons to the Marne men were marching up to and over twenty miles a day, loaded down by their equipment, in woollen uniforms, under a broiling sun, "hungry, thirsty, tired as dogs, sick with the smell of blood and the sights [they] had seen". More than anything, they suffered from their feet: "in some cases the skin of the lads' feet had peeled off with their socks and were bleeding".[1] "Literally, in many cases … their boots were half-full of blood",[2] "Their feet in a shocking way".[3]

> The men's feet were beginning to suffer terribly, for the road along which they were marching had been cobbled—cobbles, not as we know them in England, but rounded on the surface; cobbles that turned one's ankles; cobbles that the nails of one's boots slipped on, that were metallic, that

"gave" not the fraction of a millimetre. The hobnails in the subaltern's boots began to press through the soles. To put his feet to the ground was an agony, and they swelled with the pain and heat.[4]

By 3 September Corporal Denore could report:

It was the most terrible march I have ever done. Men were falling down like nine-pins. They would fall flat on their faces on the road, while the rest of us staggered round them, as we couldn't lift our feet high enough to step over them; and as for picking them up, that was impossible, as to bend meant to fall.

As if all that was not bad enough, "An aeroplane was following us most of the time dropping iron darts".[5] The cavalry fared only a little better, men falling asleep in the saddle and tumbling off, their horses also falling asleep as they walked and dropping onto their knees.[6] Despatch riders, too, fell asleep in the saddle and came croppers.[7] Men and horses literally died of exhaustion.[8] Some men committed suicide;[9] at least one horse went mad, "banging its head against a wall ... appalling to see".[10] As one officer put it, "No one at home will ever know the extraordinary way in which the Tommies came through that retreat"; testified another, "I would never have believed that men could be so tired and hungry yet still live".[11]

Yet even in circumstances as desperate as these, the San Fairy Ann spirit proved indomitable: "One man ... found a mouth-organ, and, despite the fact that his feet were bound in blood-soaked rags, he staggered along at the head of his company playing tunes all day. Mostly he played 'The Irish Emigrant', which is a good marching tune."[12]

That August retreat has gone down as one of the most memorable in history: "the Great Retreat". In length it doesn't compare with Napoleon's from Moscow or the Serbians' to Greece in 1915, and in terms of hardship these were even worse. It's the "Great" retreat because, unlike those others, at the end of it the men who had retreated stood and fought the battle that won the war; not that the Battle of the Marne was decisive in itself, but it shut down the Schlieffen Plan, and Germany's hopes of rapid victory in the West, which was necessary if she was to win a war on two fronts.

Yet how the BEF was able to maintain itself as a coherent force—even a fighting force, as its actions at Mons, Le Cateau, Landrecies and Néry prove—through this retreat, is remarkable.

The ... retreat from Mons ... will for all time be regarded as one of the finest performances of the British army. Hopelessly outnumbered from the start, and fighting on a length of front far exceeding their powers to hold, there was no way by which our troops could avoid retreat, and by all the rules of war they ought to have suffered not only defeat but annihilation.[13]

The man who made this testimony was Sir William Robertson, not notorious for overstatement, or being easily impressed.[14] Sir James Edmonds, Official Historian of the Great War, concurs in his view:

The Retreat from Mons ... was in every way honourable to the Army....
They were short of food and sleep when they began their retreat, they continued it, always short of food and sleep, for thirteen days; and at the end of the retreat they were still an army, and a formidable army.[15]

But there would have been nothing formidable about the BEF had it been broken up in the field through failure of command and control. General Joffre reported to his government that "the least check would run the risk of transforming [retreat] into a rout", and the British were even more vulnerable than the French, forming the left flank guard of the whole Allied line (after Le Cateau).

Failure was perilously close:

For the first few months after the war broke out confusion reigned supreme. Belgium and the north of France were one huge jumbled battlefield, rather like a public park on a Saturday afternoon—one of those parks where promiscuous football is permitted. Friend and foe were inextricably mingled, and the direction of the goal was uncertain. If you rode into a village, you might find it occupied by a Highland regiment or a squadron of Uhlans. If you dimly discerned troops marching side by side with you in the dawning, it was by no means certain that they would prove to be your friends. On the other hand, it was never safe to assume that a battalion which you saw hastily entrenching itself against your approach was German. It might belong to your own brigade. There was no front and no rear, so direction counted for nothing. The country swarmed with troops which had been left "in the air," owing to their own too rapid advance, or the equally rapid retirement of their supporters; with scattered details trying to rejoin their units; or with despatch riders hunting for a peripatetic Divisional Headquarters.[16]

That the army held together in such confusion was due in great part to those despatch riders hunting for their so-often-peripatetic target—and failure to find their target could result in disaster, as losses already referred to prove (see Chapter Four). Don R sometimes rode for more than a full day at a stretch, covering hundreds of miles. Corporal Corcoran averaged two messages an hour, riding "day and night",[17] some three hundred miles a day, over roads that might be "no more than … paths", and Roger West travelled almost as far as Paris trying to find a "rearguard [that] had been withdrawn four hours before [he was] ever sent out to find them"[18]—twenty days earlier! (Though he was far from idle through those days, as his DSO for blowing the bridge at Pontoise proves.)

The despatch rider's problems were exacerbated by a crippling shortage of maps. In best British muddling tradition, the departing BEF had been supplied with maps only of those "regions adjacent to the Franco-Belgian border where it proposed to operate". After the retreat began "a wire arrived [at the War Office] demanding the instant despatch of maps of the country as far to the rear as the Seine and the Marne".[19] But how to deliver these to an army on the move, and how then to get them to despatch riders who were on the go sometimes every hour of the day and night? Those maps that were made available were "useless", according to Captain Watson—too small-scale and cluttered. One of his colleagues gets lost because he is "mapless (maps were very scarce in those days)", and repeatedly Watson explains that he had no map—sometimes "it was by pure accident I found my way". Even when French maps could be found, they were "extremely unsuited to a despatch-rider's work";[20] indeed, they were unsuited to any military endeavour.[21]

Much of the despatch rider's work was back and forth along the line of retreat, ensuring coherence and transmitting orders and information backward or forward; but what could be even more important—and where lack of maps created particular problems—was transverse communication among the various units that, because of their very size, had to be split up to march along parallel roads: for if longitudinal electronic communication was difficult, transverse to the line of march it was often impossible. The five divisions of the BEF travelled along five different *major* routes, over-spilling onto any minor roads that ran in the right direction and off-road when necessary. Quite apart from the obvious problems for control and resupply this fragmentation caused, separation from one's companions, and uncertainty as to whether one was moving in the right direction, could sap morale, so the appearance of a despatch rider, to correct or confirm one's route, could be a terrific boost. To aggravate the problem of transverse communications, after Haig's uncharacteristic panic when attacked at Landrecies, his I Corps, already separated from II Corps by the Forêt de Mormal, set off on a line of retreat east of the Oise, so that for seven days the two corps of the BEF were separated by that river.[22] Inter-corps communication therefore demanded that despatch riders had to hunt for bridges, and the limitations and locations of these might hugely increase the distance travelled. No wonder men were riding up to three hundred miles a day.[23] This would be a respectable mileage even today, on modern motorcycles, over tarmacadam roads.

The value of the Motor Cycle Despatch Corps to survival of the BEF through that retreat, and the enemy's ultimately fatal failure to either break the BEF up in the field, or defeat the Western Allies at the Marne, may be measured by the Germans' very insistence on the most modern and "best" for their armies,[24] and consequent relegation of the motorcycle—of which their armies may have had over 20,000 in 1914[25]—to a lowly supportive role in the field of communications.[26] In doing this they were far too clever for their own good, for at the time wireless was primitive, and its fragile nature, together with the dangers of *en clair* communications—their wireless traffic could be picked up by the Eiffel Tower[27]—or, alternatively, unacceptable delays in ciphering and deciphering, made wireless unsuited to the needs of an army either in rampant advance or in full-tilt retreat. General von Kluck's account of the invasion reveals other problems with German methods of communication: an increasing number of troops had to be detailed to guard cable lines—"20 battalions and 4 squadrons of *Landsturm*" on 22 August, and more were to be assigned later—and commanders' mobility was restricted: "Corps commanders must keep in constant touch with their telephone stations, should they leave them, by motor-cars or other means".[28] Kluck's failure to mention motorcycles here, or in his lengthy "Order of Battle" appendix, or indeed anywhere in his account, suggests that the First Army may have had no motorcycle despatch riders at all. In a lengthy, detailed description of the various personnel and vehicles he passed through in a five-hour overtaking manoeuvre of what must have been the First Army, American war correspondent Alexander Powell nowhere mentions motorcycles.[29]

Further complicating Kluck's communications problems was the fact that "Signallers, other than telegraphists, were an ill-developed branch in Germany", which used "communications troops" (*verkshrstruppen*) who were "completely separated from both the engineers and the pioneers", despite their need to work with these branches.[30]

Kluck may have had motorcycles, despite this: one British interpreter who was wounded and captured on 1 September complains of a German motorcyclist who was "very unpleasant" (though overall he was well-treated).[31] But this man may have been the driver of a personnel- or materiel-carrier sidecar outfit, for Kluck is all but obsessed with communications through his account, and the evident value of the despatch rider to communications, coupled to Kluck's failure to mention them, is strong evidence that they were not there. Bülow's cavalry was used to effect communications between the Second and First Armies, again suggestive that motorcyclists were unavailable, but for the most part "Communication with the Supreme Command had therefore to be carried on mainly by wireless stations, which again were overworked in keeping touch with the Cavalry Corps and the neighbouring armies ".[32] In his account, Eric Ludendorff acknowledges despatch riders in this theatre, but only to mention their failure, and he does not make it clear that they were motorcycle-mounted; rather, his context suggests pedal-cyclists. Elsewhere Ludendorff credits the "magnificent work" of "volunteer motor corps" despatch riders for providing "the safest means of communication" to the German no less than to the British forces, but his context suggests the Eastern front.[33] Germany did use motorcycle-mounted DRs in the West too,[34] perhaps as early as December 1914 to judge from a *Graphic* article,[35] but overall, in combination with other circumstantial evidence, Ludendorff's testimony supports the contention that where "better" means of communication were available and could be co-opted, or laid down, as on the Western Front with its relatively smaller scale, it was these "better" means that were used—ultimately toward failure of the German cause.

The overwhelming evidence is that Moltke sent his armies into the field dependant on "radio and telephone exclusively; and with no provisions for alternate means of communication".[36] Dr Terence Zuber, who probably knows more about German forces of the time than Moltke did, writes: "I have not seen reference to motorcycles on the 1914 Organization Tables of any German units. The light wheeled vehicle of choice in the German army in 1914 was the bicycle".[37]

The BEF did of course have wireless and cable (the British Army had used wireless in the South African War, though without success), including a lorry-mounted 1.5kW Marconi wireless set, which one signaller claims "did excellent work",[38] yet its contribution could have been only small. Even during positional warfare, though it became increasingly important to day-to-day command and control, wireless might be "little used, probably owing to an objection to the laborious task of encoding messages amid the hurly-burly of battle".[39] "In the emergency [of battle], code and cipher regulations were to a great extent swept away", and delays caused by decipherment were even more hazardous in the retreat before the 1918 Spring Offensive.[40] Telephone was no better, at any rate through the Great Retreat: at Mons every word spoken over the telephone system could be listened into by anyone within miles.[41] Sometimes Signals were able to use the civilian telephone infrastructure, but this was rudimentary in places, notably in agricultural districts; there was almost none at Le Cateau for this reason, though the one in the railway station was used to link II Corps with GHQ,[42] and while Signals were able to lay enough wire to provide a connection between GHQ and I Corps, II Corps, 35 miles distant, and bearing the brunt of the fighting, had to be instructed by DR and staff car (for the telephone line from the railway station could carry only so much traffic).

Often the French were jealous in husbanding civilian networks for their own use,[43] and in some places they had sabotaged telegraphic and telephonic systems in their retreat; and always laying cable took time, which was desperately short, as was cable. So were men, so short that those detailed to communications work had to be incorporated into the fighting line as early as Mons,[44] which placed a further load on despatch riders. Cable waggons did precede the advance, but cable was in such poor supply—like all of the BEF's materiel—that precious time had to be given to reeling in as much as possible for re-use before retreating farther. Even at Mons some brigades were running short and to make matters worse, near Le Cateau the Germans captured "a complete cable detachment", a serious loss to add to cable already abandoned at Mons.[45] Corporal Tait reports being briefly attached to a "flying telegraph company—the kind of people who venture as far as possible forward, and, in the case of retreat, wait until the very last to cut the wires".[46] Despatch riders were used by these units for "spying out the routes and indicating the best way in which labour could be saved and a reliable circuit obtained in the shortest possible time".[47] After the Marne cable shortages persisted; the retreating Germans had destroyed local infrastructures, so Watson reports elatedly: "in Chouy the Germans had overlooked a telephone—great news for the cable detachment".[48]

As the August retreat proceeded, better practices developed, "and of these the most important was the allotment of certain despatch riders to different portions of the formation. This made possible a more rapid and efficient interchange of messages". The details varied from division to division, but some had evolved the practice of allocating two DRs to each brigade, a practice that was to become a permanent feature of army organisation through the war. Other divisions developed a system specifically suited to a hard-pressed army in retreat, with two riders each to the flank-, the rear- and the advance-guards, and two more to the billeting officers—though many divisions might not have even ten DRs left by the time the BEF turned on the Marne, far less the stipulated sixteen, but be reduced to "as few as six or seven". Despite their depleted numbers, "the service given by the despatch riders was superb, and though casualties to men and machines were fairly frequent, and the strength of many units was down to a minimum, touch was kept and messages cleared with exemplary promptitude".[49]

German communications were affected by the same conditions in the field, in ways even more severely than the BEF because of the scale of their armies and lack of motorcycle DRs. The sheer number of troops meant that so congested were French roads that sometimes two German corps had to share a single communications line,[50] and von Kluck admitted, "the means of communication between the First Army and those in supreme command were totally inadequate.... Orders ... did not arrive till after the most important events had already begun".[51] The Germans were forced back on "primitive codes, such as chalk-marks, the breaking of trees or branches, the disposition of squares of turf, etc"—even smoke signals, something almost unbelievable of the most technologically advanced nation on earth.[52] (Adoption of smoke signals may speculatively but not unreasonably be imputed to aficionados of Western writer Karl May, the most popular author in Germany in the years before the war—the young Hitler's favourite.)

It is tempting to dismiss such claims as merely Allied propaganda born out of a frantic need to discredit an army that seemed invincible; and indeed the source, *The War Illustrated*, was, like every other British publication of the time, under the watchful eye of the British War Propaganda Bureau. But British propaganda was always based on fact—though not necessarily, of course, on truth—and the above report dates from 1918, when the Great Retreat was part of history. Besides, such "primitive codes" were not so ancient, having been used by Napoleon barely a century before, and, though successful wireless telephony with planes and with tanks did occur in July of that year,[53] communication between aeroplanes and the ground, even in 1918, might be by "clumsy code" using a cloth panel.[54] Jomini and Clausewitz, those great military authorities of the nineteenth century, were Napoleonic scholars, Jomini indeed a veteran of Napoleon's campaigns, and their word would have been sacrosanct at the Prussian Staff College; so such "primitive" methods of communication would have been well known to German generals, most of whom had been born before the age of modern communications. And despite the huge advances in communications by then, even in the Korean War General "Iron Tits" Ridgeway used smoke signals *in extremis*.

The British Official History sums up German communication problems:

> OHL was connected to the four Armies of the left wing by telephone, to the Third, Second and First Armies by wireless alone. There was grave delay in the transmission of wireless messages, due to there being only one receiving station at OHL, and to interruptions by weather and by the French field stations, owing to the bluntness of the tuning curve. They arrived so mutilated that they had to be repeated three or four times before they could be read.[55]

These problems were "grave" not only on the march but, even more so, when the march ended at the Marne: "The critical state of the battle had impressed itself deeply on General von Moltke at OHL on the morning of [8 September]", but OHL's response was compromised by "delays of the German communication system".[56]

The BEF too, of course, suffered from failure of "modern" communication systems during the retreat, but they were not entirely dependent on them: "Cable communications were out of the question for the present, with the Huns close on our heels. It was up to the Despatch Corps now to keep ...

the British Army articulate."[57] These are the words of a despatch rider; but his superiors are in overwhelming agreement. Major Priestley, of the Royal Engineers, intimately engaged in the Great Retreat and professionally involved in communications, acknowledges:

> It is evident that the mainstay of the intercommunication system in a rapid retreat must be the despatch rider and the orderly, assisted to a small extent only by the occasional use of permanent lines ... but [in 1914] units reached their destinations so late, and had in many cases to leave so early, that it was not worth while to make the practice [of laying lines] general. As a general rule, *reliance was placed entirely on despatch riders*....[58]

It is easy to imagine the fatal chaos that might have resulted without despatch riders, given the paucity and unsuitability of wireless sets and a pace too fast to lay cable effectively. "Ground" and "air" cable (cable respectively lain on the ground and strung on trees) was provided where necessary or when possible but, besides the frantic pace, divisions were broken up along parallel roads, something that made laying cable effectively often less difficult than impossible.[59] The usefulness of such wire as was strung along the line of retreat can only have been limited, therefore, and extreme shortages meant that the Signals companies had to recover as much as possible before retreating further—unlike the Germans, who strung light disposable wire which they abandoned on their retreat to the Aisne, using it to "clothes-line" pursuing DRs. Months later, Corporal Best was hurt by such a hazard—though it appears from his account that it was a British "air" wire, blown from the trees by winter winds, that brought him down.[60]

The column rider was essential to maintaining contact between battalions, brigades, divisions and corps, and maintaining smooth uninterrupted movement along the route. Northeast France and Flanders were crammed with refugees as well as armies and traffic management was essential.[61] Don R had to advise the convoy officer on breakdowns and obstructions and organise traffic clearance,[62] when junctions could be "a mess of mixed transport standing wheel to wheel and facing in all directions".[63] He also had to round up stragglers, often carrying worn out men on his motorcycle, constant work that exhausted the rider.[64] Motorcycles alone had the speed and small size to effect rapid communication, through roads cluttered with other vehicles,[65] jettisoned materiel,[66] soldiers on the march, half-dead for lack of sleep, and fleeing civilians.[67] Sometimes it was impossible to ride even a motorcycle, such was the crush: West once had to dismount and push (primitive transmissions and lack of a hand-clutch lever made low speed control difficult).[68] DRs also performed a myriad of other duties and, perhaps in part because of the class to which most of them—in the early days at least—

belonged, their regard for duty, and sterling discharge of it, helped save the Old Contemptibles to fight another day, and seed Kitchener's New Armies with NCOs.

Positional Warfare

After October 1914, communications had to be adapted for optimum effectiveness in a war of position, and cable and to a much lesser extent wireless became established. Yet through the years of trenchlock the despatch rider sustained his position. Convoy work was constant, indeed of growing importance as the staff struggled to maintain an increasingly large army in the field, and despatch riders rode forward and backward ensuring free passage for the lorries, and organising assistance for any hold-ups that might need it. Closer to the forward area, the Despatch Rider Letter Service was established as early as 25 September 1914 and inaugurated on 29 October. The DRLS was a routine service that ran twice a day at prescribed times, and as the telegraph transmitted ever more battlefield messages, those of lesser importance were passed down to the DRLS in order to keep the lines clear; hence the service was described disparagingly by many Dons as a glorified postman's job; yet it was important to command and control and essential to morale. While speed was important in delivering urgent despatches, in the DRLS regularity and reliability was the priority. It made "two or three deliveries daily to all important signal offices, and circular runs to less important units in each formation area". During the 1917 Flanders campaigns pressure meant that the DRLS had to be streamlined, and "the offices of the various Area Commandants were utilised as the fixed centres to which letters could be delivered by motor cyclists.... Urgent traffic was disposed of once or twice daily by circular runs to these offices and a fairly efficient liaison was thus maintained throughout the Army".[69]

But Don R did not become entirely a "glorified postman", as some veterans of the Great Retreat disparaged a job they now had moved on from.[70] At the bitterly-fought First Ypres, there were times and places "where it was only possible to maintain communication by Motor-Cycle Despatch riders",[71] and even after comprehensive telegraphic networks were established urgent despatches still needed to be sent where cable and wireless did not suit or the former was "dis", transverse to the front from army to army or longitudinally from army through corps and division to battalion—and even farther forward if necessary to reach the despatch's recipient and be signed for.

Some of the onus of responsibility that had marked the Great Retreat was lifted off Don R's shoulders now, as the Signals Service established cable and wireless communication and these became more and more essential to waging modern war. Signallers' "first duty was to retain communications by patrolling and maintaining their wires in all circumstances, and their wires were cut by shellfire nearly every day".[72] At Loos Gough's Cavalry Signals sections "were running cables everywhere in record time with a flourish and style which were the wonder and envy of every other signals unit, especially the French"—this testimony from an Anglo-Frenchman.[73] In preparation for Cambrai 13,000 miles of cable were laid in less than a month,[74] something the men of 1914, scrambling frantically to recover as many yards as possible before retreating farther, must have marvelled at. By 1917 reconnaissance parties included signallers stringing wire to ensure telephonic contact,[75] but in the heat of battle problems remained with cable being destroyed by shellfire, and with the very condition of the battlefield: even such an essential as cable communication between infantry and artillery might break down;[76] one signalman records that at Third Ypres "it was useless to lay cable", and that, in some instances, communications reverted to visual (heliograph, lamp and flags).[77] Cable also was damaged by the constant heavy traffic needed to sustain an ever-growing army in the field, and when tanks came onto the battlefield their weight and sharp edged caterpillar tracks cut all but "deep-bury" cables; "tank corridors" were mapped by the Signals Service to deal with this problem, but in the excitement and confusion of battle these often were strayed from. Deployment of cavalry at Cambrai also tore down "air" cable (which must have unhorsed many a man), and as the British advanced they sometimes cut their own cable, thinking it was German (as it often was, Signals having co-opted German wire).[78]

By this time men with more thorough training in the various aspects of Signals work had arrived in the war theatres, and these could be used as motorcycle-mounted linesmen to speed repair of ground- or air-cable that had been damaged by shellfire or traffic; besides, DRs by now had been trained in all aspects of the Signals Service, and might be seconded to linesman work.[79] Better protection was accorded to cable as the war progressed, notably metal armouring and the "deep bury" system (burial to a depth of six feet was proof against all but the heaviest shells), and telephone communication on the battlefield became secure with the invention of the Fullerphone in 1916 (this used DC rather than AC, and therefore generated a far weaker induction field, too weak for the enemy to tap into). But much work remained for Don R; for no matter how efficient "modern" communications, security often demanded the integrity of personal delivery and accountability, and some messages were too bulky or otherwise were not suitable for cable or wireless transmission.

Besides, even as wire- and wireless technologies were taking over more of his work, Signals' responsibility was expanding, and Don had to shoulder his share of the extra burden. During the first winter more motorcyclists were allocated to Divisional Signals Companies, in recognition of this. As the number of pigeons was increased responsibility for them devolved onto the Signals Service and the number of Signals personnel was increased accordingly; though sometimes staff cars were used, usually it was despatch riders who delivered pigeons to the trenches,[80] as will be seen. It was only in 1916 that the artillery handed over responsibility for forward to the Signals, and though most of this communications was by wire, DRs had to be available during battle, often sleeping out beside the guns.

The huge expansion in size of the BEF in 1915 increased the demands on the Signals service.

> In the case of Armies, Corps and Divisions, the addition of an extra Corps, Division or Brigade involved a considerable increase of work. It was, therefore, definitely laid down that, for each such formation above the normal number, a corresponding increase of office telegraphists and motor cyclists should be added to the headquarters of the signal company of the higher formation.[81]

Then, in 1916, changes in tactics—what has come to be termed "the Learning Curve"—made their own demands upon the DR. Apart from the scale of the BEF, the single most important change through the war was the growth in importance and size of artillery. Gunners who had been firing field guns over open sights in 1914 were, by 1917, shooting at targets miles away according to map coordinates that had been calculated using data gathered through aerial survey combined with sophisticated flash-spotting and sound-ranging technology and mathematical triangulation. Cable kept infantry and artillery and the latter's "spotters" in touch, but the danger of wires "going down" or being "dis" meant that despatch riders had to be available always, so two were added to each Divisional Signal Company, four to each Corps Signal Company.[82]

Guns, however, shoot both ways, and the Germans' disrupted British communications. Armoured cable and "deep bury" helped, but could not guarantee reliability, so Don was needed to ensure communication within and between infantry formations as well as with the artillery and the air services. Furthermore, at least until 1916, cable only reached as far forward as the front line trenches, so the results of assaults across No Man's Land had to be communicated by visual, runner or pigeon—at least until reasonably reliable "forward" wireless sets and Fullerphone became available.[83] Experimentation was carried out with a "forward" set at Loos in 1915, and Captain Corcoran claims that this "rose magnificently to the demands of the situation, acting to its full range of five miles";[84] but Corcoran in many places betrays himself to be what one might call patriotically enthusiastic, and at this stage of the war wireless was intended for divisional communication backward; there is little evidence that it was used with great success in the forward zone; even at the end of the war a genuine forward set needed up to three men to carry it and its large, heavy "accumulator" (battery); effective tactical deployment of wireless really had to wait for another war. The Official History points out: "During battle, even when the lines were not cut, only short messages could be sent on telephones near the front, as hardly a word could be heard.... During the Somme the use of wireless was the exception rather than the rule. Its development came later".[85] In 1917, according to a wireless operator, "the Wireless Section was only then becoming of use in the trenches,"[86] and mainly as a supplement to cable.

Despite the Germans' apparent over-reliance on cable and wireless from the very outset, General von Arnim's complaints early in the Somme battles concerned not just the BEF's superiority in despatch riders (see Chapter Two), but its superiority in wireless technology, complaints that soon resulted in the distribution of Telefunken "*Umschalter*" trench sets to the German armies. Yet wireless remained very much supportive communication on both sides. Though it played an important role in mobile warfare in 1918 (see below), even then one professional signaller regarded wireless as being "in little more than its infancy"; in a signalling school less than six months before the armistice all forms of communication were studied, but the "full week" of exams that concluded the course "includ[ed] every subject in which we had been instructed excepting wireless".[87]

In 1917 greater effort was put into stringing wire immediately behind attacks, ground or poled air-cable initially but deep bury cable as soon as possible, the benefits to command and control being deemed worth the demands placed on labour and the short-term increase in casualties. Air- and ground-lines were "laddered"—two or more cables laid parallel with interconnecting "rungs"—to help ensure continuity of transmission through barrage damage.[88] Visual signalling was greatly improved by invention of the Lucas lamp, and more and more pigeons were brought forward—by Don R.

During the phase of positional warfare frontal communications and radial work were essential—though convoy riding of course remained to be done, and was particularly onerous during and in the preparation for offensives. One DR reports of this phase: "The very last thing that is likely to happen to the despatch rider[s] is to fall into the hands of the enemy, as their work will be entirely behind their own lines",[89] but frontal and radial tasks were not without danger. Frontal communications, i.e. roughly parallel to the front line, brought the DR into closer contact with the enemy, and the danger of being sniped or hit by shellfire.[90] Depending on the level of danger and urgency of the despatch, up to six men might be sent with the same message.[91] At Mons DRs had gone right up to the front line, where they could be knocked over by shellfire, and they still "rode daringly about" on the Race to the Sea,[92] but quickly it was accepted that messages to the front line were better delivered on foot. Strictly, Don's work ended at Battalion HQ, but he didn't work to rule: as war correspondent Philip Gibbs saw it, British soldiers were "men who [knew] the gravity of the game, and the risks, and the duty to which they have pledged themselves",[93] and despatch riders might be used between forward positions and Battalion HQ during the large-scale battles of 1916 and 1917, while the attack was still ongoing. Delivering despatches to the front line on foot was especially important after dark[94]—apart from personal danger, motorcycle traffic might indicate to the enemy the likely location of headquarters and Signals Centres, if radial paths could be plotted, and these might be inferred from engine noise even if lights were extinguished. Radial riding, from Divisional HQ some miles behind the line, was obviously safer, but the amount of work it called for during offensives was staggering: eighteen to twenty hours a day.[95]

Despite lurid tales of DRs travelling feverishly at up to 60 mph,[96] speeds were usually low. Watson describes "a gorgeous ride along a magnificent road … twenty odd miles in forty odd minutes",[97] or about 30 mph in favourable conditions. Usually conditions were far from favourable and speeds much lower, mandated at 20 mph maximum except when authorised, as has been seen. In addition to the often-treacherous conditions, sometimes the worn state of the motorcycle encouraged careful riding; but a more important factor was that "on a motor-cycle, if you are going rapidly, you cannot hear bullets or shells coming or even shells bursting unless they are very near. Running slowly on top, with the engine barely turning over, you can hear everything". Riding fast also is likely to induce a crouched position, in which many DRs are portrayed in art of the time, but "The experienced motor-cyclist sits up and takes notice the whole time. He is able at the end of his ride to give an account of all that he has seen on the way".[98]

In positional warfare "Excitement [gave] place to ennui" for the men who had been so pressed and so essential in the Great Retreat.[99] "We had become postmen", with merely "a couple of day messages and one each night".[100] But with Neuve Chapelle comes another frenzy of work,[101] made all the heavier as enemy shellfire cut cable to ribbons (the deep bury system had not yet been implemented), and in every battle the pressing need for security meant that Don was loaded with more and more work, messages that could not be trusted to wire or to wireless. In a 24-hour period during the second phase of the Somme battles—21-22 July—a traffic centre at Freicourt recorded the passage of 617 motorcycles; this compares with 813 lorries, at a time when supply of materiel was critical, and provides a measure of the DR's importance to control of battle.[102] "The roads were one solid mass of ordered traffic, waggons, guns, limbers, tractors, lorries, and flashing in and out among them all the motor cycles of the incomparable despatch riders".[103] These "incomparable" DRs provided greater security, they were more dependable than wire that could be cut by shellfire, and they allowed for prioritisation in a way that wire- and wireless communication, given the protocols and hierarchy of divisional administration, might not easily permit.

However the onus of his responsibility may have been eased, it is during positional warfare that war-weariness begins to affect Don R. A dull note now infiltrates some accounts; both the tone and coherence of diary entries sometimes deteriorates. Corporal Best, who had written, after a particularly gruelling night in 1914, "one takes things very calmly, as nothing seems to matter much", reports the following September: "more riding about over terrible roads and wet through to the skin. Fed up".[104] Part of the problem at the Somme was that the advance was over ground that had been absolutely pulverised, and after heavy rain unimaginably difficult; as early as September "Despatch riders from Divisional headquarters, 8 miles from Flers, found the road beyond Pommiers Redoubt impassable for their motor cycles".[105]

Corporal Grice, however, comes into his own on the Somme. Grice was a late volunteer, joining up in early 1916 and undergoing thorough training before being sent to France just after that critical battle began, so he did not have Best's sort of exhaustion to cope with. Yet it's wonderful to follow Grice as he evolves from something of a cynical ladykiller, whose main problem seems to be ennui, to the duty-driven man who emerges from the mud of the Somme, with its "unrivalled opportunity for seeing the war in all its vastness, wonder and cruelty", feeling himself to be, "An *asset* at last to King and Country". Despite "pot-holey roads" and the "shell strewn" wasteland of recently captured terrain, he reports in early August "the most wonderful journey of my life". Toward the end of September he seems to be becoming even more enthusiastic about his war, mature and confident in himself yet as excited as a child betimes, despite an often-exhausting work load: "Perfect weather and a real joy to be out riding amid the maze of horse and motor traffic. Met convoys at least 2 mile long". Toward the end of that month the rain falls and often he has to abandon his motorcycle and take lifts in lorries, yet throughout not just he but his colleagues seem to be suffering badly from cheerfulness, with many accounts of sing-songs in their tents at night. Corporal Davis, a much more jaundiced observer, nevertheless is able to take time out, while trying to traverse "engulfing mud", to admire, in his lyrical prose, the "fine picture of tent openings glowing cosily on the night, and of dusky men-figures silhouetted in evening task against brushwood fires".[106] By mid-October, with the mud getting heavier, forcing Grice to take lifts on lorries, motor ambulances and horses, not infrequently being forced afoot, he still can proclaim, "my only regret is that I was not out earlier". In November, with General Winter about to close the campaign down, Grice still is "Working frantically 24 hours", and reports: "The misery of war awful. Everything drab, muddied and exhausted. The limit in discomfort.... The utter uselessness of war.... Road conditions of the very worst sort. Horses, motors and bikes stuck in the mud. Many horses dead as a result of exposure". But though his tone is bleak he does not seem discouraged, and he "pitied" the infantry their lot.[107]

As 1917 dawns and that landmark winter tightens its grip Grice remains indomitable. "Surprised at wretched conditions under which infantry officers exist" (so how bad must things have been for the ranks?), he seems happy to be "Existing in a Nissen hut with another dozen DRs. Have a merry time telling tales and cooking on a Primus". Frost has hardened the mud and he enjoys "Moonlight nights and quite a pleasure riding. A varied life". Despite the conditions he enjoys—in what seems a very literal sense—"excellent health" until he leaves the DR corps in March to become an officer.[108]

Of all the men whose stories have contributed to this account, Corporal Grice is in ways the most intriguing. He seems to have been something of a privileged wastrel who delayed enlisting until faced with the threat of conscription and he became a despatch rider ostensibly, one may suppose, on the basis of his experience as editor of *The Autocycle* magazine—but also, one may suspect, because he was one of "the funk who wished only to evade the trenches", as one veteran DR described many of the newer sort.[109] If this is so, then the DR corps made a man of him.

A very different sort was Paul Maze. An Anglo-Frenchman, he was not a DR but had been attached to Hubert Gough's cavalry, and later the Fourth Army, as liaison officer with the French. His communications duties were similar to those of the average despatch rider, and he performed most of them while motorcycle mounted, so his experiences are relevant. After the taking of Thiepval (September 1916) he found that by motorcycle, "I got through the traffic better than I would have with a car and wasted less time. I could also venture up much further". An ability to get close to the action yet have access to a rapid method of reporting on that action could be of critical importance if shelling had rendered "dis" all cable communication. At Pozières Maze reports: "No telephone wires had survived the bombardment.... But for the runners who had succeeded in getting through, they [High Command] were cut off from the front line".[110] Maze saw runners killed, and did runner duty himself, like many DRs when called upon, as Grice's account illustrates. And with wires "dis", there was need for not just runners but DRs.

And Don R did not carry just messages: he carried those that carried more.

The Birdman of the Somme

Messenger pigeons have been used in war for centuries, by Ghengis Khan and even earlier. It was a pigeon that brought news of the outcome at Waterloo to Britain and another that brought, if not first news, at least much news of the outcome at Normandy on D-Day. The French had used pigeons for communication between the beleaguered city of Paris and the outside world in 1871, and it was the French that donated fifteen birds to the British Intelligence Corps on 11 September 1914 (the French Army had over seventy mobile lofts at the very outset). Four years later these fifteen "mickies", as they were sometimes called,[111] had become 20,000, the Signals had long taken over control of the pigeon service, and had trained some 90,000 men in bird management and deployment.[112] One of the most creative uses of pigeons was to airlift them over occupied territory on balloons carrying "a small wicker cage to which was attached a parachute and in which was a pigeon", as well as a questionnaire on enemy strength and a small capsule for attachment to the bird's leg after it had been completed by—it was hoped—some sympathetic Frenchman or Belgian (the cage was released from the balloon by timed fuse).[113]

The enemy was no less creative. At their military base in Spandau the Germans experimented in using pigeons in aerial photography; the birds carried tiny (2½ oz) cameras that took up to eight pictures, their shutters opened automatically by controlled-release compressed air. Whatever about the reliability of the technology, though, given the nature of homing pigeons, the only suitable area of deployment of such cameras was over enemy salients, and I am unaware that this was done. The Germans deployed hawks against enemy birds, as they had during the siege of Paris in 1971, though this strategy did not work as well as then, thanks to the much longer front.[114]

It was in early 1915, with positional warfare well established, that pigeons began to attract the attention of British units outside the Intelligence Service; in May that year II Corps of the BEF organised the first Corps Pigeon Service. "From this date the growth of the Forward Carrier Pigeon Service was rapid", and "by the autumn of 1915, the carrier pigeon had become a usual and most valuable supplementary method of communication";[115] training for those dealing with pigeons, including DRs, became part of the education process that marked the Learning Curve.[116] By 1917 divisions had their own lofts, and delivery times for messages improved. Now lofts were semi-mobile (though they could never be moved too far to avoid confusing the homing birds), cages being mounted on the upper decks of buses and the birds' keepers accommodated in the lower deck, the men alerted to a bird's arrival by a bell triggered by its landing.

But the service was hardly independent of Don R. Messages delivered from the trenches to lofts attached to Corps or Divisional HQ were collected by DR and brought from the lofts to HQ; from there they were relayed to Brigade HQ, to which most of them were addressed, this relaying being by wire or, if the lines were "dis", by despatch rider.[117]

Homing pigeons had a flight range of up to 200 miles, more than adequate for use in war, but for reliability birds at least two years old "that have proved good ones" were used.[118] They had the great advantage over dogs (which also were used by 1917), of being relatively immune to poison gas as they flew high above it—though gas-resistant bags were used to shield the birds when being transported in baskets. They also presented smaller targets so suffered few bullet or shrapnel casualties—fourteen were lost through the Battle of Loos, for instance.[119] (A further alleged advantage, that "Pigeons cannot talk and, if captured, will not give away their origin or destination"—is more an expression of wit by one Lieutenant Matlock than a real advantage, for, of course, captured messages could, as it were, talk, if a bird turned traitor and flew the wrong way.[120]) Against all their real advantages, pigeons could not be used in poor light or after dark—though toward the end of the war they were being trained in night flying—and might get lost if released too close to dusk. The fog that was such an infamous feature of the Spring Offensive meant that they "refused to fly", temperature as well as visibility being a factor in this instance,[121] for cold weather inhibited the birds also, and they might lose interest in their job if a cock and hen were released together. ("The pigeon is the rival to Marconi", a contemporary account light-heartedly overstates the case. "We're one better than wireless ... and nothing can jam us save death or flirtation".)[122]

Pigeons were trained to respond to whistled commands, but the capacity of any bird brain for learning must be limited and, as one expert points out, "the birds are free agents and return to their lofts or stay away, and it is only by kindness to the birds and kind treatment by the owner, that encourages them to return to their lofts".[123] Yet the birds should not be petted in the trenches, either, and certainly not fed titbits, or they might not fly home to the lofts. As with despatch riders', pigeons' messages were duplicated to improve chances of them getting through, and were written on "flimsies", paper "as thin and light as possible", rolled up tightly and inserted into "small aluminium cases" that were secured by rubber band to the bird's leg; later special clips replaced the rubber bands. Film was more likely to be mounted in "a small quill", which was fastened to a tail feather.[124]

Always the birds had to be guarded against the ubiquitous rats when in trenches. Though their value in communicating across No Man's Land was evident, after battle was joined congestion in the forward areas might prevent baskets being returned from the trenches to the lofts so leading to a shortage of birds just when they were most sorely needed—another instance of the problems in communication through this extraordinary war. At Arras, though they "had carried some useful messages, [they] had been insufficient in numbers".[125] Later in 1917, at Cambrai, the "secrecy and short period of preparation [for the operation] prevented the concentration of lofts in the neighbourhood in good time to train the birds to their new area".[126] It might be hard to locate suitable places for the lofts, as they needed to be accessible enough for messages to be delivered in timely fashion to HQ, yet not so close to the artillery that the birds were upset by the noise. In the Flanders offensives of 1917 tanks were provided with pigeons, and the experiment was "so successful that in future operations all Tanks were supplied with these birds"; but the birds' limitations remained, of course, and there remained need for "employment of Tank Corps despatch riders at the lofts".[127]

When mobility was restored in March 1918 pigeons became less useful, mobility itself interfering with their homing instincts; besides which, the speed of the German advance "thoroughly disorganised" the service and captured 40 mobile lofts. However, a year earlier plans for just such an event had been drawn up and lofts and birds were destroyed as the BEF fell back. The service never was restored after the Spring Offensive, (though pigeons continued to be used where available)[128] but through the years of position warfare it had proved a very useful supplementary means of communication, so much so, Blackadder fans may be interested to know, that shooting a pigeon was indeed a court martial offence; even at home the Defence of the Realm Act punished killing a pigeon with a £100 fine or six months in gaol. Far more swingeing penalties might attach to civilians in the war zone caught in possession of a pigeon: they were quite likely to be shot as spies. One such spy, in the early days of the war, was "an inoffensive, rather buxom-looking woman [who] had been walking around the square when one of her breasts cooed and flew away".[129] The Aliens Restriction Order banned British-resident Germans from owning pigeons, and "several prosecutions of pigeon fanciers" were pursued.[130]

By their nature homing pigeons can be a means of one-way communication only. They had to be brought from their lofts to the trenches, and it usually was Don R who delivered them to at least as far forward as Brigade HQ, and often farther.[131] They were carried in baskets on the DRs' backs, something that initially alarmed Corporal Davis, who served with the Carrier Pigeon Service of the II Anzac Corps on the Somme (and later with the X Corps Signal Company at Ypres). "These pigeon baskets, about a ¾ yard square, at first put the wind up me. Suppose aught goes wrong with bike, I murmured, or you get hit. How manage or fettle with that stifling strangling load strapped round your back? But with custom gradually forgot about these drawbacks". Securing the baskets, and keeping them secure, could be difficult, so one might see the intrepid DR "riding unconcernedly with the baskets floating around him like seaweed".[132] Presumably Davis means empty baskets here.

Standard pigeon baskets measured 10 inches by 15 inches by 10.5 inches deep. They were vertically divided into two compartments with side access doors secured by split pin and metal loops. A basket weighed three pounds without birds and without metal feeding troughs and normally Don R carried two of them, one above the other, slung by inch-wide webbing straps from his shoulders; but sometimes he carried a single cavalry-pattern basket, which used double-deck construction—this appears to be what Corporal Davis describes. Up to 24 birds were carried by each despatch rider, though on occasion this number might exceed 28, and the weight of "the load pulling and swaying at the straps used to cut into my shoulders so painfully".[133]

On his first delivery to the trenches Davis is appalled by "the chaos of the service" he finds when he hands his birds over to the infantry and wonders, "Can I introduce order?" In part, the "chaos" was due to Davis having made delivery to an Australian unit, Australians being as notorious at the time for indiscipline as they're remembered today—rightly—for their toughness and courage. "I like them", Davis says; "But they carry independence too far.... Before we took over, the pigeons have just been dumped, and they've done what they liked with them". What that means Davis does not make clear, but one suspects that Blackadder was not the only one to pot a pigeon. And it isn't just poorly managed lofts that Davis has to contend with, for the pigeons have to be transported on "the sorry steeds of the Aus Divisional DRs.... A crocked-up looking lot". In addition, "the DRs pinched things as easy as you like", and they appear to have been a rather unpleasant lot, certainly by comparison with the men of the early months. "Why should I have this task", the conscientious Davis asks, struggling with three baskets of pigeons on his back, "and those blighters have little else to do but play cards all day".[134]

Yet method may have underlain the image of "chaos": "The loftman gave you misleading figures as to the number of birds because he didn't want all to go out",[135] but this may have been understandable if the men in the trenches feared a German attack and felt a need to hold some birds in reserve.

Though he joined up in 1916, Davis appears to have been in the mould of the early volunteers; he does indeed try to improve efficiency, for instance devising a card index system for better accounting of the pigeons. (One suspects that his poor relationship with the Australians was due in part to his own righteous attitude getting up colonial noses.) Prior to his arrival on the Somme, birds had been delivered from lofts near Corps HQ to Divisional HQ, where the decision would be taken as to where they then were sent, but soon, and partly thanks to Davis's efforts, delivery was to be direct from Corps to Brigade HQ. Immediately it became clear, though, that "it was best to have a central meeting point where all brigades could come for their pigeons"; this was in "a wilderness" a few miles east of Albert, "past umpteen horse lines, turn right up the great winding hill that made you conk out because so much traffic just as you were getting up speed"—with 24 pigeons strapped to his back. The exhausting nature of Davis's work is exacerbated by the unpleasantness of his Australians, which is underlined by their cynicism and laziness, "leaving me to shift for myself instead of being matey", unlike the (British) DRs of II Corps, who always "extended unhesitating hospitality".[136]

Procedure when Davis reached Brigade HQ called for him to transfer the pigeons from his baskets to those of the infantry's "pigeon-wallah", but only if these were clean, and sometimes he had to leave his own baskets and bring away the infantry's, to be cleaned and if necessary repaired back at divisional base. At base, when pigeons were handed out, the ring numbers of all birds, as well as the name of the DR to whom they were issued, were entered in a book and signed for. A list was then compiled from the book on a daily basis, and this was supplied to the OC. This system improved accountability, and seems to have been devised by Davis himself.[137]

Davis's work extended to the lofts, located at Warloy and Senlis (though subsequently they would have moved forward with the front). Here again he had to make up for men "swinging the lead". One of the telephonists at Warloy—which seems to have been overworked—was poorly educated and excitable, so Davis sometimes had to transmit the message to Divisional HQ, "and it takes quite a time to get [the] message through, important as it may be. The man at the other end is maddeningly cool, while at this end other pigeons may be coming in". His "spare time" is spent cleaning and maintaining his Douglas, straightening leg-clips for re-use, and repairing damaged baskets.[138]

Like Grice and other DRs, when mud was too thick Davis had to abandon his motorcycle, taking lifts on lorries and limbers or going horseback or on foot. He describes the "wastes of chalk and clay" of the Somme landscape: "Bully tins, ribbed respirator tubing and gas helmets, countless heaps of cartridges thrown away by the men, dud shells, bits of shells, shell casings of brass, jam tins and biscuit tins dotted the drear valley, the very hell of colourless untidiness".[139] Within months, battlefield salvage policies would at least eradicate the waste.

Like most DRs, Davis enjoyed a good relationship with the officers—and he tells a story about General Birdwood, "a slightly battered but gentlemanly officer ... supposed to be the idol of his troops", that rather tarnishes the Birdie myth. Davis claims that Birdwood "was the man whom nearly every Anzac had abused to me ... because they reckoned it was due to him and the papers' gush about him that they always got pushed into hot fighting".[140]

After the Somme battles were run down, Corporal Davis was transferred to the Ypres sector, where he continued to give sterling service through Third Ypres, delivering pigeons, training novices in pigeon management,[141] and as an ordinary DR.

The Spring Offensive and the Hundred Days
Many of the same challenges as those of the Great Retreat re-emerged after the German breakout in 1918. So sudden and extensive was this that communications systems established during positional warfare were thrown into chaos; indeed, they were already strained by the very advances of 1917, which had brought the BEF far ahead of the deep-bury zone, and the need to extend the British front after the French mutinies left some divisions holding

up to 7,000 yards of front—over 10,000 in the case of one division—while they were being starved of men by Lloyd George.

"Within a few minutes" of commencement of bombardment on 21 March, communications systems in the forward zone were all but completely destroyed.

> The initial German barrage was ... intended to have a devastating effect on the entire British communications system. Shells ... smashed up the wireless stations and soon most of the telephone lines were severed—no matter how deeply they had been buried the larger shells seemed to sniff them out to expose them to destruction.[142]

To make a bad situation worse, the thick fog that so assisted the Germans meant that even visual communications were rendered useless and pigeons refused to fly. As the *stoßtrupptaktik* of Ludendorff's forces carried them quickly forward, and German artillery targeted main communications features farther back, the enemy overwhelmed even here much of the system that was unable to retreat in time.[143]

As movement was restored, once again Don R became the linchpin of communications.

> Between Divisions and Brigades motor cyclists did good work under great difficulties. Men were blown off their machines by the blast of shells falling near them and resumed their journeys immediately they had righted their cycles. Cases occurred of motor cyclists and machines being buried, dug out, and then carrying on as if nothing had happened. During the next few days the motor cyclist despatch rider was to experience a few short but crowded hours which recalled the early days of 1914. He was once more to be, on occasion, the sole means of intercommunication.... It was due to the activities of the motor cyclist despatch riders that a considerable proportion of the heavy guns in action on the southern front were saved from capture.

The BEF was much better supplied now, of course, with plenty of wireless and cable, but still "Signalling instruments [were] of delicate constitution and not well adapted to withstand without injury the rough usage inevitable" in a fraught retreat. Congestion once again was a problem, especially over the devastated old Somme battlefield, so that a mile an hour might be a good pace for a cable-waggon, and so dangerously slow was this that one German bombing plane was regarded as "an unmixed blessing" because after the bombs were dropped "the road was cleared of traffic by a helpful combination of anxious drivers and unmanageable horses". Besides, the very traffic, notably tanks, chopped ground cable—there was no time to prepare for tanks' passage—and the laying of lateral cable was particularly problematic, as in 1914, only now the British front was far wider, and lateral communication was much more important, as the speed of *stoßtrupptaktik* increased the danger of enemy infiltration and attacks on the flanks of formations.[144]

Though by this stage more reliable wireless was available to address problems caused by disruption of the cable system—notably in lateral communications—once again it mainly fell to motorcyclists to keep the retreating army coherent. In addition to the work done by DRs, "motor cyclist linesmen were found invaluable" in maintaining and repairing cable communications, but it was despatch riders upon whom the main load fell. Frequently uncertain of the location of their target—Corps HQ might be moved twice a day, and Divisional HQs even more often—and not infrequently under enemy fire:

> Motor cyclists were all worked exceptionally hard and were often called upon to carry out portions of their journeys under rifle or machine-gun fire. Frequently, the location of the units they were bound for was uncertain, but considerable ingenuity was displayed in unearthing headquarters. Many despatch riders did invaluable reconnaissance work in addition to their normal duties [again, as in 1914]. The men worked with little rest and less food and in the more hurried hours of the retreat were of vital importance.

So hard were they worked, indeed, that their "undue fatigue" sometimes delayed delivery of "urgent despatches".[145] And there might be worse than mere delays: "We kept sending mounted orderlies or [motor]cyclists back to division but it appears few ever got there".[146] Demand for DRs was such that men like Sapper FW Hopps had to be snatched from the ranks and mounted on motorcycles. Hopps does not have a cushy ride:

> Given a box of despatches and told to clear "to hell out of it". Did my best [but] got mixed up with party of RE's and gets bunged in trenches to hold Jerry[.] 30 of us. Jerries coming 10 deep. No bon. "Wind up". Won't see London any more at this rate. Jerry starts machine gunning us from rear. Shells flying all roads and aeroplanes machine gunning us from the air, very warm.[147]

Things got no better: "Everyman [sic] for himself. Jerries [sic] cavalry in village. Div HQ scoots north and arty [artillery] south. We go with French. Get out of Roye by skin of our teeth[;] very near thing[;] thought we were prisoners that time".[148]

Hopps is of a very different stripe to the "typical" DR. His education is relatively poor, as his English usage betrays, and in many ways he seems to be an example of the sort of man who made Lieutenant Best feel "sick of the private soldier as a companion", or what another veteran DR described as "the funk who wished only to evade the trenches".[149] He's an incessant grumbler; most towns are "dumps" and a constant refrain is "fed up with war"—or just "fed up"—and he doesn't seem to be a nice man. He plunders French shops and robs enemy dead, but others plunder too, and there would have been no finer feelings for enemy dead or concern for enemy bereaved from men who by now had been coarsened and maddened by years of war. More disturbing is his entry, "Lock girl in Bedroom"; there is no context for this remark so it's difficult to gauge its precise meaning but it's hard to imagine Watson or West doing such a thing. His frequent reference to "wind up", in his own case and that of others, is at odds with the stiff upper lip maintained by the men of 1914, but no doubt it also reflects the deterioration in morale as the war went on—and probably would have been the blunt truth throughout the war, which more self-consciously patriotic and duty-bound volunteers of the early days would have suppressed.[150] On the other hand, Hopps helps wounded companions, is kind to animals, sympathetic to nerve-broken men ("one of our kids sobbing his heart out"), and moved by the death of colleagues; he can rob souvenirs from enemy dead, yet can't bring himself to strip blankets off British corpses though he himself is freezing.

Paul Maze was very different—a man of the old school. He had volunteered in August 1914 and was forward liaison officer for General Gough during the March Offensive; but much of his work was despatch carrying and his experiences are typical of all DRs. "I rode back to Nesle, tired out, leaving behind me an uninterrupted wavering of gun-flashes. I had not been back five minutes when I was sent with a message to a French Army Headquarters in the south. I was so weary that I was only semi-conscious of the road sliding under me". This account might have been written during the Great Retreat, and indeed many of the priorities were the same: "What was vital, [Gough] said, was to see that units kept in touch with each other and didn't retire without giving warning to the units alongside them. He asked me to help in that way particularly". Given that Maze was half-French, liasing with French units became a particularly important job.[151]

But it was not an easy one, given the restored war of movement. As in August 1914:

> It takes time to find a headquarters. One has to stop and enquire.... In a short while one is sucked into the chaos of a retirement as a cork drifting on a river gets held up by current pools.... I raced off to inform Headquarters, but soon became caught in a web of columns that were being held up by

the baggage and artillery of other French units ... which cut across their path.... I noticed a French officer's car jammed in the block.

As during the Great Retreat, traffic was made worse by refugees—one stubborn donkey with his cart created a two-kilometre traffic-jam when he refused to move—and while ensuring that replacement French units kept in touch with evacuating British units, Maze "had hours of anxious wanderings on the dark roads, for everlastingly unexpected new problems kept cropping up". Again as in 1914, DRs got little sleep and lived as they could: "I felt the complete exhaustion of one who for days has had insufficient sleep". Maze "always ate when and where I could, and never failed to refill my bike with petrol whenever the opportunity offered. Later on it became difficult to find petrol, so I carried a spare tin behind me".[152]

And as in the opening weeks of the war, commanders relied on the quality of the DR's character: "Wherever you can", Maze reports Gough's instructions to him, "impress on the troops with whom you are in contact that on no account are they to retire without warning units on either flank. The line must bend and give, but the enemy must not be allowed to break through".[153]

The line did bend, which allowed a field workshop to be over-run, a serious loss "when the wastage in mechanical transport was exceptionally high",[154] and motorcycles were needed more than at any time since the Great Retreat. But by this time the English Midlands was winning the logistical war with the Ruhr,[155] and soon there were replacement Triumphs and Douglases on their way, along with the spares to keep them going; "tyres and tubes requisitioned in the morning were supplied in the evening".[156] Well mounted and supplied, Don R did his bit in stemming the German advance, and in sustaining the subsequent Allied advance, when mobility continued to ensure the need for him.

Somewhat similar problems to those that had characterised the Spring Offensive recurred in the final Hundred Days. The speed of advance meant that "lines of communication now effectively ended some 8 miles behind the new front line[;] telephone lines were being pushed forwards at a pace, but there was still a general air of confusion and a huge dislocation of command and control".[157] As in March, mists impeded visual communications, so again a great responsibility fell to despatch riders. "During the fogs that characterised the early autumn mornings, they were often, though themselves much hampered, the only reliable means of communication to supplement the Divisional wireless stations"[158] (wireless now being ubiquitous in the BEF, and its fragility manageable in a planned advance as it often had not been in headlong retreat). As Roger West had undertaken to blow a bridge back in 1914, now Paul Maze used his initiative and "commandeered a British lorry to take from a railway station some ammunition which had arrived for the

French, and which they urgently needed. There was no officer ... so I took the responsibility". Later he took unofficial command of American soldiers who had lost their officers—he now was attached to two American divisions that had been seconded to the Fourth Army.[159]

Once again Don R's work brought him into the danger zone. Poison gas "caused many casualties [to DRs] in 1918".[160] Even after the tide turned, danger remained. The pace of the Allied advance might be enough to cut off enemy troops, and Paul Maze encounters these in open country, between advanced troops and the main army behind, "about 200 yards to my left", and occasionally was exposed to fire, which he returned with his "carbine" (doubtless an SMLE; Maze carried one of these though DRs proper were armed with pistols) during the Battle of Amiens. Journeys might be shorter, as Army HQ kept moving ever closer to the line, yet still, in close proximity to the front, Don R was in danger. Apart from being fired upon by hostile troops, Maze was strafed by enemy aircraft, once being forced to dive "into the ditch to avoid another spray of bullets which made the road curl up in dust". In the close-range fighting that developed, his "motor-bike instead of being a help was then rather a source of danger", and eventually he was shot in the arm and evacuated.[161] But right to the end (and indeed beyond—see below), despatch riders, "enveloped in white dust or coated in mud, pursue their course unheeding over broken and shell tossed roads, familiar figures of the battlefield".[162]

Yet another pattern of similarity with 1914 may be discerned. After the failure of Ludendorff's offensive, as after Moltke's, Don R had time for leisure. Maze by then was attached to General Butler's III Corps—Gough having been sacrificed to the Frocks as a scapegoat for Ludendorff's breakout—and he enjoyed evening rides along a canal towpath in quietude, or longer trips to Montreuil-sur-mer for the day. "I felt some peace. The coolness of the shady banks and the calm reflections in the water were refreshing after the heat of the sun".[163]

Other Fronts—European

Coalition warfare meant that there were other fronts in the Great War than the fabled Western Front. Notably, there was the Eastern one, far longer and more mobile, where Russia fought the Central Powers with whatever help the Western Allies, and later the USA, could provide. The Bear was a shaky ally who had suffered devastating defeats at Tannenberg and Masurian Lakes, barely a month into the war, and was to be roughly handled by the Germans to the end. Thanks largely to French capital, Russia had been industrialising at a very rapid pace ever since the French Entente in 1894, but it still was backward and against the Second Reich it was at a huge disadvantage industrially and militarily.

One of the ways in which Britain helped the Russian war effort was by providing it with motorcycles, Britain being at this time the world's greatest producer, as she was to remain for over half a century afterward. All the Allies were supplied with British motorcycles, indeed. The French seem to have been greatly taken by the BSA single, but they also appreciated the 5-6HP Rover JAP-engined V-twin, which used a three-speed transmission and fully-enclosed all-chain drive; the AEF later was to appreciate the Rover as support for its ponderous Indians, Harley Davidsons and even more unsuitable machines.[164]

The main Russian requirement was for sidecar outfits, the terrain and its extent militating against speed as a primary consideration. The Russian Legion was supplied with armoured cars by the Royal Naval Air Service and these had DRs attached. These riders covered a modest 12,000 miles in fourteen months, but over dreadful terrain and in up to 57 degrees of frost. Roads in the Caucuses were mostly cattle tracks pocked with holes and with deep dust and sand-covered rocks. They reached 10,000 feet and sheer drops added to the excitement. One DR felt that the light and tractable Douglas was the nearest thing to an ideal machine for such conditions.[165]

The little Douglas was of 350cc displacement, however, and the Russians "stipulate 650cc as the minimum capacity for solo machines and an engine in the neighbourhood of 1000cc for sidecar work, which will alone serve to show the extremely difficult conditions" on the Russian front. Various British factories filled Russian orders until beyond the first revolution of 1917, notably Rover, Norton, who developed a special "Big Four" single, with all-chain drive and "exceptional mudguard clearance",[166] and AJS who provided a 6 HP V-twin that used oil-bath chain-cases for both primary and final drive in order to ensure reliability over long distances in harsh conditions.[167] "The wildest parts of Colonial bush cannot provide a worse trial ground for a motor-bicycle than the Russian steppes, especially when war conditions are added"; so demanding was the terrain that in order to forestall frame breakage 8HP Royal Ruby machines were supplied with outrigger front down-tubes that flanked the main one and were bolted to the steering head and the engine mount.[168] In 1914 the Russian government "purchased practically all the motor cycles it could lay its hands on", to the extent that, in those early days of "business as usual", the promise of further orders may have led the government to actually discourage conversion of motor plants to munitions manufacture,[169] contributing to the "shell scandal" of 1915. Such madness was matched on the far side of the Baltic: "one expert was sent to Russia, where he tackled the tough assignment of training peasants who could not speak his language to ride motor cycles in the dead of winter over icy surfaces on which he doubted his own ability to remain vertical!"[170]

After the February Revolution British manufacturers were left with "some hundreds of machines" on their hands. As the year wore on toward the October Revolution it became increasingly evident that the Russians never would collect these. Interestingly, one was sent to "the Madonnas of Pervyse" in Belgium, fitted with an Empire sidecar ambulance.[171]

Away from France and Flanders, Britain and her allies fought wherever they could or had to. These campaigns were at best diversions from the real struggle and at worst they robbed the Western Front of sorely needed troops and resources. Nevertheless there was a perceived moral need to prosecute the King's enemies wherever they were found. British and Empire forces therefore found themselves fighting in the Pacific (briefly), in Africa and in the Middle East, and propping up Allied liability Italy.[172]

Politicians whose admirable liberal sentiments recoiled from slaughter and the scale of it on the Western Front exaggerated the importance of these other fronts; surely elsewhere Britain could wear away Germany's allies without facing German technological and military superiority, "knock away the props", in Lloyd George's phrase, and force Germany to surrender? Hard facts were to the contrary: Germany rather was holding her allies up; capturing Jerusalem was never going to win the war, and ringing church bells to celebrate that capture could never do more than briefly boost civilian morale. The ultimate hard fact was that the war could be won only by defeating the strongest adversary, Germany, in the main theatre of war, the Western Front. Just as the generals ordered. "The chief mistakes in strategy [through the war]," the most honest Frock of the time—Lord Grey—acknowledged, was "'sideshows.'"[173]

When Lloyd George became prime minister in 1916 the "Easterners" found themselves in a far stronger position, and from then to the end the generals, specifically Haig and "Wully" Robertson, had to fight more than the enemy to win the war. There is no doubt that Lloyd George was horrified and outraged by the bloodletting, and frantic to cut down the butcher's bill; but his notion that "the long way round is the short way home" had less connection to reality than to the often-immoral horse-trading that politicians have to do, and which always had worked well for such an astute master of his game as Lloyd George, as well as with the man's personal immorality, which manifested itself in the blatant lies he told in his struggle with the generals, both in parliament at the time and in print over the years that followed.

That said, the first venture of the Easterners was endorsed by the greatest Brass Hat of all—at least in the public mind—Lord Kitchener, Secretary of War. In part he approved the undertaking because Gallipoli was a joint Anglo-French campaign and thereby it allowed the British to show commitment without spilling too much blood—at least not as much as they would have to were they to send partially trained troops to the Western Front. For all the horrors of Gallipoli, the death rate was much lower there than on the Western Front: of every nine men engaged, two became casualties at Gallipoli, five on the Western Front. It is also true that engaging the Turks reduced their capacity to prosecute the Russians, who were being mauled badly by the Germans; possibly the best thing that can be said for the campaign is that it deferred the Russian Revolution.

Apart perhaps from that, Gallipoli was a total failure, which the Dardanelles Commission later confirmed. Winston Churchill contributed greatly to the disaster, and for the rest of his life persisted in the delusion that the venture could have succeeded if prosecuted further. In fact, he himself had acknowledged in 1911, when First Lord of the Admiralty, that "it is no longer possible to force the Dardanelles";[174] but the myth of "knocking away the props" had quickly taken on the power of faith among the Frocks, even before Lloyd George's premiership, and all of faith's allure and beguilement and ferocious defensiveness.

Both Frock Coats and Brass Hats stand indicted by the conduct of Gallipoli. The whole campaign was less planned than cobbled together, at both the outset and throughout. In fairness to Churchill, he had advocated a joint sea-land attack, and Kitchener's agreement to a purely naval expedition in February-March served only to forewarn the Turks and ensure that when a joint campaign was launched in April it came up against reinforced resistance.

Gallipoli, with its sand, cliffs, gullies and salt lakes does not seem like a locale in which any war motorcyclist could distinguish himself. "There were no roads here when we landed", testifies Alan Baker, "and even now they are only a combination of sand and bumps".[175] The fact that motorcyclists *were* sent to Gallipoli provides further evidence of the campaign planners' ignorance. Often "The machines have to be pushed even running on low gear".[176] Both despatch riders and Motor Machine Gunners did serve in the theatre, and if they did so without marked distinction, the fault was hardly theirs.

Surprisingly, George Mead's initial reaction was that the dirt track roads, beaten down and compacted by earlier traffic, were "ideal for motorcycling".[177] Motorcycles were used between Divisional HQ and, chiefly, "Red Cross Casualty clearing stations, and Supply dumps in the Chocolate Hill and Lala Baba areas"; there also was daily DR communication between Divisional and GHQ, which was on the island of Imbros, something that involved a voyage by trawler, and a DRLS to both Imbros and Lala Baba.[178] Part of the route from one Casualty Clearing Station was over a very crude corduroy road, "railway sleepers placed 12 [inches] apart and filled in between by sand which the wind swept away causing us to make very slow and bumpy progress, thus rendering us 'sitting ducks'" for the Turkish artillery, which overlooked all of Suvla Bay.[179] The DRs determined that the gunners were firing according to a process of observation in one place in order to drop a shell on another after a measured interval, and countered the Turks by pausing in their journey until the shell went over.

Corporal Lamb was much less impressed than Mead with his Gallipoli posting. The roads, he found, "were merely tracks of deep sand with rocks half hidden, and it was something of a feat to be able to keep in the saddle at all".[180] Heat, dust and flies, and constant shortage of water were other complaints, as for Tommy Atkins. Lamb initially was based at Gully Ravine, which provided some cover by virtue of its depth—though shrapnel was a hazard—but once out of the ravine Lamb and his companions had to run a gauntlet of shells from the commanding heights of Achi Baba, "which seemed to watch over everything like some evil eye…. Anything moving caused the Turkish batteries to open fire and range on the road, the distance of which they were perfectly familiar with". Speed was the only chance a man had, and while Lamb found his Triumph "behaved marvellously", it was up against it on the dreadful roads.[181] Later, at Anzac Cove, he is supplied with a Douglas, which "behaved splendidly" over roads that were "mostly awful bumps, with long strips of soft sand and open country". Boulders buried in sand can bring a rider off, and when the rain comes it washes away much sand, exposing rocks and stripping corduroy roads of their insulating surface dust, leaving, here and elsewhere, "bumps which literally shake one to pieces. How the 'Douglas' machines stand it is a marvel! I was literally physically sick the other day while carrying a despatch, and had to get off suddenly and vomit". If sand and boulders are not enough to satisfy the intrepid DR, there's also Salt Lake: "a treacherous reach of mud".[182]

Advanced units could be reached only on foot, moving through a "maze" of mostly shallow trenches—bedrock preventing deep excavation—which were a Turkish sniper's delight. But Lamb realised that W beach was a cushy spot compared with Anzac Cove, after he was transferred to the latter, and had to take a despatch to the front line on foot. In the darkness he has to follow by hand the communications wire, stepping into rotting corpses en route, and daylight seems only to illuminate a place "full of horrors", the groaning of wounded men adding accompaniment to the sight and smell of the dead, until Lamb comes to fear that his nerve will go. "The sights one sees almost beggar description". Footslogging through the heavy sand is exhausting, yet there is no respite, for between despatches stores have to be fetched from the beach and dugouts excavated. Eventually weakened by dysentery, he is "staggering along in a weakened state, with despatches, hoping to dodge the ever-present sniper's bullet".[183]

Eventually there are only five DRs left out of a full complement of 25 and the workload is correspondingly increased, as the year moves toward its end and rain turns dust to mud. Buffeted by heavy winds, "staggering along carrying despatches on foot was wearisome beyond compare".[184] Flash floods in November fill the trenches and the Signals office, bedding is soaked—and then comes frost to freeze it solid. About twenty men were drowned and as many froze to death in this forgotten episode of a disastrous campaign.[185]

In addition to despatch riders, a Motor Machine Gun Squadron was sent by the Royal Navy to Gallipoli in March 1915.[186] Quickly it became evident that in the rocky sandy confines they were of even less value than despatch riders and their crews became machine gunners plain and simple. The only truly successful operation through the entire campaign was the evacuation, and in the course of this one Stanley West of the MMGS won the DSM "for gallantry in keeping the Turks at bay".[187]

If through the lens of history Gallipoli makes little sense, Salonika makes less. It played to the delusions of the Frocks in sustaining dreams of attacking Austria-Hungary from the south and along the Danube, and, like Gallipoli, pandered to imperialist greed. It also served to sideline French general Sarrail who threatened the career of Joffre, already on the skids. It soon became, as von Falkenhayn termed it, effectively a concentration camp of the Allies' own making.

Salonika was a despatch rider's nightmare: "The present condition of the roads in the war zone on the Western Front is like a billiard table when compared with the tracks around Salonika", reported CD Wallbank of the RE. "There are no roads, only mule tracks covered with huge boulders, etc. It is simply terrible ... all hills and mountains.... I have been all over Flanders, Belgium and France, and I can truthfully say that there is not a road there that would in any way compare with those around Salonika". So large were some of the boulders in the roads that crankcases were broken by contact with them.[188]

Another DR appears to disagree somewhat—at the outset:

> The roads are few and far between, but those that are there are quite passable, though they are gradually being ruined by the never-ceasing streams of motor lorries. [But] many of the camps are away from the roads and DRs have to make their way across all sorts of grounds to reach them. Recently we had deep snow and twenty-five degrees of frost and it was no joke riding [motorcycles], as you may imagine.

One DR, a veteran of 1914, explains further: there was a division in hardship between those DRs attached to divisions and brigades "who are stationed in the hills [and] have a much worse time than the corps men", who could use such roads as there were. Yet another DR, Irishman PJ Cox, reports roads to be in "an appalling condition"—and he was "a prominent competitor" in trials riding. Even toward the end of the war, away from the main routes gradients and roads were so bad that "riders used an average of one [inner tube] per day".[189] One captain of the RE reports: "The practically complete absence of roads [means that] it is quite common for two DRs to go out together, in order to assist each other through floods, over rivers or streams, and across gullies".[190]

When there was movement out of Salonika, it was only from the frying pan into the fire, as far as Don R was concerned. "Serbian roads were hopeless.... It was more like trick riding than motor cycling.... Everything that could shed itself came from the machines. The meagre stock of spares was soon exhausted, and we had to dismantle one good machine to get parts for the others". Yet even in such unpromising conditions Don proved his value "as all wires were cut and despatch riding was the only means of communications"—and the humble motorcycle proved its worth in other ways too: "My Douglas has done a great deal of towing of other machines".[191]

Breakdown is an apt metaphor for this campaign.

Desert Campaigns

After his spell at Gallipoli, George Mead was sent to Egypt, where he was issued with a Triumph. Apart from some good roads that ran a few miles out of Cairo and Alexandria and "a few military roads just made", there were only "camel tracks" across desert, and "if we can strike a camel track twelve inches wide and solid ground we are as happy as sandboys". Such roads as existed were hardly improved by the sudden increase in use; lorries eroded huge potholes that "filled to the level of the surrounding ground with drifted sand",[192] which could fetch the best of riders off. One of Mead's colleagues questioned the wisdom of even trying to use motorcycles here, though he praises the motorcyclists:

> Of what use are motor cyclists in a roadless country where the only means of transport is by camel?... His back wheel made snake-like movements [in the loose sand]. Now he would strike a hidden rock, and would be lifted a foot or more off the saddle; then the front wheel would slither away, and only by a violent effort would the rider correct his balance, but he conquered all difficulties, and ... the motor cyclist section remained, as before, the most efficient section of the company.[193]

This might sound like boasting, but the highest calibre of volunteer still was attracted to the DR corps at that stage of the war and one should not dismiss the claim entirely. On a raid on Siwa oasis it was "to the surprise of everybody but their riders [that] two motor cyclists managed to plough their way through from end to end". They had had to cover more than 200 miles through desert, riding convoy on 146 vehicles, and the horrendous dust that such a convoy inevitably raised.[194] In such conditions one Douglas engine "inhaled so much dust and sand that the deposit on the pistons consisted of an oil and sand sludge".[195]

As demanding, if over a much shorter distance, was the ride undertaken by Corporal Railton Holden and another DR, who set an unofficial record from Shallufa to Kabrit East, in Sinai. On their Douglases, they covered over eighteen miles in 75 minutes across glaring saltpans and sand that sometimes was so soft they had to dismount and push the bikes. They also had to push them up a steep sand hill that had earned the name "the precipice" from other riders. "My wrists were so numb with skidding, wobbling, pushing and mounting again that when we did reach the track I could scarcely feel the handle bars".[196]

Initially George Mead ran despatches between Port Tewfik and Ismailia and maintained a DRLS around the port. He was then attached to the Desert Mounted Corps and transferred to Kantara, on the Sinai bank of the Suez Canal, half way between Ismailia and Port Said. The sand presented problems, but the British had laid wire-mesh roads (described previously) and Mead found that "quite a fair speed could be reached along them". Where the wire mesh gave out DRs sometimes took to the railway lines, bouncing along the sand-infilled sleepers.[197]

Signals' responsibilities remained the same: maintaining communications by several means.

> Over the Air Line and Cable wires were daily transmitted the everyday interdepartmental messages, eventually delivered by orderly or DRLS. Coded operational orders were delivered by DR and then often in pairs. The 3 shifts were worked daily 8 am to 2 pm, to 10 pm, to 8 am. Night duty was mainly precautionary.[198]

In this regard, perhaps the most interesting experience Mead recounts is when he dismounts his rear wheel and connects the gearbox pulley to another on a cable reeler, in order to ease the laying of a temporary ground cable across the desert.[199] This reflects both the closer integration of the DR into the Signals Service and the increasing importance of cable communication.

Eventually, though, it's time to go to war in earnest, in support of Allenby's assault on Beersheba in October 1917. Palestine was characterised by harsh desert interspersed by fertile oases and the latter struck one DR, "after seven months wandering in that awful waste known as the Sinai Desert", like "the green fields of Elysium". But it was no heaven: WH Elce reports a 24-hour stint in the saddle without a break. Where road metal was laid down, it was, as always, done so with heavy transport rather than motorcycles in mind, and might consist of four-inch diameter stones, unrolled, often with sheer drops off onto the desert. Despite this, "accidents were rare".[200]

Another DR records that "ploughed fields, heavy sand dunes and mountainous 'wadi' country" meant low gear and slow times. Wadis, the steep-sided beds of seasonal rivers, "are sometimes of a sandy nature, but they are mostly made up of rocks and boulders, or may be likened to a shingly beach in many places. Consequently the going is very rough". Despite this, and the danger of being drowned in a flash flood, DRs often used wadi-beds: after all, conditions were hardly better on the wider desert, and wadis offered some shelter from the broiling sun, as well as concealment from Turks or hostile Arabs, the value of which was demonstrated in April 1918 when one DR broke down in Wadi Ghuzze (near Gaza), and found himself "almost surrounded by Turks". He was able to hide not merely himself but his motorcycle, until the Turks moved on, two days later.[201]

But it wasn't always possible to follow wadis, and crossing them was hard on men and bikes alike, their banks being "of a mountainous character and very precipitous.... The motor cycles stand up to the terrific gruelling to a degree which is little less than marvellous". Inevitably, though, they suffer problems of over-heating and tyre-creep as wheels spun on loose sand, ripping valves from tubes. Tyre-creep was addressed by fitting security bolts, but these complicated puncture repair, and wheel-slippage and the frequent need for low gear increased fuel consumption to about 25 mpg, and oil consumption to 100-120 mpg.[202]

An interesting example of ingenuity and initiative was found in the Palestine campaign, when some DRs fitted a triple rear wheel to a Douglas, in order to improve grip over sandy surfaces. The centre rim was stripped of its spokes and connected to the outer two by a dozen transverse struts. A cooling fan also was added.[203]

During the advance on Beersheba, Mead and a colleague, Burney by name, are detailed to wait behind in order to bring last-minute operational orders to Advanced Corps HQ, some 30 miles ahead. The two Dons decide that they can shorten their journey by cutting a diagonal across the desert, despite this sector being held by the Turks and peopled, besides, with hostile Bedouin tribesmen. High temperatures, loose sand and high dunes, which have to be circumvented, promise to add to the fun.

About half way to their destination, Mead and Burney are fired on by a group of Bedouins. They scare them off "by letting our engines roar away declutched, and by lifting the exhaust valve intermittently produced a sound similar to that of machine gunfire. That together with a few shots from our revolvers made them hurriedly vanish". But then the combination of high temperatures and deep sand begins to tell on the motorcycles. The engines overheat, and in addition Burney's clutch begins to slip. Sand between the plates and a tow from Mead get the pair going again, and they "arrived dead on target at Advanced HQ".[204]

No sooner arrived, though, but Mead, the next DR on the roster, had to take a despatch to GHQ, many miles away, over roads he did not know. A colleague, Gus King, who did know the road, volunteered to accompany him, and they left at 0200, in pitch darkness. After sunrise the heat of the day takes its toll, and Gus had to be left at an inter-route signal office, while Mead pressed on to deliver his despatch at 0100 next day.[205] Typical of so many men of the time, Mead's concern is "record[ing] the devotion to duty and physical endurance of Gus King"; he almost seems to regard himself as a mere witness to this.

Reward comes with a posting to Khirbeit Deiran, a Jewish colony of fewer than 1,000 then, some 40 miles north of Beersheba. With the Turk on the run, "DRLS had become a most welcome duty, we almost scrambled for the chance of a ride around the Holyland [sic]".

In Mesopotamia the main complaint was heat. "When remounting after a stop even contact with the burning saddle becomes torture ... at 110 degrees in the shade!"

There were the same problems of desert riding encountered in Sinai and Palestine, as well as some unique, as to every theatre. Washboard surfaces provided "the worst kind" of road, yet the little Douglas proved up to the DR's task. "After nearly 3,000 miles of the above, with a stud of seventeen motor cycles, we have not had one breakage or stoppage (except sooted plugs and stuck rocker arms)"—the qualifier does not undermine the assertion, given the tribological limitations and riders' expectations of the time. DR Corporal Black, though he rates the BSA as "top" (some Ariel, BSA and AJS motorcycles were supplied to this theatre, as well as the standard Douglas and Triumph), is impressed with the Douglas, "an ideal 'bus for our work.... I have never heard of a Dug overheating, even though the temperature here the last two months has averaged 122 degrees in the shade". There are, he goes on, "very few real roads here.... Often the sand is six to ten inches deep.... Here the light weight of the Douglas proves invaluable". Somewhat undermining his testimony to the BSA he concludes, "We think the Douglas is the most suitable, not from the point of reliability in particular ... but for its handiness in getting through thick sand".[206]

In the Mesopotamian Campaign distances called for relay riding, with DRs carrying all they might need to withstand being possibly isolated by breakdown or enemy action in a hostile desert. A full day's ride was normally up to 100 miles, but "Some DRs have had as many as 250 miles to do, and no roads—nothing but native paths—to use [, all] either hard and very bumpy or sandy". As elsewhere, road improvements to suit heavy transport did not necessarily benefit the motorcyclist: "There is a very long, sandy hill covered by cocoanut palm stems to prevent the wheels of a motor lorry from sinking, and a DR finds it very rough and trying to ride over these palms". Newly-cut roads in the moister delta and Tigris-Euphrates valleys might be marked by tree stumps, and another hazard, in this theatre where the Indian Army was deployed, was the holes left by elephants' "tiny feet" in the wet season; in the dry, these could be "15 inches to 2 feet deep", often filled and camouflaged with dust. One DR broke both footrests when he hit one, with "only another thirty-seven miles to go". In the delta and valleys malaria was a hazard, along with dysentery everywhere, and everywhere too was the hazard of locals used to a much slower pace of life stepping in front of a fast-moving motorcycle.[207]

Of all the sideshows, the desert campaigns seem to have been the most wasteful of men and resources, because whatever possibility there might have been in knocking out Austria-Hungary and Bulgaria and attacking Germany up the Danube, fighting Turkey anywhere away from the strategically valuable Dardanelles was not going to affect the outcome of the essential struggle. Yet in the desert, as in every theatre, the war motorcyclist proved his value: Sergeant CJ McGowan of the RE, to take an example, was awarded the DCM "for distinguished service in connection with the military operations of the British Forces in Mesopotamia".[208]

Africa

At the outset of war the British, keenly aware that their governance of millions was conditional on those millions' consent to be governed, were anxious not to encourage rebellious impulses, and hoped that the boundaries stipulated by the Berlin Conference of 1885 would be respected—in short, that war would pass Africa by. Governor Heinrich Schnee of *Ostafrika*—German East Africa, the mainland part of modern Tanzania, plus Rwanda and Burundi— hoped likewise. Unfortunately Governor Schnee's control was tenuous: the *Königsberg* began commerce raiding out of Dar es Salaam and two British cruisers entered and shelled that harbour in retaliation. The outcome was that within days of war's declaration General Paul von Lettow-Vorbeck over-ruled Schnee, his nominal superior, and initiated a campaign that was not to be lifted until weeks after the armistice, and would make for Lettow-Vorbeck the same sort of reputation that the next war would make for his compatriot, Erwin Rommel. Lettow-Vorbeck had 280 German personnel and almost ten times that number of *askaris* in his *Schutztruppe* colonial defence force, probably a little more than the two battalions of the King's African Rifles that faced him initially; but through the war the British were to send tens of thousands of men from the British and Indian armies, the Belgians were to send troops from the Congo, and the Portuguese more from what became Mozambique, after Portugal entered the war in 1916, in a vain attempt to apprehend Lettow-Vorbeck, and the war ranged over much of sub-Saharan East Africa.

Initial British concern was focused not on East, but on South Africa, where Christiaan de Wet's short-lived Boer rebellion had to be put down. Ivor Augustus was a despatch rider-cum-scout in this campaign, mounted on an outdated Sunbeam 2¾ HP single that used belt drive direct from crankshaft to rear wheel, engine power supplemented by what was euphemistically termed at the time LPA—"light pedal assistance"—as on a 1960s moped. To cover the 100 miles from Vryburg to Morokwen took four days, but this was quite good, given that Augustus had to make scouting reports and given that "roads... were fearful, generally six inches and more in dust". This dust penetrated his wheel bearings and caused them to collapse, and then abraded the wheel spindle thin enough for it to bend, but the resourceful Augustus straightened this and proceeded to Morokwen, the only DR to reach the town. His reward was a month's bonus pay and free South African rail pass.[209]

The de Wet campaign bled across the border into German *Südwestafrika* (now Namibia), where though the enemy lacked Lettow-Vorbeck's tenacity and skill, he still put up a fight. Another DR was luckier than Augustus in that he was mounted on a 1913 Douglas, which gave the same sort of service here as it was to give on the Western Front and elsewhere. "For the two months of the rebellion I was riding in rain the whole time. On several occasions I had to ford drifts with the water well over the engine, and the only trouble during the whole time was choked mudguards"—surely the greatest, most consistent problem, in every theatre. Later, during

> that great trek up the Swakop river which ended in the capture of Karib and Windhoek [from] a motor cyclist's point of view it would be impossible to picture anything worse[;] all the riders ... had to jump off and run alongside for the major portion of the way up the river bed, as the sand was so thick it was impossible for the machines to pull the riders through. Out of about sixty riders who started from Swakopmund only about twenty five arrived at Karib with the brigades, the rest having broken down *en route*, and of the twenty five only four did the journey without outside assistance.[210]

The Germans of *Südwestafrika* defeated, most of the British and South African motorcyclists were transferred to *Ostafrika*,[211] where Lettow-Vorbeck had attracted the sympathy and tacit support of many Arabs—expecting that German victory would result in restoration of the slave trade—which led to "valuable information" being furnished him. By December 1914 the German was "master of the situation".[212] As farther south and west, the terrain of the much larger East African theatre imposed its own demands on combatants, and offered daunting challenges. As early as 12 August 1914 "a motor-cycle despatch-rider service [from Nairobi] back to Kijabe was organised by the newly-formed East African Mechanical Transport Corps".[213] But, as everywhere in the Great War, motorcyclists served in many roles. Others attached to the Corps patrolled important roads and "were constantly ambushed" by the enemy. On 3 September 1914 a raid on their base at Mbuyuni sent them scattering in disorganisation, and resulted in the capture of some motorcycles.[214]

Roads were mere tracks—"there are no roads at all"[215]—and as the campaign advanced the British lines of communication and supply became more attenuated. Tropical seasonal changes meant that in the wet months "roads" could be under water or intractable with mud, while in the dry season they "were just like a frozen ploughed field, and why the frames [of the motorcycles] did not break I do not know" (of course, many did). So bad were road surfaces that this particular correspondent's car "broke up three twin-wire wheels in eighty miles!"[216] Dust meant that despite colonial-pattern air filters (filters were not normally fitted on home-market motorcycles back then), at decarbonising time piston deposits were "half carbon and half earth".[217]

Local fauna presented their own dangers: "of the rhinos one had to be very careful", one DR remarks in dry understatement.[218] Another, in poor light (twilight descends with notorious swiftness in the tropics), struck a lion and was thrown from his motorcycle. Despite a sprained ankle he managed to climb a tree before the lion realised his supper potential, and stayed there all night "without a bite of food or any covering, soaked to the skin by the tropical rain". Next morning the lion was breakfasting elsewhere but the whole plain was flooded, and his sprained ankle left Don unable to start his motorcycle, so he had to limp on with his despatch. Another DR "achieved the remarkable performance of covering 200 miles over appalling ground, mostly consisting of sand patches and hills, in 33 hours".[219]

As the campaign advanced, heavy lorries of the Mechanical Transport Corps degraded such roads as there were. (An enduring benefit to local people was the infrastructure of good roads that had to be laid down to serve the war effort as it became evident that Lettow-Vorbeck was not going to come quietly.) "The going was exceedingly bad in places, as the road is practically confined to heavy baggage convoys which play havoc with such a soft foundation. In many places the sand had filled up large holes to a depth of about fifteen inches, making a trap for the unwary". A Douglas rider, who rode almost 200 miles from Dar-es-Salaam to Kilossa, was grateful to find "better" going where "dust was seldom more than two inches deep, and pot-holes of any size only occurred at intervals of about 150 yards". Caught out by the short tropical twilight he covered eight miles in darkness, but conditions deteriorated and he slept in a broken-down car he came across. Further deterioration of the road led to his having to push the Douglas through deep dust.[220]

Dust was not a problem in the rainy season, but this could create "one big swamp ... quite impassable even to ox waggon transport let alone motor cycles.... I have had my machine ploughing through mud that reached half way up the crank case, which eventually brought it to a standstill and required the strength of three natives to lift it out again".[221] Even in less extreme conditions mudguards clogged in the wet season, as on the Western Front.

Apart from the Russian, the East African was the most mobile front of the war, and this offered great military potential to motorcycles—but presented great challenges too. A Motor Cycle Corps did much to vindicate Major Casserly's claims for a motorcycle-mounted infantry force, as many citations in various Supplements to the *London Gazette* prove.[222] In one "recent scrap" the Corps engaged an enemy force that numbered about 1,200, instead of the expected 500, and suffered five killed, twenty wounded and seventeen captured.[223] As well as its combat cyclists, the Motor Cycle Corps had 50 DRs attached—these were in addition to those attached to the Mechanical Transport Corps, and to many other units.

Motor Machine Guns also were deployed in East Africa, where "the mobility of the units was of great value and they saw considerable action".[224] They worked well in association with the Motor Cycle Corps: in an assault on a strongly-fortified enemy position at Tschenene "a battery of armoured motors ... helped materially to make short work of the defence and defenders".

> From this point, to anticipate the moving up of enemy troops to Dodoma, [Colonel SAL] Berrangé was sent on ahead with two battalions of infantry, a motor cycle corps, and a strong detachment of mounted scouts. He was in Dodoma four days later.... By this prompt seizure of the railway one of the chief advantages of von Lettow-Vorbeck's move into the Nguru district was nullified.[225]

Douglases and perhaps a few Triumphs were the usual DR's mount across the East African theatre,[226] as on the Western Front, but all active-combat motorcyclists—those in the Motor Cycle Corps—were "mounted on 4¼HP BSAs, and a stronger machine and more powerful engine would be hard to find", one rider testifies.[227] The BSA was all but a flagrant copy of the Triumph, and had the advantages that went with this, but it also had a far more robust front fork and better brakes, the former in particular a great advantage in this theatre; the apparent preponderance of Douglases over Triumphs here may have a great deal to do with the latter's weak front fork. The BSAs did have problems, but given the conditions it would be amazing if they did not, and engines seem to have given little trouble, despite dust-penetration of the air filters and temperatures that could reach 120 degrees in the shade, heat that lifted patches from repaired tubes as well as adding to rider misery.[228] In the dry season water was always short, and brush fires were a hazard. "One considerable fire was caused by a motor-cycle skid, the machine bursting into flames as the rider fell"[229] (apparently this was not a BSA).

There is no reason to doubt that the BSA was as robust a bike as most men claimed—it used a caged roller bearing in the con-rod big end, when most bikes used crowded rollers[230]—but its ground clearance was inadequate to the rough terrain, and lack of a handlebar-mounted clutch lever increased problems of control. Its American-made magneto gave some trouble, and shortage of spares meant that bikes had to be cannibalised to keep the rest going. One gearbox needed replacement of a bearing as inadvertently it had been run without oil.[231] Gearing was lowered in order to cope with load and ground, the engine breathers needed to be modified to prevent dust and sand from being sucked into the crankcases, and homemade cloth washers were cut to help protect wheel-bearings. Oddly enough, despite the rough terrain and spear-like thorns, punctures were relatively few.[232] The terrain, and the great weight carried, overloaded both wheel-spokes and forks, and wheel building seems to have been something of a regular maintenance chore. The need for constant mobility, in pursuit of Lettow-Vorbeck, meant that the motorcyclist, DR or combat soldier, "has no base billet [so] must carry absolutely every atom of his kit and equipment with him, and the luggage carried … would have made some of our home riders open their eyes"; total weight was about 140lbs.

> Firmly strapped across the carrier were a large kit-bag and a roll of blankets done up in a waterproof sheet, surmounted by a mess-tin and a tin of "bully". On the near side a spare belt was coiled up under the pannier bag, and on the off side a despatch and map case. The saddle down tube carried a spare inner tube in its leather case and a spare water bottle. Bags holding flour, coffee, and sugar were tied to the handle-bar, together with an enamel drinking mug and a tin of beef fat. Attached to the front fork was a long rifle holster, in which were a rifle and signalling flags…. A spare pair of puttees wrapped round the tank served as knee-grips.

An unusually robust front brake—a dummy belt-pulley rather than a rim-stirrup—helped stopped the considerable weight, but carriers broke under their loads and footboards were ripped off against rocks and in deep sand.[233]

In the teeth of these problems, all 400 BSAs supplied survived the campaign—at least according to George H Frost.[234] George was no disinterested reporter, though, but what now would be regarded as a PR executive for BSA; however, there is tentative support for his claim. The Motor Cycle Corps' chaplain testifies: "after 2,800 miles, with the cycles very much overloaded and used over the worst roads in the world, there is not one machine that cannot take to the road at once".[235] This tribute is not necessarily at variance with the fact that some machines had to be cannibalised, for these may have been stripped in emergencies and restored when spares eventually were supplied. One rider claims that up until 1917 at least "We have still our original number of machines";[236] another describes how tribes were paid for recovering broken-down motorcycles,[237] a practice that could help account for sustaining numbers. There can be no doubt that some motorcycles were lost—those in the German raid on Mbuyuni, for instance, and at least one that was accidentally burned—but all 400 BSAs may well have been conserved.

The fact that the BSAs were fitted with fully enclosed chain drive helps explain their impressive reliability, for the loads they carried would have overwhelmed a belt's friction drive, and the terrain they had to cover would have worn out exposed chains within a thousand miles. (A transmission shock absorber eased some of the harshness inherent in all-chain drive at the time.) But doubtless a significant reason why they all survived was because replacing them, in such a remote theatre, would have been extremely difficult. Another reason is that despite the harshness of the terrain, and the wiliness of the enemy, the East African theatre was nowhere nearly as demanding as the Western Front.

The East African campaign reflects well on the military capabilities of all concerned but especially on the African troops, who bore the brunt of the fighting, and perhaps more than any on the Germans' *askaris*, who remained undefeated—though of course without leadership and the discipline imposed by their German officers they never could have been so effective. Lettow-Vorbeck proved himself not only a wily and worthy foe but also a decent human being who respected British non-combatants and cared for his *askaris*: in an almost pathetically-ironic footnote to history, the surviving *askaris* of Germany's East African campaign of the First World War were paid pensions by the ultimate victors of the Second, the USA, thanks to the efforts of Lettow-Vorbeck through the agency of his old adversary Jan Smuts, by now his old friend. Smuts, erstwhile Boer commander, later a field marshal in the British Army, recently a founder of the United Nations, passed the call on to the USA, now banker of the Western world, and in the waxing antagonism of the Cold War the USA responded, underwriting the pensions of those of the *Schutztruppe* still alive. This contradiction of the usually brutal imperial German attitude to "mud races" is made poignant by the fact that Lettow-Vorbeck was himself poverty-stricken when he made his appeal.[238]

If cynicism may be discerned in the motives of the underwriters of the scheme—given the jockeying for position between the superpowers across the Third World—it's difficult to impute anything but the best in human nature to Lettow-Vorbeck's campaign for justice for his old *askaris*, or in his old African warriors' response. Many of these had lost their discharge papers over the decades that had elapsed since they had lain their rifles down, undefeated in the field, and to eliminate impostors while being as fair as possible in administering the relief scheme, someone came up with the notion of issuing drill commands in German to all claimants.

Not one old soldier failed the test.

Neither did the British despatch rider sent to find Lettow-Vorbeck with news of Germany's surrender.[239]

The Easter Rising

On 24 April 1916 what one might term the Far Western Front was opened when an alliance of dissident republicans and militant socialists raised rebellion in Ireland with the help of "gallant allies"—the Butchers of Belgium.[240] The Easter Rising had no chance of military success, something both the rebels and their cynical German paymasters realised, and that it lasted almost a week took its own leaders by surprise. But its effect on the war effort was of longer duration, as a whole division (the 59th) was sent to secure Ireland, rather than to France in the build-up to the Somme offensive, and the hostility elicited by the ham-fisted response by the British to the Rising continued to divert men, resources and attention until the War of Independence erupted two months after the Armistice.

Chief among the rebel leaders of 1916 was Pat—latterly Padraig—Pearse, son of an Englishman and Commandant General of the Irish Volunteers, a rump of the National Volunteers, most of whom had helped form the 16th Division in 1914. Even as the rebellion was playing itself out, some of these comrades were being gallantly gassed at Hulloch by their old friends' new allies. Pearse was an impressive and limpidly sincere man, described by the British general who pronounced his death sentence as "one of the finest characters I have ever come across".[241] Undoubtedly he was well intentioned, like many of his comrades, but in his case at least a terrifying naiveté was coupled to the elitism of all radical nationalists. Until a couple of years previously Pearse had been a constitutionalist and less than two months before taking up arms had acknowledged that "if any nation can obtain its freedom without bloodshed it is its duty to so obtain it".[242] He may have been able to square this statement with raising armed rebellion while Home Rule was pending in the same way that he seems to have enigmatically envisaged such rebellion resulting, in a densely populated city, and in an age of artillery and high explosives, in his own heroic self-sacrificial death alone—certainly no civilian casualties. These greatly outnumbered those of combatants on both sides, and the rising death toll of the innocent played a part in inducing Pearse, to his credit, to surrender.

Commanding the other rebel faction, the Citizen Army, was James Connolly; like Pearse a well-intentioned if cranky man, a Scottish-born veteran of the British Army, now working to bring down international capitalism by fighting for Irish nationalism. Another do-gooder, thinking with his Marxist ideology, convinced that no decadent empire would destroy the property of its capitalists—in the teeth of more than a year's evidence to the contrary from France and Belgium—he was certain that the rebels would not be bombarded out.[243] One of the first acts of Connolly's defenders of the working class was to steal the handcart of a working man; when the man tried to recover his livelihood his whimsical defenders shot him dead.

In charge of military operations was a dying consumptive, Joseph Mary Plunkett. One of the rebels later described their military rationale as "little short of madness": an early military operation saw trenches dug in Stephens Green, where they were overlooked by four storeys on four sides.[244] Meanwhile, back in the GPO, after declaring a *republic*, Pearse and Plunkett discussed establishing a *kingdom*: "an independent Ireland with a German Prince as King. They even named the Prince, Joachim"—the Kaiser's son.[245]

Anyone who thinks that one might look for more collective intelligence, imagination and commonsense in a henhouse than at Rebel HQ ought to peek into the enemy camp. First response by the British called for mounted lancers to charge the General Post Office, which was defended by riflemen behind limestone walls a couple of feet thick. The outcome was as predictable as that dead horses will stink in the sun.[246] Most Crown casualties were inflicted in the assault on a fortified position on Mount Street Bridge, one that easily could have been bypassed, isolated and reduced at leisure. After the Rising had been quelled, the British executed the leaders after trial by secret military courts, protracting the executions to add insult to Irish injury, thereby reversing public opinion and sending things into a downhill spin from a very low point of departure.[247]

Despite thinking with their ideologies, the rebels got a few things right. They captured some half-dozen strongpoints around the heart of Dublin, and established their HQ in the GPO. This meant that the British could not safely use telephones, and besides the rebels cut communications—they themselves had to use a tin can on a string to send messages from the GPO to an outlying strongpoint across Sackville Street.

Combination of sabotage and lack of security effectively rendered modern communications systems "dis"—as a Signaller would put it—and called for despatch riders to effect communications among the various units called in from the Curragh (the British Army's main base in Ireland), from Athlone, and from Britain herself, and to coordinate the assault on rebel positions.

Despatch riders gained favourable mention in General Maxwell's account of the fighting: they "fearlessly carried despatches through streets infested with snipers"[248]. One Don, Corporal J Healy from Cork, who had been invalided home from Gallipoli, was sent to Dublin and "for gallantry during the Dublin rebellion he was promoted to sergeant". Sergeant Healy evidently was a manly sort of chap: he had raced a BSA in the 1914 TT and, as well as gaining promotion for delivering despatches, he also was decorated by the Royal Humane Society for rescuing a woman from the River Liffey.[249] Corporal HA Wallen, a local man, possibly like Healy on leave and pressed into service at short notice, also earned praise from General Maxwell for the "useful work" he did on a 6HP AJS sidecar outfit (which may have been supplied by Wallen's father, "a well-known Dublin motor cycle trader").[250]

Contemporary reports prove the validity of Maxwell's endorsement of Don R. There was indeed great danger from snipers, unarmed soldiers on furlough being fired on in the opening stages before they realised what was going on,[251] but for obvious reasons despatch riders became priority targets once the military response came. One might ask how good these snipers could have been, and the answer would have to be "better than one might think". The rebels might not be the Old Contemptibles, but they did have Mausers and Lee Enfields, as well as motley other guns,[252] and the politically sensitive situation in Ireland had meant that the administration had allowed private armies to march and drill for two years. According to one—albeit partisan—account, a British officer compared his own men's accuracy most unfavourably to that of youthful rebels,[253] and certainly some men, like Andy Conroy of the Citizen Army, were recognised sharpshooters.[254] One hundred and twenty five military deaths prove that the rebels knew how to shoot, and their *Gewehr* 1871 Mausers (the "Howth rifles") fired 11mm dumdum bullets, which could do fearsome damage.[255] Maxwell's account, though propagandistic and self-serving, hardly overstated the danger to his men, and his tribute to Don R certainly was not misplaced. Thomas Harborne, a volunteer DR with the Crown forces, was killed in action.[256]

The rebels too depended on couriers and despatch riders, one of whom was shot dead outside Trinity College by an Anzac on furlough. Though one account describes him as a "motor dispatch rider", this man most likely was one of a trio of fast-riding bicycle-mounted DRs.[257] But the rebels certainly did use motorcycles: after the rising had been suppressed, one was discovered inside the GPO, and despite the shelling and fires, this was "perfect, tyres uninjured and petrol in the tank";[258] one may reasonably infer that it was one of two motorcycles ridden into the city from Joseph Plunkett's house on Easter Monday, for use in despatch carrying.

Outside Dublin city, motorcycles were more important. It was a "motorcycliste", Marie Perloz, of the Dublin *Cumann na nBan*, who notified the Cork volunteers of the Rising,[259] and another despatch rider brought the news to the Wexford volunteers, encouraging these to seize Enniscorthy the day after the Dublin insurrection; the garrison held out until after Pearse's surrender.[260] The impressive success of the County Dublin Fifth Battalion was due in large part to the military skills of Dick Mulcahy—second in command of the battalion; later IRA Chief of Staff in the War of Independence—but also because its commandant, Thomas Ashe, rode a motorcycle. The battalion was bicycle-mounted, and ranged over much of North County Dublin and parts of East Meath, picking targets of opportunity that its leader's speed of mobility allowed it to spot. At least one other rebel, James Quigley, was motorcycle mounted, and acted as a scout,[261] and the rebels seem to have used despatch riders to effect communications long before the rebellion erupted,[262] no doubt inspired by the UVF's successful use of motorcycle despatch riders in the Larne gun-running operation.

Not that Ashe's rebels had things all their own way: motorcycle-mounted Constable Eugene Bratton, attached to Navan RIC station, won the Albert Medal for breaking out of an Ashe ambush and bringing help to his beleaguered colleagues.[263]

Outside Dublin and Meath there was little rebel activity, but this did not mean that there were no rebels-in-arms abroad, so the British forces conducted sweeps in various parts of the country to flush them out. Involved in one such operation was a young man from Loyalist Belfast, CA Brett.[264] Brett, a law student, was soon to find himself an officer in France, but at the time of the Easter Rising he was still in training, stationed in Cork, and by lucky chance the proud owner of a little two-stroke Levis motorcycle. He was appointed despatch rider cum billeting officer to his unit, which was scouring counties Waterford and Wexford for rebels in flight—obviously Enniscorthy had been a priority target and some rebels had slipped out of town before the garrison surrendered. By this time two motorcycle-mounted billeting officers had been attached to each division in the BEF,[265] so we see the lessons of the Great War being applied to Ireland—not for the last time, as shown by Brett's fear later on of being "clothes-lined" (see Chapter Three), and captured rebel DRs swallowing their despatches during the War of Independence.

The Easter Rising remains contentious—more so than ever as its centenary approaches. An increasing number of Irish nationalists, no longer so cowed as formerly, contend that it proved ultimately disastrous for their cause and their country, leading as it did to years of conflict and decades of bitterness, as well as ensuring permanent division of the island—its most deadly sabotage of nationalist aspiration. Yet even some who are appalled by the Rising's elitist, anti-democratic impulse, by the tragic and unnecessary deaths it caused— then and in subsequent years—remain impressed by the men who raised it. General Blackader's tribute to Pearse was echoed by Tommy Atkins' to the rebels' courage and the clean fight they made. Some who stood sentry over the doomed leaders' last hours did so in tears.[266] "They all died like men", one witness reported, "but MacDonagh died like a prince."

Thomas MacDonagh was a poet, not a prince, and another Irish poet, Frank Ledwidge, was to die at the Somme a few months later. Ledwidge's last poem, "Thomas MacDonagh", was a lament for his old friend who had died in the "enemy" camp.

The Easter Rising serves as something of a microcosm of the Great War. The two World Wars have been described as a European Civil War, and the Rising had the bitterness of a family quarrel about it, with Dublin Fusiliers putting down insurrection on the streets of their own city; brothers might find themselves pointing guns at each other and—perhaps the most telling example of the complexity of that struggle—William Kent, brother to Eamonn Ceannt, signatory of the Proclamation and one of the "martyrs of Easter Week", was killed in action by his brother's "gallant allies". As the punitive peace of Versailles sowed the seeds of the strife that Hitler harvested in 1939, so the "peace" that General Maxwell imposed by his long-drawn-out executions of the rebel leaders, imposition of martial law, and harassment of peaceful people, sowed the seeds of the War of Independence.

Yet—not to excuse the man but to explore the microcosm further—how better could Maxwell have done in a time of war? He was "a mediocrity" doing his best at a time that called for far more great military minds than the world could supply. Had he been a genius he would have been in France, providing too valuable leadership to be spared to deal with a few troublesome "traitors" in an old stagnant backwater of Empire.[267] His boss, General Haig, was shooting serving soldiers for desertion, cowardice, or even insubordination; how better could he, subordinate General Maxwell, deal with Paddies who had cast their lot with Fritz? This was no small consideration at a time when Britain was fighting for her very life, and the opening of a "Far Western Front" was potentially calamitous: had the Rising been successful, the Provisional Government planned to join the Central Powers;[268] and encouraged by the Rising and the widespread resentment elicited by the disastrous British response, the Germans planned further intervention in Ireland in early 1917: *Aufgabe P.*[269]

Scuppering of nationalist ambition had less to do with the rebels' military failure or war's ironies than with the Rising's confirming Unionists' prejudiced views that Papists could never be trusted and that Fenians were bloodthirsty murderers. This confirmation ensured that division of the island, on the cards since 1911 yet negotiable in its terms, would become non-negotiable and permanent. The Rising, and the misjudged British response to it, led to years of warfare, "troubles" in every decade since, and an enduring national schizophrenia about the use of violence toward political ends. If the

Rising indeed serves as microcosm of a greater European civil war, the fact that to this day dissident republicans continue to murder their fellow Irishmen and -women is a measure of the long shadow cast by the Great War.

Après la guerre fini

This was another term that, though it never suffered such inhumane mispronunciation, came to acquire the same sardonic overtones as *San Fairy Ann*—a sort of Big Rock Candy Mountain of impossible aspiration. And there is more than something of San Fairy Ann in what happened immediately after the armistice.

As is well known, the first and last British casualties of the war were sustained at Mons. Less well known is that from Mons, in 1918 as in 1914, began a long and gruelling march by soldiers of the BEF, this time not in flight from rampant Germans but as rear escort to beaten armies, this time winter's cold and wet adding to the misery rather than summer's heat and dust. John Jackson's account is enough to generate a frisson of déjà vu:

> This constant marching day after day, following closely on the strenuous fighting prior to the Armistice was terribly hard on us, the roads, after the passage of the heavy German artillery and other weighty machinery of war, were in a fearful state, which was made worse by the continued wet weather. We floundered along, up to the ankles in mud and mire....

Again, men's feet suffer, "blood oozing from their dilapidated boots at times", and again food is scarce, supply lines being attenuated.

And again, "There were no wires ... all communications of any distance being done by motor-cycle despatch riders".[270]

Don R, in victory as in impending defeat, did his essential bit.

Endnotes

1 George Coward, *Coward's War: An Old Contemptible's View of the Great War*, pp. 27, 34.
2 Lt-Col Osborn, "Epic Story of St Quentin: How Tom Bridges Saved Two Regiments", p. 96.
3 Andrew Hamilton and Alan Reed (eds), *Meet at Dawn, Unarmed: Captain Robert Hamilton's account of Trench Warfare and the Christmas Truce in 1914*, p. 47.
4 Captain Arnold Gyde, "The Terror and Tribulation of those Fateful Days", p. 68.
5 Corporal B J Denore, "'Sleep-Walkers' of the Great Retreat", p. 105.
6 Richard van Emden (ed), *Tickled to Death to Go: Memoirs of a Cavalryman in the First World War*, pp. 59-60.
7 WHL Watson, *Adventures of a Despatch Rider*, p. 79.
8 Lynn Macdonald, *Ordeal by Fire*, pp. 16-17; Norman Stone, *World War One: A Short History*, p. 44.

9 Malcolm Brown, *The Imperial War Museum Book of 1914*, p. 95.
10 Emden, ibid, p. 59.
11 Brown, ibid, pp. 96, 97.
12 Denore, ibid, p. 102.
13 Sir William Robertson, *From Private to Field Marshall*, pp. 206-07.
14 "I've 'eard different", was a frequent line of his when fielding Lloyd George's glib lies.
15 James Edmonds, *History of the Great War: Military Operations France and Belgium, 1914*, p. 284.
16 Ian Hay, *The First Hundred Thousand*, pp. 228-29.
17 AP Corcoran, *The Daredevil of the Army: Experiences as a "Buzzer" and Despatch Rider*, pp. 39-40.
18 Roger West, "Diary of the War", pp. 16, 111.
19 Charles Edward Callwell, *Experiences of a Dug-Out*, p. 21.
20 Watson, ibid, pp. 26, 55, 61, 203.
21 Philip Warner, "Le Cateau", p. 210.
22 Barbara Tuchmann, *The Guns of August*, pp. 396-97.
23 Corcoran, ibid, p. 39.
24 Corcoran, ibid, pp. 125-26.
25 This claim was made in a German technical magazine during the war, though it is unverified—see *The Motor Cycle*, 27 September 1917, p. 304.
26 In a seven-page appendix, "Order of Battle of the First Army, 1914", General von Kluck nowhere includes despatch riders or motorcycles, though he does detail telephone, wireless and balloon; nor does he anywhere mention either in his main text. See Alexander von Kluck, *The March on Paris and the Battle of the Marne, 1914*, pp. 169-75
27 Edward Spears, *Liaison 1914: A Narrative of the Great Retreat*, p. 300.
28 Kluck, ibid, pp. 42, 50.
29 E Alexander Powell, *Fighting in Flanders*, pp. 116-17. Powell describes this army as the Ninth, but it can only have been the First or Second, and would seem more likely to have been von Kluck's First.
30 *The Times History of the War*, Vol. I, p. 238.
31 "An MP", *Mons, Anzac and Kut*, p. 48.
32 Kluck, ibid, p. 98, 86.
33 Erich von Ludendorff, *Ludendorff's Own Story*, pp. 36, 42, 102, 121.
34 *Motor Cycling*, 21 November 1916, pp. 47-48, 62.
35 *The Graphic*, 19 December 1914, front page. The illustration accompanying the headline, "The Captured Dispatch Rider: A German Motor-Cyclist in Belgian Hands", is clearly posed and may even be faked to give a lift to Christmas readers. It's impossible to identify the fallen and disabled motorcycle, but it has direct drive from the crankshaft pulley, an arrangement that would have dated it by German Army standards—though the Germans did commandeer civilian motorcycles, including, one may presume, those of older designs.
36 Samuel G Myer, "The Fourth Arm", p. 169.
37 Personal communication.
38 AP Corcoran, "Wireless in the Trenches", p 795,
39 Cyril Falls, *History of the Great War: Military Operations, France and Belgium, 1917*, p. 238.
40 RE Priestley, *The Signal Service in the European War of 1914-1918 (France)*, pp. 243, 273.
41 Priestley, ibid, p. 58.
42 Walter Reid, *Douglas Haig: Architect of Victory*, p. 185.

43 Priestley, ibid, pp. 17-19; Robin Neillands, *The Old Contemptibles: The British Expeditionary Force, 1914*, p. 145.
44 Neillands, ibid, p. 116.
45 Priestley, ibid, pp. 30, 18-19.
46 WH Tait, IWM document PP/MCR/161, 28 August 1914.
47 Priestley, ibid, p. 28.
48 Watson, ibid, p. 100.
49 Priestley, ibid, pp. 24, 31.
50 Hew Strachan, *The First World War: Volume I: To Arms*, p. 240.
51 Kluck, ibid, p. 109.
52 Tighe Hopkins, "German Spies in France: Facts and Fictions of Germany's Secret Service", www.greatwardifferent.com/Great_War/Spies/Spies_France_01.htm.
53 JFC Fuller, "The Application of Recent Developments in Mechanics and other Scientific Knowledge to Preparation and Training for Future War on Land", p. 246.
54 Priestley, ibid, p. 145.
55 James Edmonds, *History of the Great War: Military Operations France and Belgium, 1914*, p. 317.
56 Edmonds, ibid, p. 330.
57 Corcoran, *The Daredevil of the Army*, p. 37.
58 Priestley, ibid, pp. 18, 21-22. Emphasis added.
59 Corcoran, *The Daredevil of the Army*, p. 32; West, ibid, p. 102.
60 OH Best, IWM 87/56/1, 10 February 1915.
61 Niall Ferguson argues that Moltke's stripping of the German right wing made no difference to the outcome of Schlieffen's invasion plan: the road network was so choked that even a single division could not have made a fighting difference. This may be a controversial claim, but it helps convey the problems a despatch rider had to contend with.
62 *Motor Cycling*, 5 January 1915, p. 220.
63 West, ibid, p. 31.
64 West, ibid, pp. 15-16; pp. 46, 57, 65; Watson, ibid, p. 34. Convoy work remains an important part of a DR's work today.
65 West, ibid, pp. 33-34.
66 West, ibid, p. 43.
67 Watson, ibid, pp. 38; West, ibid, p. 83.
68 West, ibid, p. 33.
69 Priestley, ibid, pp. 51-52, 186, 309.
70 WG Mead, "Forty Thousand Hours of War", p. 20; Watson, ibid, p. 270.
71 Malcolm Brown, *The Imperial War Museum Book of the Western Front*, p. 36.
72 JF Lucy, *There's a Devil in the Drum*, p. 301.
73 Paul Maze, *A Frenchman in Khaki*, pp. 131-32.
74 Priestley, ibid, p. 232.
75 Alexander Paterson, "Bravery in the Field?", p. 256.
76 William Carr, *A Time to Leave the Ploughshares: A Gunner Remembers 1917-18*, pp. 57, 61, 108.
77 Coward, ibid, p. 123.
78 Priestley, ibid, pp. 233, 237-38, 240, 246.
79 Priestley, ibid. p. 34.
80 Priestley, ibid, p. 53.
81 Priestley, ibid, p. 156.
82 Priestley, ibid, p. 156-57.
83 Priestley, ibid, pp. 224-25.

84 Corcoran, "Wireless in the Trenches", p. 796.

85 James Edmonds, *History of the Great War: Military Operations France and Belgium, 1916*, pp. 70-71.

86 B. Neyland, "A Wireless Operator", p. 123.

87 John Jackson, *Private 12768*, p. 205.

88 Priestley, ibid, pp. 213-20.

89 *Motorcycle and Bicycle Illustrated*, 26 July 1917, p. 14.

90 Corcoran, *The Daredevil of the Army*, pp. 41, 49-50, 54-55; West, ibid, pp. 32, 93; *Motor Cycling*, 6 July 1915, p. 221.

91 *Motor Cycling*, 5 January 1915, p. 220.

92 JF Lucy, *There's a Devil in the Drum*, pp. 113, 202.

93 Gibbs, ibid, p. 356..

94 Watson, ibid, p. 123; *Motor Cycling*, 6 July 1915, p. 220.

95 *Motor Cycling*, 5 January 1915, p. 220.

96 See, for instance, Corcoran, *The Daredevil of the Army*, p. x; Max Pemberton's account: "Battle of the Great High Road and How the Despatch Rider Came Home", www.greatwardifferent.com/Great_War/Despatch_Rider/Despatch_Rider_01.htm. (Sixty miles an hour *would* have been a feverish speed at the time.)

97 Watson, ibid, p. 58.

98 Watson, ibid, p. 114. Don R learned again in the next war the potential danger from engine noise and the need to ride constantly on the lookout for danger—especially, in this war, from above. See Chisholm, ibid.

99 Corcoran, *The Daredevil of the Army*, p. 46.

100 Watson, ibid, pp. 270, 138.

101 Corcoran, *The Daredevil of the Army*, pp. 47-48.

102 AJP Taylor, *English History 1914-1945*, p. 60.

103 *Official History of the New Zealand Engineers During the Great War, 1914-1919*, p. 87.

104 Best, ibid, 22 November 1914, 3 September 1915.

105 Col H Stewart, *The New Zealand Division 1916-1919: A Popular History Based on Official Records*, p. 89.

106 OH Davis, IWM document PP/MCR/180, p. 67.

107 TW Grice, IWM P391, 31 July 1916, 11 August 1916, 12 August 1916, 14 August 1916, 20 September 1916, 8 October 1916, 14 October 1916, 7-8 November 1916, 11 November 1916, 30 November-1 December 1916.

108 Grice, ibid, 16 December 1916, 4 January 1917, 6-7 January 1917, 22-24 January 1917, 8 March 1917.

109 *The Motor Cycle*, 2 August 1917, p. 108.

110 Maze, ibid, p. 175, 188.

111 OH Davis, IWM document PP/MCR/180, p. 64.

112 Priestley, ibid, p. 53.

113 Clayton, *Forearmed: A History of the Intelligence Corps*, p. 34.

114 *The Illustrated War News*, 14 March 1917, pp. 10-11.

115 *The Illustrated War News*, 27 March 1918, p. 28.

116 Davis, ibid, p. 220.

117 Priestley, ibid, pp. 89-91, 221.

118 AH Osman, "Pigeons for Sport and War", p. 108.

119 Priestley, ibid, p. 92.

120 AFU Green, *The British Home Guard Pocket-Book*, p. 121.

121 Peter Hart, *1918: A Very British Victory*, p. 71.

122 *The Illustrated War News*, 27 March 1918, pp. 26, 28.

123 Osman, ibid, p. 110—Osman was antebellum editor of *The Racing Pigeon* magazine.

124 Davis, ibid, p. 73; Osman, ibid, pp. 107-08; John Jackson, *Private 12768: Memoir of a Tommy*, p. 175.

125 Falls, ibid, p. 238.

126 Priestley, ibid, p. 241.

127 Priestley, ibid, p. 247.

128 Priestley, ibid, 264-65, 276.

129 *Motor Cycling*, 11 May 1915, p. 15

130 *The War Illustrated*, Vol. I, p. 341; James Hayward, *Myths & Legends of the First World War*, p. 14.

131 Staff cars might be used, but this appears to have been relatively uncommon, red tabs perhaps being reluctant to have cars rendered smelly and dirty by freighting pigeons.

132 Davis, ibid, pp. 62, 189.

133 Davis, ibid, pp. 69, 76.

134 Davis, ibid, p. 65, 67, 68, 76..

135 Davis, ibid, p. 62.

136 Davis, ibid, p. 62-63, 69.

137 Davis, ibid, pp. 93, 258.

138 Davis, ibid, pp. 73, 84, 85.

139 Davis, ibid, pp. 81, 92.

140 Davis, ibid, p.82.

141 Davis, ibid, p. 226.

142 Hart, ibid, p. 70.

143 Priestley, ibid, p. 258, 260, 262.

144 Priestley, ibid, pp. 264, 246, 268-69.

145 Priestley, ibid, pp. 268, 270, 276.

146 Brown, ibid, p. 304.

147 FW Hopps, 06/54/1. "Warm", of course, refers not at all to weather conditions.

148 Hopps, ibid, 23 March 1918.

149 *The Motor Cycle*, 2 August 1917, p. 108.

150 An untypical account of the early months is Captain Burgoyne's of the "*beastly slovenly*" "curs", "brutes" and "loafers" of his command. He literally kicks and punches them into shape. Yet he is far from devoid of concern and even affection for them, and his harsh treatment reflects the firm paternalism of the British Army. See Gerald Achilles Burgoyne, *The Burgoyne Diaries*, passim.

151 Maze, ibid, pp. 287-88, 293-95.

152 Maze, ibid, pp. 290, 296, 298-99, 315.

153 Maze, ibid, pp. 294-95.

154 War Office, *Statistics of the Military Effort of the British Empire during the Great War 1914-1919*, p. 856.

155 An apt description by Dr Rob Thompson: "'Everything Bar the Shouting': BEF Logistics on the Western Front 1914-1918", Lecture, Fulwood Barracks, Preston, 1 November 2008.

156 Maze, ibid, p.336.

157 Hart, ibid, p. 344.

158 Priestley, ibid, p. 329.

159 Maze, ibid, pp. 307, 336, 347, 349.

160 Priestley, ibid, p. 207.

161 Maze, ibid, pp. 304, 313, 336-37, 347, 352.

162 JFB Livesay, *Canada's Hundred Days*, p. 347.

163 Maze, ibid, pp. 322-23.

164 *Motor Cycling*, 22 January 1918, p. 197; 5 March 1918, p. 334.

165 *Motor Cycling*, 24 April 1917, p. 566.

166 *The Motor Cycle*, 22 March 1917, p. 262.

167 *The Motor Cycle*, 5 April 1917, p, 309. Fulfilling Russian orders was to cause headaches for British riders in succeeding years, for the Russians—very sensibly—insisted that magnetos on their motorcycles were shifted from in front of the engine—the usual location then—to behind, in order to protect the essential magneto from mud and water thrown up by the front wheel, which could short-circuit the spark. Economies of scale meant that factories extended this arrangement to civilian models, so that into the 1930s riders of Matchless V-twins had to cope with the inexact ignition timing that inevitably stemmed from an attenuated magneto drive as the chain wore, and that became more problematic as engine performance was improved.

168 *Motor Cycling*, 15 January 1918, p. 175, 22 May 1917, p. 43.

169 *The Motor Cycle*, 6 January 1916, pp. 1-2.

170 Ixion, *Motorcycle Cavalcade*, p. 125.

171 *The Motor Cycle*, 13 September 1917, p. 252; 15 November 1917, p. 471.

172 Italians made for unfortunate allies. Mussolini's ill-advised Greek adventure in 1941 may well have cost Hitler victory in the Second World War. In the First, a fair case can be made that the Italian declaration against the Central Powers stiffened the resistance of even Slavs within the Austro-Hungarian forces to fight their "traditional" enemy; and certainly Lloyd George's stripping of divisions from the Western Front in the wake of the Caporetto disaster, right between Third Ypres and Cambrai, did the BEF no favours.

173 George, H Cassar, *Kitchener: Architect of Victory*, p. 487.

174 Robert Rhodes James, *Gallipoli*, p. 4.

175 *The Motor Cycle*, 5 August 1915, p. 139.

176 *Motor Cycling*, 13 July 1915, p. 352.

177 Mead, ibid, p. 43.

178 Mead, ibid, pp. 43-44.

179 Mead, ibid, p. 45.

180 Lamb, ibid, p. 25.

181 Lamb, ibid, pp. 25-26.

182 Lamb, ibid, pp. 41, 45.

183 Lamb, ibid, pp. 32, 34, 39, 36.

184 Lamb, ibid, p. 50.

185 A vivid and harrowing account of this forgotten episode is Lieutenant-Colonel FWD Bendall's "The Flood at Suvla Bay, pp. 305-11.

186 *The Long, Long Trail*, www.1914-1918.net/mmg.htm.

187 *The Motor Cycle*, 16 March 1916, p. 254.

188 *The Motor Cycle*, 6 January 1916, p. 17; 2 March 1916, p. 214.

189 *The Motor Cycle*, 13 January 1916, p. 33; 24 October 1918, p. 374.

190 *Motor Cycling*, 14 November 1916, p. 42.

191 *The Motor Cycle*, 3 February 1916, p. 116B.

192 *The Motor Cycle*, 30 November 1916, p. 468; 28 June 1917, p. 603; 11 January 1917, p. 26.

193 *Motor Cycling*, 23 January 1917, pp. 288-89.

194 *Motor Cycling*, 20 March 1917, p. 461.

195 *The Motor Cycle*, 17 February 1916, p. 158.

196 *Motor Cycling*, 6 November 1917, pp. 508-09.

197 Mead, ibid, p. 59.

198 Mead, ibid, p. 67.

199 Mead, ibid, p. 71.

200 *The Motor Cycle*, 27 December 1917, p. 615; 20 June 1918, p. 595.

201 *Motor Cycling*, 9 July 1918, p. 155.

202 *The Motor Cycle*, 6 December 1917, p. 547; 31 January 1918, p. 104.

203 *The Motor Cycle*, 7 March 1918, p. 223.

204 Mead, ibid, pp. 75-78.

205 Mead, ibid, p. 80.

206 *The Motor Cycle*, 27 July 1916, p. 71; 17 May 1917, p. 446; 11 October 1917, p. 353.

207 *The Motor Cycle*, 22 November 1917, p. 486.

208 *The Motor Cycle*, 5 September 1918, p. 223.

209 *The Motor Cycle*, 27 May 1915, p. 512.

210 *The Motor Cycle*, 17 February 1916, p. 158.

211 *The Motor Cycle*, 23 November 1916, p. 452.

212 *The Times History of the World*, Vol. XII, p. 78-80.

213 Charles Hordern, *History of the Great War: Military Operations: East Africa, Volume 1*, p. 19.

214 Hordern, ibid, pp. 35-36.

215 *The Motor Cycle*, 21 September 1916, p. 244.

216 *The Motor Cycle*, 24 August 1916, p. 160.

217 *The Motor Cycle*, 10 May 1917, p. 420.

218 *The Motor Cycle*, 21 September 1916, p. 244.

219 *Motor Cycling*, 22 August 1916, p. 345; *The Motor Cycle*, 7 September 1916, p. 203, 23 November 1916, p. 452; *The War Illustrated*, 9 September 1916, p. 81.

220 *Motor Cycling*, 29 January 1918, p. 211-13.

221 *The Motor Cycle*, 21 September 1916, p. 244.

222 Too numerous to list but, for instance, 6 August 1916, p. 9223; 17 December 1917, p. 13202; 29 November 1918, p. 14103; 1 April 1919, p. 4201; 5 June 1919, p. p. 7260; for others see the *Gazette*'s website, http://www.london-gazette.co.uk/search.

223 *Motor Cycling*, 29 May 1917, front page.

224 The Long, Long Trail, http://www.1914-1918.net/mmg.htm.

225 Edmund Dane, *British Campaigns in Africa and the Pacific 1914-1918*, pp. 127-28.

226 *The Motor Cycle*, 4 July 1918, p. 10; *The Times History of the War*, Vol. XII, p. 95.

227 *The Motor Cycle*, 21 September 1916, p. 244.

228 *Motor Cycling*, 29 January 1918, p. 213.

229 Hordern, ibid, p. 359.

230 *The Motor Cycle*, 19 November 1914, p. 555.

231 *Motor Cycling*, 29 May 1917, front page.

232 *Motor Cycling*, 31 August 1915, p. 412.

233 *The Motor Cycle*, 23 November 1916, p. 452.

234 George H Frost, *Munitions of War: A Record of the work of the BSA and Daimler Companies during the world War 1914-1918*, pp. 55-60.

235 *The Motor Cycle*, 12 October 1916, p. 324.

236 *The Motor Cycle*, 10 May 1917, p. 420.

237 Gordon Wood, *I Was There*, p. 52.

238 Before Hitler, German racism was probably no more objectionable than that of other Europeans. The Second Reich certainly was merciless in its oppression of Africans, but when word of the horrors of this eventually got back home (after subjection of the Maji-Maji rebellion in 1907), popular outrage turned German imperialism into a conscientious taking up of the White Man's Burden.

Lettow-Vorbeck had lost an eye to the Maji-Maji, but he overcame any bitterness this may have engendered, and later became an early opponent of Nazism, to the detriment of his military and political career and, eventually, to his impoverishment.

239 Paul von Lettow-Vorbeck, *My Reminiscences of East Africa*, p. 207.

240 Ireland for long had been seen as the back door to England. Italians, Spaniards and French variously had landed troops there between the sixteenth and eighteenth centuries; but it comes as a surprise to learn that the French had explored the possibility of invasion, with Russian help, as recently as 1902, when Gallic pride still was smarting after Fashoda and British military weakness had been exposed in the South African War. Germany had been factoring Ireland into its plans probably since the first Moroccan crisis, and especially since Roger Casement's 1913 essay, "Ireland, Germany and the Next War", published in the *Irish Review*. See Gabriel Doherty and Dermot Keogh (eds), *1916: The Long Revolution*, pp. 30-31.

241 Brian Barton, *From Behind a Closed Door: Secret Court Martial Records of the 1916 Easter Rising*, pp. 109-10.

242 Joseph Lee, *The Modernisation of Irish Society, 1848-1918*, p. 150.

243 Connolly, however, like the canny Scot he had been born, hedged his bet: while insisting that capitalists would never hesitate to send the khaki proletariat to its collective death rather than damage bourgeoisie property, he forecast that bombardment of Dublin would imply the end of British rule in Ireland—not a bad stab at the future, as things transpired.

244 These are the words of William T Cosgrave, later first president of the Free State. Plunkett, however, was no more a fool than Connolly: he was a schemer who had helped forge the "Castle Document", which sought to hoodwink the nominal leader of the Irish Volunteers, Eoin MacNeill, into endorsing rebellion (the Volunteers had been charged with defending Home Rule, not with raising rebellion). Digging trenches in Stephens Green may have been initiated not on Plunkett's order but on that of Connolly—whose Citizen Army faction took the Green—or that of Connolly's second-in-Command, Michael Mallin.

245 Desmond FitzGerald, *Desmond's Rising: Memoirs 1913 to Easter 1916*, p. 143.

246 Criminally insane though it may appear, the charge needs to be evaluated in the circumstances and the thinking of the time, when up to four paramilitary forces (the Ulster Volunteers, the National and Irish Volunteers, and the Irish Citizen Army) had been drilling in public under the indulgent eye of Dublin Castle for more than two years. Possibly the Castle (the centre of British administration in Ireland) had so persuaded itself to believe that these forces were all mere bluff (Chief Secretary Birrell had remarked, "I don't take these people seriously"), that it came to imagine that a show of "real" force would bring these impudent Paddies to heel. This interpretation is supported by the thoughts of Margaret Skinnider, a (bicycle) despatch rider for the rebels—see her memoir, *Doing My Bit For Ireland*, p. 109.

247 Three decades later, apparently having learned nothing from their catastrophic misjudgements in 1916, some British were anxious to shoot the top Nazis out of hand.

248 *The Long, Long Trail*, www.1914-1918.net/frenchs_ireland_despatch.htm

249 *The Motor Cycle*, 31 January 1918, p. 104.

250 *The Motor Cycle*, 18 May 1916, p. 476.

251 Jeff Kildea, *ANZACs and Ireland*, p. 65.

252 There may have been as many as 66,000 rifles among the various paramilitary organisations in Ireland by early 1915. Though some report that most were "a

grab-bag assortment of outdated weapons" (Doherty and Keogh, ibid, pp. 59-60), one eyewitness points out that those arms held by the Dublin rebels "were of various kinds, but all of them were formidable" (Barton, ibid, p. 43).

253 Skinnider, ibid, p. 19.
254 Peter Woods, "The Week to Come", www.rte.ie/radio1/doconone/player.html?feedUrl=/radio1/doconone/atom/2568132.xml&play=true&position=0&volume=-1.
255 These Mausers, with their ammunition, had been withdrawn from German colonial service, and dumdums often were used in colonial conflicts in those insouciantly racist days. Pearse deplored these bullets, but there is no doubt they were fired.
256 *Sinn Fein Rebellion Handbook*, p. 58.
257 Kildea, ibid, p. 64.
258 Mrs Hamilton Norway, *The Sinn Fein Rebellion As I Saw It*, p. 71.
259 Charles Townshend, *Easter 1916: The Irish Rebellion*, p. 235. One suspects that Miss Perloz took the train from Dublin, beginning her motorcycle ride in Cork city.
260 Wells, Warre B and N Marlowe, *A History of the Irish Rebellion of 1916*, p. 184.
261 *Sinn Fein Rebellion Handbook*, p. 113.
262 Ibid, p. 182.
263 Ibid, p. 260; *Motor Cycling*, 13 March 1917, p. 433.
264 CA Brett, "Recollections".
265 Stephen Bull, *An Officer's Manual of the Western Front*, p. 59.
266 Barton, ibid, pp. 235, 249.
267 In yet another qualifier to this account of a most complex episode: though he has been called, with good reason, "the man who lost Ireland for the Empire", Maxwell was not a callous fool—or the "mediocrity" as which he is often dismissed. He was described by a contemporary as "a clever man, broad-minded and open to argument", and, though no Hibernophile, he personally donated £200—a very significant sum at the time—to relief of distress that the Rising had caused to the poor of Dublin. Ironically, part of the reason for a dismayed government's choice of Maxwell to "sort things out" was the likelihood of his acceptability to the Irish because he had been vigorously opposed to the Gallipoli campaign (itself a reflection on his intelligence), in which many Irish had died without, it was widely felt, their efforts having been recognised. See Barton, ibid, pp. 42, 47, 48.
268 Barton, ibid, p. 6.
269 Doherty and Keogh, ibid, p. 42.
270 Jackson, ibid, pp. 225-26, 231.

8

San Fairy Ann?

Does It Matter?

Does it matter—losing your legs?…
For people will always be kind,
And you need not show that you mind
When the others come in after football
To gobble their muffins and eggs.

Does it matter—losing your sight?…
There's such splendid work for the blind;
And people will always be kind,
As you sit on the terrace remembering
And turning your face to the light.

Do they matter—those dreams from the pit?…
You can drink and forget and be glad,
And people won't say that you're mad;
For they'll know that you've fought for your country,
And no one will worry a bit.

Siegfried Sassoon[1]

THE SPLENDIDLY BITTER Sassoon is perhaps the archetypal protest poet of the Great War. English professors may insist that Wilfred Owen is a more accomplished artist; and they would be right in their pedantic way; and the best of Owen's poems indeed convey the horror and the pity of war as little else does. Yet Sassoon has an edge that gentle Owen lacks; for in the poetry of "Mad Jack" is an all but tangible rage so powerful that it can draw a red mist down before the eyes of even those who know better than what faux-liberals shrilly insist the war was: futile; a waste—all the clichés.

We all know better now than Sassoon or Owen did then; or at least we have the perspective that they never could have had, and we can know more than poets and generals put together, if we care—or maybe dare—to inform ourselves.

Though there remain things we will never know: for we have been lucky enough to be able to follow Sassoon's admonition in another poem: to "… never know / The hell where youth and laughter go".

But there is another side to the story told by Owen and Sassoon. Not all poets shared their vision, but those who didn't were excluded from ready public access by the anthologists of the 1930s and—especially—the 1960s and since, for political reasons. Few, therefore, have read Gilbert Frankau, and even fewer have been forced to confront his quite shocking poem, "The Other Side", far less to engage with its troubling conclusion:

> And if posterity should ask of me
> What high, what base emotions keyed weak flesh
> To face such torments, I would answer "*You!*
> Not for themselves, O daughters, grandsons, sons,
> Your tortured forebears wrought this miracle;
> Not for themselves, *accomplished utterly*
> This loathliest task of murderous servitude;
> But just because they realised that thus,
> *And only thus*, by sacrifice, might they
> Secure a world worth living in—*for you*.

And then there are those who looked back on the war not even ambiguously but with downright yearning, something that no canonical poet aspired to express. Yet Charles Carrington speaks for a great many veterans when he claims: "the companionship of the trenches, about which sentimentalists spouted, was in some unexplained sense a reality…. [I]n spite of everything, my two years in France had been 'the happiest of my life'."[2] Guy Chapman was perversely captivated for the rest of his long life by the "indescribable charm in the distraught landscape churned up by successive bombardments, a nightmare beauty such as no one would see again". Not merely the "distraught landscape", but what had created its "nightmare beauty", fascinated Chapman: the week-long "drumfire" bombardment preceding the opening of the Somme battles, which drove some men out of their minds, exhilarated him; for him it

> was not a noise, it was a symphony. It did not move, it hung over us. It was
> as though the air were full of a vast and agonised passion…. It was poised
> in the air, a stationary panorama of sound, a condition of the atmosphere,

not the creation of man…. And this feeling, while it filled one with awe, filled one also with triumphant exaltation.[3]

Chapman was haunted by his experiences, in a perversely positive way, to his death: "*La guerre, mon vieux, c'est notre jeunesse, enselvie et secrete*", he quotes more than once.[4] "I had known that unsought sharpening of awareness, of the mind and body. Familiarity did not blunt it. I shall never see or hear so clearly again". He was conscious of how incongruous, even grotesque, his emotions must seem: "To anyone with no experience of that war this must seem foolish. It is only at moments that I realise how much less alive I am than I was then…. What is missing is the sense, fleeting beyond price, of living in every nerve and cell of one's body and with every ghostly impulse of one's mind".[5]

Chapman was no perverse shellshock victim. He had a successful career and his marriage to Margaret Storm Jameson was, by all the evidence, enviably happy. Yet Margaret knew and accepted that even for her, her husband's war would always remain "Occupied territory. A country of your mind I shall never be able to enter".[6]

A great many men shared Chapman's complex emotions. Lyn Macdonald interviewed "One old soldier [who] remarked, 'In a way I lived my whole life between 19 and 23 and anything that happened after that was merely an anticlimax.' Coming from a man in his late 70s who had led a successful and interesting life it is a chilling thought."[7] Even the most unlikely men were affected. Olaf Stapledon felt that the war was senseless and perverse, yet also that he needed to "do his bit" in some way, so he joined the Friends' Ambulance Unit—though he was not a Quaker, or even a pacifist—and served with the French Army. The Friends were of course non-combatants, but, like those other British volunteers in the French forces, the sidecar ambulance drivers in the Vosges, they could be so close to the line that they suffered bombardment, and "after twenty-four hours of this" Stapledon could feel his nerves beginning to "give out…. Yet deep down in my mind, and difficult to introspect, was a strange quietness, an aloof delight". Like Chapman, he could "catch surprising glimpses of a kind of superhuman beauty in the hideous disaster of war itself".[8]

This is not to argue that the war was in any way a good thing; but it was not experienced by all who fought it as the unmitigated brutal horror that simplistic idealists or political partisans would insist we believe it was. And it was necessary to defeat German militarism. The price demanded was high but for most people the price of peace was morally beyond consideration as long as that menace remained. At the time, and for long afterward—to the end of their lives in the case of many—the people of Britain regarded the war as a necessary sacrifice that was, all told, worthwhile.

Where would Don R have stood on this issue? To some extent, the answer to that question depends on when Don joined up. The early volunteers, as we have seen, tended to be the sort of men many nowadays would dismiss as either fools or liars; men who spelled *Duty, Service, King* and *Country* as they spelled *God*—with a reverential capital. For such a man social responsibility utterly eclipsed petty consideration of individual rights. For him responsibility meant that he simply had to do his bit—no question. Corporal Watson had no illusions of personal bravery but "Physical coward or no physical coward—it obviously had to be done".[9] Such a man's life was his Country's, his soul his God's, and his greatest and most sacred Duty was, if necessary, to die for King and Country and go to God thus shriven. Such a man's greatest sense of gratification came from knowing that his Duty had been discharged—that he could stand before God or King and be acknowledged as worthy by both. Despatch rider Creighton Richard Storey, who wrote, "We feel as if we were fighting to save the world, and to die in such a cause we consider an honour", was honoured as he would have wished.[10] Lieutenant A Sang, gloomy and recklessly brave, had volunteered out of despair, having been crossed in love; he actually "hated motorcycles and motorcycling" but felt that as a motorcyclist he had the best chance of getting into the war and giving his life in a worthy cause, and his death wish was granted at the Marne.[11]

Such men might be made of stern stuff, but they were no humourless moralists. "I really believe there were no happier boys in the Army than our DRs," recalled one. "We used to grouse, this being a soldier's privilege, but we had a rattling good time, and those who have since taken commissions, frequently sigh for the good old days in the ranks".[12] And one cannot dismiss such sentiments as nostalgia, for they are contemporary, and OH Davis contemporaneously reports more than one of his fellow DRs, like himself, "having the finest time of his life—it was great".[13] Captain Watson concludes his introduction to *Adventures of a Despatch Rider*, a book that is "ugly with sorrow", with a prayer for a future in which "the publishing of a book like this will be regarded with fierce shame"; yet despite the hardships and loss of many friends, he clearly enjoyed his war.[14] Corporal Grice deplores "The utter uselessness of war", as he observes it at the Somme, but he betrays no bitterness—rather, the feeling of being "An *asset*, at last, to King and Country", elates him.[15] Bill Foster's son describes how his father "always recalled his service through the Great War with great interest and happy memories. He rarely spoke of the horrors but remembered the warm camaraderie among the troops [and] his eyes would light up when he recalled wartime experiences".[16]

Perhaps George Mead best sums it up for Don and Tommy both: "Despite the hardships of that War I do not regret one moment of my Service to my

Country and being OHMS".[17] One can imagine Mead and other old Dons wistfully reciting an unpretentious piece of doggerel of their glory years:

"DR": A Companion
1917
Scudding through the darkness
Half across the plain,
With the wind against you, and a biting rain,
Skidding where the pools lie
Dank amid the clay,
Knowing there's a strafing
If the mails delay.

Then you think of firesides
With a long regret,
Peaceful, easeful evenings—
Book and cigarette,
Eiderdowns and pillowslips,
Coffee cups and frills
Late pm on P and M—
Home's a thought that thrills.

19?
Dreaming after office hours
By electric light,
In a stuffy sitting room—
Of another night!
Civilised and sanely clad,
Cleaned and groomed and fed,
Shall we ache for those glad rides
In the days long dead?

Can we come again, chum,
To the things that seem
Sweet and so alluring
In a war-time dream?
Will other thoughts then thrill us,
Restless as we are,
When the old world claims us,
Chum, beyond the bar?

Sophie C Eliott-Lynn[18]

"Restless as we are..." George Mead was not the only despatch rider who shared the sentiments of Carrington and Chapman. Many must have looked back on "things that seem / Sweet and so alluring", for within a month of the armistice a Despatch Riders' Club was formed, under the patronage of the Auto Cycle Union. The club's objective was described by ex-DR GA Cade as "perpetuating the comradeship of motor cyclists who have been RE despatch riders. Many firm friendships have been made in the Service".[19] The club became the Association of RE Despatch Riders, and in 1934 this had almost 1,500 members.[20] Reading through the names on the association's list, the modern researcher finds "old friends" whose accounts have helped make this one possible; names like OH Best, Oswald H Davis, H Etherington, HAJ Lamb, WG Mead, and William H Tait; but other names are missing—notably, perhaps, Sproston, Watson and West. Some old Dons may have died in the interim—Watson and Corcoran, for example—but many were still alive in 1934, as the dates of their memoirs, or testimony from their descendents, show. Others were abroad—West emigrated to America (as did Corcoran).

All this proves is that despatch riders, like other soldiers, did not all feel the same about their war service. Many wished to get back to their "real lives" and try to forget those years; for instance, Graham Oates evidently thought his post-war competition riding, and transcontinental rides in Canada, were far more interesting.[21] Many more DRs, conscripts from later in the war, would not have been the sort to join an association that retained some of the socially elite quality of the early DRs; others could not have afforded to: eight shillings and sixpence for the Annual Re-Union Dinner might have been more than some were getting on the dole in the pits of the Depression. The expense of this dinner might suggest that it was the better-off men, the social elite of the early years, who were most enthusiastic about their war service.

Yet there were few enough DRs at the outset, so the fact that almost fifteen hundred men were in the Association twenty years after the war's outbreak, ten times the original DR strength, despite all wastage, indicates that many old Dons of more modest background cherished their years of service, welcomed the opportunity to meet others who felt the same, and did indeed "ache for those glad rides / In the days long dead".[22]

Evaluation of the DR Corps must wait until, with a bit of luck, this exploration has prompted further scholarship. What may be said at this juncture is that DRs in the Great War were a truly unique bunch of men. They had an aura of daring and romance that earned them popular comparison with "our air boys".[23] They were privy to confidential information, which they put together with other facts they observed in their movements and pooled with their colleagues.[24] They also had maps—though these were faulty or totally absent in the early war of movement[25]—and because of these, and the intelligence they shared, they were frequently consulted by officers,[26] intensifying their aura of importance. Though often they were hard pressed, all told they had a cushy number, with "plenty of leave" and an easy workload.[27]

something they appreciated, and sometimes bursts of exhilaration in the open air under friendly skies, when they might "capture sometimes those sharp delightful moments of thirsting interest that made the [Great] Retreat into an epic and the Advance a triumphant ballad". Captain Watson acknowledges:

> We were awkwardly privileged persons—full corporals with a few days' service. Motor-cycling gave superlative opportunities of freedom. Our duties were "flashy" and brought us into familiar contact with officers of rank.... In short, we who were soldiers of no standing possessed the privileges that a professional soldier could win only after many years' hard work.[28]

John Lucy claims that the "news wallahs" of the Signals Corps "regarded themselves as privileged because their job was important, and they took advantage of this";[29] but Watson's account, written in 1915, decades before Lucy's, suggests that, in the case of despatch riders, privilege had been accorded, not self-awarded. In fairness to Lucy, he is merely reporting, not grumbling; rather, he is ungrudging in his personal admiration for the Signals Corps. And there seems no way of avoiding the conclusion that, during the Great Retreat at least, the despatch rider was so vital that without him the BEF could hardly have held together to make the critical contribution it was to sustain until the end.

Yet not to overstate Don's importance: he was a cog in a huge military machine, and though betimes he bore a disproportionate part of the load imposed on that engine of war he never did so alone. In the Great Retreat he owed his own survival in part to the cavalry, a force that since has been almost as denigrated as Don's role has been forgotten. Quite apart from its historic action at Néry, by its scouting and screening the cavalry gave invaluable cover to the BEF throughout the Great Retreat. Under that cover, and with the heroic endurance of the Poor Bloody Infantry, Don held the force together, to fight another day, and another, up to that last eleventh hour. Yet the *RUSI Journal*, through the war and for years afterward, contains much material on cavalry and virtually not a mention of motorcycles; and though cavalry was more valuable, actually and potentially, than the donkey-walloper school of cynicism would portray it, nevertheless it seems clear that the motorcycle rider did far more to win the war than the trooper—or indeed the "tanker".

So why has he been so overlooked, when the tank and even the cavalry continue to be accorded far more attention?[30]

The freight- and personnel-sidecar helped the British economy to function from Business As Usual through Total War; it made a significant, but hardly essential, contribution. Sidecar ambulances were of value at home and in the Vosges sector, but again they made no critical contribution to winning the war—though the *Service de Santé Militaire* bolstered British credibility when there were mutterings that perfidious Albion was fighting her war with French lives. The MMGS, though it vindicated itself in 1918, likewise was no war-winner.

But the despatch rider made a contribution that further research may well prove to have been essential to victory. He too was no war-winner, but, as Admiral Jellicoe was the only man who might have lost the war in an afternoon, Don R might have lost it too—not in an afternoon, but in the protracted retreat to the Marne in 1914. Had the BEF been broken up in the field through those fraught days, it is hard to see how Germany would not have won the war. Even had Joffre contained the invaders on the Marne after the moral and military disaster of his ally's collapse, and consequent exposure of the Fifth Army's flank, his armies would have, in his own words to Haig, "ceased to exist" before the Somme battles opened, haemorrhaging as the French were at Verdun. Presuming survival then, without the British attack at Third Ypres the Germans surely must have attacked and broken the then-demoralised French armies. At Mons and Le Cateau the BEF's fighting retreat had proved that it was no Contemptible Little Army, and the fact that it was still together at the Marne may well have been a factor in Kluck's decision to make his fatal turn.[31] In clogging the wheels of Schlieffen's—or Moltke's—plan, and in securing Ypres, the BEF made a critical contribution to preventing defeat.

Failure of the Schlieffen Plan illustrates Colonel Fuller's point on the importance of information to command and control[32]—and the value of the British DR in reflection of that failure: "German failure at the Marne in 1914 can be traced in a large part to the failure of their signal net". Moltke sent his armies into the field dependant on "radio and telephone exclusively; and with no provisions for alternate means of communication".[33] For all their fabled technological advancement, and their invention of the motorcycle, the Germans underestimated the value of the motorcycle despatch rider at the start, and the rate of their advance outpaced the speed of their ability to lay cable.[34] The nature of retreat rendered cable all but redundant to the BEF, and the Germans' over-reliance on wireless and cable contributed to their communications problems through the Great Retreat. It was Don R who, more than anyone, held the BEF together through those awful days, so that it could fight another day. The commander-in-chief himself acknowledged

> the splendid work which has been done throughout the campaign by
> the [motor]cyclists of the Signal Corps [who] have been conspicuously
> successful in maintaining an extraordinary degree of efficiency in the
> service of communications. Many casualties have occurred in their ranks,

but no amount of difficulty or danger has ever checked the energy or ardour which has distinguished their Corps throughout the operations.[35]

Such service is all the more remarkable given that DRs were, for the most part, very young men with no more than a couple of weeks' army training, if any at all, "amateurs at [a] professional game".[36] Theirs was an astonishing achievement.

Don R did not win the Great War. But it's hardly exaggeration to say that he prevented it from being lost. From the dreadful first day of the Somme, through the French Mutinies, the Italian collapse, the defeat of Russia, the setbacks of the Spring Offensive and the advance of the Hundred Days, the BEF carried the fight to the Kaiser's armies, and in November 1918 had secured territory, guns and prisoners out of all proportion to its sector. But had it not survived that fraught retreat in the opening weeks it could not have done any of those things. One authority estimates, with more than seven decades of perspective: "At no time in this century has signals intelligence affected campaigns more significantly than at the very hour of its birth, in 1914".[37] And who was the linchpin of Signals then, when both cable and wireless more often than not were "dis"? Don R.

Yet Don has been forgotten. Why? If his importance really was so great, how could he come to have been so overlooked?

One factor is his passé technology. Though telegraph and wireless had been used in previous wars—wireless in the Second Boer War (though unsuccessfully by land forces), telegraph as far back as the Crimean—the motorcycle nevertheless seemed "primitive" by comparison to electronic communication. In the next war wireless came into its own, and electronics and radio development led to everything from RADAR and SONAR to ENIGMA and the means that broke that code. Belt-driven wheels and chuffing engines must have seemed so last-century by comparison. Engines might be cutting-edge—but only when fitted into aeroplanes and tanks. And those that were seemed merely to highlight the obsolescence of the motorcycle's primitive specifications. Capturing the popular imagination was no longer Colonel Fiske's young motorcyclists but Captain Johns' Biggles.

Perhaps as important as its crudity and humility, the motorcycle was everywhere, used by a great variety of military personnel, so ubiquitous it became all but transparent, its importance hidden in full sight, easy to overlook, especially as it could not be used directly in combat. Yet the motorcycle's essential value in the Great War was so evident to the military that a decade later its use into the future was acknowledged by the *RUSI Journal*.[38] Despite that, though, the *Journal*, through the war and for years afterward, contains hardly another mention of motorcycles. Post-war developments in planes and tanks served to further sideline public awareness of the motorcycle. British monied and propertied classes were hostile to the motorcyclist, as shown by the often-swingeing penalties for speeding handed down by magistrates even to soldiers home on leave. After the war, up to 40,000 surplus motorcycles were dumped on the market, and the motorcyclist became more proletarian, his importance, perhaps, easier to dismiss in a still socially stratified world.

Another factor that led to the motorcyclist being overlooked is that the Great War was won not by motorcycles, or even by tanks or warplanes, but by a combination of changes in infantry tactics and a virtual revolution in artillery, and over the years the infantryman in the trenches came to define experience of that war. Don R, by his own ready admission, had a cushy time compared with Tommy Atkins: "The duties of a Dispatch Rider were risky and arduous, but were nothing in comparison with the ordeal suffered by the men who manned the front line trenches";[39] "The brunt of battle is borne by our comrades who push the bayonet or fire the gun; our ultimate purpose is to serve their needs, and it is our pride to spend ourselves in that service".[40] His relatively comfortable war may have been interpreted at some level in the dim public consciousness that Don R could hardly have been very important; and as Victorian and Edwardian values came to be rejected by a disillusioned public, the class to which most early DRs belonged reinforced this negative perception. They would have seemed far more Donkeys than Lions, to those even aware of them any more; the sort of "patriotism and physical courage" that drove, say, Roger West to brave an advancing German army and scale a bridge to lay explosives, while crippled with an infected foot, was exactly what left-wing intellectuals felt they ought to "snigger" at, according to Orwell. "And it's not for the sake of a ribbon'd coat / Or a season's fame" that West and men like him did their bit: their code of honour would have scorned anything like self-proclamation of their worth.

Finally, in a war that was marked more than any other by irony, failure and disappointment, Don may have become a victim of his very success: because "[he] is likely to become conspicuous only when he fails in the task assigned him",[41] he came to be overlooked by history because he *didn't* fail. Had he failed, it's difficult to see how history would not have been different.

So, for whatever reasons, and despite the contribution that he made to history, Don has been forgotten.

And, to echo Sassoon, does that matter? San Fairy Ann? Against the loss of life and limb and mind on a colossal scale, loss of memory of one cog in a huge machine can't matter very much, surely? Don himself might well agree, self-effacing fellow that he was. It doesn't matter, what he did, now that he's in his grave, in France or Flanders, Africa, Palestine or Mesopotamia—wherever he fell off his Trusty Triumph or little Douglas. Or went from despatch rider to bookie's runner before he died in neglected old age.[42] Gone to whatever reward there may be. Which maybe is only the war that was won, and in the winning of which he and his chums played their part. They only fought for their country, after all, so no one need worry a bit. Especially now they're all dead. San Fairy Ann.

Yet of course it matters. It matters to historians, whose job it is to tease out the threads of the past. Even more so, it matters—or it should—to all of those in whose cause Don, like Tommy, did his bit and sometimes gave his all. We must not allow ourselves to forget all that was done, by all involved, for our sake. *We* are the *"You!"* of Frankau's strident, challenging poem. We are the fruits of the Duty they discharged, to the point of death. What is our duty to them?

San Fairy Ann? Don't think so.

Endnotes

1 Copyright Siegfried Sassoon; by kind permission of the Estate of George Sassoon.
2 Charles Carrington, *Soldier From the Wars Returning*, pp. 218-19.
3 Guy Chapman, *A Kind of Survivor*, pp. 63-64. A vivid description of what enchanted Chapman comes from Irish poet Frank Ledwidge: "you can scarcely understand how bright the nights are made by ... rockets. They are in continual ascent and descent from dusk to dawn, making a beautiful crescent from Switzerland to the sea. There are white lights, green, and red, and whiter, bursting into red and changing again, and blue bursting into purple drops and reds fading into green. It is all like the end of a beautiful world."
4 Chapman, ibid, e.g. pp. 76, 288.
5 Chapman, ibid, p. 125.
6 Chapman, ibid, p. 163.
7 Lyn Macdonald, "Oral History and the First World War", p. 138.
8 Olaf Stapledon, "Experiences in the Friends' Ambulance Unit", pp. 370, 374
9 WHL Watson, *Adventures of a Despatch Rider*, p. 4.
10 *Motorcycle and Bicycle Illustrated*, 19 July 1917, p. 34.
11 Roger West, "Diary of the War: Retreat from Mons to the Battle of the Aisne", p. 15a.
12 *Motor Cycling*, 9 May 1916, p. 6.
13 OH Davis, PP/MCR180, 23 July 1916.
14 Watson, ibid, pp. xi, xii.
15 TW Grice, IWM manuscript P391, 14 November 1916, 12 August 1916; emphasis in original.
16 William Hayden Foster, "Distant Guns", p. 30.
17 W George Mead, "Forty Thousand Hours of War", Introduction; OHMS: On His Majesty's Service.
18 *The Motor Cycle*, 20 December 1917, p. 578. The P & M in "Late pm on P & M" refers to the motorcycle used primarily by DRs in the air arms.
19 *The Motor Cycle*, 12 December 1918, p. 524.
20 *Association of RE Despatch Riders: Names & Addresses* (London: Association of RE Despatch Riders/Auto-Cycle Union, 1934).
21 Bill Snelling, *Aurora to Ariel: The Motorcycling Exploits of J Graham Oates.*

22 The association seems to have closed its books as its members died or fell away; but in 1979 Bert Thurling founded the still extant Ex-Royal Signals Dispatch Riders' Club.

23 *Motor Cycling*, 15 August 1915, p. 327.

24 Watson, ibid, pp. 113, 183.

25 Watson, ibid, pp. 26, 55, 203; Roger West, "Diary of the War: Retreat from Mons to the Battle of the Aisne", pp. 32, 69, 71, 74.

26 Max Burns and Ken Messenger, *The Winged Wheel Patch: A History of the Canadian Military Motorcycle and Rider*, p. 29.

27 Watson, ibid, p. 254; AP Corcoran, *The Daredevil of the Army: Experiences as a "Buzzer" and Despatch Rider*, pp. 44-45.

28 Watson, ibid, pp. 199, 266.

29 John Lucy, *There's a Devil in the Drum*, p. 301.

30 A good treatment of the exaggerated importance given to tanks can be found in James Hayward, *Myths & Legends of the First World War*, Chapter 6, "Lions, Donkeys and Ironclads".

31 Kluck's lines were over-attenuated; his troops were exhausted; the fortuitous direction of the French rail network north of Paris probably influenced his decision; the move had the capacity to separate the French Sixth Army and the Paris garrison from Joffre's other armies and the BEF, offering the enticing potential to defeat the two forces in detail, as Ludendorff and Hoffmann just had the Russians at Tannenberg and Masurian Lakes; and, as Terence Zuber argues, there may never have been a Schlieffen Plan. Nevertheless, the BEF no doubt gave Kluck pause, and critically affected the fall of the iron dice.

32 JFC Fuller, "The Application of Recent Developments in Mechanics and other Scientific Knowledge to Preparation and Training for Future War on Land", p. 241.

33 Samuel G Myer, "The Fourth Arm", p. 169. See also John Ferris, *The British Army and Signals Intelligence During the First World War*, p. 5, for the consequences for the German advance of *en clair* communication.

34 Myer, ibid, p. 170.

35 RE Priestley, *The Signal Service in the European War of 1914 to 1918 (France)*, p. 42. The reference is to Sir John French's despatch of 20 November 1914.

36 Corcoran, *Daredevil*, p. 2.

37 Ferris, ibid, p. 5.

38 General Percy Hambro, "The Horse and the Machine in War", p. 95; Major HCH Eden, "A Mobile Light Division", p. 57.

39 ER Booth, "The Musings of a Nonagenarian", The Western Front Association website, http://web.westernfrontassociation.com/thegreatwar/articles/individuals/erbooth.htm.

40 R Chevenix Trench, "Signal Communication in War", p 308

41 Corcoran, "Wireless in the Trenches",

42 Paul Vallely, "Living in the nation's memory".

Appendix 1

Motorcycles—Numbers

Makes and quantities of motorcycles and sidecars in possession of the British Armed Forces at the time of the Armistice:[1]

Make*	Overseas**	At Home	Total	Remarks
AJS	262	8	270	250 in Italy
Ariel	27	25	52	
Autocarrier	-	12	12	Three-wheelers
Bradbury	1	14	15	
BSA	322	766	1,088	245 in East Africa
Clyno	642	1,150	1,792	478 in France
Douglas	9,515	8,800	18,315	Including 13,477 2¾ HP solos and 4,816 sidecars
Humber	2	9	11	
Indian	33	140	173	105 with Canadian contingent
James	155	8	163	155 in Italy
Matchless	1	135	136	Also 8 sidecars
New Hudson	7	14	21	
New Imperial	88	338	426	646 fitted with Sunbeam sidecars
Norton	-	232	232	
Phelon & Moore (P&M)	135	3,248	3,383	Standardised by RFC/RAF; also 150 sidecars
Premier	6	50	56	
Rover	20	366	386	Also 210 sidecars
Royal Ruby	51	104	155	Some with sidecars
Royal Enfield	1	160	161	Some with sidecars
Rudge Multi	18	377	395	Also 4 with sidecars
Scott	-	411	411	Also 1 with sidecar
Sunbeam	1	78	79	Also 326 with sidecars
Triumph	9,813	8,185	17,998	Mainly 4 HP models; 306 with sidecars
Warwick	-	15	15	
Zenith	5	304	309	

1 Bart H Vanderveen, *Motorcycles to 1945*, p. 26.

* Only those makes with more than ten units in service are tabled. Other makes include:

Abingdon—1	Harley Davidson—1	OK Junior—1
Bat—2	Imperial—1	Quadrant—8
Brennabor—2	JAP—2	Regal—1
Burney &	Lea-Francis—9	Rex—1
Blackburne—1	Levis—1	Singer—1
Calthorpe—1	LMC—1	Sparkbrook—1
Campion—4	Magnet—1	Sun—1
Centaur—1	Motosacoche—1	Wanderer—1
FN—1	NUT—7	
Griffon—1	NSU—2	

Also listed are 243 Empire sidecar outfits.

** Motorcycles in use overseas at the time of the Armistice were:
East Africa—563
Egypt—1,461
France—15,978
India—289
Italy—1,022
Malta—17
Mesopotamia—1,314
Russia—40

Salonika—976

Grand total overseas: 21,660.

The total of all these motorcycles, solos and sidecars, is 48,175 units. Total wartime production of all motorcycles for the Armed Forces is unknown, but the total number of new and remanufactured British machines must have been well over 100,000.

Main marques used:

BSA: Birmingham Small Arms made excellent motorcycles until about ten years before the firm folded in 1973. Its first engine, made in 1910, was a 499cc side valve single suspiciously like the Triumph Model H (both not merely look alike but share displacement dimensions of 85x88mm) and it soon proved itself comparable in performance and reliability. A 557cc version of this engine (85x98mm), the 4¼ HP Model H, was to power most of the BSAs used through the war, driving through a three-speed countershaft gearbox with chain primary- and belt final drive. In addition to a caged-roller big-end in the engine, the BSA was relatively advanced in having a stout front brake, a dummy pulley into which a block bore, rather than a cycle-type stirrup brake acting on the wheel rim.

Though used in good numbers by the French, the BSA was not an officially-sanctioned mount for the British DR—the factory was too busy making Lee Enfields and Lewis guns—but 400 of them served in the East African Campaign as mounts of the Motor Cycle Corps. It seems that all 400 came through. These bikes were fitted with the three-speed gearboxes but all-chain drive, the rear chain being fully enclosed against the dust and mud of that demanding theatre, and a transmission shock-absorber both easing the loading on the chains and smoothing the harshness of all-chain drive (harsh compared to a belt). So heavy was the demand on BSA that, its Small Heath factory being given over to arms manufacture and expansion there impossible, a new factory for motorcycle and parts manufacture had to be opened in Redditch.

Clyno: This was the machine recommended for service in the MMGS by Winston Churchill, after observed tests; about 1,800 were supplied to the BEF through the war. The sidecar was manufactured by the Clyno cycle company working in close association with Vickers in order to maximise suitability as a machinegun platform, and it was mounted to the motorcycle using four socket fittings; this ensured solid mounting but permitted the sidecar to be quickly removed (for maintenance or repair) and almost as quickly reattached without losing the wheel geometry necessary for good handling and frugal tyre wear. It used all-chain drive and is believed to be the very first motorcycle to use pressed aluminium chaincases, which excluded dirt and ensured that chain lubricant did not turn into grinding paste, thereby ensuring long chain life and reliable running.

Because it was designed for sidecar work the Clyno was fitted from the start with a kickstarter acting through a three-speed countershaft gearbox when most other motorcycles depended on pedals turning the rear wheel which then turned the engine—that or push-starting; it also used a clutch to disconnect the drive at standstill and for pulling away, long before most other bikes had such refinement. It had a stout braced front fork that swung on two pair of links, one at the top, the other at the bottom of the long, strong steering head, and used two springs. Though the front brake was a conventional stirrup-type acting on the rim, the rear used twin shoes expanding inside a drum, an advanced design for the time. Wheels mounted 3.5-inch wide tyres when 2.25-inch were commonplace, and of all British motorcycles, the Clyno was closest to the American V-twins in its ruggedness but it was lighter and more manageable.

The engine was an AJS air-cooled side-valve V-twin displacing 744cc (76x82mm dimensions) and rated at 5-6 HP by the system of measurement used at the time. Later in the war the factory used an 8 HP JAP engine, but these were designed for Russia and none seem to have been used by the MMGS.

Douglas: At 350cc in displacement, and rated at 2¾ HP, the "Duggie" was the smallest motorcycle approved by the WO, yet it became second only to the Triumph in popularity, and in certain situations is was actually better. Its compactness and light weight made it easier to manhandle out of ditches or pick up on an icy road, and its lower centre of gravity gave great stability.

The Douglas used a fore-and-aft horizontally-opposed ("boxer") twin, side-valve in operation, with each piston measuring 60.8mm in diameter; given a stroke of 60mm, this meant that the engine was "over-square", unusual for the time, which helped shorten the unit and made for greater compactness. An outside flywheel allowed the crankcase to be compact and strong while retaining the engine-tractability essential for duty in wartime conditions. It used chain primary-drive to a two-speed gearbox mounted under the rear cylinder, with belt drive to the rear wheel.

Douglas also produced the Model B, a motorcycle with larger 593cc engine (74.5x68mm—again, an over-square boxer), rated at 3½ HP, for use as a sidecar tug. Some of these were used by the RNAS to haul mobile radio equipment.

P&M: Phelon & Moore made a 500cc (actually 475cc; 82.55x88.9mm) single-cylinder side-valve engine, rated at 3½ HP, which in the pioneer years was regarded as one of the best engines in the world, while the motorcycle was advertised as "perfected", with such nice touches as control cables routed inside the handlebars. In 1913 trials it made an impression on the RFC, and the P&M was to be the standard motorcycle used by all the air arms; after the Triumph and the Douglas, it was the most numerous of the British war motorcycles, with about 3,500 supplied to the air arms. The engine was steeply inclined, taking the place of the front frame down-tube and therefore a stressed member—a good design feature given the number of front down-tubes that failed in service. The front fork, too, was a notably robust item. Evidence suggests that the P&M was the only motorcycle that was produced to the high pre-war standards throughout the war—quality control in all others declined to some extent.

The P&M's unusual enclosed two-speed transmission used twin primary chains driving to a single transmission shaft with a dog clutch engaging either of the two sprockets to the final drive, which was by enclosed chain rather than belt.

Scott: The Scott was not one of the machines stipulated by the War Office for supply to the forces, but it almost was at the outset, with a specially made sidecar designed to carry a machinegun. Scott only ever made two-strokes, but they were uncommonly reliable, fast machines (one had won the 1912 Isle of Man TT, after leading from the very start), and after the prototype was tried out by the Admiralty and endorsed by Winston Churchill, like the Clyno, an order for 300 was placed, to be supplied to both Admiralty and WO. Later a "Guncar" three-wheeler prototype was supplied; this was like a car but with one wheel on one track "leading" the rear on the other, something that gave the advantages of a sidecar with the structural integrity of a car. This used a similar two-stroke twin engine, liquid cooled, but with more advanced features. By then, however, the unsuitability to war service of a sporty two-stroke, however well made, were evident, and the Scott was dropped.

Triumph: Triumph made the first motorcycle that was reliable and truly suited to everyday motorcycling, and it was to become almost synonymous with despatch riders of the Great War. The Model H displaced 550cc (85x88mm) and was of side valve operation; from late 1914 it operated through a three-speed countershaft gearbox with chain primary- and belt final drive. Some 30,000 were supplied to the war effort, and with the Douglas the Triumph was the "standard" despatch-rider mount after 1915. Triumph also manufactured the Gloria sidecar.

Appendix 2:
Awards and Recognitions

Sample of decorations and recognitions received by motorcyclists during and after the war:

Name/Unit	Nature of Action	Award/Recognition	Source
DR Corps	"…splendid work … has been done throughout the campaign by the Cyclists of the Signal Corps … [They] have been conspicuously successful in maintaining an extraordinary degree of efficiency in the service of communications"	Mentioned in Sir John French's despatch of 20 November 1914	Priestley, *Signals Service*, p. 42.
South African Motor Cyclist Corps and DRs	"… constant hard work [and] indefatigable energy of despatch riders"	Mentioned in General E Northey's despatch, 10 March 1917	*The Long, Long Trail* www.1914-1918.net/ hawthorns_second_ despatch.htm
Motor Machine Guns	For "invaluable" work rendered in the fighting line	Official acknowledgment by BEF HQ	*The Motor Cycle*, 29 April 1915
Cpl WL Anderson	"His [DR] work has been admirable"	DCM	Supplement to the *London Gazette*, 3 September 1919
Cpl Bert Bennes	"I don't know what I got it for. It just came in the mail"	MM	Burns and Messenger, p. 29
Mr J Bower		*Croix de Guerre* with bronze star	*Motor Cycling*, 5 February 1918
Cpl JA Boyd	"… great initiative … while carrying despatches"	DCM	Supplement to the *London Gazette*, 18 February 1918
Sjt CD Bulman	"… conspicuous gallantry and devotion to duty…"	DCM	Supplement to the *London Gazette*, 18 February 1918

OH Davis	"… for devotion to duty…" "I'm not the kind of man who expected that kind of thing, sir … I never dreamt I should be worth one"	MM	IWM document PP/MCR180, p. 196. See also *Triumph on the Western Front: Diary of a Despatch Rider 1915-1919.*
L Cpl O Dufour Clark		DCM	*The Motor Cycle*, 29 June 1916, p. 611.
DR CT Evans		Mentioned in General Haig's despatches	*The Motor Cycle*, 29 June 1916, p. 611.
Cpl Eric Goodhart		Mentioned in Sir John French's Despatches; DCM	*Motor Cycling*, 22 December 1914
Cpl WN Gurdon	"…for carrying important despatches under fire by day and night"	DCM	*London Gazette*, 3 June 1915
Mr AA Hannay		*Croix de Guerre* with silver star	*Motor Cycling*, 5 February 1918
Mr E Hartley Hacking		*Croix de Guerre* with bronze star	*Motor Cycling*, 5 February 1918
The Hon C Hill-Trevor		*Croix de Guerre* with silver star	*Motor Cycling*, 5 February 1918
DR LEA Karg	"For conspicuous gallantry and devotion to duty"	DCM	Supplement to the *London Gazette*, 18 February 1918
Mr WD Linsell		*Croix de Guerre* with bronze star	*Motor Cycling*, 5 February 1918
"The Madonnas of Pervyse"—Baroness de t'Serclaes and Mairi Chisholm	Humanitarianism	MM 1914 Star Order of Leopold Order of Queen Elizabeth of Belgium Order of St John of Jerusalem	*Elsie and Mairi Go To War* by Diane Atkinson
DR Patrick Mahony	Delivered despatch under fire and enabled "isolated body of troops" to rejoin main force	DCM	*Motor Cycling*, 28 May 1918

Sgt CJ McGowan		DCM	*The Motor Cycle*, 5 September 1918
Paul Maze		DCM MM with bar *Croix de Guerre.*	Paul Maze, *A Frenchman in Khaki*, introduction
A/Cpl JHH Peterson	"For conspicuous gallantry and devotion to duty"	DCM	Supplement to the *London Gazette*, 18 February 1918
"Motorcyclist Simpson"	"… for taking provisions to an isolated detachment at great personal risk"	*Croix de Guerre*	*Motor Cycling*, 23 November 1915
Sec Lt LS Smith		Mentioned in despatches	*The Motor Cycle*, 1 July 1915
(Sir) Charles Symonds		*Medaille Militaire*	*Oxford Dictionary of National Biography*
WH Tait	For services during the retreat from Mons	*Medaille Militaire*	Imperial War Museum, folder PP/MCR/161 www.iwm.org.uk
WHL Watson	"For conspicuous gallantry and resource on numerous occasions in carrying messages under shell and line fire…"	DCM	*London Gazette*, 18 February 1915, p. 1706.
Lt Roger West	For blowing a bridge in the teeth of the German advance in August 1914	DSO	Roger R West, IWM document 67/122/1, p. 120 and obituary dated 26 November 1975 that accompanies IWM folder
Cpl Eric Williams	For "services rendered at Neuve Chapelle"	DCM	*The Motor Cycle*, 24 June 1915, p. 619.

This sample gives a flavour of the work done and risks taken by motorcyclists in various units. It is impossible to be definitive because, quite apart from the scale of tracing all motorcyclists through the war, citations for awards may mention only "for carrying despatches", which might have been on foot. To give some indication of scale of DR service in one action—albeit a desperate one—one despatch rider "can vouch for the following awards" to other DRs in the March retreat of 1918: in one (unidentified) division: two MMs, one DCM; in another: two MMs; in a third division: four MMs; in a fourth: two MMs.

Appendix 3:
Riders of the Storm

Most of the salient accounts from which this one has drawn may be inspected in the Imperial War Museum, Lambeth, London, whose resources and staff both are terrific assets to any student or researcher. But this list of DRs is more representative than comprehensive, if only because the names of so many who contributed to this book have been lost forever. Other accounts, though, are out there. They deserve to be discovered and made known.

Best, Lieutenant OH, IWM document 87/56/1

Best served as a motorcycle despatch rider, with the rank of corporal, on the Western Front from September 1914 to August 1915, and later in Egypt and Palestine. His account provides much detail on not just a DR's duties and living conditions, but on the character of his fellow soldiers and his training as a subaltern at an RE signal depot. He served to the end of the war.

Corcoran, AP, author of *The Daredevil of the Army: Experiences as a "Buzzer" and Despatch Rider*

Austin Patrick Corcoran was born in Co Cork in 1890 and travelled widely in his youth, hunting in Africa and ranching in South America. He enlisted in the same spirit of adventure and seems to have been invalided out of the army for in 1916 he moved to New York where he met and married another Irish-born writer, Norah. They led an interesting and peripatetic life until Austin died of pneumonia in 1928.

I suspect that Corcoran's book is at least in part compiled from first-hand accounts rather than based on personal experience; nevertheless it's an informative read, and an enjoyable one, enlivened by reluctance to let unembellished truth stand in the way of a good story.

Davis, OH, IWM document PP/MCR/180

Oswald Davis enlisted in the Royal Engineers in November 1915 and served as a despatch rider, mainly with the Carrier Pigeon Service, on the Western Front, from July 1916, initially at the Somme, later at Ypres. A recipient of the Military Medal yet not afraid to admit to fear, a hard-working modest man with a strong sense of duty and affection for his chums and humanity in general, he has an equally strong sense of fair play that can provoke scathing outrage. His account is informative and often very readable in rude typescript (though equally often hard to decipher through typos and abbreviations)—

even lyrical: "The slope of the hill we had captured showed up gently dun and dim and desolate and swart and on it stood up like dark tusks the few tree-stumps remaining"; one is hardly surprised to learn that he was a published poet. After the war he became a successful writer, notably of biographies of George Gissing and Arnold Bennett. His account recently has been published by FireStep Books as *Triumph on the Western Front: Diary of a Despatch Rider 1915-1919.*

Etherington, Lieutenant HE, IWM document 81/23/1

Rather strange person—though maybe it's unfair to so summarise a man based on the brief entries in a pocket diary kept while he was serving as a despatch rider, mostly around Ypres. That he gained his king's commission suggests that Etherington wasn't such a caricature of inefficiency and callousness as some of his "brief diary entries" suggest (though one can never discount the San Fairy Ann factor.) Whatever the truth, he did his bit, and if he really was as neo-sociopathic as some of his diary entries suggest, his human failings counterbalance, to the relief of ordinary mortals, the impossible heroism of, say, West and Grice.

Foster, Lieutenant WH, IWM document 99/36/1

Foster's short, very readable account was actually written by his son but his file also includes extracts from wartime correspondence which records his service on the Western Front as a despatch rider from October 1914 to November 1915, when he took a commission. A very valuable account.

Grice, Lieutenant TW, IWM document P391

A splendidly intriguing character, Grice seems to have been something of a wastrel who delayed enlisting until faced with the threat of conscription and he became a despatch rider ostensibly, one may suppose, on the basis of his experience as editor of *The Autocycle* magazine—but also, one may suspect, because he was one of "the funk who wished only to evade the trenches", as one veteran DR described many of the newer sort. If all this speculation is well founded, then the DR corps made a man of him. He evolves from a peacetime ladykiller, whose main problem seems to have been ennui, to a duty-driven man proud to be "An *asset* at last to King and Country". He's enthusiastic, excitable as a child betimes, and a chronic sufferer from cheerfulness after he joins up and quits taking himself so seriously. Like so many DRs, he becomes an officer, in his case with the 190th Machine Gun Company. A man to look out for in Valhalla.

Hopps, FW; IWM document 06/54/1

By his own account, Hopps seems to be exactly the sort of man who makes the urbane Lieutenant Best feel "sick of the private soldier as a companion". He's an incessant grumbler and he doesn't seem to be a nice man. He complains that "DRs have hell of a job", yet is "very sorry" to lose his temporary position. He plunders French shops and German corpses—but others plunder too, and there would have been no fine feelings for enemy dead or concern for enemy bereaved in the heat of war. His frequent references to "wind up", in his own case and that of others, contrasts with the stiff upper lip maintained by men like Watson and West, but no doubt it also reflects the deterioration in morale as the war went on—and probably would have been the blunt truth throughout the war. On the other hand, Hopps is kind to animals, sympathetic to wounded companions and nerve-broken men, and moved by the death of colleagues. For all his superficial unpleasantness he leaves an impression of a humane and oddly appealing character, both witness to war's horrors and victim of them.

Lamb, 2nd Lieutenant HAJ, IWM document 01/9/1 & PP/MCR/187

Lamb gives insight into training and living conditions of DRs after the first frantic weeks and along with Best's and Mead's, his descriptions of a despatch rider's duties at Gallipoli and in Mesopotamia are excellent. Most notable, perhaps, is his account of the Gallipoli floods of November 1915. Commissioned in January 1917, he was appointed to the Divisional Artillery Signal Section and helped set up a Signal School.

Maze, Paul; author of *A Frenchman in Khaki.*

Maze was a comfortably-off Anglo-Frenchman who bought a new motorcycle with the express purpose of volunteering it and himself for the war effort. He was not a DR but was quickly attached to Hubert Gough's cavalry, and later the Fourth Army, as liaison officer with the French. His communications duties were similar to those of the average despatch rider, and he performed most of them while motorcycle mounted or as a runner. He narrowly escaped being shot as a spy in the course of the Great Retreat and was wounded four times; his last wound, sustained in the Hundred Days campaign, took him out of the war. He was awarded the DCM, the MM with bar, and the *Croix de Guerre.*

Mead, WG, IWM document PP/MCR/7

Mead served as a despatch rider at Gallipoli from August to December 1915, and his account covers the landing at Suvla Bay, motorcycle rides in that grotesque theatre, and journeys to other headquarters and Casualty Clearing Stations around Suvla as well as by ferry to GHQ on Imbros. Later he served in Egypt and Palestine, and his description of motorcycling in exotic theatres makes Mead's account invaluable.

Watson, Captain WHL; author of *Adventures of a Despatch Rider*.

As easily as Maze, Watson stepped in off the street and bought a new motorcycle so that he might ride off into war on it. He published his account of the Great Retreat quite early in 1915. There's something seminal about this account, given that it was not merely drawn from letters scribbled in the heat of action, but written by something like the very archetype of the "original" DR: a son of privilege, a graduate of public school and Oxford, a self-confessed coward who, as slave to duty—"it obviously had to be done"—evolves into something that no reasonable human being would begrudge acknowledging a hero.

William Henry Lowe Watson was born in 1891 in Westminster, the second son of a clergyman, and died in Wimbledon in 1932. Commissioned in 1915 he went on to become a temporary major in the Tank Corps, his substantive rank that of captain. He married in 1916, obviously while on leave. He was mentioned in despatches and awarded the DSO; earlier, while a corporal, he had been awarded the DCM.

Watson was an impressively good-looking man and an even more impressively tall one; at 6ft 5½ins he was a veritable giant in those days. As well as *Adventures of a Despatch Rider*, he wrote *A Company of Tanks*. Humane, witty, intelligent, modest and brave, Willie epitomised the DR of the early part of the war.

West, Roger Rolleston, DSO; IWM document 67/162/1.

West died in California in 1975, a successful petroleum geologist and engineer. But really, how can anyone sum up a man who, with no military training, and an infected foot, blows up a bridge in the enemy's teeth? How San Fairy Ann can you get?

Abbreviations and glossary

ADS: Advanced Dressing Station.
AEF: American Expeditionary Force.
ASC: Army Service Corps.

BEF: British Expeditionary Force.
Brass Hats: army generals.

Ca ne fait rien: see San Fairy Ann.

Dis: disabled or disconnected cable communication.
"Don" and "Don R": despatch rider.
DR: despatch rider.
DRLS: Despatch Rider Letter Service.
DCM: Distinguished Conduct Medal.
DORA: Defence of the Realm Act.
DSC: Distinguished Service Cross.
DSM: Distinguished Service Medal.
DSO: Distinguished Service Order.

Frocks / Frock Coats: politicians.

HP: horsepower—at this time a nominal value, measured by piston displacement.

IWM: Imperial War Museum.

MC: Military Cross.
MGC: Machine Gun Corps.
MIRA: Motor Industry Research Association.
MM: Military Medal.
MMGB: Motor Machine Gun Battery.
MMGS: Motor Machine Gun Service.
MO: Medical Officer.
MT: Mechanical Transport.

OC: Officer Commanding.
OHC: overhead camshaft.
OHMS: On His Majesty's Service.
OHV: overhead valve.

PBI: Poor Bloody Infantry.

RAF: Royal Air Force, created on 1 April 1918 from amalgamation of RFC and RNAS.
RAMC: Royal Army Medical Corps.
RAP: Regimental Aid Post.
RE: Royal Engineers.
RFA: Royal Field Artillery.
RGA: Royal Garrison Artillery.
RHA: Royal Horse Artillery.
RFC: Royal Flying Corps.
RNAS: Royal Naval Air Service.

San Fairy Ann: see *Ca ne fait rien.*
Stoßtrupptaktik: Storm trooper tactics, adopted by the Germans in 1917.
SV: side valve.

VAD: Voluntary Aid Detachment, providing care to wounded soldiers.
VC: Victoria Cross.

WO: War Office.
WD: War Department.

References

Alexander, William, and Arthur Street. *Metals in the Service of Man* (Middlesex: Penguin, 1962)

Allen, CE. "A Motorcyclist at War", in *Motorcycle Sport*, July 1975, October 1975, March 1976 (London: Ravenhill, 1975, 1976).

---. *Titch: The Founder's Tale* (Banbury: Live Wire Books, 2007).

Allen, George H, Henry C Whitehead and FE Chadwick. *The Great War, Second Volume: The Mobilisation of the Moral and Military Forces* (Philadelphia: George Barrie's Sons, 1916).

Ansell, David. *The Illustrated History of Military Motorcycles* (London: Osprey, 1996)

Arthur, Max. *Last Post* (London: Weidenfeld & Nicolson, 2005).

Association of RE Despatch Riders: Names & Addresses (London: Association of RE Despatch Riders/Auto-Cycle Union, 1934).

Atkinson, Diane. *Elsie and Mairi go to War: Two Extraordinary Women on the Western Front* (London: Preface, 2009).

Bacon, Roy. *Military Motorcycles of World War 2* (London: Osprey, 1985).

Bailey, Jim. *The Sky Suspended: A Fighter Pilot's Story* (London: Bloomsbury, 2005).

Barnett, Corelli. *Britain and Her Army 1509-1970* (Middlesex: Pelican, 1974).

Barton, Brian. *From Behind a Closed Door: Secret Court Martial Records of the 1916 Easter Rising* (Belfast: Blackstaff Press, 2002).

Barton, Peter, Peter Doyle and Johann Vandewalle. *Beneath Flanders Fields: The Tunnellers' War* (Stroud, Gloucestershire: Spellmount, 2007).

Bean, CEW. *Letters From France* (London: Cassell & Co, 1917).

Belfast Evening Telegraph, The, 25 April 1914.

Bendall, FWD. "The Flood at Suvla Bay", in Purdom CB (Ed). *On the Front Line: True World War I Stories* (London: Constable, 2009).

Best. Lieutenant O H. Unpublished memoir (London: Imperial War Museum, document reference 87/56/1).

Birmingham, GA. *Minnie's Bishop and Other Stories* (New York: Hodder and Stoughton, 1915).

Blunt, Lt Col GCG, DSO, OBE, RASC. "Mechanised Transport in Small Wars" in *RUSI Journal*, Vol. LXXIII, August 1928.

Bly, Nelly. "Champion of her Sex", in *New York Sunday World*, 2 February 1896.

Bond, Brian. *"Disenchantment Revisited"*, in *A Part of History: Aspects of the British Experience of the First World War* (London: Continuum, 2008).

--- & Nigel Cave. *Haig: A Reappraisal 80 Years On* (Barnsley: Pen & Sword, 2009).

Bonser, HP. "A Sapper in Palestine" in *On the Front Line: True World War I Stories* (London: Constable, 2009).

Booth, ER. "The Musings of a Nonagenarian", Western Front Association website (http://web.westernfrontassociation.com/thegreatwar/articles/individuals/erbooth.htm)

Brett, CA. "Recollections"; unpublished memoir (Belfast: Linenhall Library).

British Medical Journal, The: The Journal of the British Medical Association, London.

"British Divisions of 1914-1918, The" in *The Long, Long Trail* (www.1914-1918.net/britdivs.htm).

Brown, Malcolm. *The Imperial War Museum Book of the First World War* (London: Guild, 1991).

---. *The Imperial War Museum Book of the Western Front* (London: Pan, 2001).

---. *The Imperial War Museum Book of 1914* (London: Pan, 2005).

Bull, Stephen (complier). *An Officer's Manual of the Western Front 1914-1918* (London: Conway, 2008).

Bulletin, The, October/November 2007, Number 79 (Macclesfield: The Western Front Association, 2007).

Burgoyne, Gerald Achilles. *The Burgoyne Diaries* (London: Thomas Harmsworth Publishing, 1985).

Burns, Max and Ken Messenger. *The Winged Wheel Patch: A History of the Canadian Military Motorcycle and Rider* (St Catharines, Ontario: Vanwell Publishing, 1993).

Callwell, Charles Edward. *Experiences of a Dug-Out* (London: Constable & Co, 1920).

Camp, Charles Wadsworth. *History of the 305th Field Artillery* (New York: The 305th Infantry Auxiliary, 1919).

Carr, William. *A Time to Leave the Ploughshares: A Gunner Remembers 1917-18* (London: Robert Hale, 1985).

Carrington, Charles. *Soldier From the Wars Returning* (Barnsley, S Yorks: Pen & Sword, 2006).

Cassar, George H, *Kitchener: Architect of Victory* (London: William Kimber, 1977).

Casson, Stanley. *Steady Drummer* (London: Bell & Sons, 1935).

Chapman, Guy. *A Kind of Survivor* (London: Victor Gollancz, 1975).

Chesney, George. *The Battle of Dorking* (Oxford: OUP, 1997).

Chevenix Trench, Major R. "Signal Communication in War" in *RUSI Journal* Vol. LXXII, February-November 1927.

Chisholm, DH. *Memories: the wartime recollections of a Royal Signals despatch rider*, http://www.southampton.ac.uk/~mic/Dad/index.htm "

"Christmas Truce 1914-1999" (www.hellfire-corner.demon.co.uk/chums.htm).

Classic Motor Cycle, The, August 1985 (Peterborough: EMAP Publications).

Claxton, William J. *The Mastery of the Air* (London: Blackie and Son, 1915).

Clayton, Anthony. *Forearmed: A History of the Intelligence Corps* (London: Brasseys, 1996).

Clew, Jeff. "The Sound of Something Special" in *The World Of Motorcycles: an Illustrated Encyclopedia* (London: Orbis, 1979).

Coleman, Frederic. *From Mons to Ypres with French* (Toronto: William Briggs, 1916).

Corbett-Smith, A. *The Retreat from Mons: By One Who Shared In It* (London: Cassell and Company, 1916).

Corcoran, Captain AP. "Wireless in the Trenches" in *Popular Science Monthly*, May 1917.

---. *The Daredevil of the Army: Experiences as a "Buzzer" and Despatch Rider* (New York: EP Dutton & Company, 1919).

Coward, George H. *Coward's War: An Old Contemptible's View of the Great War* (Leicester: Matador, 2006)

Croft, Brevet Lieutenant Colonel WD, DSO. "The Application of Recent Developments in Mechanics and other Scientific Knowledge to Preparation and Training for Future War on Land" in *RUSI Journal*, Vol. LXV, May 1920.

Dane, Edmund. *British Campaigns in Africa and the Pacific 1914-1918* (London: Hodder and Stoughton, 1919).

Davis, OH. Diary (London: Imperial War Museum, document reference PP/MCR180).

Dawson, Lieutenant Coningsby. *The Glory of the Trenches: An Interpretation* (New York: John Lane, 1918).

DeGroot, Gerald J. *Blighty: British Society in the Era of the Great War* (London: Longman, 1996)

Denore, Corporal B J. "'Sleep-Walkers' of the Great Retreat", in Hammerton, Sir John (Ed). *The Great War: I Was There Volume One* (London: The Amalgamated Press, 1938).

Divisional Signals Company Royal Engineers, www.fairmile.fsbusiness.co.uk/signals.htm.

Doherty, Gabriel, and Dermot Keogh. *1916: The Long Revolution* (Dublin: Mercier Press, 2007).

Dunn, Captain JC. *The War the Infantry Knew, 1914-1919: A Chronicle of Service in France and Belgium* (London: Abacus, 1994).

Eden, Major HCH, MC. "A Mobile Light Division" in *RUSI Journal* Vol. LXXII, February- November 1928.

Edmonds, Brigadier-General Sir James E. *History of the Great War: Military Operations, France and Belgium 1914* (London: Macmillan & Co, 1933).

--- and GC Wynne. *History of the Great War: Military Operations, France and Belgium 1915* (London: Macmillan & Co, 1927).

---. *History of the Great War: Military Operations, France and Belgium 1916* (London: Macmillan & Co, 1932).

Emden, Richard van (ed.). *Tickled to Death to Go: Memoirs of a Cavalryman in the First World War* (Staplehurst, Kent: Spellmount, 1996).

Eden, Major HCH. "A Mobile Light Division" in *RUSI Journal*, Vol. LXXII, February 1928, No. 489.

Etherington, HE. Unpublished memoir (London: Imperial War Museum, document reference 81/23/1).

Ex 2337318. "Motorcyclist at War", in *Motorcycle Sport*, August 1976, Vol. 17, No. 8 (London: Ravenhill Publishing Company Ltd, 1976).

Falls, Cyril. *History of the Great War: Military Operations, France and Belgium 1917: Volume I: The German Retreat to the Hindenburg Line and the Battles of Arras* (London: Macmillan & Co, 1940).

Ferris, John (Ed). *The British Army and Signals Intelligence During the First World War* (Stroud, Glos: Alan Sutton, 1992)

Fiske, Colonel James. *Facing the German Foe* (New York: Saalfield, 1915).

---. *The Belgians to the Front* (New York: Saalfield, 1915).

FitzGerald, Desmond. *Desmond's Rising: Memoirs 1913 to Easter 1916* (Dublin: Liberties Press, 2006).

Fitzhugh, Percy K. *Tom Slade: Motorcycle Dispatch Bearer* (New York: Grosset & Dunlap, 1918).

Fletcher, David. *War Cars: British Armoured Cars in the First World War* (London: HMSO, 1987).

Foster, Lieutenant WH. "Distant Guns" (London: Imperial War Museum, unpublished memoir, document reference 99/36/1).

Frankau, Gilbert. *Peter Jackson, Cigar Merchant* (London: Hutchinson & Co, 1920).

Frost, George H (compiler). *Munitions of War: A record of the work of the BSA and Daimler Companies during the world war 1914-1918* (Birmingham and Coventry: The BSA Co Ltd & Daimler Co Ltd, undated).

Fuller, Col. JFC, DSO. "The Application of Recent Developments in Mechanics and other Scientific Knowledge to Preparation and Training for Future War on Land" in *RUSI Journal* Vol. LXV, May 1920.

---. "Progress in the Mechanicalisation of Modern Armies" in *RUSI Journal* Vol. LXX, February-November 1925.

Fyfe, Hamilton. "At Army Headquarters" in *The War Illustrated*, 9 March 1918 (www.greatwardifferent.com/Great_War/Hamilton_Fyfe/Army_Headquarters_01.htm).

---. "What Canadian MM Gunners did" in *The War Illustrated*, 29 June 1918 (www.greatwardifferent.com/Great_War/MM_Guns_01.htm).

Gibbs, Philip. *The Soul of the War* (New York: Robert M McBride, 1916).

---. *The Way to Victory* (New York: George H Doran Company, 1919).

Gilson, Captain Charles. *Motor Scout in Flanders: or, Held by the Enemy* (Glasgow: Blackie & Son, undated).

Gleichen, Edward Lord. *The Doings of the Fifteenth Infantry Brigade August 1914 to March 1915* (London: William Blackwood & Sons, 1917).

Glendinning, Frank. "Engineers Extraordinary" in *The World Of Motorcycles: an Illustrated Encyclopedia* (London: Orbis, 1979).

--- "Triumph: Living on Former Glory" in *The World Of Motorcycles: an Illustrated Encyclopedia* (London: Orbis, 1979).

Graphic, The. London: 2 October 1915.

Great War in a Different Light, The: Accounts and Galleries from Great War Period Books, Magazines and Publications (www.greatwardifferent.com/ Great_War/index/htm).

Green, Brig-General AFU. *The British Home Guard Pocket-Book* (London: Conway, 2009).

Greenhalgh, Elizabeth. "Why the British Were on the Somme in 1916" in *War in History, Vol. 6, No. 1,* 1999.

Grice, Lieutenant T W. Unpublished memoir (London: Imperial War Museum, document reference P391).

Gudmundsson, Bruce. *The British Expeditionary Force 1914-15* (Oxford: Osprey, 2005).

Gyde, Captain Arnold. "The Terror and Tribulation of those Fateful Days", in Hammerton, Sir John (Ed). *The Great War: I Was There Volume One* (London: The Amalgamated Press, 1938).

Hamilton, Andrew and Alan Reed (eds). *Meet at Dawn, Unarmed: Captain Robert Hamilton's account of Trench Warfare and the Christmas Truce in 1914* (Walton: Dene House, 2009).

Hammerton, Sir John (Ed). *The Great War: I Was There Volume One* (London: The Amalgamated Press, 1938).

Hanbro, General Sir Percy. "The Horse and the Machine in War" in *RUSI Journal*, Vol. LXXII, February 1927, No. 485.

Hankin, BD. "Communication and Control of Military Forces" in *OR*, Vol. 4, No. 4 (Birmingham: Operational Research Society, 1953).

Hart, Peter. *1918: A Very British Victory* (London: Phoenix, 2009).

Hay, Ian. *The First Hundred Thousand: Being the Unofficial Chronicle of a Unit of "K(1)"* New York: Houghton Miflin, 1916.

Hayward, James. *Myths & Legends of the First World War* (Stroud: The History Press, 2010).

Holden, Michael. "Training, Multi-National Formations, and Tactical Efficiency: The Canadian Motor Machine Gun Brigades in 1918", University of New Brunswick, www.cda-cdai.ca/symposia/2003/holden.htm.

Hopkins, Tighe. "German Spies in France: Facts and Fictions of Germany's Secret Service" in *The War Illustrated*, 2 February 1918 (www. greatwardifferent.com/Great_War/Spies/Spies_France_01.htm).

Hopps, FW. Unpublished diary (London: Imperial War Museum, document reference 06/54/1).

Hopwood, Bert. *Whatever Happened to the British Motorcycle Industry* (Yeovil, Somerset: Haynes, 1981).

Hordern, Charles. *History of the Great War: Military Operations, East Africa, Volume 1, August 1914- September 1916* (London: HMSO, 1941).

Horne, Alastair. "Verdun and the Somme" in *Purnell's History of the 20th Century*. (London: BPC Publishing, 1968).

Horner, Arnold. "Ireland's Time-Space Revolution: improvements to pre-Famine travel", in *History Ireland*, September/October 2007 (Dublin: History Publications Ltd, 2007).

Imperial War Museum, London.

Isacker, E Van. "The Diary of a Dispatch Rider Attached to the Belgian General Staff" in *The War Illustrated*(www.greatwardifferent.com/Great_War/Dispatch_Rider/Dispatch_Rider_02.htm)

Ixion. *Motorcycle Cavalcade* (London: Iliffe, 1950).

Jackson, John. *Private 12768: Memoir of a Tommy* (Stroud: Tempus, 2005).

James, Robert Rhodes, *Gallipoli* (London: Batsford, 1965).

Jarrett, Charles. *Ten Years of Motors and Motor Racing 1896-1906* (London: Foulis, 1956).

Jebens, Captain FH. "Transport of Infantry Machine Guns" in *RUSI* Journal, Vol. LXXV, November 1930.

Jeffrey, Keith. "Nationalisms and gender: Ireland in the time of the Great War 1914-1918" (http://www.oslo2000.uio.no/program/papers/r13/r13-jeffery.pdf).

Jervis-White-Jervis, Lieutenant Henry. *Manual of Field Operations* (London: John Murray, 1852).

Jourdain, HFN. *The Connaught Rangers, Volume II* (London: Royal United Services Institute, 1926).

Kanter, Buzz. *Indian Motorcycles* (Osceola, WI: Motorbooks International, 1993).

Kildea, Jeff. *ANZACs and Ireland* (Cork: Cork UP, 2007).

Kipling, Rudyard. *France at War: On the Frontier of Civilisation* (New York: Doubleday, Page & Co, 1915).

Kluck, Alexander von. *The March on Paris and the Battle of the Marne, 1914* (London: Edward Arnold, 1920).

Kuhl, General von. "The Operations of the British Army, August-September 1914" in *RUSI Journal* Vol. LXVI, February-November 1921.

Laffin, John. *British Butchers and Bunglers of World War One* (Godalming: Sutton Publishing, 1998).

Lafone, HC. "The Motor's Place in War" in *War Facts and Figures* (London: The British Dominions General Insurance Company Limited, 1915).

Lamb, Lieutenant HAJ. "As You Were: Being a narrative of the Great War 1914-1918 as seen by the Author, a soldier in the ranks of the British Army, from the commencement as one of 'Kitchener's Men', and latterly as an officer" (London: Imperial War Museum, unpublished memoir, document reference 01/9/1).

Lauder, Harry. *A Minstrel in France* (London: Andrew Melrose Ltd, 1918).

Lee, Joseph. The Modernisation of Irish Society, 1848-1918 (Dublin: Gill & Macmillan, 2008).

Lewis, David. *The Man Who Invented Hitler: The Making of the Führer* (London: Headline, 2004).

Little, Alan. "A frontier between civilisations", BBC News, 13 March 2005 (http://news.bbc.co.uk/1/hi/programmes/from_our_own_correspondent/43437 91.stm).

Livesay, JFB. *Canada's Hundred Days* (Toronto: Thomas Allen, 1919).

London Gazette, The (www.london-gazette.co.uk/)

Long, Long Trail The www.1914-1918.net.

Lowe, Lieut. Col. TA. *The Western Battlefields: A Guide to the British Line* (Aldershot: Gale & Polden, 1920).

Lucy, JF. *There's a Devil in the Drum* (Uckfield, East Sussex: Naval & Military Press, 1993)

Ludendorff, Erich von. *Ludendorff's own Story: August 1914-November 1918* (New York and London: Harper & Brothers, 1919).

Lupfer, Timothy T. "The Dynamics of Doctrine: The Changes in German Tactical Doctrine During World War One, in *The Leavenworth Papers* (Fort Leavenworth, KS: US Army Command and General Staff College, 1981).

Macdonald, Lyn. *Ordeal By Fire: Witnesses to the Great War* (London: The Folio Society, 2001).

---. "Oral History and the First World War", in *A Part of History: Aspects of the British Experience of the First World War* (London: Continuum, 2008).

Macnaughtan, S. *My War Experiences in Two Continents* (London: John Murray, 1919).

Malloch, Hedley. "Behind the Lines: The Story of the Iron Twelve, Part One", in *Stand To!: The Journal of the Western Front Association*, December 2009/January 2010, Number 87.

Manning, Frederic. *Her Privates We* (London: Serpent's Tail, 1999).

Margerison, John S. "Spotting For The Guns: Adventures of an Observation Officer of the Kite Balloons" in *The War Illustrated*, 5 January 1918 (www.greatwardifferent.com/Great_War/Balloon/Balloon.htm).

Marshall, Logan. *A History of the Nations and Empires Involved and a Study of the Events Culminating in The Great Conflict* (http://www.gutenberg.org/dirs/etext03/ecigc10.txt).

Masters, David. "M-5054", in *Classic Bike*, December 2007.

Maze, Paul. *A Frenchman in Khaki* (London: Heineman, 1934).

McCance, Captain S. *History of the Royal Munster Fusiliers, Vol II* (Schull, Co Cork: Schull Books, 1995).

McKenzie, FA. "Winter in the West" in *The War Illustrated*, 11 December 1915 (www.greatwardifferent.com/Great_War/Winter_1915/Winter_1915.htm).

Mead, W George. "Forty Thousand Hours of War" (London: Imperial War Museum, unpublished memoir, document reference PP/MCR/7).

Memorial of the Great War, 1914-1918: A Record of Service (Montreal: The Bank of Montreal, 1921).

Messenger, Charles. *Call-To-Arms: The British Army 1914-18* (London: Cassell, 2005).

Minton, David. *The Triumph Story: Racing and production models from 1902 to the present day* (Yeovil: Haynes Publishing, 2002).

Montague, CE. *Disenchantment* (London: Chatto & Windus, 1924).

Morgan, Captain FS. "The Development of Communication and Command", in *RUSI* Journal, Vol. LXXVI, February-November 1931.

Morgan, JK. *Leaves from a Field Note-Book* (London: Macmillan, 1916).

Mosier, John. *The Myth of the Great War: A New Military History of World War One* (London: Profile Books, 2001).

Motorcycle and Bicycle Illustrated (New York: Motorcycle Publishing Co, 1917).

Motor Cycle, The 1914-1919. (Archives held by The Vintage Motorcycle Club Ltd, Allen House, Wetmore Road, Burton Upon Trent, Staffs., DE14 1TR).

Motorcycle Sport (London: Standard House, 1976).

Motor Cycling 1914-1919. (Archives held by The Vintage Motorcycle Club Ltd, Allen House, Wetmore Road, Burton Upon Trent, Staffs., DE14 1TR).

"MP, An". *Mons, Anzac and Kut* (London: Edward Arnold, 1919).

Myer, Lieutenant Samuel G. "The Fourth Arm", in *Military Affairs*, Vol. 8, No. 3. (Autumn 1944).

Nason, Anne (ed). *For Love and Courage: The Letters of Lieutenant Colonel EW Hermon from the Western Front 1914-1917* (London: Preface, 2008).

Neillands, Robin. *The Old Contemptibles: The British Expeditionary Force, 1914* (London: John Murray, 2005).

Neyland, B. "A Wireless Operator", in Purdom CB (Ed). *On the Front Line: True World War I Stories* (London: Constable, 2009).

Nicholson, ES. *Adventures of a Royal Signals Despatch Rider* (Peterborough: UpFront Publishing, 2003).

Norway, Mrs Hamilton. *The Sinn Fein Rebellion As I Saw It* (London: Smith, Elder & Co, 1916).

Official History of the New Zealand Engineers During the Great War, 1914-1919 (Wanganui: Evans, Cobb & Sharpe, 1927).

Orsi, Douglas J. "The Effectiveness of the US Army Signal Corps in Support of the American Expeditionary Force Division and Below Manoeuvre Units During World War I" (Fort Leavenworth, KS: Master's Dissertation, 2001).

Orwell, George. *The Lion and the Unicorn: Socialism and the English Genius* (London: Secker and Warburg, 1941).

Osborn, Lt-Col. "Epic Story of St Quentin: How Tom Bridges Saved Two Regiments", in Hammerton, Sir John (Ed). *The Great War: I Was There Volume One* (London: The Amalgamated Press, 1938).

Osman, AH. "Pigeons for Sport and War" in *War Facts & Figures* (London: The British Dominions General Insurance Company, 1914/1915).

Pakenham, Thomas. *The Scramble for Africa, 1876-1912* (London: Abacus, 1992).

Paterson, Alexander. "Bravery in the Field?", in Purdom CB (Ed). *On the Front Line: True World War I Stories* (London: Constable, 2009).

Pemberton, Max. "Battle of the Great High Road and How the Despatch Rider Came Home" in *The War Illustrated*, 6 January 1917 (www.greatwardifferent.com/Great_War/Despatch_Rider/Despatch_Rider_01.htm).

Powell, E Alexander. *Fighting in Flanders* (Toronto: McClelland, Goodchild & Stewart, 1915).

---. *Italy at War and the Allies in the West* (New York: Charles Scribner's Sons, 1919).

Priestley, Major R E. *The Signal Service in the European War of 1914 to 1918 (France)* (Chatham: W & J Mackay and Co, 1921).

Purdom CB (Ed). *On the Front Line: True World War I Stories* (London: Constable, 2009).

Robertson, Sir William. *From Private to Field Marshall* (London: Constable & Co, 1921).

Rogerson, Sidney. *Twelve Days on the Somme: A Memoir of the Trenches, 1916* (London: Greenhill Books, 2006).

Royal Automobile Club Journal, The (London: Royal Automobile Club, 2 December 1909; 9 December 1909).

Ruhl, Arthur. *Antwerp to Gallipoli: A Year of the War on Many Fronts—and Behind Them* (New York: Charles Scribner's Sons, 1916).

Salopek, Paul. "Shattered Sudan", in *National Geographic*, February 2003.

"Sapper". *The Lieutenant and Others* (London: Hodder and Stoughton, 1915).

Schilling, Phil. *The Motorcycle World* (New York: Random House, 1974).

Sellers, William E. *With Our Fighting Men: The Story of their Faith, Courage, Endurance in the Great War* (London: The Religious Tract Society, 1915).

Setright, LJK. "Oil to All Parts" in *The World Of Motorcycles: an Illustrated Encyclopedia* (London: Orbis, 1979).

---. *Drive On: A Social History of the Motor Car* (London: Granta, 2003).

Shaw, Francis J. "'Cast A Cold Eye': The Rising of 1916 in the Context of Irish History" in *Studies: An Irish Quarterly Review*, Summer 1972 (Dublin: The Society of Jesus).

Sheffield, Gary (ed). *Leadership and Command: The Anglo-American Military since 1861* (London: Brassey's, 2002).

---. *The Somme* (London: Cassell Military Paperbacks, 2003).

--- and Dan Todman (eds). *Command and Control on the Western Front: The British Army's Experience 1914-18* (Stroud: Spellmount, 2004).

Sheldon, James. *Veteran and Vintage Motorcycles* (London: Transport Bookman, 1971).

Shepherd, CK. *Across America by Motor-Cycle* (London: Edward Arnold, 1922).

Sinn Fein Rebellion Handbook (Dublin: The Irish Times, 1917).

Skinnider, Margaret. *Doing My Bit For Ireland* (New York: The Century Co, 1917).

Smith, Peter. Private postcard collection.

Snelling, Bill. *Aurora to Ariel: The Motorcycling Exploits of J Graham Oates* (Laxey, Isle of Man: Amulree Publications, 1993).

Sparks: A Motorcycle Monthly Vol 1, No 1, July 1909, pp. 4-5, http://w6rec. com/duane/bmw/M_M/page5.jpg

Spears, Sir Edward. *Liaison 1914: A Narrative of the Great Retreat* (London: Cassell, 1999).

Sproston, Corporal AJ. "Four Months Under Fire: Despatch-Rider's Adventures" (*The Daily Mail*, London, 14-19 December 1914).

Stapledon, Olaf. "Experiences in the Friends' Ambulance Unit", in *We Did Not Fight 1914-18: Experiences of War Resistors* (Ed. Julian Bell; London: Cobden-Sanderson, 1935).

Stewart, Col H. *The New Zealand Division 1916-1919: A Popular History Based on Official Records* (Auckland: Whitcombe and Tombs, 1921).

Stewart, Herbert A. *From Mons to Loos: Being the Diary of a Supply Officer* (Edinburgh: Blackwood and Sons, 1916).

Stone, Norman. *World War One: A Short History* (London: Penguin, 2008).

Strachan, Hew. *The First World War: Volume I: To Arms* (Oxford: Oxford UP, 2001).

Strandman, Hartmut Pogge von. "Germans in Africa 1900-14: A Place in the Sun", in *Purnell's History of the 20th Century* Volume 1 (London: BPC Publishing, 1968).

Strang, Herbert. *The British Army in War* (London: Humphrey, Milford, OUP, 1915).

Suffering From Cheerfulness: The Best Bits from The Wipers Times (London: Little Books, 2007).

Tait, WH. Unpublished diary (London: Imperial War Museum, document reference PP/MCR/161).

Taylor, AJP. *English History 1914-1945* (Oxford: OUP, 1965).

Times History of the World, The (London: *The Times*, 1915).

Todman, Dan. *The Great War: Myth and Memory* (Hambledon Continuum, 2005).

Townshend, Charles. *Easter 1916: The Irish Rebellion* (London: Penguin, 2006).

Toye, Richard. *Churchill and Lloyd George: Rivals for Greatness* (London: Macmillan, 2007).

Tuchman, Barbara. *The Guns of August* (New York: Bantam, 1976). University of Birmingham Centre for First World War Studies (www.firstworldwar.bham.ac.uk).

Valley, Paul. "Living in the nation's memory" in *The Independent*, 11 November 2000.

Vanderveen, Bart H. *Onyslager Auto Library: Motorcycles to 1945* (London: Frederick Warne & Co, 1975).

Verma, Ritu. *Gender, Land and Livelihoods in East Africa: Through Farmers' Eyes* (Ottawa: International Development Research Centre, 2001).

Vivian, E Charles. *A History of Aeronautics* (New York: Harcourt, Brace and Co, 1921).

Walker, Mick. *NSU: The Complete Story* (Marlborough: Crowood Press, 2009).

Walker, Neil. *The King's Shilling* (www.bbc.co.uk/ww2peopleswar/stories/38/a8542938.shtml).

Ware, Pat. *The Illustrated Guide to Military Motorcycles* (London: Arness Publishing, 2010).

War Facts & Figures (London: The British Dominions General Insurance Company, 1914/1915).

War Office. *Statistics of the Military Effort of the British Empire during the Great War 1914-1919* (London: HMSO, 1921).

Warner, Philip. "Le Cateau", in *Purnell's History of the First World War*, Volume 1, Number 8 (London: BPC Publishing, 1969).

Watson, Frank. "A Territorial in the Salient", in Purdom CB (Ed). *On the Front Line: True World War I Stories* (London: Constable, 2009).

Watson, Captain WHL. *Adventures of a Despatch Rider* (Edinburgh: Blackwood and Sons, 1915).

Wells, Warre B, and N Marlowe. *A History of the Irish Rebellion of 1916* (Dublin and London: Maunsel & Company, 1916)

West, Lt Roger Rolleston, DSO. "Diary of the War: Retreat from Mons to the Battle of the Aisne" (London: Imperial War Museum, unpublished memoir, document reference 67/122/1).

Westerman, Percy F. *The Dispatch-Riders: The Adventures of Two British Motor-cyclists in the Great War* (Glasgow: Blackie & Son, 1915).

Wharton, Edith. *Fighting France: From Dunquerque to Belport* (New York: Charles Scribner's Sons, 1915).

Whitman, Roger B. *Motor-Cycle Principles and the Light Car* (New York and London: Apppleton and Co, 1920)

Willis, Chris. *Motorcycles, Murder and Misogyny* (www.chriswillis.freeserve.co.uk/Sayersbikes.htm).

Winnifrith, Douglas C. *The Church in the Fighting Line* (London: Hodder and Stoughton, 1915).

Winter, Denis. *Haig's Command: A Reassessment* (London: Classic Penguin, 2001)

Wise, David Burgess. "Churchill's Choice" in *The World Of Motorcycles: an Illustrated Encyclopedia* (London: Orbis, 1979).

--- "Pioneers: How It All Began" in *The World Of Motorcycles: an Illustrated Encyclopedia* (London: Orbis, 1979).

Wood, Gordon. *I Was There* (Ilfracombe: Arthur H Stockwell, 1984).

Woods, Peter (producer). "Week to Come, The", *Radio Telefis Eireann* documentary, www.rte.ie/radio1/doconone/player.html?feedUrl=/radio1/doconone/atom/2568132.xml&play=true&position=0&volume=-1

Wright, Edward. "The Great Work of Salving War Material", in *The War Illustrated* (www.greatwardifferent.com/Great_War/Garbage_of_War/Garbage_of_War_01.htm).

Wyatt, Horace G. *Motor Transport in War* (London: Hodder & Stoughton, 1914/1915).

Young, Mike. *Army Service Corps, 1902-1918* (London: Leo Cooper, 2000).

Young, Brigadier Peter. "The Great Retreat", in *Purnell's History of the First World War*, Volume 1, Number 8 (London: BPC Publishing, 1969).

Index

207-08, 209, 211-27, 229, 242-49.
--- character of: 28-29, 132-33, 135,
  137-38, 142, 202, 204-05, 207.
--- evaluation: 108, 136-37, 147-49,
  189, 205, 229, 244-49, 256-58.
--- German treatment of: 109, 112.
--- in German army: 89, 187-88, 189.
--- in popular fiction: 46.
--- of Irish rebels in 1916: 226-27.
--- of Ulster Volunteer Force: 46, 54,
  227.
--- on home front: 47, 53, 54, 118, 119.
--- organisation and training: 54, 119-
  28, 124, 126, 128, 189, 193-94,
  Illustration 3.
--- pay and conditions: 138-140.
--- requirements of: 126, 132-38.
--- uniform and equipment: 113, 106,
  141-47, Illustrations 5, 6 and 11.
--- War Office calls for: 55.
--- women: 53-54, Illustration 9.
--- youngest: 46, 152.
Despatch Rider Letter Service: see
  DRLS.
"Dis": 87, 120, 192, 194, 198, 199,
  225, 247.
Discipline: 129, 162, 202, 223.
Dispatch rider: see Despatch rider.
Dogs: 110, 133, 199.
"Donkey" school of thought; "donkey-
  walloper": 18, 19, 31, 91, 161, 169,
  171, 210, 245, 248.
Don R: see Despatch Rider.
Douglas motorcycle: 45, 54, 58, 62,
  63, 64, 66, 67, 69, 71, 72, 73, 74,
  77, 78, 79, 81, 82, 84, 85, 86, 90,
  130, 134, 203, 207, 209, 212, 214,
  215, 216, 217, 219, 220, 221, 248,
  251, 254, Illustrations 5 and 12.
DR: see Despatch Rider.
DRLS: 48, 121-22, 192, 211, 215,
  217.
Dunn, Captain JC: 58, 108, 123, 133,
  136, 137.
Dust (hazard): 14, 44, 60, 66, 72, 77,

103-04, 107, 208, 209, 212, 214-
  15, 218, 219, 220, 221, 222, 229,
  253.
Duty, devotion to/sense of: 15, 16, 18,
  26, 27, 28, 29, 45, 46, 53, 67, 74,
  112, 122, 133, 134, 135, 137, 156,
  180, 192, 196, 197, 206, 217, 224,
  240, 242, 249, 256, 257, 258, 259,
  260, 262.

E

East Africa Campaign: see African
  campaigns.
"Easterners": 210.
Easter Rising: 58, 125-26, 164, 224-
  29.
Edmonds, Sir James: 185.
Egalitarianism: 29, 134.
Egypt: 88, 163, 164, 168, 169, 214,
  252, 259, 261.
Electronics: 23, 35, 36, 37, 67, 88,
  118, 125, 148, 186, 247.
Enfield motorcycle: 51, 156, 158, 159,
  251.
Engine, internal combustion: 39, 41,
  42, 46, 47, 49, 51, 52, 59, 60-66,
  67, 68, 69, 70, 71, 73, 75-76, 78,
  80, 84, 85, 86, 89, 90, 125, 129,
  132, 137, 155, 160, 161, 173, 177,
  178, 179, 196, 209, 215, 216, 219,
  221-22, 247, 252-55.
Entente: see Allied politics.
Etherington, Lieutenant HE: 107, 136,
  244, 260.
Exhaustion (hazard): 108, 126, 140,
  184, 191, 197, 202, 207, 212, 250.
Explosives: 36-37, 56, 224, 248.

F

Falls (hazard): 69, 72, 80, 106, 108,
  119, 144, 145.
Faux-liberal: 20, 38, 90, 239.
Fenian: 38-39, 228.
Field Postal Service: see DRLS.
Fiske, Colonel James: 46, 47, 119, 247.